To: Barbara

My best wishes for your success as a Universal Design Professional.

Roberta Null

Universal Design

UNIVERSAL DESIGN

Creative Solutions for ADA Compliance

*Roberta L. Null, Ph.D.
with Kenneth F. Cherry*

Professional Publications, Inc.
Belmont, California

On the cover: The interior lobby of the Terraces of Los Gatos, California, an outstanding example of universal design for a senior's housing facility. (Reprinted with permission from Interior Arts, Inc., Fresno, CA. Interior designers: Pat Hennings, ASID, IDEC, and Vivian Coats, ASID. Photographer: Tamela Ryatt.)

Acquisitions Editors: Elizabeth Fisher, Wendy Nelson, and Mary Fiala
Production Manager: Aline M. Sullivan
Copy Editor: Jessica R. Whitney-Holden
Typesetter: Yvonne Sartain
Illustrator: Yvonne Sartain and American BookWorks Corporation
Proofreaders: Jessica R. Whitney-Holden and Aline M. Sullivan
Cover Designer: Charles P. Oey
Original Text Production: American BookWorks Corporation

UNIVERSAL DESIGN: CREATIVE SOLUTIONS FOR ADA COMPLIANCE

Copyright ©1996 by Professional Publications, Inc. All rights are reserved. No part of this publication may be reproduced, stored in a retrieval system, or transmitted, in any form or by any means, electronic, mechanical, photocopying, recording, or otherwise, without the prior written permission of the publisher.

Printed in the United States of America

Professional Publications, Inc.
1250 Fifth Avenue, Belmont, CA 94002
(415) 593-9119

Current printing of this edition: 2

Library of Congress Cataloging-in-Publication Data
Null, Roberta L., 1934-
    Universal design : creative solutions for ADA compliance / Roberta
L. Null, Kenneth F. Cherry.
      p.   cm.
    Includes bibliographical references and index.
    ISBN 0-912045-86-8
    1. Architecture and the physically handicapped--United States.
2. Physically handicapped--Legal status, laws, etc.--United States.
I. Cherry, Kenneth F., 1953- .   II. Title.
NA2545.P5N85 1996
720'.42'0973--dc20
                                                  95-23842
                                                      CIP

Contents

Foreword ix
Acknowledgments xiii
Introduction xvii

1. **What Is the Americans with Disabilities Act?** 1
    Related Legislation 4
    The Reasoning Behind the ADA 5
    Title I: Employment 6
    Title II: Public Services 13
    Title III: Public Accommodations and Services
        Operated by Private Entities 17
    Title IV: Telecommunications 19
    Title V: Miscellaneous Provisions 20
    What the ADA Means for the Future 23

2. **What Is Universal Design?** 25
    Four Cornerstones of Universal Design 27
    Other Benefits of Universal Design 29
    Universal Design and an Aging Population 33
    Strategy: Universal Design for the Preschool Child
        by Jannis Shea, Ph.D., and Marjorie Inman, Ph.D. 35
    Strategy: Universal Design for the Elderly
        by Marjorie Inman, Ph.D., and Jannis Shea, Ph.D. 37

3. **The Universal Design Process** 45
    Empathy and Universal Design 46
    Universal Design Techniques 47
    Case Study: Mendelsohn House: Milestone in Low-Income
        Housing for the Elderly
        by Robert Herman 53
    Case Study: San Diego Center for the Blind:
        Design as a Team Effort 56
    Techniques: Environmental Programming
        by Ann Warble-Nienow and Roberta L. Null, Ph.D. 62
    Strategy: The Oral History Interview
        by Karen Hirsch 66
    Strategy: User Considerations in an ADA Task Force
        by Joel I. Kahn 69

4. **Implications for Facility Managers** 71
   Universal Design Implications for Facility Management
      by Timothy J. Springer, Ph.D. 72
   Case Study: Accessibility for Customers: Guidelines for Making
      Your Small Business Accessible
      by Mary H. Yearns, Ph.D., and Arvid E. Osterberg, D.Arch. ... 81
   Case Study: Purdue University's ADA Compliance Plan
      by Owen J. Cooks. 88
   Strategy: Occupational Therapy Accessibility, Assessment,
      and Consultation
      by Shoshana Shamberg, OTR/L 95
   Case Study: Facility Management: A Cultural Universal
      Design Perspective
      by Nancy C. Canestaro, Ph.D., and James C. Canestaro, AIA . 100

5. **Enabling Products** 103
   Strategy: Universal Design for Products
      by James L. Mueller 104
   Strategy: Using Customer Feedback for New Product Design:
      A Study of Appliance Controls
      by Sandra S. Thurlow, Ph.D. 113
   Case Study: Re-Creating the School Lunch Kit: Research
      in Universal Product Design
      by Elizabeth B. N. Sanders, Sheila Zwelling,
      and Susan Russell 115
   Case Study: "Discovery" Seating and Fixtures Furniture 120
   Case Study: Seating Posture Theories: A Research Approach to
      Ergonomic Chair Design
      by Johan Ullman, M.D. 124

6. **Universal Design in the Office** 133
   The Universal Office
      by James Postell 134
   Strategy: Universal Design for the Computer Environment
      by Diane Davis. 147
   Strategy: Chemical Sensitivities
      by Cindy Paulson-Schiefelbein, M.A., OTR 161
   Case Study: Cornell University's International Facility
      Management Program
      by Franklin Becker and William Sims 164

7. **Design in Public and Commercial Environments** 177
   Strategy: Defining and Designing Public Places
      by Kerry A. Nelson, ASID, IDEC. 178
   Case Study: Redesigning a Child Development Center
      by Henry Sanoff, Ph.D., AIA 180
   Case Study: Airport Interior Design: An Integrated Approach
      by Bradley A. Knopp, the HTM Group, and Joseph A. Maxwell,
      Joseph A. Maxwell Industrial Design 191
   Strategy: Design for Acoustic Environments
      by Anne E. Seltz, M.A., CCC-A 205
   Case Study: The ADA and High-Speed Railcar Interiors: Creating
      Equal Access for All Travelers
      by Alan P. Wier 210

Case Study: One Restaurant's Efforts at ADA Compliance
  by Susan Zavotka, Ph.D., and Jillianne Pfeifer 214
Case Study: Camden Yards Ballpark: A State-of-the-Art Facility
  for Accessibility
  by John P. S. Salmen, AIA. 216

8. Universal Design in the Home 219
Strategy: Applying Universal Design Philosophy to Housing Design
  by Lois J. Moore, M.S., and Edward R. Ostrander, Ph.D. . . . 224
Case Study: The Bartlett Independent Living Laboratory
  by DeVonna L. Cervantes and Margaret J. Weber, Ph.D. . . . 230
Strategy: The Universal Kitchen
  by Carol V. Dagwell, Ph.D. 231
Strategy: Universal Bath Design
  by Joan M. Eisenberg 240
Case Study: Residential Redesign for Accessibility
  by Lee Meyer 246
Case Study: An Innovative Home Renovation: Making Use of a
  Residential Elevator
  by Betty Jones. 247

9. Marketing Universal Design 251
Case Study: The Peaks and Valleys of Marketing Accessible Housing
  by William K. Wasch 255
Case Study: Home ReVisions:
  Marketing Tools for Independent Living
  by Sheila Zwelling 263
Case Study: The Friendly Home
  by Gail Hartwigsen, Ph.D. 265
Strategy: Marketing Universal Design Products to an Aging
  Population
  by Joseph A. Koncelik. 268
Case Study: Marketing Universal Design as a Public Service:
  A Nonprofit Resource Center
  by Rae Duncan-Lyle 272
Strategy: Marketing Universal Design as a Consultant
  by Susan Behar, ASID. 275
Strategy: New Marketing Strategies for Universal Design
  by Amy Harden, Ph.D. 280

10. Resources 285
Americans with Disabilities Act: Government Resources 285
Americans with Disabilities Act: Nongovernment Resources . . . 287
Organizations 288
Publications. 289
Technology. 290

Appendix A: Chemical Sensitivities 293
Products and Resources. 293
Books and Articles. 295

References 297

Contributors 303

Index 315

Foreword

Designers are currently facing a revolutionary challenge: to redesign the built world—its interiors, exteriors, products, and furnishings—so that it will be usable by all people. This challenge has developed out of the expanding population of people with disabilities and advancing years, their increasingly vocal demands for recognition, and their ability to command the attention of the marketplace through sheer weight of numbers.

If you stop to consider the full scope of abilities and age groups that need to be accommodated by any given design, the terms *barrier-free* and *accessible* seem to defy definition. The issues are complex: What is barrier-free for a person in a wheelchair may not be for someone who has a vision or hearing impairment. Similarly, the auditory signals that are helpful to the visually impaired are inaudible to the hearing impaired, illustrating the need for multiple cueing. Simple removal of barriers does not fulfill the responsibility of designers to provide environments that can be fully interpreted and experienced with quality.

Designers must consider the entire lifespan—including periods of temporary disability—of individuals who may wish to use the space or product being designed. In short, they must begin to create *universal designs*. This work by Dr. Roberta L. Null assists us in this task by defining and illustrating a universal design approach—designing all products, buildings, and exterior spaces to be usable by all people to the greatest extent possible. She brings together a diverse group of individuals to reveal how universal design is being approached in a number of fields, and she puts forward a coherent and compelling philosophy of a general theory of universal design process.

Clients are beginning to react to the aging of the population and to new legal strictures brought on by such legislation as the Americans with Disabilities Act; thus, "better for everyone" and "planning ahead for your family's needs" is beginning to replace "handicapped" and "elderly" as marketing approaches. As comfort, safety, and flexibility become more important marketing tools, emerging technologies will continue to respond to the needs of people of all ages, abilities, and sizes. It will thus be up to designers to decide whether reluctant compliance with minimum accessibility standards will be replaced by creative, sensitive, and comprehensive design services, such as those proposed in this book. Since disabilities have no racial, social, or economic barriers, almost every family and business will eventually feel the impact of these laws. Perhaps more than any other group, the design profession will be required to develop the expertise to deal effectively with the requirements of these laws.

As new legislation and changing social values force housing providers and business owners to question their stereotypical assumptions about people with disabilities, a "no-market" misconception has begun to give way to a more humanistic recognition of the difference between "physical disability" and "environmental handicap." The designer, motivated to eliminate environmentally induced handicaps, can assist in empowering people with all types of physical or cognitive disabilities to be integrated as fully as possible into the mainstream of daily life.

One of the key points of Dr. Null's work is that disability is a normal condition of life and should be taken into account in all that is designed and produced. Even if there is no apparent market for accessibility in a particular instance, it will often become necessary to design for accessibility anyway, because people with disabilities are unable to visit inaccessible housing and businesses. Conversely, designing for accessibility can arrest the vicious cycle of denial and lack of use, providing flexibility for users and a positive influence on the bottom line of the client's financial statements. In today's society, where mass production is the method used to reduce costs, it will always cost more to build a few special and different features than to mass produce all of them to be usable by everyone. And, if we are to fairly balance the costs related to accessibility, then all costs must be considered—economic, aesthetic, functional, and opportunity costs. Among the practical cost trade-offs in the consumer's or user's analysis may be reducing the need for dependence on attendants, avoiding placing a family member in an institution or nursing home, avoiding moving to a new home, or avoiding finding a new job.

It is a virtual certainty that the public consciousness surrounding rights for people with disabilities will continue to grow in the coming years, especially given the passage of the Americans with Disabilities Act. Predictions for future trends include the following:

- The aging of the population will propel the issues of accessibility to the forefront of national consciousness. Faced with the prospect of forced dependence on an inadequate number of specialized care facilities, older Americans will migrate toward homes and other environments that support independent living.

- There will be a trend toward universal design as design professionals react to the new laws and discover innovative ways to reconcile aesthetics, functionality, and costs.

- The "better for everyone" and "planning ahead for your family's needs" approaches will begin to replace specialized "handicapped" and "elderly" marketing of universally designed products, homes, commercial buildings, and outdoor environments. Terms such as *lifespan design*, *comfortable*, *safe*, *flexible*, and *adaptable* will be commonplace marketing tools.

- New and emerging technologies will continue to arise in response to needs of people of all ages and abilities, particularly as the marketing advantages are better understood, making it easier for designers to specify appropriate components for universally designed products and architecture.

- Attitudes toward people with disabilities will continue to change in a positive way, although not as quickly as many would hope. As a greater percentage of the population joins the community of people with disabilities, either through their own life changes or those of family members or friends, there will be less fear and misunderstanding of what people with disabilities want.

The design profession holds the key to empowering people with all types of physical and/or cognitive disabilities to move as fully as possible into the mainstream of daily life. Legislated changes notwithstanding, designers will decide whether accessibility will take the form of better design for everyone, or simply unattractive, costly, Band-Aid™ solutions to annoying code requirements. Basic compliance with the minimum requirements in the building codes must be replaced by the creative, comprehensive design services of practitioners who are well trained and sensitive to the full range of human needs in the environment and who actively support a philosophy of maximizing abilities and independence for people of all ages, physical sizes, and abilities. Dr. Null's book embodies and explores this philosophy, showing how universal design can be practiced throughout our society.

—Ronald L. Mace

Acknowledgments

To my mentors and advisors throughout my formal education at:

South Dakota State University: (B.S.—Home Economics Education) Elaine Luchsinger, who piqued my interest in kitchen design and challenged me to consider graduate school.

University of Minnesota: (M.A.—Home Economics Education) Marjorie Brown, Roxana Ford, and Amy Jean Holmblade-Knorr, who helped me see home economics and education as fields of intellectual inquiry and suggested interior design as an additional field of study.

Ohio State University: (Ph.D.—Home Economics Education and Environmental Design) Julia Dalrymple, Home Economics Educator, who provided the flexibility and support to build a meaningful doctoral program; and Bill Sims, from City & Regional Planning in the School of Architecture, who guided my entrance into the world of environmental design research and helped me understand the importance of designing supportive environments.

To my students and professional colleagues throughout my academic career at:

Purdue University: where, under the leadership of Kathleen Johnston, I was able to develop and teach courses in housing and design, and, through the support of Residence Hall Administration, to conduct research on residence hall environments.

San Diego State University: where I discovered the power of forming coalitions of students, design and social service professionals, and other community leaders and where my students had the opportunity to learn socially responsible design through participation in the renovation project at the San Diego Center for the Blind (described in Chapter 3). Through my work with Kim Gibbons and a dedicated staff at the Center for the Blind, I came to appreciate the tremendous changes that the aging of the population has necessitated in rehabilitation strategies for persons with sensory disabilities. The kitchen renovation project (featuring a complete showroom donated by "Kitchens by DeLuca" in La Mesa, CA) received the 1986 Environmental Design Award from the Education Foundation of ASID, and that led to further community involvement with the San Diego ASID Chapter. Jan Bast, Project Director, coordinated the award-winning (ASID Community Service award and President Bush's "Point of Light" award) project with support from private donations and two community block grants. The involvement of Professor Kerry Nelson and interior design students from SDSU and the ASID community project is described in Chapter 3.

My participation in a faculty writing workshop taught by Laura Emery provided a supportive environment for perfecting writing skills; but more importantly, it helped me find Ken Cherry, the talented writer who shares my philosophy of universal design and has helped turn my ideas into reality. His ability to magically integrate the writing styles of our many contributors into a unified, comprehensive whole has made this a "universally designed" manuscript.

My approach to universal design has been influenced directly and indirectly by contacts and conversations with a large, diverse network of persons with disabilities. I first heard Ron Mace at a Handi-Tap Seminar in Columbus, Ohio in 1979 (I still have my notes from his presentation). His common-sense approach to providing accessible and adaptable environments had, and continues to have, a profound impact on my research, teaching, and writing.

As part of "Operation Turn-About" (a program of tutoring and support for students with learning disabilities, started by Sandy Ball), I was invited to attend the 1993 meeting of the President's Committee on Employment of Persons with Disabilities. At a recognition luncheon for Sandy and her students, we were able to meet Jim Brady and several staff members from the National Organization for Disability (NOD). At the same meeting I was also introduced to Reverend Wilke (pictured in Chapter 1 at the ADA signing ceremony), who helped me discover some of the work being done to make places of worship accessible (including the wonderful book, *That All May Worship*, by Ginny Thornburg of NOD).

Sandy Ball is a former student of my twin sister, Ruby L. Trow, Home Economics Teacher Educator at Cal Poly-Pomona. I have been fortunate to have my networking opportunities expanded through a continuing dialog with my life-long best friend, fellow home economist, and identical twin.

Another member of my personal support group is my husband, Loyd Carlson. His amazing patience and good humor have strengthened our partnership.

I also want to express my appreciation of the leaders in the universal design movement who have provided information, encouragement, and emotional support thoughout this project, especially:

Ron Mace from the Center for Universal Design in Raleigh, North Carolina, and Jan Reagan, Librarian at the Center, who promptly answered questions, filled requests for drawings and information, and always knew what was happening.

James Mueller and John Salmen, who I first heard in the early '90s at a universal design seminar in the Herman Miller Showroom at the Pacific Design Center during West Week. Mueller is an industrial designer who, in addition to his book *The Work Place Workbook* (featured in several locations in this manuscript), has created two outstanding videos on universal design.

John Salmen, an architect who is publisher of *The Universal Design Newsletter*, completed the extremely useful technical review of this manuscript. In addition, thanks to John Raeber, FAIA, FCSI, CIS, of San Francisco; David Kent Ballast, AIA, Architectural Research Consulting, of Denver; and Tom Deniston, Accessible Design Associates, of Colorado Springs; who also completed a technical review of this manuscript.

Elaine Ostroff and the Universal Design Education Project, for major contributions to universal design and the incorporation of universal design concepts into design curricula throughout the United States.

Nancy Canestaro, who took major responsibility for editing a special universal design issue of *Housing and Society*, a journal of the American Association of Housing Educators. This special issue features creative teaching, research, and public policy strategies for universal design and was planned as a supplement to this book.

In addition to the contributors whose biographies are included in the "List of Contributors," I would like to express special thanks to Pat Henning-Smith, an interior design educator from Fresno, California, whose award-winning senior housing design is featured in the cover photograph and in the book. Also, thank you to the many contributors of drawings and photographs of products and designs that are featured throughout the book, and to Dara Baldridge, a recent graduate of the Miami University Interior Design program, who redrew several floor plans.

And finally, to that special group of editors at Professional Publications, Inc.: Wendy Nelson, Liz Fisher, Mary Fiala, and Aline Sullivan, who have provided support through the trials and tribulations related to the publication of this manuscript.

Introduction

Throughout my career as an educator and design professional, my research and teaching interests have focused on the design of supportive environments. When I was in graduate school at Ohio State University, I was introduced to environmental design and research by my advisor, Bill Sims, who is now Director of Cornell University's International Facilities Management Program. My focus at the time was on student residence design, and my work with Dr. Sims helped me see a new way of thinking about designed spaces in relation to specific activities. Later, while teaching at San Diego State University, I was involved in the redesign of a service center for people with vision loss, especially the low-vision elderly.

This evolution in my interests from student populations to the needs of the elderly to those with particular disabilities always contained a central essential element in the design process, drawing on the knowledge of a diverse team of experts and end users while translating research and knowledge of user needs into design criteria or directives. That approach is particularly crucial for creating universal designs. It is reflected in the choice of contributors for this book and is stressed within the individual chapters.

Universal Design: Creative Solutions for ADA Compliance grew out of my desire to show that the knowledge gained and the environment created by relying on a multidisciplinary team can be fundamentally different from the work one does individually. I also wanted this book to reflect this belief. Consequently, this book is a collaborative effort. I sought out and received submissions from a diverse group, and rather than merely reporting on their experiences, I provided them with a common platform from which to tell their stories and share their ideas.

These voices come from educators at colleges and universities; from product, industrial, and residential designers; from architects;

and from furniture and appliance manufacturers; as well as from individuals who have disabilities. The book's focus is on the design of environments that adapt, support, and enable all people—young and old, male and female, with disabilities and without.

This is not a "how-to" of design (although there are elements of direction here and there, and case studies are presented that may prove useful in your own work). Instead, it is a book of ideas and examples, descriptive more than prescriptive, a book to awaken your creativity rather than to follow as one might a recipe. Although focusing often on the ADA and acknowledging the usefulness of various guidelines, the central theme of this book is that the spirit of the law is its main connection to the designed world, not the letter of its requirements.

The first chapter presents an overview of the Americans with Disabilities Act, discussing its major points in straightforward language. I have kept to the general format of the legislation as much as possible, but I have dealt in more depth with the sections that are particularly pertinent to the design community.

Each of the remaining chapters begins with a general theoretical discussion followed by a number of selected readings in the form of "Universal Design Strategies," "Universal Design Techniques," and "Case Studies." The Strategies and Techniques sections deal with a specific aspect of the built environment that can be better designed to meet the needs of a redefined population. For example, in the readings for Chapter 2, general guidelines are suggested for creating environments to foster independence in preschool children and the elderly—two groups that have been underrepresented in past designs. Later Strategies look at small business accessibility, kitchen design, and marketing techniques. Case Studies present examples of how working designers, architects, and educators have used universal design principles in actual practice. As the book progresses, Case Studies make up the bulk of the text since they better enable the reader to understand how universal design can be applied in the various environments discussed.

Chapters 2 and 3 define and develop the concept of universal design and utilize several case studies to illustrate the principles introduced. Chapter 4 discusses the impact of the ADA on Facility Managers, the group largely responsible for implementing the changes required in reaching ADA compliance. The chapter shows how universal design can alleviate many of the financial concerns the ADA may have raised for facility managers and illustrates how better environments can be created for all their workers and clientele.

Chapter 5 considers how best to use available products within the designed world to support people's needs, and it describes some guidelines for creating new products. Then, through general discussions, illustrations, and further case studies, Chapters 6–8 explore how universal design concepts can be used in a variety of environments: the office, with special attention given to computer workstations and alternative approaches to the traditional 9 to 5 work world; the commercial and public world, which has been deeply affected by passage of the ADA; and the home, which, although exempt from ADA legislation, has a greater impact on most individuals than any other environment. It is also the environment where much universal design work has already been done and from which much can be learned.

Chapter 9 offers some suggestions for marketing universal design to a possibly unknowledgeable public, with studies detailing the experiences of several individuals and companies who have sought to turn universal design products and environments into successful businesses. The chapter closes with some ideas on where it may be best to turn in the future with marketing efforts. The final chapter provides a brief listing of resources that can be used for further study of universal design and the ADA.

—Roberta L. Null, Ph.D.

What Is the Americans with Disabilities Act?

1

The most often-cited number of Americans with disabilities is 43 million. This represents over 17 percent of the total population that is directly affected by the passage of the Americans with Disabilities Act (ADA). But that number may be vastly underestimated because the statistic is drawn from government information on disability-related payments (and the latest census now reports the number at 49 million), and it does not take into account individuals who are secure enough financially to not seek aid or those who have disabilities that they learn to live with without seeking assistance from government agencies.

Medical equipment manufacturers and suppliers estimate the number to be more than double the official figure, as does Ronald Mace, the president of the Center for Universal Design (formerly Barrier Free Environments, Inc.) in Raleigh, North Carolina, although for slightly different reasons. Mr. Mace's estimate is based on a broader definition of what constitutes a disability (including the fact that each day millions of people find themselves temporarily disabled for varying lengths of time from accidental injuries). The medical community bases its figure on actual equipment demand.

A reasonable assumption would be that the number of Americans with disabilities that interfere with their day-to-day functioning is 80 million or more (or about 32 percent of the total population). There are some 37 million Americans with arthritis alone, most of whom could benefit from the universal application of lever door handles (as discussed in Chapter 2), and many of whom qualify for accommodation under the ADA.

> **Disability in America**
>
> 43 Million, According to the ADA
> - Hearing-impaired: 22 million (including 2 million deaf)
> - Totally blind: 120,000
> - Legally blind: 60,000
> - Epileptic: 2 million
> - Partially or completely paralyzed: 1.2 million
> - Wheelchair users: 1.4 million
> - Developmentally disabled (cerebral palsy, for example): 9.2 million
> - Speech-impaired: 2.1 million
> - Mentally retarded: 2.5 million
> - HIV-infected: 1 million (estimated)
>
> Source: Office of Special Education and Rehabilitative Services, Centers for Disease Control

The Americans with Disabilities Act (Public Law 101-336) is essentially an extension of the Civil Rights Act of 1964. In much the same manner as the Civil Rights Act established protection on the basis of race, color, national origin, sex, and religion, the ADA provides protection against discrimination on the basis of disability in the areas of employment, public accommodation, state and local government services, and telecommunication services.

The ADA, however, differs from the Civil Rights Act in a very important way: It requires that accommodation be made to remove any barriers to full participation by people with physical or mental impairments. It thus reflects a changing view about the nature of a disability. Underlying the act is the belief that a disability is brought about by an environmental or attitudinal barrier, not by the person with a physical or mental impairment. The ADA exhorts Americans to find ways to remove those barriers, thereby minimizing the effects of the disability and providing equal opportunity for a historically isolated and ignored group.

The ADA was passed by the House of Representatives on July 12, 1990, by a margin of 377 to 28. The Senate followed the next day by a margin of 91 to 6. President George Bush signed the Act into law on July 26, 1990 (see Figure 1-1).

A Blessing for the Presidential Signing of the Americans with Disabilities Act

The White House
July 26, 1990
Rev. Dr. Harold H. Wilke

The reverend's address blessed the assembly with the following prayer:

Today we celebrate the breaking of the chains which have held back millions of Americans with disabilities.

Today we celebrate the granting to them of full citizenship and access to the Promised Land of work, service, and community.

Bless this gathering…this joyous celebration.

Bless our President as he signs the Americans with Disabilities Act and strengthen our resolve as we take up the task, knowing that our work has just begun.

Bless the American people and move them to discard those old beliefs and attitudes that limit and diminish those among us with disabilities.

1-1. The Reverend Harold H. Wilke, without arms, accepts with his foot a pen from President George Bush following the 1990 bill signing ceremony for the Americans with Disabilities Act on the south lawn of the White House. Rev. Wilke is a founding director of the National Organization on Disability. *(Reprinted with permission from Rev. Harold Wilke, Director, Healing Community.)*

Related Legislation

Several other federal acts either directly influenced or strongly affected the enactment of the ADA, and they continue to play a supportive role in creating equal rights for Americans with disabilities. The three most significant of these were the Equal Education for All Handicapped Children Act of 1975, the Architectural Barriers Act of 1968, and the Rehabilitation Act of 1973.

The Equal Education for All Handicapped Children Act of 1975

The Equal Education Act directed all public school systems to offer free, equivalent education to children who had been segregated, isolated, or ignored—in short, children who were being discriminated against on the basis of a disability that kept them out of consideration for a mainstream education.

The "mainstreaming" that occurred as a result of this legislation brought about two important events. First, it introduced thousands of Americans to populations they had had little or no contact with, and as people began to interact more fully with children who happened to have disabilities, many preconceived notions about capabilities and "limitations" began to change. The particular child began to take precedence over the particular disability.

Second, a generation of Americans with various physical and mental impairments have now been formally educated in a mainstream setting. And these individuals expect equal opportunity in employment and services. The ADA provides that opportunity.

The Architectural Barriers Act of 1968

The Architectural Barriers Act (PL90-480) mandated that all facilities funded partially or wholly by federal funds and intended for public use should be designed and constructed in an accessible manner. The act applied to new construction, renovations, and leased facilities.

The ABA had little application to general public spaces, such as shops, theaters, restaurants, and private offices, and offered no consequences for noncompliance. It also did not cover those parts of leased buildings not occupied by federal programs. Thus a federal office might be located on the third floor of an inaccessible building, making its programs unavailable to many people with disabilities.

The Rehabilitation Act of 1973

While the Architectural Barriers Act was directed at accessibility, the Rehabilitation Act of 1973 was most concerned with discrimination. Not only did this act prohibit discrimination against those with disabilities in all federal agencies or programs receiving federal financial assistance, it also mandated affirmative action for people with disabilities.

Section 504 of the act specifically requires that federal programs be conducted in barrier-free environments, but allows (as does the ADA) services to be provided in alternate sites. Thus, the act does not specifically require retrofitting of an environment since its primary aim is to provide equal access to programs.

The Rehabilitation Act is in many ways the model for Title I of the ADA, which deals with employment. For all federal agencies, all recipients of federal financial assistance, and any contractors or subcontractors who received more than $2500 in federal contracts, many of the ADA provisions of non-discrimination on the basis of a disability have been provided since the mid-1970s. The Rehabilitation Act is not superseded by the ADA for covered entities: The ADA does not exempt a federal contractor from following the affirmative action provisions of the Rehabilitation Act even though the ADA does not specifically set similar requirements for its covered entities.

The Rehabilitation Act has provided some important lessons. Access to the work world was gained for the first time by many individuals who had found it difficult, at best, to find supportive employment. The history of their employment has shown that people with disabilities are capable of working and are willing to work, and that accommodations that assist them in their work are available and relatively inexpensive. The basic groundwork for newly covered entities under the ADA has already been lain.

The Reasoning Behind the ADA

The text of the Americans with Disabilities Act lists two reasons for its enactment. First, discrimination against people with disabilities based on historical isolation, misunderstanding, and stereotype is unjust and counter to the spirit of the Constitution. Second, such discrimination is extremely costly: More than 60 billion dollars are spent each year on maintaining a population that wants to be independent. The ADA seeks to integrate these individuals into the mainstream work world and into society as a whole.

The ADA addresses each of these concerns in its five titles, setting forth guidelines for employment and access to goods and services while defining who is covered under each of its provisions and establishing means of redress against discrimination. The ADA also presents some important defenses for entities that are unable to reasonably accommodate individuals covered by the law. Each of these titles will be examined in the sections that follow, with special consideration given to Titles I and III, since these will have the most significant impact on design decisions.

> ## What Is a Disability?
>
> Under the ADA, a disability is:
>
> I. A physical or mental *impairment* that *substantially limits* one or more *major life activities;*
>
> II. A record of such an impairment; and/or
>
> III. Being regarded as having such an impairment.
>
> The first definition has some important qualities that need to be examined in detail:
>
> A. *Impairment* means
>
> - Any physiological disorder, cosmetic disfigurement, or anatomical loss; or
> - A recognized mental or psychological disorder.
>
> Physiological disorders include speech, hearing, and vision impairments, as well as mobility or dexterity loss (for example, from arthritis). They also include medical conditions such as cancer and diabetes. Mental or psychological disorders include conditions listed in *The Diagnostic and Statistical Manual* (the encyclopedia of conditions used in the mental health professions) as well as learning disabilities such as dyslexia, identifiable stress disorders, and mental retardation.
>
> B. *Substantially limits* means that for an impairment to be considered a disability it must cause the individual to be unable to perform, or be significantly limited in performing, one or more of the major life activities.
>
> C. *Major life activities* are walking, talking, seeing, breathing, hearing, learning, caring for self, working, and so on.
>
> A person who has a history or record of an impairment is protected under the ADA even if the disability is no longer "active" (such as when cancer is in remission).
>
> A person who is rumored or thought to have an impairment is protected under the ADA from discrimination to the same extent as he or she would be if there was an actual disability. Thus, a person who is rumored to be HIV-positive cannot be discriminated against on the basis of that belief.

Title I: Employment

The first section of the ADA establishes guidelines to be followed by private employers, state and local governments, employment agencies, labor organizations, and joint labor-management committees. All employers of 15 or more are covered by the law. This number includes part-time employees who have worked for 20 or more weeks in the current or previous year. Also, foreign-based U.S. companies, their subsidiaries, and firms controlled by Americans must comply with the ADA in their employment of U.S. citizens unless such compliance would violate a foreign country's laws.

> ## Who Is a Qualified Individual with a Disability?
>
> There are two related definitions given in the ADA that describe who is to be considered qualified for protection under the act. One deals with employment and the other with accommodation and services.
>
> ### Title I: Employment
>
> Under the Employment provisions of the ADA, a qualified individual with a disability is one who can perform the *essential functions* of a job with or without reasonable accommodation.
>
> An essential function is any part of a job that must be done by the individual holding that position. Since the ADA lists reassigning nonessential job tasks as one way to reasonably accommodate an employee, the employer must be able to define the essential functions of any job.
>
> Under this definition, a qualified person with a disability would be one who met the educational and skill requirements and who could perform the major (that is, essential) tasks of the job with or without one or more reasonable accommodations.
>
> ### Title III: Public Accommodations and Services
>
> Under Title III, a qualified individual with a disability is anyone who could take advantage of a public accommodation or service if he or she did not have a disability. The entity providing the service must modify its operation and facility (removing architectural, communication, and transportation barriers and providing auxiliary aides and services) to make the accommodation/service usable by the individual with a disability.
>
> NOTE: See the sections "What Is a Reasonable Accommodation?" and "Defenses Against Charges of Discrimination" in this chapter for related information.

Employers of fewer than 15 workers are exempt from ADA compliance (although many may be covered by the Rehabilitation Act of 1973), as is the Executive Branch of the Federal government (covered by the Rehabilitation Act of 1973), corporations fully owned by the U.S. government, Native American nations, and bona fide private membership clubs (except labor organizations) if they are exempt from taxation.

Religious organizations are not exempt from Title I of the ADA, but they are allowed to give preference to members of their own religion.

Managing Employees under the ADA: An Example

You are the human resource manager for Common Places, Inc., a mid-sized (35 employees) architectural and design firm that has hitherto been exempt from federal employment regulations. You have a new position opening for a computer-aided design (CAD) specialist in your corporate offices.

With the ADA in place, you realize that you need to reconsider how you will handle filling open and new positions. Your first concern is the job description itself. One of the more important distinctions called for by the ADA is that an individual must be able to perform the essential functions of a job. Consequently, your task is to define what those functions are, and you will probably want to state them in the job listing and certainly in any longer job description you create. This prepares you for identifying whether an individual with a disability will be able to perform the job with or without some reasonable accommodation.

The position has historically included some minor job tasks, such as holding training sessions for interested designers and architects on new releases of the software used within a classroom setting. One of your applicants has a speech disability that makes it difficult for some people to understand her. You might then consider whether the training is central to the position you're offering, whether other specialists can conduct the training (an equivalent task that the applicant could manage would then be traded in kind), or whether the training could be done in a different way by a person with such an impairment. You cannot simply refuse to consider this applicant on the basis of a belief that she will not be able to teach in the manner hitherto used. However, you can ask her to describe how she would be able to manage this task if you do decide it is part of the essential functions of the job. She might suggest creating a self-guided multimedia training package, solving the need for dedicated training personnel.

In considering the "essential functions" requirement, you need to also consider the "reasonable accommodation" requirement, realizing that such accommodation may call for some creativity and communication on your part and on the applicant's part (see "What Is a Reasonable Accommodation?").

You've written the description of the job, listing the essential functions as they are currently conducted. If you are going to post the position both company-wide and in the local paper, you'll want to consider offering large-print copies for any present employees who may have a visual impairment. You should also consider the possibility that you'll need an assistive device or qualified translator if a person who is hearing impaired decides to apply for the opening. (If the position requires that the applicant take a test to determine skill level, you'll want to consider similar alternatives to the test itself and the test environment). Note however that it is the prospective applicant's responsibility to inform you of any accommodation needed at this stage. You are not expected to plan for every disability.

You receive more than a hundred résumés and decide to follow up with several people who look promising. Thus, you send each an application to fill out prior to your meeting, asking for more specific information about their education, the computer software packages they're proficient in, and their prior employment. Note that you cannot ask for any information that might reveal a disability. Your next step is the initial phone contacts.

The first applicant you call informs you that he uses a wheelchair and asks if your office is accessible. Fortunately, you're located on the ground floor of a multi-story building that has automatic doors opening into its lobby, and your hallways and office doors are wide enough for wheelchair access. However, another applicant informs you through a Telecommunication Device for the Deaf (TDD) operator that she is deaf, and although she reads lips, she would be much more comfortable with a sign-language translator.

You panic for a moment, wondering how you'll locate a translator, how you'll explain to your boss about the added expense, and whether this is a reasonable request (i.e., accommodation). But, lucky for you, the applicant informs you she has contacts through a local support agency that provides such services free of charge. So you set up an interview date and continue making calls.

In the event that the second applicant had not made the offer of assistance, you would have needed to consider whether your company had the resources to supply such an accommodation. The ADA does not establish specific "equations" to determine whether any given company is capable of, and thus liable for, reasonable accommodations. The federal government has, however, provided several examples of what it considers to be a reasonable accommodation. And it also allows an "undue hardship" defense to any claim of discrimination (see "Defenses," for a detailed explanation, page 14). The validity of that defense will depend on the total resources of your company, and any claims of discrimination will be decided on a case-by-case basis. In this example, it would be reasonable to expect that you could provide such a service if it was requested of you. It is reasonable to expect you as a human resource manager to know of the services available in your community, especially given the requirements of the ADA. Also, had you not been so lucky as to work out of an accessible facility, you would have had to set up an interview with the person using the wheelchair in an accessible space, even if you knew the person would not be able to access his or her workspace on a day-to-day basis given the present layout of the building.

You set up ten interviews, and one of your applicants seems to you to have fairly severe arthritis. You think to ask about this, but then catch yourself. Under the ADA you cannot inquire about or even refer to a real or perceived disability. You can, however, ask the individual to explain or demonstrate how he or she would perform an essential job function. Then it would be the applicant's responsibility to point out his or her capabilities with or without a reasonable accommodation.

After the interviews, you think you know the best person for the job, who turns out to be none of the applicants just mentioned. However, in a conversation you have with her former employer you're told about some drug problems, and you're concerned. You'd like to ask her straight out or have her submit to a medical screening before you offer her the job, especially since the second-best applicant is the man who uses a wheelchair, which you feel will be only a minor obstacle to overcome. What can you do?

There are some things you cannot do. First, you cannot require a medical test before you make a conditional offer of employment. Second, you cannot require a test at all if it is not required of all employees in the same position. Again, lucky for you, your company has had a prescreening policy in place for over a year, so you make the offer conditional on the medical exam.

The exam turns up two things. First, while taking down her medical history, the physician learns that she did have a drug (cocaine) problem, for which she received treatment. You cannot, however, now withdraw your offer based on that information. Under the ADA, a past drug addiction (but not mere casual use) that has been successfully treated qualifies as a disability. The exam also reveals through testing that she has recently used amphetamines (without a prescription). Consequently, because you have a policy in place requiring drug testing because you do not wish to hire a person currently using illegal drugs, and because the ADA does not cover individuals who currently use illegal drugs, you withdraw the offer.

You call your second choice, make him an offer, and he passes the medical exam without any problems. Although he has a disability, he is well qualified for the position and you are able to make reasonable accommodations to ensure that he works efficiently and happily. These accommodations include purchasing an adjustable workstation (or modifying an existing one); ensuring a clear path of travel to his work area and to common areas such as rest rooms, copy rooms, meeting rooms, and the cafeteria; and ensuring that each of these areas is accessible and usable by the person with the disability (see Figure 1-2).

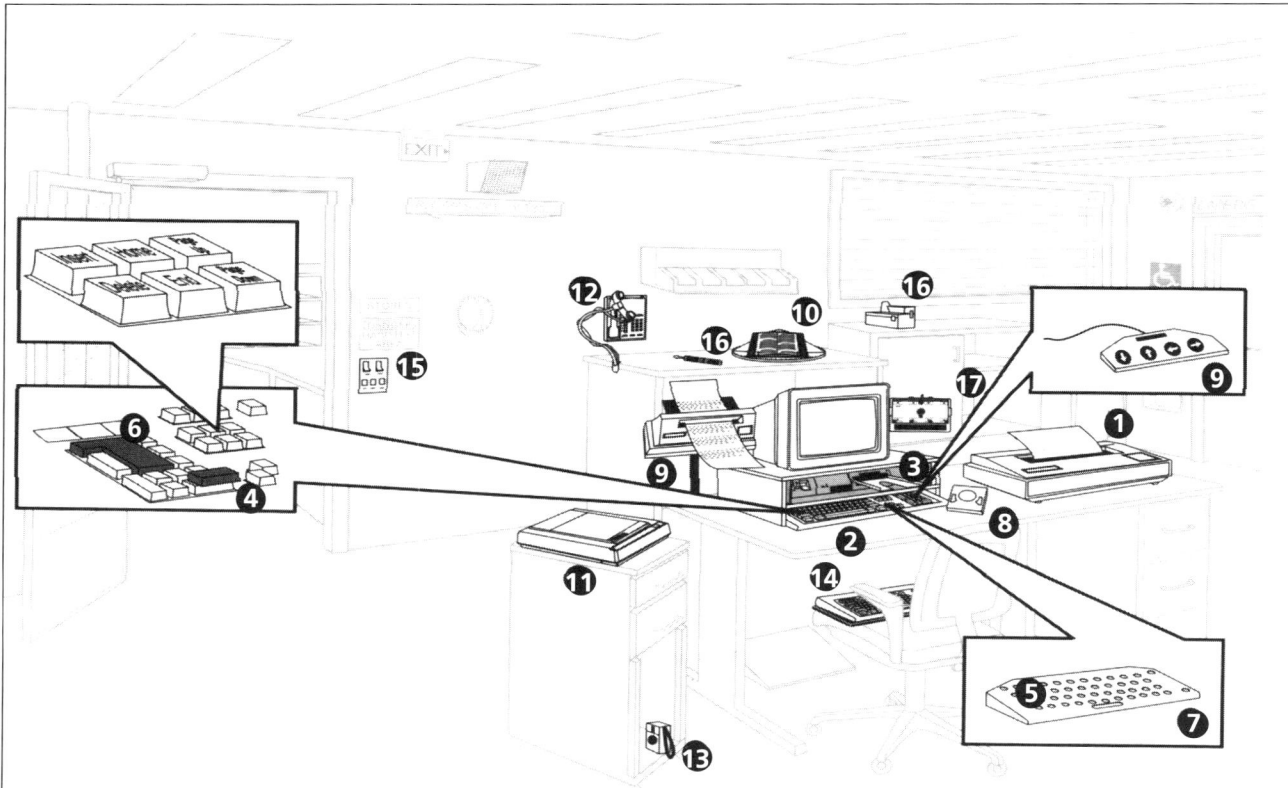

Computers

1. Provide printer paper-handling hardware, e.g., single-sheet feeder.
2. Stabilize keyboard and copy stand at most convenient height and angle.
3. Minimize manipulation—store data on hard, rather than floppy, disks (or provide guides for inserting disks).
4. Provide keycover or keyguard (keyshield).
5. Provide expanded keyboard or keyboard emulator, or adjust sensitivity.
6. Eliminate simultaneous keystrokes with keylocks, sequential or "sticky-key" software, or foot pedal.
7. Use alternative input hardware, e.g., membrane keyboard or miniature keyboard (to minimize finger movements).
8. Provide mouse or mouse emulator. "Remap" keyboard to most efficient configuration. Augment hard/software for environmental control. Accelerate input with abbreviation expansion, word prediction, or macros. Provide graphics software for illustrations.

Information Displays

9. Provide copyholder with electric scrolling.
10. Provide lazy Susan carousel bookstands for multiple source documents, or to position documents at ideal height/angle.
11. Minimize document handling through microfilm or computer information access (use CD-ROM technology or scan documents onto disk with optical character recognition); integrate document transfer (FAX/modem) into computer system. Provide "go/no-go" gauges for precision measuring instruments.
12. Provide headset, speaker phone, or "gooseneck" for receiver with switch for phone cradle buttons.
13. Provide tape recorder for short messages.
14. Provide portable keyboard with memory and/or printer or cassette recorder for notes or dictation. Provide telephone auto-dialer.

Controls

15. Limit activating force to 2 lb (add levers if necessary).
16. Use powered equipment where possible, e.g., staplers, letter openers, screwdrivers.
17. Install alternative switches sensitive to pressure, tilt, magnetic, pneumatic, auditory, or infrared input by sip-and-puff, voice, eye-gaze, eye-blink, or chin/head/tongue/eyebrow/forehead/foot movement. Provide remove-control door latches in secured areas. Avoid need for quick response. Fit levers to dial controls. Facilitate operation with flat of hand, fist, or other gross upper extremity motion. NOTE: Complete remote control systems are also available as substitute for manual control.

1-2. An example of a work area with accommodations in place for an individual who has difficulty in manipulating (from James Mueller's *The Workplace Workbook 2.0*, HRD Press, pp. 80–81). *(Reprinted with permission from the Dole Foundation for Employment for People with Disabilities.)*

Who Is Protected?

The ADA provides protection from discrimination in employment for any qualified individual with a disability. (See "What Is a Disability?" for a discussion of what constitutes a disability.) According to the ADA, a qualified individual with a disability is one who "meets the skill, experience, education, and other job-related requirements of a position held or desired, and who, with or without reasonable accommodation, can perform the essential functions of a job." There are two important qualifying definitions: *reasonable accommodation* and *essential function*. (See "Who Is a Qualified Individual?" and "What Is a Reasonable Accommodation?" for clarification of these terms.)

Also protected are those people who have a record of having a disability and those who are regarded as having a disability. In the first case, an individual who had a history of drug addiction but who has been successfully rehabilitated and has remained drug free is protected from discrimination under this provision of the ADA.

In the case of an individual being regarded as having a disability (for example, a young man is rumored to have a multiple personality disorder and does not), the same protection applies as would be given for a true impairment.

Who Is Not Protected?

The ADA specifically notes certain individuals as not being protected by its regulations. These include anyone who currently uses drugs illegally, and people with the following sexual and behavioral disorders:

- Transvestitism, transsexualism, pedophilia, exhibitionism, and voyeurism

- Compulsive gambling, kleptomania, or pyromania

- Psychoactive substance use disorders resulting from current use of drugs

The ADA does not prohibit the use of drug testing in the workplace. Protection is not extended to those individuals who currently use illegal drugs or to those who drink on the job when policies exist against such activity.

Employment Practices Covered by the ADA

An employer cannot discriminate against a person with a disability at any stage of his or her employment, and that coverage extends to individuals who become disabled while they are employed. The law requires that reasonable accommodations be made to provide equal opportunity for all employees at every stage of their employment.

The list of protected employment practices includes the application process, testing, hiring, assignments, evaluation, discipline, training, promotion, medical examinations, layoff/recall, termination, compensation, leave, and benefits.

The law applies to a present employee to the same extent it applies to a new applicant. An employee with a disability is also entitled to equal access to all activities offered to other employees, including parties given at a private home or public club, sporting events, picnics, retreats, and so on. This aspect of the ADA reveals the far-reaching impact of the law on everyone's lives. It is important to be aware of just how many barriers exist in a world of motion, sound, and visual acuity that go largely unnoticed. Steps need to be taken to dismantle those barriers and to start building environments that accommodate everyone.

Accommodating Employees with Disabilities

The most constructive approach an employer can take to complying with the ADA is to talk to employees about what they need to manage their work environment. Once their suggestions have been obtained by the employer or designer, the particular accommodation can be planned for and implemented.

Most people with disabilities have plenty of experience accommodating themselves to the world. They know the tools and tricks of creating a workable environment for themselves. (See Karen Hirsch's article on personal history interviews in Chapter 3 for more on this.) In fact, the ADA does not allow an employer to provide an accommodation that is not acceptable to the individual with the disability. A solution must be offered that is mutually agreeable. The case study offered by Owen Cooks on Purdue University's ADA compliance plan in Chapter 5 points out that soliciting input from individuals with disabilities *before* changes are implemented can actually save money and may show that the employer has made a "good-faith" effort to make reasonable accommodations. (See "Defenses Against Charges of Discrimination" for more on the good faith defense.)

In some cases employers will need to be creative, imagining themselves in the place of the employees, seeing through their eyes. (Chapter 3 offers some strategies for facilitating this process.) The government has set up several programs to assist employers: The Job Accommodation Network, for example, offers toll-free assistance to help create workable solutions to accommodating any number of disabilities. Their services are available by phone, TDD, and modem (see Chapter 10).

> ## What Is a Reasonable Accommodation?
>
> In general, an accommodation will fall into one of three categories:
>
> - Making the workplace/facility accessible
> - Changing the way a job/service is normally handled/provided
> - Providing or modifying equipment or assistive devices
>
> If a person who uses a wheelchair could perform a programming job given an adjustable workstation, horizontal files, and clear access to a workspace and common areas, then it would be a reasonable accommodation for most companies to make the requisite changes to allow such a person to hold that position. A person with a hearing impairment can reasonably expect to have an assistive device available at a theater open to the general public, and he or she should be able to work, live, and relax in a well-designed acoustic environment that can be adapted to specifically accommodate his or her impairment. People with visual impairments can reasonably expect to encounter environments that are free of hazards and that offer clear signals for navigation. They should also be provided with large-print materials or alternative media such as recordings, braille prints, software enhancements that enlarge print on a computer screen, or even a reader both on the job and at places of public and private service (a library, for example).
>
> Other examples of reasonable accommodation are:
>
> - Installing an entry ramp
> - Enlarging doors and making at least one rest room accessible
> - Installing redundant alarms that alert by visual, auditory, and tactile clues
> - Using sound-absorbing materials on office dividers to cut down on background noise
>
> Reasonable accommodation can also include offering a flexible work schedule, part-time work, and reassignment to a vacant position (in a case where an employee becomes disabled and can no longer perform the essential functions of his or her current job).

Title II: Public Services

Title II has two subsections: The first deals with general state and local government services, the second with transportation concerns.

In most cases, state and local governments have been covered by the Rehabilitation Act of 1973, because most receive some measure of federal funding. Consequently, in employment, they are in many ways required to meet stricter standards in hiring people with disabilities than those required by the ADA. Virtually all state and local governments are bound by the same employment provisions for private entities in Title I.

> ### Defenses Against Charges of Discrimination
>
> The ADA sets up several specific defenses for any entity accused of discriminatory practices against an individual with a disability. There may be times when compliance with the ADA seems unattainable, and the law has established several categories from which to draw a defense.
>
> I. *Undue hardship/burden:* This defense can be used in cases of employment and accommodation. If an entity can show that making an accommodation (such as installing a ramp, providing a translator, and so on) would involve a substantial difficulty or expense, it might be granted an undue hardship exemption. Note that there are no set guidelines for determining what constitutes undue hardship. Cases are decided individually.
>
> II. *Direct threat:* This defense is used in cases where an entity considers the inclusion of an individual with a disability to pose a substantial risk of harm to the safety and health of herself or others. It must be based on valid medical knowledge or objective evidence, not on speculation. The requirement must be the same for all other individuals, and the entity is required to attempt to eliminate or reduce the risk with a reasonable accommodation before it can claim this defense.
>
> III. *Readily achievable:* This defense is used mainly in reference to removing architectural barriers. Such removal must be both easily accomplishable and able to be done without great expense. Installing an entry ramp may in some instances be unreasonable (the slope of land may be too great, or the company's resources may be too small). Note that even in such cases where physical removal of a barrier is unreasonable, the entity may still be required to provide other means of service (home delivery/pickup, for example).
>
> IV. *Fundamental alteration to nature of goods and services:* This defense is used in Title III to protect entities for whom making certain types of accommodations would fundamentally change the way they do business or the goods being offered.
>
> V. *Good-faith effort:* If an entity has made several attempts to accommodate a person with a disability but has been unable to do so, this defense is taken into account when deciding what remedies will be required, if discrimination is found.

Subtitle A: General Services

Subtitle A of Title II guarantees qualified people with disabilities equal access to all services and programs or activities provided by a public entity. This includes all public meetings, schools, recreational facilities, and libraries, for example. Virtually any activity open to the public at large that is the province of a state or local government must be accessible to individuals with disabilities. Accessibility in this case may require removing architectural barriers; making facilities fully accessible; and providing assistive devices, alternative means of presentation, or readers and translators (see Figure 1-4).

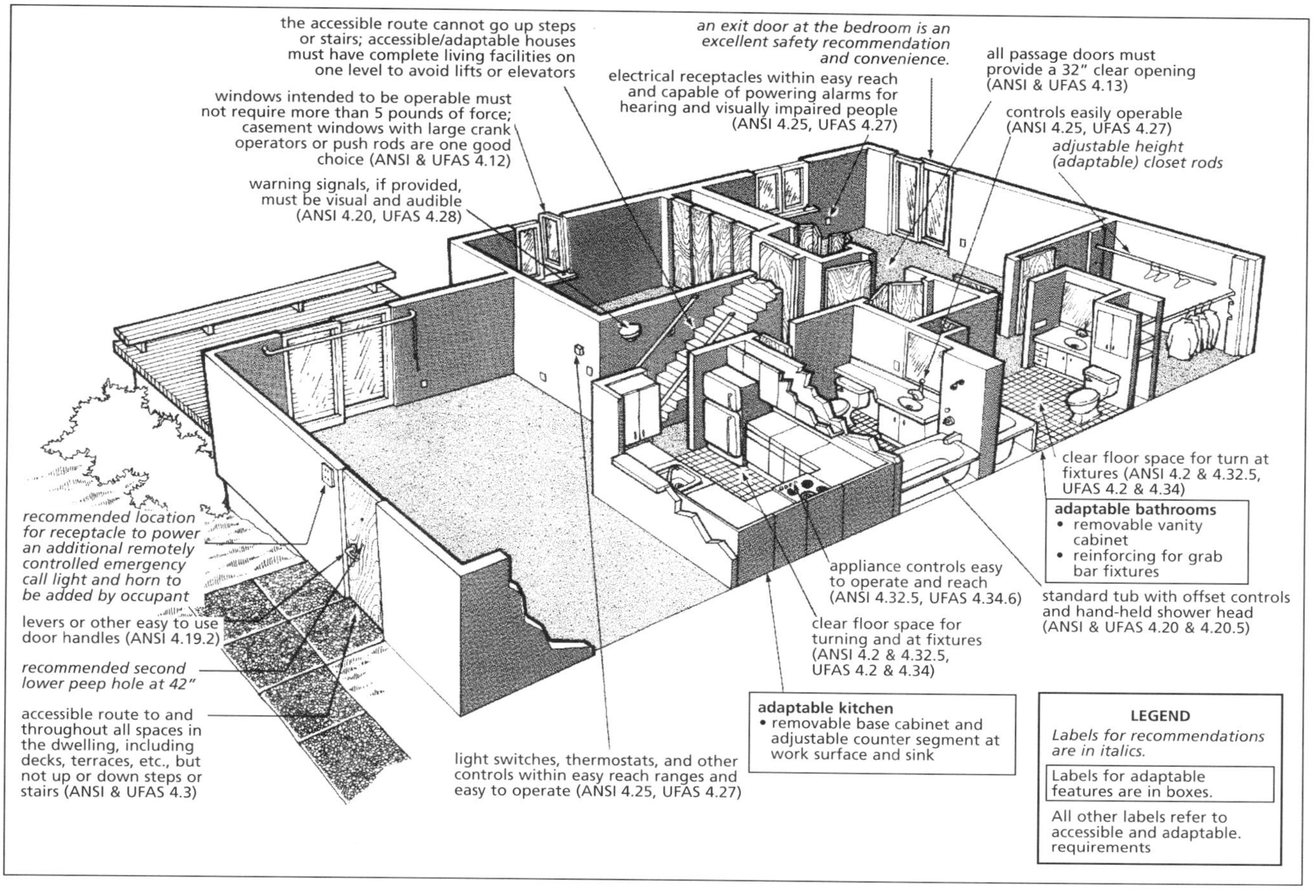

What Is the Americans with Disabilities Act?   15

[Figure showing cutaway view of an accessible/adaptable house with numerous labels:]

- the accessible route cannot go up steps or stairs; accessible/adaptable houses must have complete living facilities on one level to avoid lifts or elevators
- an exit door at the bedroom is an excellent safety recommendation and convenience.
- electrical receptacles within easy reach and capable of powering alarms for hearing and visually impaired people (ANSI 4.25, UFAS 4.27)
- all passage doors must provide a 32" clear opening (ANSI & UFAS 4.13)
- windows intended to be operable must not require more than 5 pounds of force; casement windows with large crank operators or push rods are one good choice (ANSI & UFAS 4.12)
- controls easily operable (ANSI 4.25, UFAS 4.27) *adjustable height (adaptable) closet rods*
- warning signals, if provided, must be visual and audible (ANSI 4.20, UFAS 4.28)
- *recommended location for receptacle to power an additional remotely controlled emergency call light and horn to be added by occupant*
- clear floor space for turn at fixtures (ANSI 4.2 & 4.32.5, UFAS 4.2 & 4.34)
- **adaptable bathrooms** • removable vanity cabinet • reinforcing for grab bar fixtures
- levers or other easy to use door handles (ANSI 4.19.2)
- appliance controls easy to operate and reach (ANSI 4.32.5, UFAS 4.34.6)
- standard tub with offset controls and hand-held shower head (ANSI & UFAS 4.20 & 4.20.5)
- *recommended second lower peep hole at 42"*
- clear floor space for turning and at fixtures (ANSI 4.2 & 4.32.5, UFAS 4.2 & 4.34)
- accessible route to and throughout all spaces in the dwelling, including decks, terraces, etc., but not up or down steps or stairs (ANSI & UFAS 4.3)
- light switches, thermostats, and other controls within easy reach ranges and easy to operate (ANSI 4.25, UFAS 4.27)
- **adaptable kitchen** • removable base cabinet and adjustable counter segment at work surface and sink
- **LEGEND** *Labels for recommendations are in italics.* Labels for adaptable features are in boxes. All other labels refer to accessible and adaptable requirements

1-3. ANSI, UFAS, and ADA Accessibility Guidelines (ADAAG) share the same numbering system, making cross-referencing between various standards relatively easy.

New construction and alteration to existing facilities must meet the standards set forth by the Americans with Disabilities Act Accessibility Guidelines (ADAAG). These guidelines are similar—and sometimes identical—to the earlier guidelines set by the American National Standards Institute (ANSI) A117.1. ANSI guidelines are voluntary suggestions (although they are widely adopted as code by states and municipalities); ADAAG are minimum requirements that must be met (see Figure 1-3).

The ADA accessibility guidelines contain general design standards for building and site elements, such as parking, accessible routes, ramps, stairs, elevators, doors, drinking fountains, bathrooms, alarms, signs, telephones, and automated teller machines. They also contain specific technical standards for restaurants, medical care facilities, libraries, and transient lodgings. Selections from these guidelines appear throughout this book, but the designer should be familiar with the complete set while remaining aware that these represent minimum standards. Selections throughout

1-4. An example (from AIKCO) of wall sconces that meet the ADA's 4" protrusion limitation (the major compliance feature). *(Reprinted with permission from AIKCO.)*

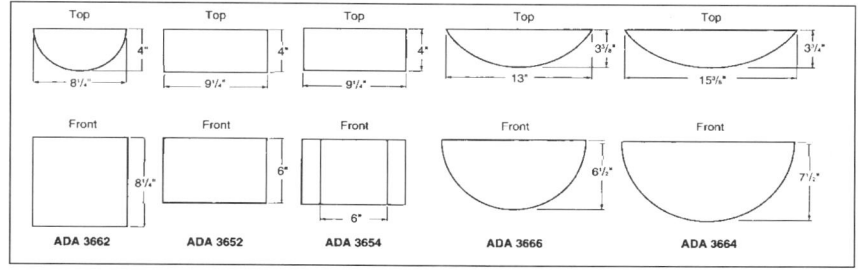

the book stress the importance of moving beyond any mere set of guidelines for creating universal design.

Subtitle B: Transportation

Part I

Subtitle B covers public transportation and is further divided into parts I and II. Part I concerns public transportation by bus, light and rapid rail, or any other vehicle that operates on a fixed-route schedule. The purpose of this part is to ensure that such systems be made available to individuals with disabilities as rapidly as possible.

Any new vehicle ordered after August 25, 1990, must be usable by individuals with disabilities, including those who use wheelchairs. (Temporary relief may be granted for this requirement if the public entity makes an effort to purchase an accessible vehicle but finds that none is available.) Also, any vehicle that is remanufactured and can be expected to be in service for five or more years must be made accessible during that remanufacturing. (Used vehicles are also covered by this rule, unless accessible vehicles can be shown to be unavailable.) An exception to the rule exists for historical vehicles, if making them accessible would fundamentally alter the character of the vehicle. (See "Defenses Against Charges of Discrimination" for a definition of this and other defenses.)

Public entities are also required to provide a paratransit (equivalent and accessible) system for individuals with disabilities if they offer a fixed-route system. The paratransit system must be comparable to the regular system (that is, pick-up time must be similar). However, public entities that can show that implementing such a system would result in an undue financial burden can petition for an exception.

If the public entity offers a demand responsive system (such as a senior center bus), then that system must meet the same accessibility standards for new vehicles detailed above, unless they offer an alternative system that provides an equivalent service for those with disabilities.

All new transportation facilities must be accessible as outlined in the ADAAG. Also, any alterations must follow these guidelines to the maximum extent feasible. Section 227 specifically mandates that all key transportation stations after January 26, 1995, must have become accessible; however, extensions of up to 30 years may be granted in cases that present extraordinary difficulties.

In general, public entities are bound by the same rules that apply to Title III (Public Accommodations).

Part II

This subsection of Title II deals with intercity and commuter rail transportation. The same rules governing Part I apply here. Some compliance dates, however, differ. Accessibility standards must have been met by July 26, 1995, and all key stations must have been made accessible by July 26, 1993 (again, extensions are available in some cases). In Chapter 7, Alan Wier describes a design project in which high-speed rail cars were designed to meet all of the requirements of the ADA.

Title III: Public Accommodations and Services Operated by Private Entities

Title III affects nearly every business imaginable: every grocery, restaurant, theater, zoo, museum, gas station, and laundromat. If a service is offered to the public at large, it is covered by the ADA.

There are 12 general categories listed in the ADA as public accommodations:

1. Places of lodging
2. Establishments serving food or drink
3. Places of exhibition or entertainment
4. Places of public gathering
5. Sales or rental establishments
6. Service establishments
7. Stations used for specific transportation
8. Places of public display or collection
9. Places of recreation
10. Places of education
11. Social service center establishments
12. Places of exercise and recreation

There are two specific exceptions to coverage given in the ADA—religious organizations and private clubs (as defined by the Civil Rights Act of 1964). Even though religious organizations are exempt from compliance, voluntary compliance is urged by many church leaders (see Figure 7-14). All other private entities that have dealings with the general public and whose operations affect commerce are prohibited from discriminating against an individual on the basis of a disability. They must attempt to accommodate the needs of all individuals by allowing full access to and participation in the services offered. A private entity is required to remove existing architectural and communication barriers in existing facilities

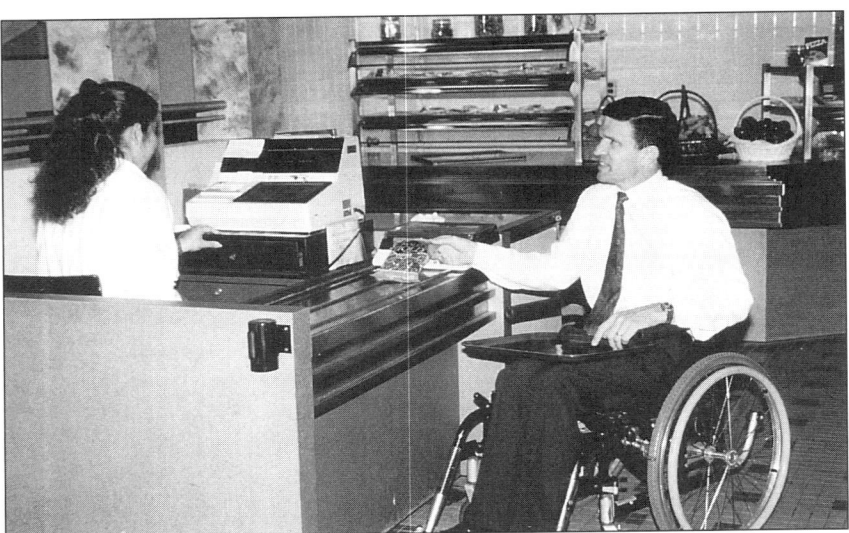

1-5. Stores with check-out aisles must be made accessible under the ADA. This photo shows a strategy that works well for both the individual using a wheelchair and the clerk, who is then not required to stand for hours without opportunity to sit. *(Reprinted with permission from the Eastern Paralyzed Veterans Association.)*

and transportation barriers in existing vehicles, where such removal is readily achievable. If the means are not readily achievable, that entity must provide alternative service that is equal in kind.

Furthermore, such access and participation must be offered on an equal basis in an integrated setting. Thus, a person with a hearing impairment has the right to an assistive device when attending a movie and should not have to sit in a special section apart from the general public to make use of that device. Likewise, a person using a wheelchair has the right to enjoy a film while sitting in a central part of the theater, not just in a special section removed from the general audience (see Figure 1-5).

Transportation

The transportation guidelines under this title are similar to those in Title II. However, the standards are different for a private entity that provides some transportation services (a hotel shuttle service, for example) but that is not primarily in the business of transportation. An exception is available for historical vehicles whose character would be fundamentally altered if made accessible.

New Construction and Alteration

All new construction of commercial facilities must be accessible except where it is structurally impracticable to do so (note that this exception does not apply to the Title II regulations for public, that is, government, facilities). Consequently, such construction must at minimum meet the standards set forth in the ADAAG. All alterations must be accessible to the maximum extent feasible, to include parking, entry ways, rest rooms, water fountains, and telephones (TDDs). The ADA specifically exempts the requirement for elevators in buildings of fewer than three stories with under 3000 square feet of space per story, unless that facility is a shopping mall or center or contains health care providers (the Attorney General has the authority to add to this list).

Examinations and Courses

All facilities where examinations and courses related to applications, licensing, certification, or credentialing for secondary or postsecondary schooling, or for educational, professional, or trade purposes are given must be accessible or made available at an alternate site. All material must be available in a variety of accessible formats to accommodate specific disabilities (on tape for the visually impaired, for example).

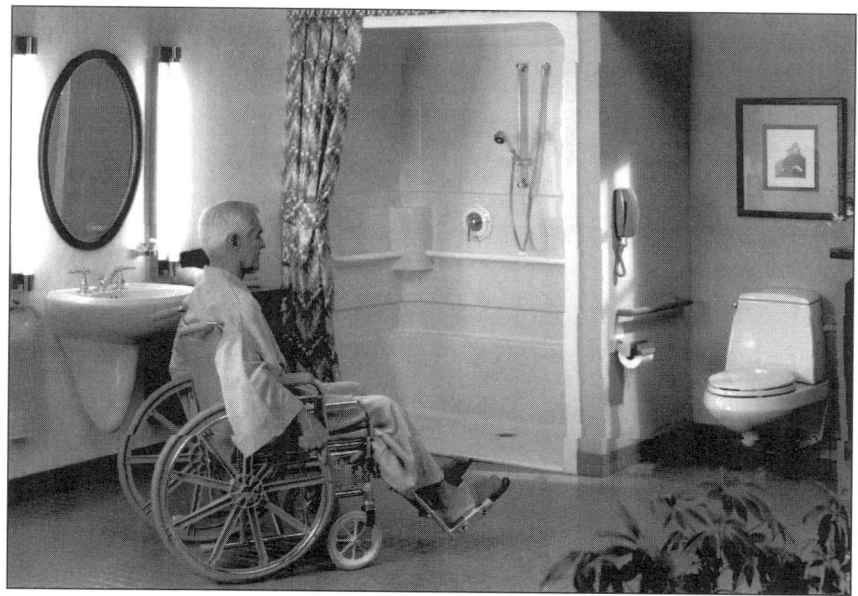

1-6. Universal design features that meet ADA standards for bathroom fixtures in commercial or residential spaces include wall-hung lavatory and toilet, an accessible shower unit with adjustable shower wand, well-placed grab bars, and good lighting. *(Reprinted with permission from Kohler Co.)*

Title IV: Telecommunications

Title IV amends the Communications Act of 1934 in two significant ways, affecting both individuals with speech and hearing impairments, and public and private entities faced with providing alternative communication devices (such as TDDs) as reasonable accommodations and auxiliary aids.

Tax Incentives for Businesses

Disabled Access Tax Credit

Internal Revenue Code Section 44 allows an eligible small business to elect a tax credit equal to 50% of eligible access expenditures between $250 and $10,250 for a credit of up to $5000 in any given year.

An *eligible small business* is one that has gross receipts for the preceding year of less than $1 million or had no more than 30 full-time employees. Eligible access expenditures include any amounts spent to remove barriers, purchase assistive devices, provide readers, and so on (that is, any reasonable accommodation expense).

This credit can be elected in more than one tax year.

Tax Deduction to Remove Barriers

Internal Revenue Code Section 190 allows any entity that must remove a barrier to accommodate a person with a disability (including transportation barriers) to take up to a $15,000 deduction each year for such alteration. However, the alteration must meet the standards set by the Architectural and Transportation Barriers Compliance Board.

Expenses for new construction are not eligible.

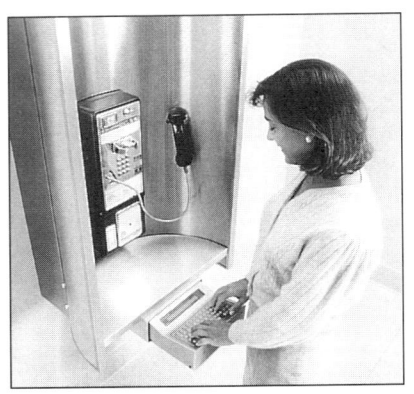

1-7. Telecommunication devices for the deaf (TDD), such as this pay phone from Ultratec, are one example of the accommodations that entities serving the general public will need to make. *(Reprinted with permission from Ultratec, Inc.)*

The ADA amends Title II of the Communications Act by requiring the implementation of telecommunication relay services both within and between states. These services allow communication by print over existing phone lines to a special operator who verbally relays the message to the recipient and then sends the reply back to the originator by print.

Title IV also amends Section 711 of the Communications Act, requiring that all public service broadcasts produced or funded in whole or in part by the Federal Government be closed captioned. The producer is responsible for this provision; however, if an individual television station receives the captioning but fails to broadcast it, then that station is liable.

Title V: Miscellaneous Provisions

Title V addresses several concerns that are pertinent to the rest of the act but that may require further clarification. These are brief sections that are important but somewhat disconnected.

Section 501

The first section of Title V declares that no part of the act should be interpreted as allowing lesser standards to be applied than are otherwise required by existing federal, state, and local laws (the Rehabilitation Act of 1973 and pursuant regulations are noted). This section also points out that the ADA does not affect rules about smoking in places of employment, public accommodation, or transportation. Nor does the ADA place restrictions on insurance companies, except to specify that insurance plans cannot be used to discriminate against a person with a disability.

This section repeats the rule noted elsewhere in this chapter and in the ADA that individuals with disabilities are not required to accept accommodations, aids, services, opportunities, or benefits that they do not want. The belief that the entity and the individual must work together to find a mutually agreeable solution to any problems of discrimination is underscored throughout the ADA.

Other Sections

Section 502 waives a state's immunity from prosecution (as established in the 11th amendment to the Constitution), allowing a state to be sued for discrimination under the ADA.

Section 503 protects an individual who is filing a complaint or suit of discrimination from any form of harassment or retaliation.

Section 504 sets the deadline for accessibility guidelines to be issued (ADAAG) by the Architectural and Transportation Barriers Compliance Board.

Section 505 allows for attorney fees to be collected for the prevailing party in any judgment (federal government is excluded).

Section 506 sets guidelines for the creation of technical assistance manuals and programs, including disseminating information to appropriate parties through publications and training programs. This section also establishes that failure to receive technical assistance cannot be used as a defense against a discrimination charge.

Section 507 requires a study to be conducted of the policies of the Federal Wilderness Areas to see if they inhibit the ability of individuals with disabilities from full access and enjoyment. It also reaffirms that wilderness areas cannot prohibit the use of wheelchairs.

Section 508 specifically notes that transvestitism is not considered to be a disability; thus, individuals are not covered by the act solely on the basis of their being transvestites.

Section 509 extends the coverage of the ADA in all its provisions to the House of Representatives and the Senate.

Section 510 underscores earlier statements in the act that current illegal use of drugs is not protected under the ADA, and it specifically states that nothing in the act is to be construed as affecting current policies on drug testing.

Section 511 defines some categories of individuals or conditions that are not considered to be disabilities as defined by the ADA: homosexuality and bisexuality; transvestitism, transsexualism, pedophilia, exhibitionism, voyeurism, gender identity disorders that are not the result of physical impairments, and other sexual behavior disorders; compulsive gambling, kleptomania, or pyromania; and psychoactive substance use disorders resulting from current use of drugs.

Section 512 amends the Rehabilitation Act of 1973 to include the ADA definitions of disabilities in terms of alcohol and drug addiction.

Section 513 encourages the use of alternative means of dispute resolution.

Section 514 allows individual provisions of the act that are found unconstitutional to be removed without affecting the remainder of the ADA.

Remedies for Discrimination

The ADA provides for various remedies and courses of action to be taken in cases of discrimination. Specific steps are outlined for each of the act's titles.

Title I

The employment section of the ADA is enforced by the Equal Employment Opportunity Commission (EEOC) using the same procedures used to enforce the Civil Rights Act. To report any discrimination, individuals must contact their local EEOC office (on their own behalf or on behalf of another; individuals are protected from retaliation for reporting). The EEOC will investigate and try to resolve any discrimination found. If no resolution is possible they will either file suit or issue a "right to sue" letter.

Remedies include hiring, reinstatement, promotion, back pay, front pay, restored benefits, reasonable accommodation, attorneys' fees, expert witness fees, and court costs. Punitive and compensatory damages are also available in cases of intentional discrimination or where no good faith effort has been made, limited to the following amounts:

No. of Employees	Maximum Damages
15–100	$ 50,000
101–200	$100,000
201–500	$200,000
500+	$300,000

NOTE: Punitive damages are not available against state and local governments.

Title II

Lawsuits can be brought by private parties, or complaints can be filed with appropriate federal agencies (Agriculture, Education, Health and Human Services, and so on). Complaints filed with the Department of Justice will be referred to the appropriate agency. Remedies under this title are the same as for Section 504 of the Rehabilitation Act of 1973. Attorneys' fees are awarded to the prevailing party.

Title III

Private parties can bring lawsuits to stop discrimination. In these cases, attorneys' fees may be awarded. Suits can also be brought by the Attorney General in cases of gross abuse. In these cases monetary damages (but not punitive damages) and civil penalties can be awarded: up to $50,000 for a first offense; up to $100,000 for subsequent violations.

What the ADA Means for the Future

A person who has a disability may see the Americans with Disabilities Act as a welcome relief to a system of neglect and disregard, but is possibly a bit skeptical that sweeping changes will be seen within the first several years. Given the history of other civil rights movements and legislation, this skepticism is probably justified. However, the nature of this act—especially its requirement that employers and business and governments work with individuals to find reasonable accommodations—will bring about some necessary changes. A person with a disability also can find some support in the legal means of redress available for the first time (see "Remedies for Discrimination").

The majority of Americans should look at the ADA as an opportunity for enriching their experience of others and for finding competent and willing workers and consumers. For designers, the ADA and the growing interest in universal design presents an opportunity for creatively changing the built world. The ADA and subsequent information generated about meeting the needs of people with disabilities will change every environment for the better, providing spaces and products that support people throughout their lifespans.

What Is Universal Design? 2

Over the past few years the term *universal design* has been showing up in advertisements for a variety of products, has been cited in the text of the Americans with Disabilities Act and its accessibility guidelines, and has appeared on the course offerings at many design and building conferences across the nation. There has been a wellspring of interest in the concept, but at the same time, there is a clear lack of any fully realized definition of what exactly is meant by universal design.

Some people define universal design as simply "good" design. This only replaces one word with an equally imprecise term. In the broadest terms, universal design is "design for all people." Universal design, also known as *lifespan design*, seeks to create environments and products that are usable by children, young adults, and the elderly. They can be used by people with "normal" abilities and those with disabilities, including temporary ones. Still, like many generalities, "designing for all people" provides a nice slogan but doesn't do enough to further understanding and use of the quite remarkable, indeed revolutionary, concept behind the mere definition. This book is meant to provide both a theoretical and a practical base from which you can build a working understanding of what it means to achieve universal design.

Ronald Mace, the architect who coined the term "universal design," says that one of the more important changes brought about by the use of this term is the elimination of the label "special needs" from segments of the population who are working to maintain or gain their independence. Universal design and the ADA both ask that people be viewed as equal in nature, as having

People First: Using Language that Dignifies

Instead of Saying:	Use:
• Handicapped person	• Person with a disability
• Mute, dumb, deaf, blind… person	• Person who cannot speak, has a hearing impairment, visual impairment, and so on
• Palsied, CP, or spastic	• Person with cerebral palsy
• Mongoloid	• Person with Down's syndrome
• Cripple	• Person who has a physical disability
• Retarded, crazy, mental defective	• Person who has a mental disability
• Epileptic	• Person who has epilepsy
• Alcoholic or addict	• Person who is chemically dependent

similar rights and obligations, and as deserving of equal opportunity in every facet of society. The approach used by both is "people first," which is the guiding principle of this book and which is reflected in the now-accepted method of referring to people with disabilities: person as a noun followed by disability as an adjective.

One of the problems with the phrase "special needs" is that the disability is given more attention than the person (special needs implies that "they" are lacking something "we" have). This results in the individual being further discriminated against by being made to feel separate, different, in need. (Think of the times you've seen wheelchair accessible entrances for buildings located in the back, separate from the regular entryway.)

Universal design features are good for almost everyone, and as they become incorporated into the everyday world, the similarities between people, as well as their needs for similar products and environments, will become more readily apparent.

Historically, design has met the needs of people with varying abilities by creating specialized (and thus expensive), rather unattractive products and

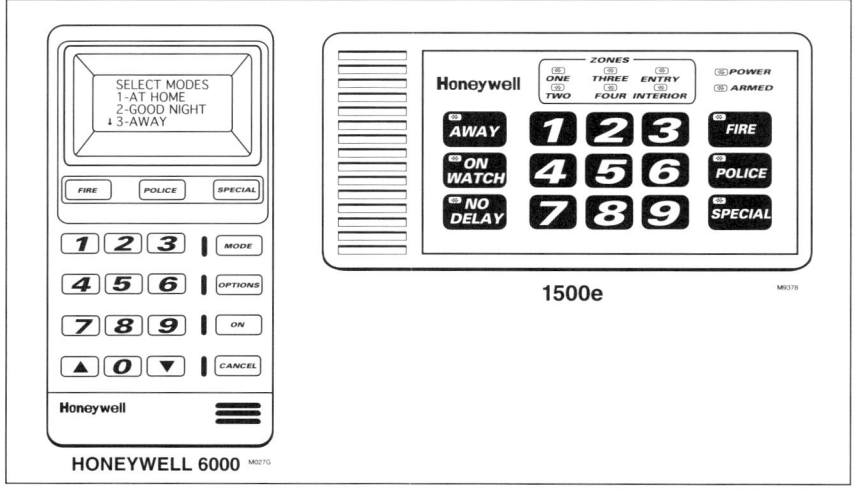

2-1. Home automation systems, such as these from Honeywell, are other examples of security systems that provide support through easy-to-use controls. *(Reprinted with permission from Honeywell, Inc.)*

environments to make up for a "missing" ability (prosthetic design) or by removing a barrier to access (accessible, or barrier-free design). Universal design incorporates the features of both of these design styles but goes a step further by looking at people with a more encompassing eye. It defines ways of thinking about and designing environments and products that work for the greatest number of people possible, regardless of their range of ability, body size, or age. One easily recognizable example is the use of levers instead of round knobs on doors. Levers can be used by people with arthritis, small children, and anyone who has confronted a closed door while holding two armfuls of groceries in a sudden downpour of rain (see Figure 2-2).

Universal design asks that designers create spaces and products that adapt to people as individuals and that strengthen their sense of themselves as capable and independent, or even as their needs change, or even if they have a disability that historically would have severely limited their ability to work, play, or do much more than simply exist in the world.

A prevalent example of such adaptable design is the ergonomic office chair that adjusts for height and for forward and backward leaning support (see Figure 2-4). (Ergonomic design is discussed in detail in Chapter 6.) This type of design can also be more fully utilized in the home, where people also come in different sizes and deserve decent support. Throughout this book, illustrations of products for both office and home are offered as examples of universal design. As home offices become increasingly accepted, more of the same careful design currently being used in office furnishings will be applied to the home.

Four Cornerstones of Universal Design

Susan Behar, ASID (see Chapter 9—Marketing), views universal design as "an enhancing business strategy needed for survival and renewed opportunities for design professionals. The four A's—accessibility, adaptability, aesthetics, affordability—address the education and design values necessary for incorporating universal design into our environment." Similarly, but with a slightly different focus, this book posits that the following four underlying principles be considered essential for creating a universal design. Universal design must be:

1. Supportive
2. Adaptable
3. Accessible
4. Safety oriented

2-2. Lever door openers are a simple, inexpensive example of universal design, widely used in Europe and becoming more prevalent in the United States. *(Reprinted with permission from HEWI, Inc.)*

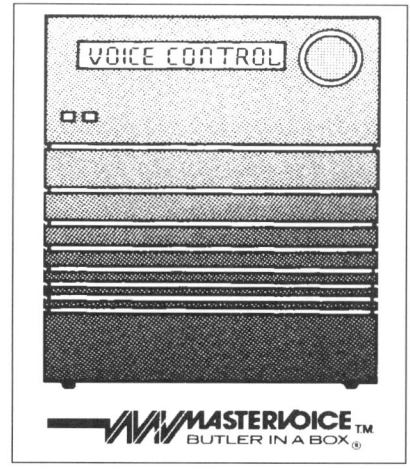

2-3. Products such as the Butler in a Box® home automation system can be very supportive additions to a design and have been used in some model homes (see Bill Wasch's case study in Chapter 9). The Butler in a Box® can be made to manipulate up to 256 devices (phones, televisions, draperies, and so on) by touch control and up to 42 devices by voice control. Voice recognition is an especially useful and supportive universal design feature. *(Reprinted with permission from AVSI.)*

2-4. An ergonomic chair is one of the most important components in an adaptable work space. This one, from Girsberger Office Seating, provides pivot points under the knee, to the floating lumbar support area, and to the upper back panel; ribbing for upper back flexibility; removable cushions for cleaning or replacement; levered vertical and horizontal position controls; and dual-wheel casters on a five-point base for safety and ease of movement. *(Reprinted with permission from Girsberger Office Seating.)*

These four interrelated aspects of a design provide useful standards for the measurement and evaluation of new and existing products and environments.

Supportive Design

The first test of universal design is that it must be *supportive:* It should provide a necessary aid to function, and it must not, in providing such aid, create any undue burden on any user (see Figure 2-4). Consider the lighting used to illuminate a work surface or space. Lack of appropriate lighting can actually lead to decreased visual acuity. And as people grow older, they need more light to see as well. Depending upon the environment (home, work, windowed, enclosed), people need to be able to adjust for different levels and directions of light to support everyday activities. Or consider a kitchen countertop, which should be glare-free and easy to clean. If it lacks these supportive features, it will actually add stress to day-to-day living.

Adaptable Design

Adaptable means that a product or environment should serve a majority of individuals who have a variety of changing needs. One example was mentioned earlier: the ergonomic chair. Adjustable workstations are another example of design that adapts to meet a variety of needs (see Figure 2-5). Desks that adjust in height, with wraparound or detachable surfaces, meet the test of adaptability. Adjustable stands for keyboards and monitors also meet this requirement, as do software programs that allow a computer to display text in varying fonts and sizes. Products such as these are useful for people with visual impairments and for anyone whose eyesight "isn't what it used to be," one of the most common complaints of aging.

Accessible Design

Accessibility means removing barriers. For universal design and the ADA, such barriers are both attitudinal and physical. By encompassing a broader range of human abilities, universal design subtly empowers individuals, changing a physical environment that currently hinders or harms many people unnecessarily. Universal design promotes accessibility because most barriers (to mobility, communication, or well being) inhibit most people. For example, curb cuts work for bicyclists and parents pushing carriages as well as for people using wheelchairs. However, universal design suggests looking closer at the design of curb cuts by also considering how they affect people with visual impairments. Once this is done, designers may decide to use placement and texture, or a contrasting color or pattern, to alleviate possible accidents that may arise from visual limitations.

Examples of accessible design include placing wall sockets at an 18-inch height from the floor for ease of reach from a wheelchair, using wider, standardized doors, and creating a travel path free of obstacles. These are all features that would benefit everyone—higher wall sockets mean less bending from a standing position, wider doors provide more room for maneuvering packages and furnishings, and a clear travel path helps prevent accidents. Accessible design means rethinking space and equipment to better enable use by all people (see Figure 2-7).

Safety-Oriented Design

Safety-oriented design promotes health and well being. It is corrective and preventative. Using contrasting colors or patterns to mark changes in floor level helps protect against tripping injuries (see Figure 2-6). Desks and cabinets with rounded edges are safer than those with sharp edges. Redundant alarms that have both audible and visual signals are safer than those that use only a single cue. A smoke alarm that also provides a light source can save time in exiting a burning building and can also mark the path of exit.

There is more to safety, however, than overcoming physical threats. Safety also entails a sense of psychological well being, of belonging, of self-esteem and self-worth. Any environment impacts both the physical and the psychological, and design must be directed toward both. Safe design must recognize and deal with both physical and psychological challenges.

Products and spaces that allow their users to gain a high level of competence support a state of psychological health. They protect individuals from the loss of independence as they cope with changes that occur naturally as they age. When people no longer work as well within a given environment because of changes in their physical capabilities, they should not have to curtail their activities or lower their expectations about what they can accomplish. Rather, the environment should be flexible enough to accommodate changing human needs and abilities.

Other Benefits of Universal Design

Universal design has several beneficial features besides the four already noted. First, universal design is economical. It does not focus on creating products and environments for an individual disability (since each person manages a disability in a unique way), but instead goes beyond specialization, not only by utilizing existing products in different ways but also by standardizing those

2-5. The Trakker™, from Haworth Inc., is an example of adjustable design. The touch control provides continuous adjustment to work surfaces from 26" to 42" for sitting or standing work and can easily accommodate people in wheelchairs. *(Reprinted with permission from Haworth, Inc.)*

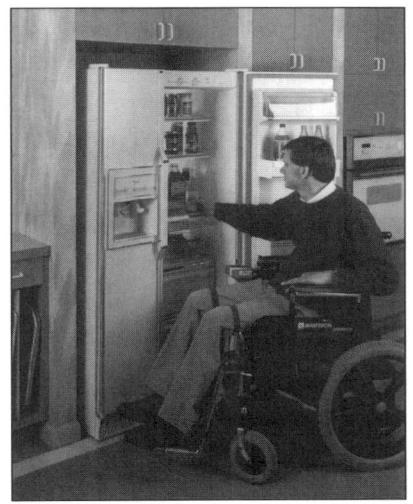

2-6. Side-by-side refrigerator/freezers provide easy access for people of all statures and abilities. *(Reprinted with permission from Whirlpool Corporation.)*

2-7. This universal kitchen provides several safety features, including the contrasting floor pattern that tells people with vision impairments (as well as running children and preoccupied parents) that a solid surface is ahead. Kitchen design by Joan Eisenberg, CKD. *(Reprinted with permission from American Ceramic Olean Tile.)*

things that can be beneficial to everyone. Here, the call for a standard door width (3 feet) stands out because it not only provides access for people using wheelchairs and walkers, but also saves time and money for builders, designers, and manufacturers. A wider door is also more convenient for people who need to move furniture through doorways.

The most narrow doors in a house are into bathrooms because early builders thought that no one would be moving furniture in and out of one. Unfortunately, this standard has remained, even though more and more people use wheelchairs and walkers and consequently must have a wider access into the bathroom. Wider halls also need to become a standard within housing. Anyone who is ever in need of emergency service that requires a stretcher will find her care severely hampered by narrow hallways that don't allow turns into and out of rooms.

Universal design is also aesthetically pleasing; products and environments do not stand out as different or necessary. Designers for "special needs" often give little consideration to appearance, and so people with certain disabilities are surrounded by institutional-looking products. Often the world at large thinks all products that meet varying abilities need to be cumbersome and ugly, a bit like living in a stereotypical sterile hospital ward. The products themselves add to the problem by calling unwelcome attention to the disability at the expense of the individual's need for an aesthetically pleasing environment. Universal design, on the other hand, adapts products that are already accepted by the population at large, or creates ones that will be pleasing to everyone (see Figure 2-8).

2-8. Grab bars, long associated with an "institutional" and thus unappealing look, now fit within any decor and even add a new level of attractiveness. *(Reprinted with permission from Lumex.)*

Finally, universal design is marketable. Millions of Americans want to buy what universal design can provide. As the baby boom generation has changed, so have the main areas where their money is spent. When "boomers" had their own babies, lots of money was spent on products for children. And as boomers grow into later adulthood, more money will be spent on products and environments that allow them to maintain their independence.

Another important marketing consideration is that the ADA will provide access to a fuller lifestyle for millions of people with disabilities who have been kept out of the mainstream. The ADA will bring millions of people who must be accommodated through assistive devices and accessible environments into the workplace. And it will bring these same people into the social world of restaurants, grocery stores, theaters, and so on. Virtually all owners of businesses or services need to consider how universal design can help make environments accessible to these individuals.

Products will have to be developed and provided, and environments will have to be created or adapted, that provide access for people who have been shut out due to a physical or mental impairment. As people in general begin to interact more fully with a broader population that has been socially isolated, more people will want to live in home environments that not only meet changing personal needs but also make it possible to entertain friends who have disabilities. There will be a huge demand for designs and products that provide such opportunities.

Universal design products that fulfill all of these standards will be the best alternative to mere prosthetic design and will be among the most highly demanded. As the demand increases so will the production levels, leading to lower costs and greater availability.

Characteristics of Aging *by Joseph Koncelik*

Changes in Vision
- Yellowing of the lens
- Opacity of the cornea
- Weakening of the muscle controllers
- Crazing of the cornea
- Flattening of the lens (farsightedness)
- Loss of sensitivity to intensity of color
- Loss of sensitivity to blue color (and other "cool" colors)
- Less ability to discriminate closely related colors
- Slower adaptation rate in light-to-dark conditions
- Loss of ability to discriminate fine detail
- Less ability to discriminate closely related distances (curbs and steps)

Changes in Hearing
Hearing losses begin to occur at about age 40—at first imperceptibly, but later with gradually increasing loss. As with all normal age losses, the rate of onset is different for different individuals. However, one specific loss is very closely identified with aging: *presbycusis*, or selective frequency hearing loss (especially the higher frequencies), resulting in a confusion of sounds and mixing of conversation and background noise.

Losses in the ability to distinguish low-volume sound also occur with greater frequency among the aged population. This is a problem that is beginning to affect everyone due to the level of environmental noise that constantly surrounds us.

Changes in Human Strength, Flexibility, and Mobility
- Loss of strength in the lower extremities, causing a "drop" to chair surfaces when sitting
- Less ability to bend the knee joint to an acute angle in order to position the center of gravity (CG) over the heels for egress from a chair
- Greater reliance upon arm strength to lift the CG from the seated surface and stabilize the body for transition from standing to sitting
- Longer seated durations, yet earlier onset of discomfort, owing to tissue loss over the ischial tuberosities (load-bearing points on the base of the hips that press against muscles of the buttocks)
- Gradual transition from normal walking gait to a "shuffling" gait whereby the aged adult thrusts feet forward out from under the CG.

Factors that are closely related to these changes are:
- "Tremor" experiences in early morning and at end of day.
- Loss of grip strength in palm (from 95 lb in youth to as little as 5 lb)
- Loss of "pinching" or tip prehension strength in the fingers (from 30 lb to 0 for some)
- Greater need to use whatever appendage of the environment presents itself for stability when walking, climbing, or changing position
- Early onset of fatigue on inclined walkways or ramps
- So-called "kick space" around sofas, low-base tables, and other household furnishings is too small at current 3" level (needs to be 8")
- Need for armrests on dining chairs that fit below table surface, with solid back support. (Aged adults do not lean forward when dining, but use backrest of chairs for support.)

Universal Design and an Aging Population

It has often been stated that either everyone has disabilities or that all are merely temporarily abled. This can be better understood by considering some of the natural effects of aging and the number of people who are rapidly approaching the latter third of their lives, the time when their bodies begin to change in ways that don't work as well within the present, built environment (see "Characteristics of Aging").

Within the next 30 years, the population of retirement-aged persons will steadily increase until it reaches about 24 percent of the total population, with 42 elderly individuals for every 100 working-age people. And there is a trend of retirement-aged individuals returning to the workforce, even being courted to do so. These individuals will need universally designed products and environments since their needs in the workplace will require accommodation.

But this group may have difficulty lobbying for itself. Older Americans must first risk the stigma of being considered "disabled," after a lifetime of relative independence and competence. The squinting middle-aged professional male holding a report at various arm lengths and still not finding the proper focal point is something of a cliché, but it points to the difficulty of identifying a need in a population that jealously guards its competence. Few are willing to admit that their bodies are changing, their demands on their environments are changing, and their capabilities need some assistive devices. Consider a nearing-retirement-age couple who finally get to buy their dream house and still believe they will be happiest in a three-story building with winding stairs and lots of long hallways. As the couple ages, there's a good chance their bodies' changing needs will not allow them to fully enjoy the features of the house they have long felt were most attractive. As

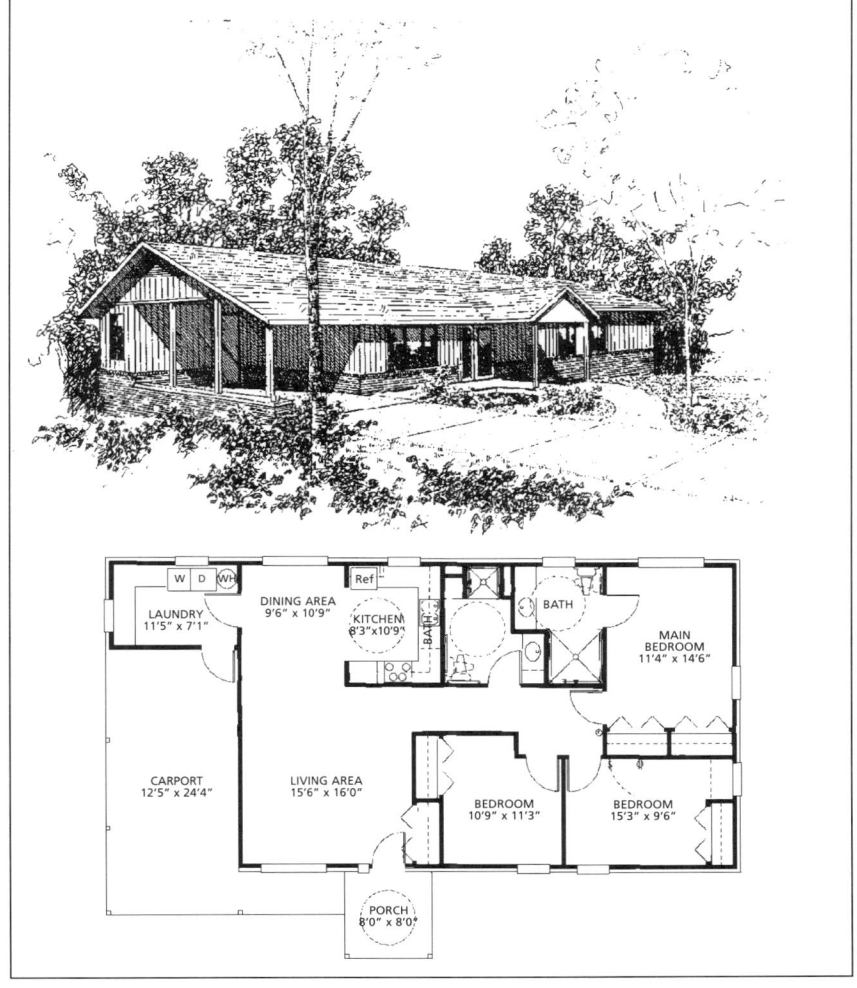

2-9. More and more people will begin to demand universal (adaptable) housing as they begin to realize the benefits of owning a home that can change to meet their changing needs and abilities. A universally designed modular house developed by Ronald Mace in collaboration with Excel Homes. *(Reprinted with permission from Ronald L. Mace, Accessible Stock House Plans #6A, 1993, Center for Accessible Housing.)*

individuals become more aware of what they should be able to expect from their environments, they will begin to change their dreams without losing the joy of maintaining their independence and homes (see Figure 2-9).

Lorraine Hyatt, an environmental psychologist working with elderly populations, reported in 1982 on several barriers to implementing lasting changes:

- Most people think nothing can be done about impairments experienced in aging.
- There have been few models for using the available tools effectively.
- The environment has been undervalued in comparison to other resources (shared activities and family care, for example).
- The type of changes seen as necessary have been thought to be complicated and needing the input of "experts."
- Many people want their environments to remain as they have been throughout their lives; thus, they resist making changes, fearing that the "feel" of their environments will then change.
- Professionals (such as physicians) have not understood or stressed the importance of the environment as part of the overall support system for the individual; often, they don't even think of how the home environment can be altered to accommodate the needs of the changing person.

Although there has been some improvement in the years since Dr. Hyatt made these observations, the situation remains largely unchanged. However, universal design holds the promise of alleviating each of these problems. For example, OXO International produces a line of kitchen tools with large, sure-grip handles (see Figure 2-10).

As environments and products that empower all individuals through supportive, adaptable, accessible, and safe designs (that is, universal design) become widely available, people will be able to reconstruct their built worlds in ways that allow them to maintain their independence, that perhaps even allow them to become more capable and competent. Then the requirements of the ADA will be met and exceeded, and the move toward true design for all people will be realized.

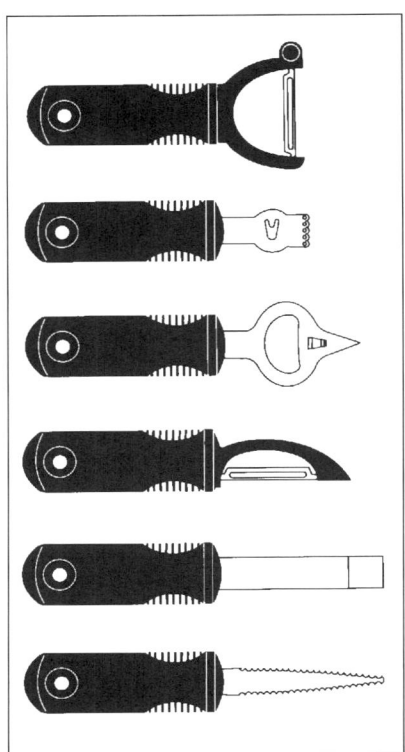

2-10. A sample of products designed for ease of gripping from OXO International.
(Reprinted with permission from OXO International.)

Universal Design Strategy
Universal Design for the Preschool Child
by Jannis Shea, Ph.D., and Marjorie Inman, Ph.D.

The attitudes, feelings, and perceptions of their living environments felt by young children can greatly affect their emotional development. Piaget's view of cognitive development serves as a guide to understanding how a child begins to view his or her world (1973). According to Piaget, the preschool child is able to represent his or her world in many ways through play, imitation, drawing, and language. The home and the spaces occupied by children are important frames of reference in early childhood for establishing a sense of well being and a view of the environment beyond the home.

Only a few researchers have studied young children in their environment, especially in their residential settings (Sweaney et al., 1986). Gaunt (1980) investigated rooms that children use and the activities they pursued in these rooms and concluded that children's access to space in the home should be improved, and parents should learn more about children's needs in the residential environment.

Several studies indicate that a place for possessions and a space of their own were both very important criteria in the design of residential spaces that include children (Webb, 1984; Lindberg, 1960; Proshansky, 1973; Hildreth and Hoyt, 1981). Others show that overcrowding in the home can limit the space needed for privacy, which is an important aspect of development of the preschool child. Rohe found that household density has an effect on personal satisfaction and behavior (1982). Additionally, Loo reported some evidence that young children appear to be more reactive to crowding than older children (1978).

A study of 100 preschool children (Sweaney et al., 1986) showed that families who were least crowded were the most cohesive, while the most crowded families were found to be most organized and scored highest on achievement orientation. The least crowded families were most likely to use the living room for interactions, while the more crowded families used a variety of rooms. An interesting finding from this study showed that the child's bedroom was selected both as the favorite room of preschoolers as

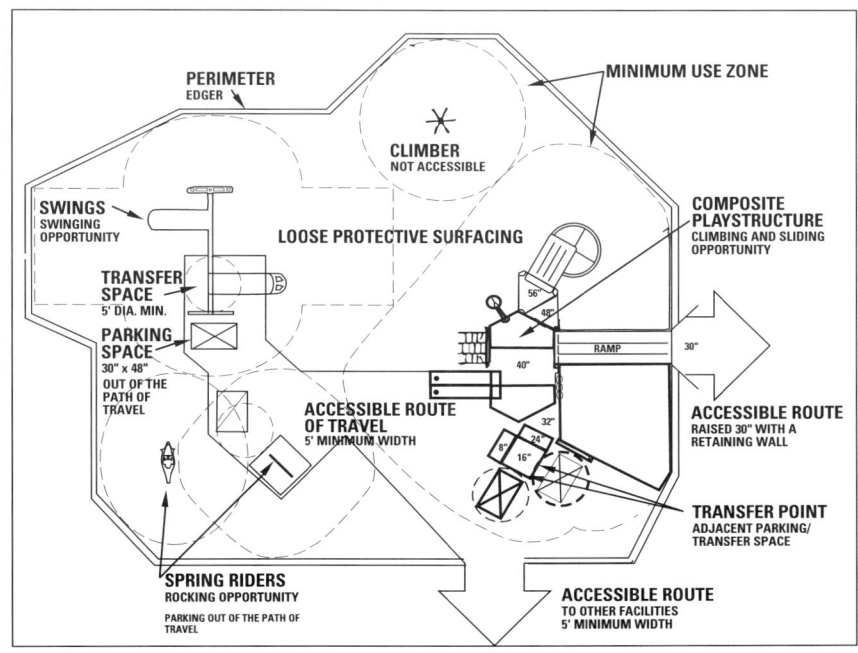

2-11. In an attractively landscaped setting with gardens, water and bird feeders, a well-designed play structure can offer a multi-sensory outdoor experience for visitors of all ages and abilities. This accessible design from Landscape Structures, Inc., includes the following features: TuffTurf™ provides an accessible route of travel to the structure; the structure itself has a transfer point with grab bars and a ramp from a berm. *(Reprinted with permission from Landscape Structures.)*

well as the room where they were most likely sent when being disciplined. If the child's bedroom is perceived to be of such importance to the child, then the design of that room should be carefully laid out to stimulate interests and should reflect the favorite activities and colors of the child who will occupy it.

There are several important criteria to consider when planning spaces for the preschool child. The following list serves as a guide for insuring that the needs of children are considered when planning a universally designed environment:

1. *Prime location:* Consider safety of the neighborhood where young children can develop a sense of trust in other adults as they encounter friendly neighbors and experience safe play environments.

2. *Privacy and territoriality:* Plan spaces that children can call their own, where they can play out their fantasies and begin to discover their abilities and limitations.

3. *Personalization/storage:* Design spaces for children to store personal belongings that foster a sense of identity, such as drawings, writings, treasured collections, and hobbies.

4. *Security:* The environment must foster a sense of well being and of a safe haven from outside intruders.

5. *Floor space:* Open spaces that are free from fragile furniture and accessories accommodate the development of large muscle control.

6. *Furniture:* Furnishings must be designed for safety and durability with consideration for appropriate anthropometric standards for young children.

7. *Bathroom:* Fixtures, walls, and floor surfaces must be designed to assure safety and ease of cleaning and fixtures must be scaled to foster a child's independence.

8. *Social space:* Provide areas for entertaining friends.

9. *Lighting:* Adequate lighting ensures safety and can be adjusted for various activities. Provide easy-to-reach controls.

10. *Flooring:* Surfaces must be easy to clean, durable, and free of hazards that might cause tripping or slipping.

11. *Maintenance:* Surfaces and textures that are durable, easily cleaned, and nontoxic must be selected.

12. *Aesthetics:* Sensory stimulation can be provided through sight, sound, and touch and should include the use of bright colors, sounds, and varied textures.

13. *Outdoor space:* Areas for play must include consideration for safety and aesthetics.

The designer's consideration of these elements will help children grow into responsible, independent young adults and support their expectations of a lifetime of healthy experiences.

Universal Design Strategy
Universal Design for the Elderly
by Marjorie Inman, Ph.D., and Jannis Shea, Ph.D.

Developing a plan for meeting the housing needs of the elderly begins with understanding what it means to grow old in this society. For all people, growing older means adapting to physical and functional changes as well as to a changing social environment. Aging is likely to result in feelings of despair and loss of personal control over one's destiny (Rotter, 1971). The autonomy one gains in youth creates a sense of internal control over one's life; however, in old age decreased income, role loss, and diminished vigor and social status combine to leave many with a sense of being controlled by external circumstances. To correct the imbalance, residential environments for the elderly must be designed that ensure safety, health, comfort, convenience, and most importantly, independence—features that provide a psychological feeling of internal control over the environment.

According to Brown and Davis (1992), residential design for the elderly should address eight "opportunity elements":

1. Socialization
2. Growth and development
3. Transportation
4. Entertainment and cultural activities
5. Work
6. Communications
7. Healthful rest
8. Personal expression

Design for socialization might include such features as a front porch or a common meeting place in a retirement village plan. Personal growth and achievement can be fostered by including built-in bookshelves in a residence, a media center, or computer systems and software that engage individuals and encourage them to continue exploring ideas and activities. Transportation means locating the residence in an accessible place within the community, and also refers to independent movement within the dwelling itself. Entertainment is provided through television and the stereo components of a media center. Work includes not only the care of the home, but also the provision of space for activities and hobbies. Communication includes the telephone as well as an emergency call system. Healthful rest includes privacy, quiet surroundings, a firm bed, and seating within and outside of the dwelling. Finally, personal expression means the individual's ability to select the decor of the residence and the opportunity to surround oneself with expressions of individuality.

Paralleling and supplementing these 8 opportunity elements are 25 universal design criteria developed by M. Boschetti and M. Inman (Inman et. al., 1992):

1. *Prime location:* The dwelling should be located near transportation, good shopping, dependable medical facilities, educational and recreational opportunities, and so on.

2. *Privacy:* Public and private spaces should be clearly separated within the residence.

3. *Personalization:* Areas to display personal items should be provided and should allow the individual to have a reflection of his or her life history.

4. *Territoriality:* The residence should be designed to give a feeling of being able to control one's own territory.

5. *Security:* The environment must be safe from intruders, use strong locks, and have interested neighbors nearby, eliminating some of the fear that comes with increased frailty.

6. *Floor space:* Adequate space must be given to accommodate major items of furniture that have family or personal meaning.

7. *Living or family room:* Furniture should include a comfortable chair with a head rest, washable if necessary. Tables should be placed next to seating for telephone, reading materials, and other hobbies and necessities.

8. *Dining facilities:* There should be room in the kitchen to eat, as well as in one other location.

9. *Kitchen:* The space should include well organized, easy-to-reach storage, safe appliances and controls (front operated), and adequate counter space.

10. *Bedroom:* The room should include a comfortable bed and chair along with tables at the sides of the bed and chair to hold a telephone and reading material.

11. *Bathroom:* Space should be designed with a large circulation area (room for wheelchair and walker), safety grips, shower with seat, easy-to-clean surfaces, easy-to-reach storage, door swings that insure no one can be trapped inside room, bidet for cleanliness, and elevated toilet seat.

12. *Laundry facilities:* The washer and dryer should be located at accessible heights with easy-to-read instructions.

13. *Place for entertaining and hobbies:* Flexible space to accommodate recreational interests and social relationships is desirable.

14. *Adequate storage spaces:* Room for personal possessions, including clothing, household equipment, and personal mementos should be included.

15. *Quiet spaces:* Places where one can be free of unwanted background noise for reading, writing, or rest should be part of the design.

16. *Lighting*: Adequate lighting should be provided with easy-to-reach outlets and controls and no extension cords that might cause tripping.

17. *Climate control:* Adequate heating, cooling, and ventilation with easy-to-read-and-use controls should be provided.

18. *Flooring:* Nonslip flooring, easily maintained and durable, and no loose rugs that might cause falls are important for safety.

19. *Stairways*: Eliminate stairs and steps where feasible; provide ramps for wheelchairs and walkers where altering access is not possible.

20. *Maintenance/cleaning:* Surfaces and textures should be easy to clean and maintain.

21. *Windows:* At least one window should be provided with a view to nature and neighbors.

22. *Display areas:* Places to display memorabilia and personal collections, which provide ties with the past, should be included.

23. *Outdoor space:* Places with pleasing views to sit and enjoy the out-of-doors are important features.

24. *Aesthetics:* Bright colors, varied textures, and designs for sensory stimulation are desirable.

25. *Affordability:* Since income may be limited, the housing should be selected within budget constraints.

By utilizing the 8 opportunity elements as a starting point for designing environments for the elderly and by keeping the 25 more detailed design features in mind, a living space that supports the continued independence of this growing segment of the population can be provided.

2-12. The Apple Valley Care Center in Apple Valley, California, is a skilled nursing facility designed by Interior Arts Inc., Fresno, CA. The Skilled Nursing Facility lobby offers wide clearance for wheelchair use, allowing residents to draw up face-to-face with guests, helping those with visual and auditory impairments to communicate. The seating combines shallow seat depths and seat heights with long arms and knobs or grips to help seniors stand up. Because the average 70-year-old requires three times the amount of light as the average 20-year-old, high levels of non-glare and indirect lighting with adequate illumination and even light levels are used throughout the facility.
(Figures 2-12 through 2-15 reprinted with permission from Interior Arts, Inc., Fresno, CA 93711. Interior Designers: Pat Hennings, ASID, IDEC, President; Laura Watkins, ASID; Vivian Coats, ASID. Facility: The Terraces of Los Gatos.)

2-13. At the Apple Valley Care Center, bright colorful wallpaper borders and residential-style, cherry nightstands and dressers keep rooms from appearing institutional. Ergonomics has played an important role in the design. For example, hospital beds in this Skilled Nursing Facility are customized to accommodate the smaller stature of residents, particularly women. By making the beds smaller, more living area is provided in the rooms.

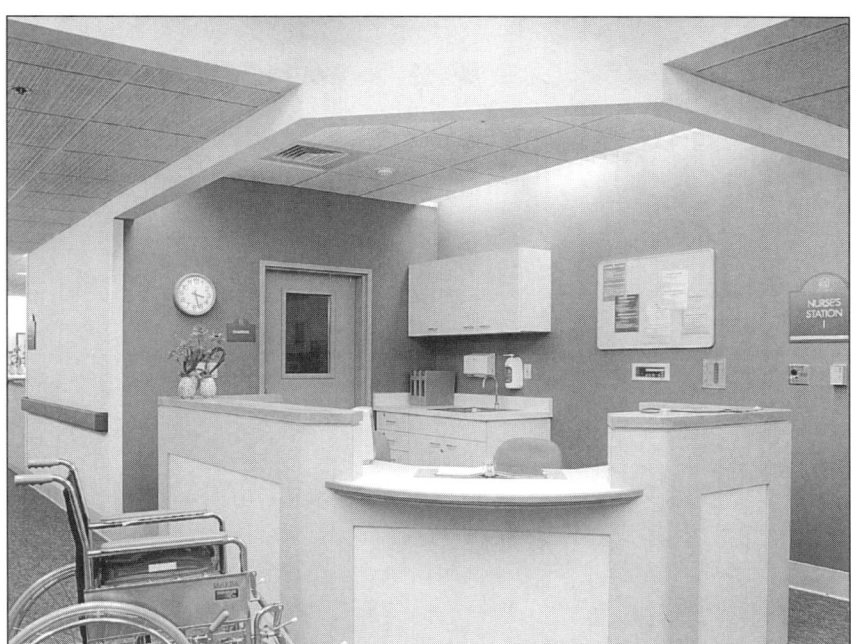

2-14. The Terraces of Los Gatos Nurses Station displays ADA signage with raised letters and braille, ADA handrails, a lowered counter, and high contrasting colors to assist residents who are visually impaired.

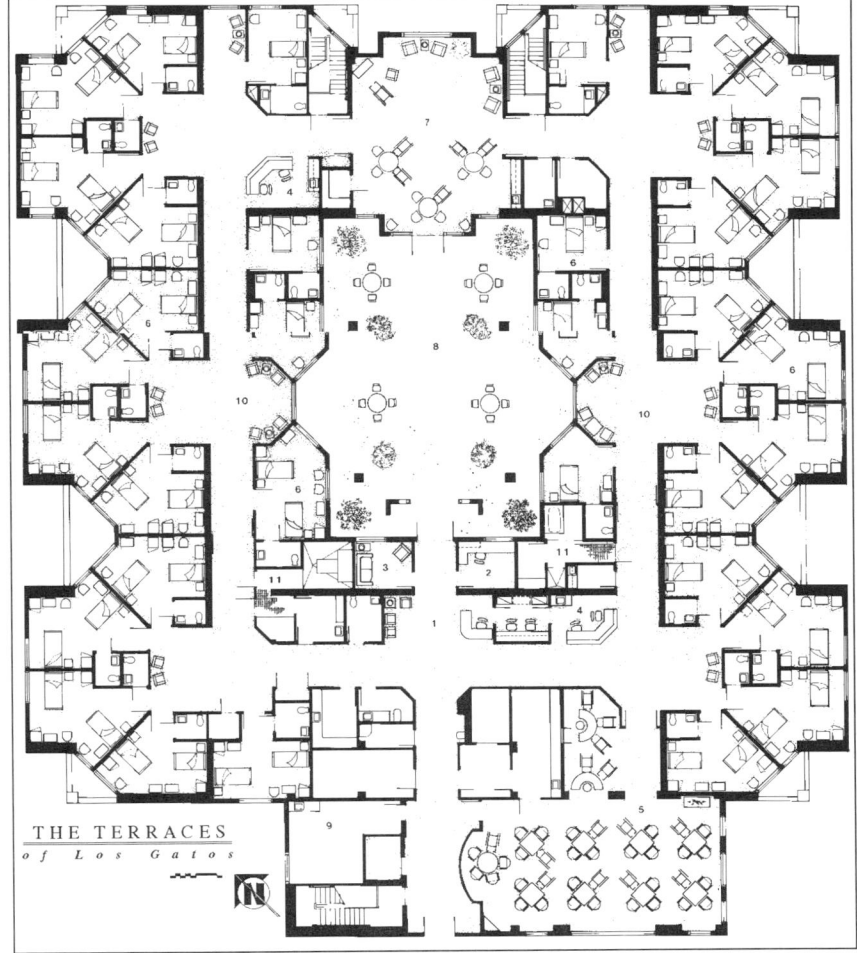

2-15. The floor plan of the Skilled Nursing Facility of The Terraces of Los Gatos shows that residents live in large double rooms with roommates. A toe-to-toe configuration is used in the rooms providing separate windows and controls for each resident on his or her side of the room. Common areas adjacent to the Skilled Nursing Facility include a library, an ice cream parlor, a sewing room, and a game room. Outside, the grounds are professionally landscaped with gazebos and benches for sitting and talking with friends or visitors.

2-16. These floor plans and accompanying checklists illustrate universal design criteria for kitchens and baths (in this instance, a renovation project of a senior rental housing development). *(Reprinted with permission from Dana G. Stewart and Jill A. Osiowy, Housing Studies, Research and Development Program, Fac. of Architecture, University of Manitoba.)*

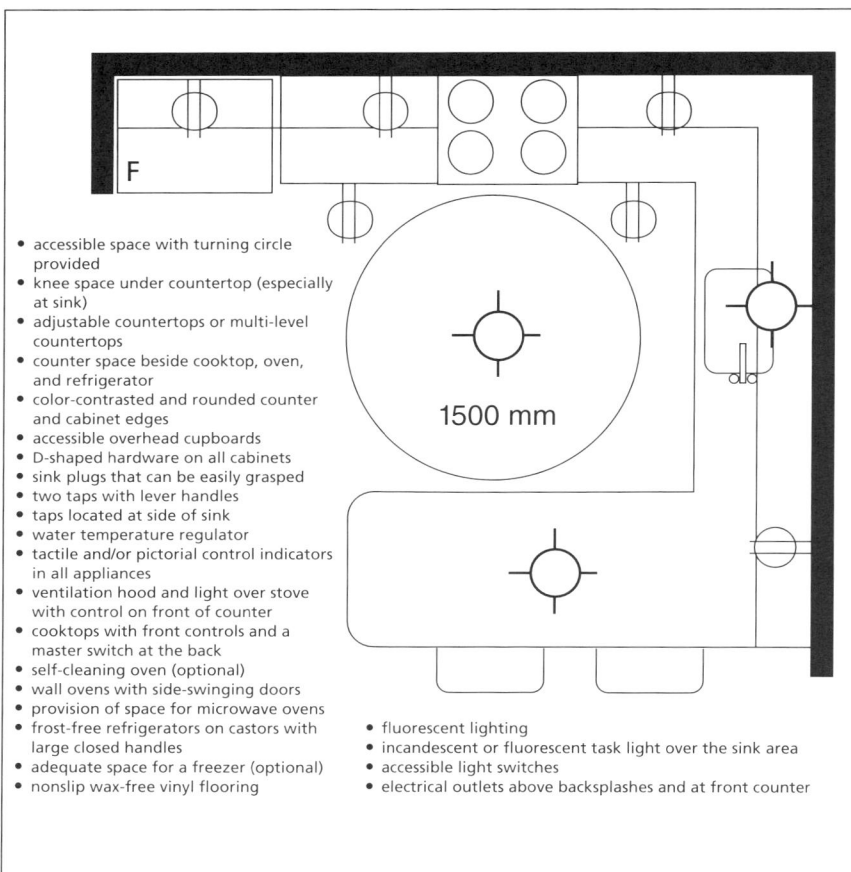

- accessible space with turning circle provided
- knee space under countertop (especially at sink)
- adjustable countertops or multi-level countertops
- counter space beside cooktop, oven, and refrigerator
- color-contrasted and rounded counter and cabinet edges
- accessible overhead cupboards
- D-shaped hardware on all cabinets
- sink plugs that can be easily grasped
- two taps with lever handles
- taps located at side of sink
- water temperature regulator
- tactile and/or pictorial control indicators in all appliances
- ventilation hood and light over stove with control on front of counter
- cooktops with front controls and a master switch at the back
- self-cleaning oven (optional)
- wall ovens with side-swinging doors
- provision of space for microwave ovens
- frost-free refrigerators on castors with large closed handles
- adequate space for a freezer (optional)
- nonslip wax-free vinyl flooring
- fluorescent lighting
- incandescent or fluorescent task light over the sink area
- accessible light switches
- electrical outlets above backsplashes and at front counter

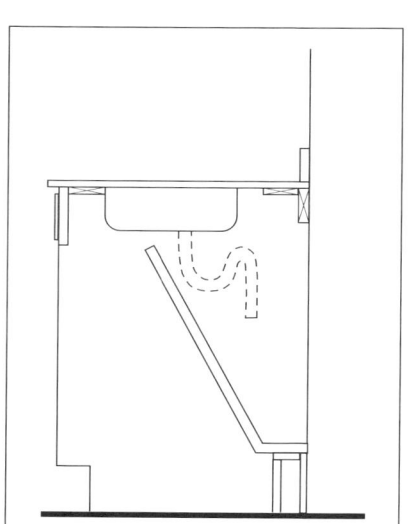

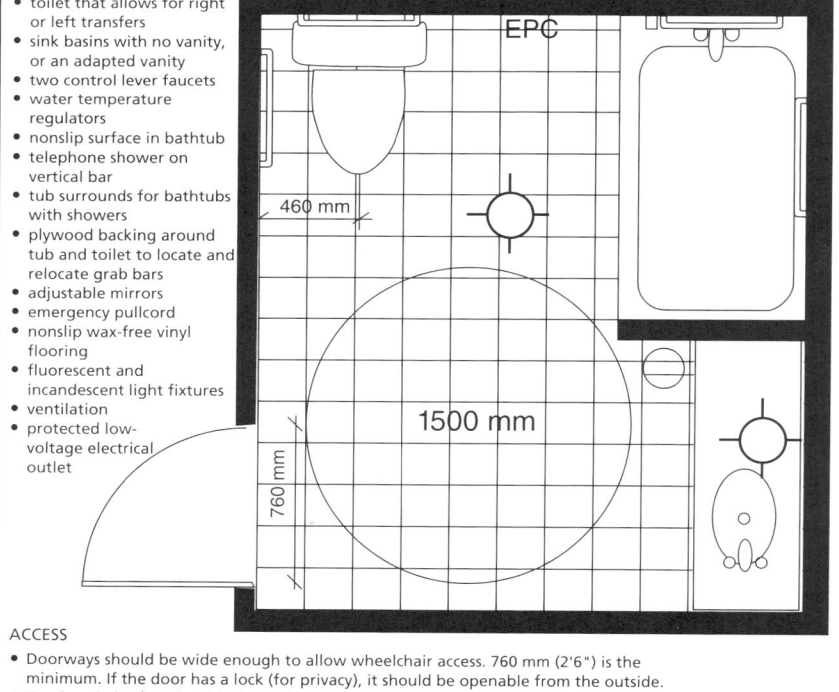

- toilet that allows for right or left transfers
- sink basins with no vanity, or an adapted vanity
- two control lever faucets
- water temperature regulators
- nonslip surface in bathtub
- telephone shower on vertical bar
- tub surrounds for bathtubs with showers
- plywood backing around tub and toilet to locate and relocate grab bars
- adjustable mirrors
- emergency pullcord
- nonslip wax-free vinyl flooring
- fluorescent and incandescent light fixtures
- ventilation
- protected low-voltage electrical outlet

ACCESS
- Doorways should be wide enough to allow wheelchair access. 760 mm (2'6") is the minimum. If the door has a lock (for privacy), it should be openable from the outside.
- Turning circles for wheelchairs, walkers, and scooters should be provided. The minimum space required for wheelchairs is 150 mm (5'0").

What Is Universal Design? 43

One Bedroom Floor Plan

Bath
- toilet placement does not allow for side transfer
- no grab bars at toilet or bath
- layout does not allow wheelchair turn radius 1500 mm (5'0")

Bedroom
- sliding closet doors are preferred to folding

Circulation
- doorway width too narrow for wheelchair minimum 760 mm (2'6")
- hall width too narrow to allow for wheelchair turn

Kitchen
- counter space of 300–450 mm (12–18") should be available beside range and refrigerator
- counter and cabinet edges should have rounded edges
- wall oven with side-swinging door should be provided

Storage
- bi-fold doors should be avoided; sliding doors are preferred
- secondary storage should be provided in another part of an apartment building as many seniors move from houses into smaller apartments

One Bedroom Floor Plan, Adapted

Bath
- adequate turning radius for wheelchair 1500 mm (5'0")
- sink basin with no vanity below
- grab bars at toilet and bath
- toilet allows for side transfer

Bedroom
- adequate turning radius for wheelchair
- storage with sliding doors
- accommodates two double beds and a dresser

Circulation
- door width allows wheelchair access, 760 mm (2'6")
- hall width allows wheelchair movement, 1100 mm (3'6")
- turning circles at all enclosed spaces, bath, bedroom, entry, kitchen

Kitchen
- counter space beside cooktop, oven, refrigerator
- adequate turning radius for wheelchair
- wall oven with swinging door

Storage
- linen closet at entry, broom closet in kitchen, walk-in storage and plenty of bedroom storage
- sliding doors

Living Room
- adequate space for flexible furniture arrangements
- layout allows for wheelchair turning radius

2-17. Floor plans of a proposed renovation project for senior rental housing in Winnipeg, Manitoba, Canada, reveal problems and indicate possible universal design interventions. *(Reprinted with permission from Dana G. Stewart and Jill A. Osiowy, Housing Studies, Research and Development Program, Fac. of Architecture, University of Manitoba.)*

One Bedroom Floor Plan
Electrical and Lighting

One Bedroom Floor Plan, Adapted
Electrical and Lighting

The Universal Design Process   3

When people engage in any creative activity, they are, in effect, designing. And this range of creative human activity is enormous. Making a decision is creating—it is choosing from a vast array of possibilities to meet the present needs.

Decisions surrounding the outfitting of a home office with a workstation, chair, and storage equipment require a creative act. One has to consider the space the items will occupy, the present color scheme, the general layout of existing furnishings, the lighting, and the types of uses the office will serve (reading, writing, drafting, computer use). Preferences of style and materials (and perhaps the desires of others who might use it) must be considered and then balanced with budgetary constraints. Finally, the furnishings can be purchased.

Once everything is in place, one has to evaluate how successful the design was: Does the color scheme work? Do the desk and cabinets fit within the room size and furnishings? Is it comfortable for long-term work? This evaluation may even lead one to return the desk or chair and begin the process over again.

All these processes will be going on either covertly or overtly. Design is often done as part of a team, enlisting the aid of potential users or a professional designer, or at least asking the sales representative's advice. A checklist can be used to evaluate the success of the design. Or one may have the good fortune of doing everything right the first time without any serious, conscious planning at all. However, as the design process becomes more complex, as projects demand more expertise from the designer, accountability increases. The designer must be able to draw on a wealth of knowledge from a variety of sources.

When designers and other professionals decide to be involved in working toward a universal design, they must welcome (and even ask for) new supportive technologies such as wheelchairs that climb stairs and other barriers (thus truly empowering their users), computers that make it possible for people with virtually any disability to interact more fully with their world, and air quality control devices that make the unseen world healthier. Designers also welcome innovations in established policies including companies that empower their workers by giving them the choice of working out of home offices, or that focus on responsibility and accomplishment (not just on adherence to established routine), and that take seriously human rights laws, such as the Americans with Disabilities Act, that provide protection against discrimination.

Each of these design innovations may make the world work better. To the extent that they accomplish that goal, they will gain recognition for their success, and their principles will be adopted throughout the culture. The creativity they display will then serve as a model, leading to further innovations. These are all examples of universal design.

Empathy and Universal Design

Consider again the "people first" approach introduced in Chapter 2. A firm grasp of this concept will be driven by one's capacity to *empathize* with people in a variety of circumstances. More than anything else, universal design is defined by empathy. Empathy is the foundation from which all good design is built. It is the quality that makes each individual's self-worth something that can be nurtured. The ability to empathize and act on the awareness it awakens is the critical factor in creating a universal design. But empathy is not a quality that suffuses American life. The work world is not generally considered an empathetic environment; workers are often considered to be present to fulfill the employer's needs, with little regard given to their own needs. The same is true of many social agencies.

One of the subtlest requirements of the Americans with Disabilities Act is its demand that people reevaluate how they interact with each other, in addition to looking at how physical environments are constructed. At that level, the act signals a shift in how people are managed at work, how services and entertainment are provided, and how people treat one another. If the ADA is merely seen as a requirement to make environments accessible, the main point of the legislation is missed since compliance can often be met in the physical environment by following the ADAAG to the letter and making any minor changes that may be requested by a qualified person with a disability.

But what is central to the ADA and the universal design movement is a belief that the built and imagined world does not work for many. Universal design can be further defined as "informed, empathic, creative activity focused on altering the known environment." The known environment is not just physical space and objects, but also human beings interacting. As such, universal design encompasses every discipline. It's a unifying circle within which designers, architects, lawyers, sociologists, psychologists, educators, and managers interact. The universal design process begins with empathy, while the techniques needed to accomplish whatever goal one has in mind will follow (as the first case study in this chapter will show).

Everyone is doing some kind of design most of the time. But often, that design means simply going through the motions, repeating what is already there because it's what is known. The universal design process is not just the methodological design of building a house or tinkering with a few specifications to make a slightly different version of an existing environment: Universal design asks for the design of an entirely new creature. Designers are being asked to embrace the chaos of discovery, to put imagination before skill—and in the process re-create the world.

Universal Design Techniques

In addition to asking whether a design meets the criteria described in Chapter 2 (supportive, adaptable, accessible, and safe), the designer can also utilize several techniques throughout the process to help create a universal design: participatory design, modeling and role playing, and post-occupancy evaluations.

Participatory Design

The universal design process is essentially participatory design. The basic steps are outlined briefly here and will appear again in many of the case studies throughout the book. These studies reveal a variety of approaches to participatory design—all of which are useful, none of which should be taken as the only approach.

No matter what type of project one is involved in, once the tasks to be completed have been identified, there are certain key techniques to help define goals and realize solutions.

In the design community, this stage is often termed *programming* and includes the following activities:

- *Establishing goals:* working with all involved parties to determine the general parameters of the project

- *Conducting research:* learning about the people and spaces involved, and also educating everyone in relevant areas of study

- *Uncovering concepts:* identifying the pieces of the conceptual framework that is guiding the project

- *Determining needs:* stating the constraints on the project (financial, spatial, time, and so on) to help define the proper approach

- *Stating problems:* drawing on all of the above to divide the project into logical components that can be solved through design directives

These activities are further delineated in the "Environmental Programming" Technique section later in this chapter. Environmental programming reveals how techniques that develop design criteria (such as those in put forth in the Strategy sections of Chapter 2) can greatly simplify the design process.

Perhaps the most important, and often most neglected, step is *research*, which has several methods proven to work well for gathering information:

- Background reading
- Interviews
- Surveys and questionnaires
- Observation
- Focus groups

Background Reading

There will always be information to be gathered that applies specifically to each project. However, some broad areas of study should be considered that affect the design of all environments including, but certainly not limited to, the trade journals for design, aging, and disabilities. Research available on the elderly is especially useful when one is interested in the design needs of people with disabilities. As noted in Chapter 2, the population is aging rapidly, and as people age they encounter many of the disabilities that must be accommodated under new laws. A great deal of data exists on the specific needs of this population group as their bodies change, all of which is pertinent to the creation of a universal environment.

Interviews

The more people one can interview about the project—their specific needs and especially current dissatisfactions—the better. Interviews should include as many of the people involved in a project as possible: current and prospective users, architects and designers, psychologists and sociologists (if pertinent), financiers, and so on. Karen Hirsch, a designer, discusses the importance of personal history interviews in the Strategy section later in this chapter. Her article offers very useful advice on ways to get needed information from prospective users. Similarly, at the end of the chapter, Joel I. Kahn, an engineer with Procter & Gamble who has multiple sclerosis, tells of his own personal involvement on an ADA Task Force. His article points out that the inclusion of people who will actually be affected by decisions is crucial to the process.

Surveys and Questionnaires

It is important to create a general profile of the audience. Surveys and questionnaires are one way of doing this. Designers need to do research on creating questions that do not point an audience to a specific response as well as modifying existing questionnaires that have proven effective in other areas. Questions should try to establish how people are currently using the environment and the ways they would like to see things improve. A good example of the use of surveys and questionnaires appears in Owen Cooks' description of Purdue University's ADA Compliance Plan in Chapter 4.

Observation

Oftentimes one can gain a better understanding of a project and its audience by observing people in action, either within an existing environment for a renovation, or within a similar environment if it's something new. For example, time-lapse photography could be used to build an observation profile of patterns of use for an airport waiting room, or for the use of a social space at a retirement community. Such observations can serve as useful supplements to the feedback given through the survey/questionnaire.

Focus Groups

By holding meetings with a cross-section of an audience, focused on specific aspects of the project, designers can generate creative solutions to known problems and further identify the issues under consideration.

The approach outlined here has been called *participatory design*, which requires designers to allow the people who will be affected by their decisions to play a significant role in shaping the project. This approach may also lead to a partnership of sorts with a wide range of professionals and laypeople. For some projects one may want to actively involve psychologists, architects, designers, engineers, facility managers, project managers, people with specific disabilities, and so on. The more knowledge gathered up front, the

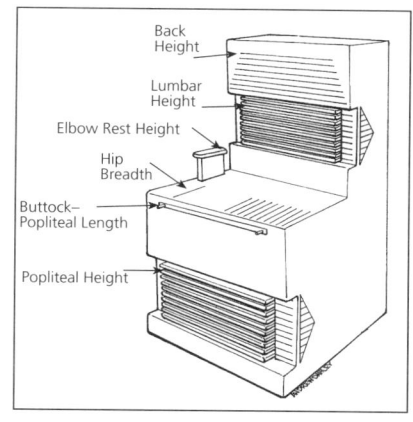

3-1. William Dowell, a research program manager at Herman Miller, Inc., designed this Anthropometric Percentile Estimation Device to collect size data for individuals in a particular workplace (floor-to-back-of-knee length, buttock-to-back-of-knee length, lumbar region height and depth, and elbow rest height). Software used with the device allows comparison to those same measurements for the whole of the United States. (The source for the normal population is the 1988 Anthropometric Survey of U.S. Army Personnel, the most ambitious anthropometric survey ever undertaken—9000 men and women.) *(Reprinted with permission from Herman Miller, Inc.)*

less chance there will be for unnecessary problems to develop after the project has been completed. See the case study on the San Diego Center for the Blind in this chapter for an example of participatory design.

Once enough background data has been collected, one will be able to develop a number of design concepts to reach the goals set for the project. Design concepts set down specific strategies for solving individual aspects of a project; for example, if privacy is an issue, one of the design concepts will be to identify ways to ensure that concern is met while keeping within the overall design plan.

Modeling and Role Playing

Once design concepts have been developed, goals have been set, and a plan of action has been created, the designer may feel ready to begin the actual implementation of the design. However, there are a few further steps needed to ensure against unexpected failures. The first of these is *modeling*.

A designer does this to some extent when putting the design onto paper or creating a mock-up of the environment as it is projected to be when finished. Consider taking this process one step further by doing a full-scale working model of one representative space (a typical work space in an office, for example). By doing so, aspects of the environment that may not have been planned for can be identified: furniture management and lighting problems, for example. Alan Wier utilized such a mock-up in creating the design of a high-speed rail car (see Chapter 7).

A second technique to consider is *role playing*. This can be as simple as taking part in the regular routine of the intended audience, or as complicated as utilizing some of the new technology available that puts one within an environment before it's been constructed. Computer-aided design (CAD) programs with full-motion animation have proven very useful for this purpose, while virtual reality is fast on the way to becoming available to designers who are more serious computer users.

As work is done implementing a design, there is frequently a need to reevaluate goals and design concepts. Through such activities as modeling and role playing, one may discover that preliminary designs are not as effective as they could be. Perhaps the project as a whole may be redefined, and in the process this particular environment will be brought closer to a fully supportive, universal design.

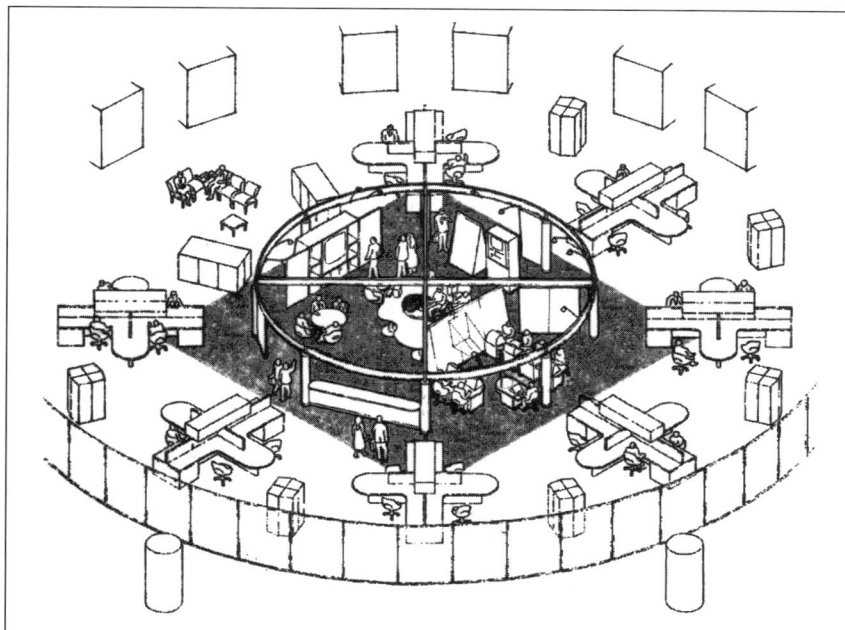

3-2. The trend toward teamwork in American business inspired the development of Steelcase's Personal Harbor™ Workspace. Today's office workers are coming together to solve complex problems requiring the talents and perspectives of many different disciplines. As more teams work together, additional team spaces are required in which office workers have access to both the team and their own individual working environment. Multiple meetings can take place in the same open area in the Commons, a concept that Steelcase, Inc., is testing to make more effective use of underutilized open office space. Easels on wheels and markerboards that hang on tracks from beams provide space division. *(Reprinted with permission from Steelcase, Inc.)*

Post-Occupancy Evaluation

Designers evaluate each project in some manner from the first day they began to consider what it will demand. Evaluation is an ongoing process. However, a specific form of evaluation that too often gets ignored needs to be focused on here: post-occupancy evaluation (POE).

A post-occupancy evaluation uses many of the same techniques that constitute participatory design. Observation, interviews, questionnaires, surveys, and focus groups can also be used to get feedback on the design after it has been executed. From such feedback shortcomings can be corrected in any of the techniques used, each of the design directives can be tested against the results, and the designer can thus learn to better define and resolve issues in the future. Basically, the designer must ask, "Did my design work? How well? What things could I improve on? What have I learned from the process?"

A well-known research designer speaks and writes eloquently on the importance of evaluation, defining a POE as a study of how well a newly designed interior environment supports the behavior, performance, and satisfaction of its users. Design is considered a hypothesis about how a future environment will affect people's behavior and feelings. Therefore, a POE is the *verification* of that hypothesis.

Robert Herman, in this chapter's first case study, credits the use of post-occupancy surveys with the increasing success he has found in each of the stages of the project he describes. By combining pre-occupancy surveys/evaluations and research with continuing post-occupancy evaluations, he was able to move closer to providing a completely supportive environment for the seniors who were his clientele.

When the Mendelsohn House project (the third phase of the case study described) first began to unfold, the architects and non-profit housing organization used surveys and interviews to determine the needs of prospective end users, thus involving seniors in the design process from planning to post-occupancy. The planning stage took approximately four months to complete, including the time to take the photographs necessary for explaining the choices to end users. Small group sessions were held (four to ten people) where slides were presented depicting various design strategies. From these sessions, specific design directives unfolded:

1. Include an active street edge, with some commercial use on the ground floor to connect with the neighborhood.

2. Include commercial shops that serve the needs of residents.

3. Design a building that looks modern (this was not what the architects had expected to hear since most of the users had previously lived in residential hotels of Victorian vintage).

4. Maintain a positive, dignified image through style and details (for example, carpeting, fine art, use of subtle colors).

5. Include a lobby for security and consistency with users' experience in residential hotels.

6. Include balconies in the apartments.

7. Ensure safety at the entryway and throughout the building.

Through the use of post-occupancy surveys and interviews, observation, and ongoing research into the needs of the elderly, Woolf House, the Ceatrice Polite Apartments, and Mendelsohn House evolved to meet more completely the occupants' needs. These research results elicited the need for:

- Real kitchen hoods, not charcoal-filtered recirculating fans

- Better access and clearances for wheelchairs in some areas

- Protection of lower walls inside units designed for the disabled

- Places for grandchildren to play

- Automatic opening on main entry doors

- Desk clerk to electrically control the main entry doors; not just residents buzzing people in from their unit intercoms

Mendelsohn House is completely wheelchair accessible, with 19 apartments specifically outfitted for disabled occupants.

Several principles guided the design decisions:

- Establishing continuity with the residents' backgrounds through the use of familiar architectural features

- Avoiding isolation from the outside world by including neighborhood businesses at the ground level and bay windows in residents' apartments for "eyes on the street"

- Encouraging social interaction among residents through a variety of activity areas

- Enhancing a sense of pride and dignity by including more than the "basic daily minimum" of services

- Treating time as an important feature of life measured by natural changes—sunlight, shadows, rainwater, wind, and color, all encouraging a state of alertness

A personal sense of security, actual and perceived, was also an essential design goal. Balancing the need for reassuring security devices with their presence as reminders of threatening conditions was a key consideration. The best security originates with the residents themselves, who provide surveillance for all well-designed, needed spaces.

The project received a 1991 National Honor Award for Design Excellence from the American Institute of Architects, one of 19 projects selected from over 650 considered. Mendelsohn House also received the first-ever People in Architecture award in 1990 from the California Council/ American Institute of Architects. As Mr. Herman points out, "Subsidized housing has rarely been the recipient of design awards. Just 20 years ago such housing was a social, political, and aesthetic embarrassment within our cities." Mendelsohn House was selected as a winner not only from among other housing developments but from a range that included museums, hotels, marketplaces, a symphony hall, and a post office.

Case Study

Mendelsohn House: Milestone in Low-Income Housing for the Elderly
by Robert Herman

About 30 years ago, urban renewal bulldozers cleared a downtown neighborhood in San Francisco of nearly 4000 low-income housing units to make way for a new convention center. Many of the displaced people were seniors who subsequently went to court and won a landmark settlement requiring the city to provide 1500 units of replacement housing, to be built by nonprofit developers (see Figure 3-3).

The court settlement, made in 1973, arranged for construction funding by raising the city's hotel tax by only ½ percent, principally

3-3. Map of downtown San Francisco showing the location of the three replacement housing developments for seniors designed by Herman Stoller Coliver Architects. *(Figures 3-3 through 3-5 reprinted with permission from Herman Stoller Coliver Architects, San Francisco.)*

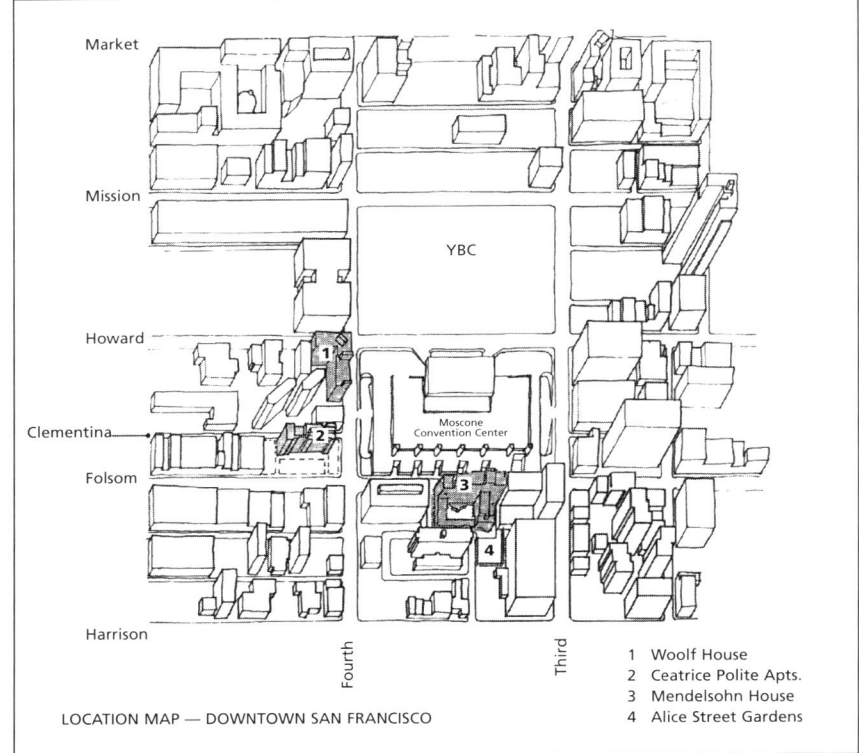

1 Woolf House
2 Ceatrice Polite Apts.
3 Mendelsohn House
4 Alice Street Gardens

LOCATION MAP — DOWNTOWN SAN FRANCISCO

taxing those who would benefit from the new convention center. Since that time, three replacement housing developments for seniors have been designed by Herman Stoller Coliver Architects for non-profit developer Tenants & Owners Development Corporation (TODCO) of San Francisco: Woolf House (182 units) in 1972, Ceatrice Polite Apartments (91 units) in 1982, and Mendelsohn House (189 units) in 1988. As post-occupancy surveys and experience have fed into a learning curve, each development has become more carefully and humanely designed than the last (see Figure 3-4).

Affordability was maintained by containing unit sizes to HUD limitations, although amenities such as bay windows and recessed balconies greatly enhance livability for the residents. The building structure is painted, poured-in-place concrete with infill plaster panels. Added expense was reserved for design features where it counted most: the main entrance canopy, decorative tiles, window patterns, arched openings, and finishes for ground-level shared areas.

One enters the building through a lobby reminiscent of a comfortable residential hotel (the type of residence most of the clientele had been living in). Residents' common spaces overlook a central courtyard. At the front door, seating is arranged for inconspicuous people watching. Spaces are organized to encourage mingling and a feeling of independence through the interior architectural layout and choice of furnishings. Handrails are an integral design element, as important for appearance as for utility. As used here, they lend a friendly quality, accentuating the curves

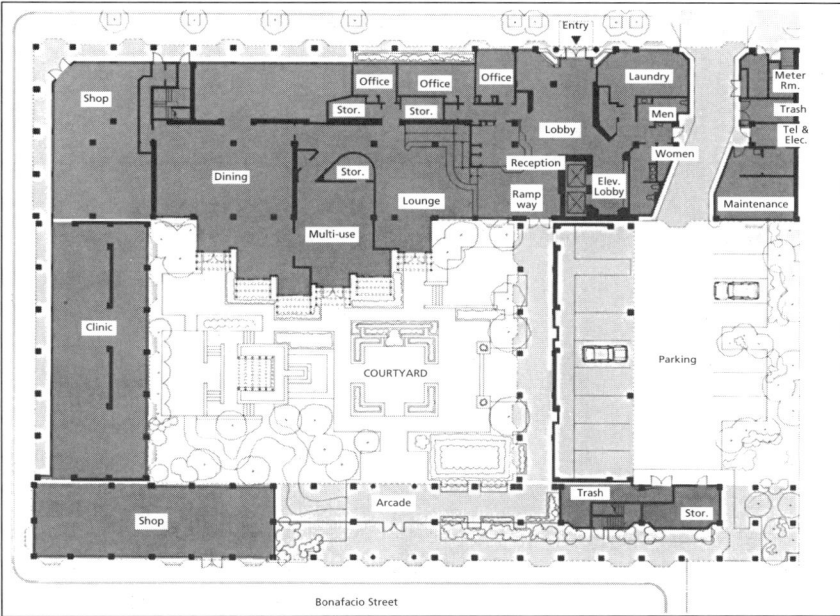

3-4. Artist's rendering of Mendelsohn House. Detailed floor plan.

of ramps and corridors. A variety of period furniture, harmonized by color and fabric selection, resemble a typical family's collections gathered over a generation or more.

A "history wall" containing photos of the history of the neighborhood, including the residential hotels bulldozed by the redevelopment agency, lines the edges of the public lounge space. Small lamps at the reception desk animate the entry. Structural columns with decorative capitals characterize the ground floor, integrating the lounge, ramp, entry, and elevator foyer.

The courtyard, arcaded on two sides, is luxuriantly planted. A fountain and pool, hard-surface exercise area and grassy gathering place for special events, meandering paths for strolling, and a tot lot for visiting grandchildren complete a variety of carefully designed spaces. Two large rooftop vegetable gardens provide an opportunity for productivity and sense of growth for all residents.

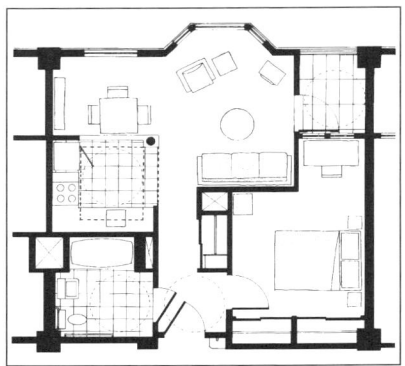

3-5. Floor plan of a representative one-bedroom apartment in Mendelsohn House, featuring a bay window, flower balcony, and windows that open onto a single-loaded corridor.

Within the residential 2nd–9th floors, corridors are punctuated by package shelves, deeply inset front doors, decorative apartment numbers, and kitchen windows that borrow light from across single-loaded corridors. Each apartment has a bay window and most have balconies recessed from the wind, encouraging people who have difficulty getting out to remain visually connected to the rest of the world, much as the traditional front porch on single-family homes connected people to their neighborhood (see Figure 3-5).

Kitchens in one-bedroom apartments and in many of the studios are located in the midst of living areas, not isolated, encouraging the person cooking to comfortably talk with someone seated nearby. All units and public areas are wheelchair accessible, with 10 percent of the apartments outfitted for residents with disabilities. All apartments are *adaptable*; that is, they can be made fully accessible with minor additions. Based on the experience gained from POEs of Woolf House and Ceatrice Polite Apartments, only 10 percent needed to be fully accessible.

Orientation to the sun was a key factor in the shaping of the building. The 7th–9th story wing casts its shadow over a main street while shielding the garden courtyard from street noise. Lower and narrower building wings complete the sunny and amply sized inner courtyard.

Case Study
San Diego Center for the Blind: Design as a Team Effort

The San Diego Center for the Blind (SDCB) is a nonprofit, independent rehabilitation facility founded in 1972 to help people

3-6. Floor plans for the kitchen area of the San Diego Center for the Blind.

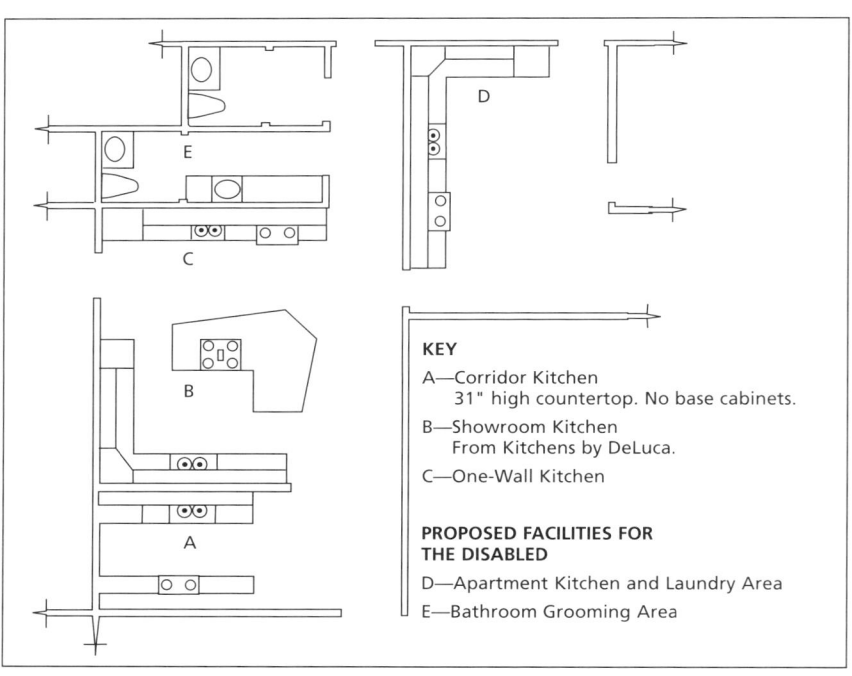

who are blind or otherwise visually disabled reach their highest potential for independence and self-reliance. SDCB accomplishes this through ongoing classes and counseling in such areas as orientation and mobility, activities of daily living, and communication skills. A large segment of the clientele are elderly, with a lifetime of sighted habits, who have a great deal at stake in being able to maintain their independence in their own homes. They need to relearn much that they have taken for granted.

SDCB has, since its inception, inhabited a 9000-square-foot building on a busy street near the San Diego State University main campus. The building originally housed a health spa/gym and later a bank. Due to funding concerns and a lack of expertise, the building SDCB inherited in 1972 remained little changed until 1985 when a class of undergraduate design students from the university (as a class project) took on the task of redesigning the existing kitchen facilities, which were being used to train people with varying degrees of visual disability.

The redesign of the kitchen space prompted SDCB administrators and at least one of the students to ask the professor (this book's main author) if there was anything that could be done to make the students' plans a reality for the center. Dr. Null started making phone calls. Within a few months over 70 companies had donated over $60,000 worth of equipment and a design team had been formed to oversee a remodeling project—a team that included kitchen designers, Dr. Null, social service personnel, other designers, a low-vision lighting specialist, and the public relations home economist for the local utility company who was able to secure volunteer services from labor unions and other community groups to carry out the renovation. The board chairman for the SDCB was a retired contractor who supervised the actual construction.

By November of 1985, the one-wall, outdated kitchen (which lacked even basic adaptations such as large-print controls/instructions) had been transformed into three working models of state-of-the-art kitchen designs (see Figure 3-6), representing the types of kitchen layouts often found in people's homes. The following year the project was awarded the American Society of Interior Designer's (ASID) prestigious Environmental Design award for the students' part in the remodeling.

As with remodeling projects everywhere, when one thing changes everything else seems to needs changing. A snowball effect took place when the center's staff and design team asked themselves and each other, "Why not?" They recognized that the overall design of the building was not supportive of the workers or the clientele, and they set out to rethink and rebuild the facility with the assistance of an expanded team, including the community service committee of the San Diego chapter of ASID, headed by interior designer Jan Bast;

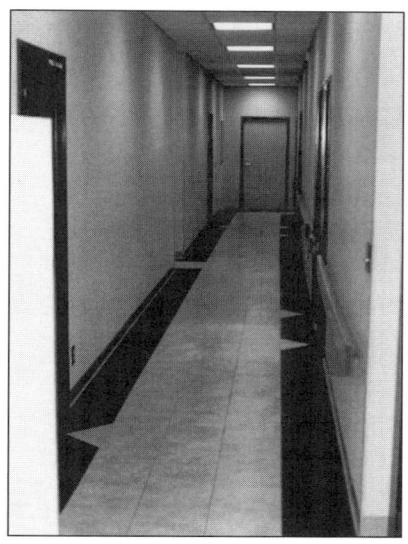

3-7. One of the hallways in the recently remodeled SDCB facility showing these universal design features:
- Good overall lighting
- Contrasting colors to assist in wayfinding and marking door locations

3-8. Unisex bathrooms have these universal design features:
- Contrasting colors in door, door frame, walls, flooring, and handrails
- Lever handles

3-9. A client, Margaret LiDrazzah, is shown in the main teaching/demonstration kitchen (Kitchen B), which was donated by Kitchens by DeLuca in La Mesa, CA. Universal design features include:
- Contrasting color between cabinets, countertops, and cabinet handles, and between electrical switches and outlets
- Accessible controls on range
- Magnetic induction cooktop unit that is safer to use since the surface remains cool to the touch. A warning bell is sounded if a burner is not turned off when a utensil is removed.
- Under-cabinet lighting that provides solid lighting for all work surfaces

(Reprinted with permission from Margaret LiDrazzah.)

3-10. An instructor demonstrates adaptive measuring techniques in Kitchen C (one-wall unit). Universal design features include:
- Contrasting edge and backsplash integrated into the Avonite® countertop
- D-shaped cabinet door handles
- Sliding cabinet doors that promote safety by not projecting into room

environmental psychologist Ann Gero-Stillwell, who provided a pre-design baseline study (from interviews, surveys, and focus group meetings) and a post-occupancy evaluation (using the same techniques); ASID professional members; and a continuing number of students from several design courses at SDSU taught by Kerry Nelson (who all learned from the work being done and contributed to the final product—see the enamel plaques in Figure 3-13). Funding for this new project was secured through private donations, government grants, and a community block grant from the city of San Diego, totaling over $500,000. The general goals of the project team were to:

1. Improve the feel of the space to create a cheerful and professional image

2. Improve wayfinding through special cues and a logical space plan

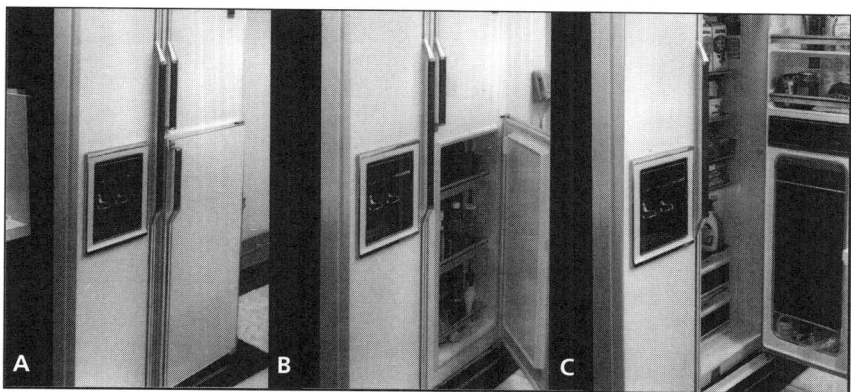

3-11. Refrigerator (donated by Whirlpool Corporation) in Kitchen B reveals several universal design features:
- Side-by-side configuration allows freezer and refrigerator access at any height (A & C).
- Mini-door allows easy access for frequently used items (B).
- Access to ice and water is provided without opening the door.
- Handles are easy to grasp and contrast with doors.
- Full-length refrigerator access is also provided.

3. Make the building easier to use for the elderly and for people with disabilities by utilizing universal design techniques

Wayfinding concerns covered areas such as space planning to group similar activities; traffic flow to ensure a logical movement from entry to activity and to protect against obstacles; use of clear, consistent signage; and contrasting color and texture to serve as cues to changing function.

Universal design concerns included increasing the overall lighting in the facility, reducing glare, using task lighting and lighting within handrails, and creating contrast in color and shade in doors, door frames, door handles, and walls, as well as in carpet and tile to mark areas and changing levels. Other universal design features (see Figures 3-7 to 3-12) included:

- D-shape or lever handles on doors and cabinets
- Visible and accessible storage using pull-out shelves and lazy Susan corner cabinets
- Storage inserts for pantry and other cabinets
- Adjustable shelves within cabinets
- Sliding doors on cabinets
- Side-by-side refrigerator/freezers with slide-out shelves, water and ice dispensers in doors, and mini-doors for frequently used items
- Large print directions, braille overlays, and easily grasped controls on appliances
- Arrangement of appliances in order of their use within kitchens
- Ranges with front controls
- Magnetic-induction cooktops that are cool to the touch and sound a warning when a pan is removed or improperly placed
- Pull-out boards below microwave and other side-opening oven doors

3-12. Kitchen A, a corridor kitchen, with these universal design features:
- Contrasting border in floor covering
- Corian® countertop with contrasting edge
- Absence of base cabinets and lowered (32-inch) countertops provide access to work spaces by clients who use wheelchairs

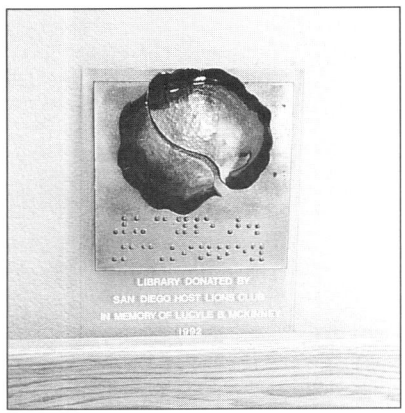

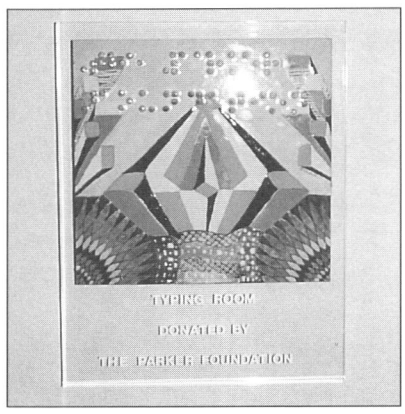

3-13. To show their appreciation for the opportunity to participate in the ASID renovation project at the San Diego Center for the Blind, interior-design students at San Diego State University designed donor recognition systems. The design chosen for use at SDCB featured plaques (such as this one by Diane Montag) created and donated by members of the Enamelist's Guild.

- Rheostats for incandescent lighting
- Automatic faucets with preset temperature controls
- Single-lever faucet controls
- Faucets with spray attachments in kitchen
- A variety of heights in tables and counters
- Nonslip grab bars
- Adjustable desks and workspaces
- Ergonomic furniture for offices, "boxy" furniture for group use to safeguard against protruding edges

The project also called for the creation of a model apartment that would be used as both a demonstration facility and a training center for adapting one's home to be more fully supportive of activities of daily living.

The team wanted to utilize design features that would maximize the self-sufficiency of all parties concerned and that could easily be applied to most other public and private facilities, not just those serving people with visual impairments. They also understood that the population they were dealing with was not one that needed to have only their visual disability accommodated. Many of the clientele were elderly; many used wheelchairs, walkers, and canes; many had arthritis or some other disability. The design team wanted to create a facility that would be supportive of all people and all their various abilities. While the project was not covered by ADA regulations (since it was begun before enforcement dates), the design team's decisions and implementations met and in many cases exceeded the requirements of the ADAAG.

As often happens when remodeling an older building, unexpected setbacks occurred. Soon after construction had commenced, it was discovered that asbestos insulation had been used in the original building; its removal proved costly and time consuming, forcing a reduced scope of the project.

The reconstructed facility was "completed" in 1991. The post-occupancy evaluation revealed some dissatisfaction with the end product, much of it owing to the inability to carry out all of the design plans (some new furniture and signs were lacking, for example). The POE also revealed some new problems that were the direct result of the redesign:

- The preliminary study had identified the need/desire for staff and student lounges, which after the reconstruction began to be used as storage centers.
- Some offices were made smaller, and thus less room was available for seeing-eye dogs (prevalent in the facility).

- Since all the offices were grouped at the front of the building, there were some security concerns about the rear entrance, especially after hours.

There are clear solutions to some of these problems: The lounges can be turned into offices, providing more space and giving back some measure of security to the rear of the facility. Existing offices may then need to be redefined to also provide more space for dogs (see Figures 3-14 to 3-16).

The three overall goals were met: more professional image, better wayfinding, and use of universal design features. The POE clearly shows how much has been accomplished and how much remains to be achieved. Thus, it's serving double duty: Not only is it offering a means of evaluating the project, but it can now be used as a baseline study for the next phase of the project. So, just as the initial kitchen redesign led to a reconsideration of the facility as a whole, the overall remodeling has led to a further refinement of

3-14. These cabinets in the model apartment open to allow access to a pull-down bed unit, which adds flexibility to a size-constrained facility. The bed is used to demonstrate bed-making techniques.

3-15. The activity/community room at the SDCB now provides these universal design features:
- Flexibility and adaptability: Attractive wood folding doors can be used to divide the space and also provide access to a large storage area for the long folding tables.
- Accessibility: The Bola® chairs donated by Fixtures Furniture are lightweight yet sturdy and comfortable.
- Color contrast for safe maneuvering.

3-16. New facade for SDCB showing a unique braille sign.

goals. The recent award of another community block grant further improved the facility, including an updating of the much-used training kitchens, upgrading the HVAC systems, and creating a new facade for the building (see Figure 3-16).

The SDCB building was dark, monotonous, cavernous, and confusing (due to haphazard organization). One of the statements made during the pre-design interviews was that the service looked "hard up," that is, not professional or capable. That image has now been made over. The facility is brighter, with a clear layout and logical plan. Obstacles have been removed, and universal design details have been incorporated to make the building safer and easier to negotiate. The facility is now gaining recognition throughout the country as a model for other such programs—both for its designs and for the methods used to carry out those designs.

Universal Design Techniques
Environmental Programming
by Ann Warble-Nienow and Roberta L. Null, Ph.D.

Identifying user needs is essential to any successful design activity. Environmental programming is a flexible design tool that encourages designers, students, and facility managers (i.e., anyone with an interest in universal design) to emphasize the development of design criteria and the analysis of client needs before approaching a graphic design solution. Environmental programming also provides a design approach that can be used successfully by anyone who does not have high-level graphic design skills, since it instead requires a focus on the social and psychological aspects of an environment. In the case studies describing airport design and high-speed railcar design (Chapter 7), the complexity of the projects actually made use of environmental programming in addition to many types of graphic design skills. This process can be used early in the research programming phase.

Environmental programming encourages the designer to emphasize the development of design criteria and analysis of client needs before they approach a design solution. It thus provides a designer with the means to communicate with clients about their needs and desires. Or it could be used by the client to analyze their needs and communicate them to the design professional.

Following a development of profiles for users and the environmental setting, design criteria are formulated that can:

- Be supportive for a chosen user group in a specific physical setting
- Facilitate or support a particular social process
- Meet the needs of a person with a disability

The following example is a complex analysis of a suburban shopping center in relation to how it met the needs of an elderly population. The figures were completed by housing/interior design graduate student Ann Warble-Nienow as an independent study project. In this case, environmental programming was basically used as a post-occupancy evaluation with recommendations for adapting the environment rather than as an initial problem-defining programming effort.

A Coastal Resort Shopping Center Example

The purpose of this environmental assessment project was to analyze a suburban shopping center in relation to how well it met the needs of the permanent residents in a southern resort area. By using behavioral science research techniques to analyze the problem and develop design criteria for architectural adaptation, an evaluation model was developed. This model can be used by businesses or community action groups to study shopping facilities in a variety of settings. The techniques may also be expanded to include universal design and ADA compliance evaluations.

The Setting and Clientele—Pineland Mall

Due to the mild climate on the South Carolina Coast, Pineland Mall was designed with a covered walkway connecting the stores and a small lagoon in a park-like setting in the center of the mall. The mall's clientele consisted mainly of permanent residents of this resort area. Many were retired or semi-retired individuals in the upper-middle to upper income level.

Human Traffic Problems

Observation revealed that the front edges of the mall were the most heavily traveled. Close parking spaces were vied for by people just running in for groceries. The space between the grocery and drugstore was one of the busiest in the mall, while the other heavily used stop was the dry cleaners on the front corner of the mall. This site had a buildup of illegally parked cars, resulting in street congestion while people popped in to pick up their cleaning. The fringes of the front edge and the "near" lagoon area in the center of the mall got semi-heavy use (see Figure 3-17).

3-17. Human traffic movement, Pineland Mall.

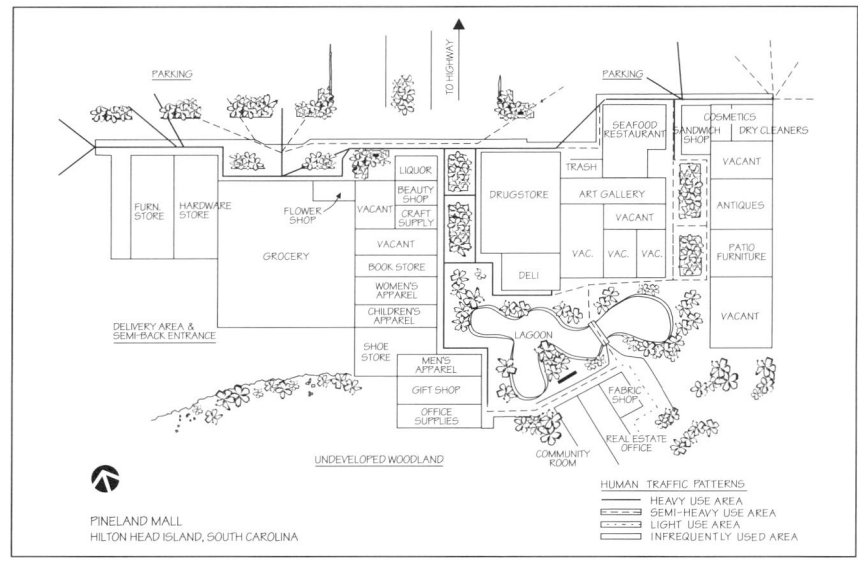

Environmental Programming Requirements for the Elderly

In order to plan adaptations of a shopping facility to make it a supportive environment for the elderly, recognition had to be made of the diversity and needs of this age group. The environment needed to be free of architectural barriers, which were barriers that discouraged elderly persons from orienting themselves to the environment. Other types of barriers prevented the elderly from passing easily from one area to another and prevented them from manipulating the equipment in the environment. The architectural barriers were identified (see Figure 3-18), and design criteria were established for recommended changes in the shopping environment. Design criteria were based on what was learned about the elderly through observation and other forms of behavioral research reported in the environmental design literature.

3-18. Architectural barriers, Pineland Mall.

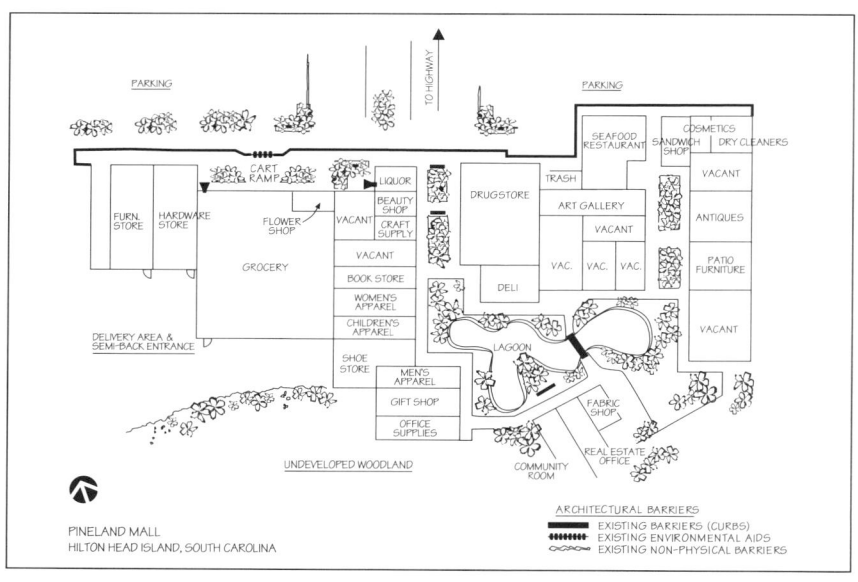

Environmental Revisions

Even though the recommended adaptations (see Figure 3-19) of the mall were planned to create a supportive shopping environment for the elderly, these adaptations were practical for everyone shopping there. Easy access to stores, adequate restroom facilities, places to sit and rest with pleasant views, adequate mapping, and identification of store locations are good design for everyone. In fact, many merchants have discovered the hard way that elderly customers don't see themselves as elderly and will shun merchandise and facilities planned for older people. Meeting the varied needs of customers is simply good business.

Specific revisions and adaptations for Pineland Mall included the following:

- Numerous benches provided for resting, socializing, and waiting

- Public rest rooms located to service the whole of the mall were designed to accommodate persons with disabilities

- Mechanical boosters on all entrance and exit doors for ease of use by all

- Ramp-type curbing at various points along the front edge of the mall

- Parking for use by those with disabilities designated according to code

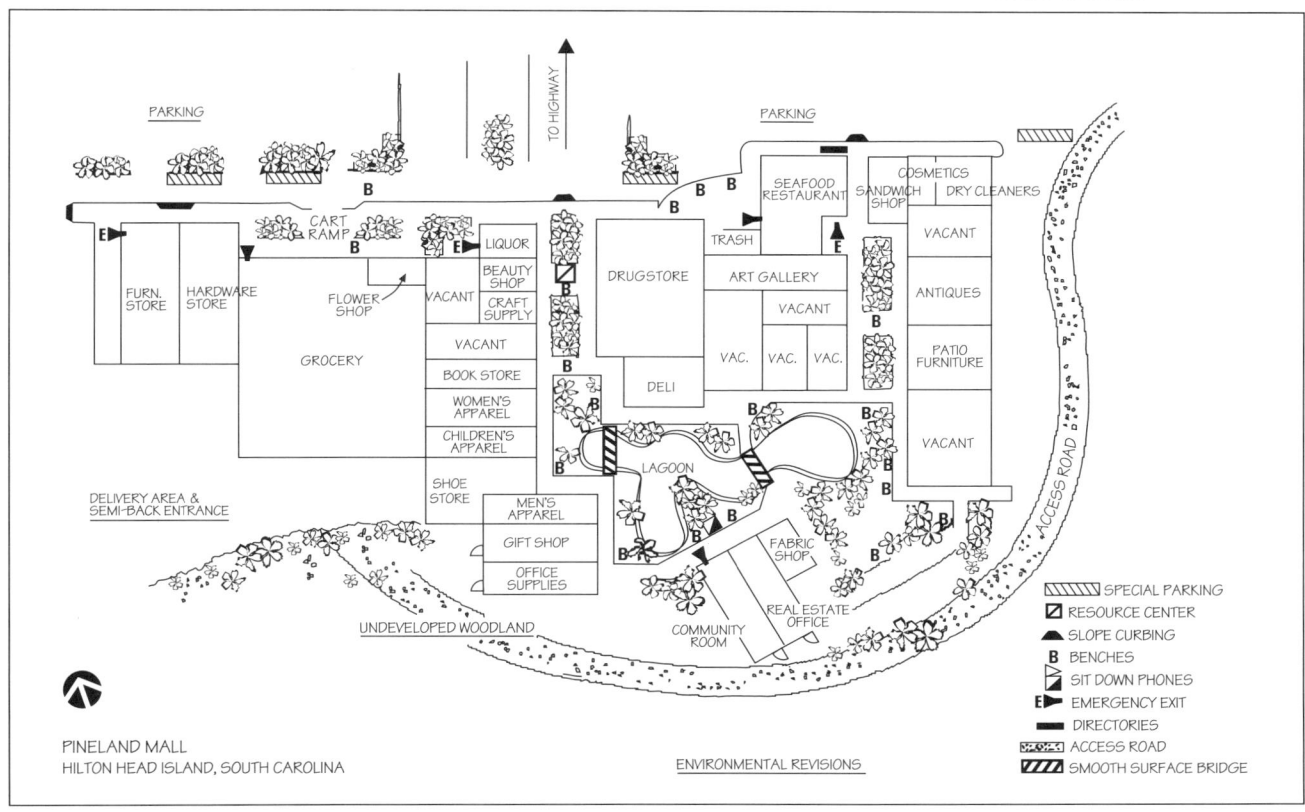

3-19. Environmental revisions, Pineland Mall.

- Directories redesigned to produce signs legible to those with failing eyesight

- Two additional directories added to the site to aid in wayfinding

- Creation of a road through woods behind the mall, providing emergency access and relief of congestion at the front of the mall

Universal Design Strategy
The Oral History Interview
by Karen Hirsch

Oral history interviews represent a powerful way for people often ignored by society to add their voices and their perspectives to the writing of history that interprets the past, to the understanding of the values that govern the present, and to the planning for the decisions that will influence the future. The use of personal oral history research with people with disabilities can serve many purposes, some of which are relevant to designers.

If designers are interested in creating an environment that can accommodate everybody, the needs of people with disabilities must be included from the beginning. The best way of assuring that these needs are met is to involve people with disabilities directly in the process of planning and designing the environment. Oral history interviews constitute an effective way of letting people with different kinds of disabilities contribute to the task of eliminating architectural barriers.

Various members of the disabled community have different accessibility needs, and sometimes the removal of a barrier for one group has been done in ways that create problems for another. It is therefore important for designers to include people with all kinds of abilities and disabilities in the design process. While people using wheelchairs need an environment that is free of architectural barriers, people who are blind need a multitude of concrete environmental clues to aid them in their task of orientation and navigation without the use of sight. Thus, curbs represent effective barriers to people in wheelchairs, while they are helpful guides for people who are blind. Oral history interviews with both groups of people could reveal other areas of conflicting needs as well as some creative solutions, such as using textured surfaces on curb cuts, that could work for both groups.

In addition to making their needs known to designers, people with disabilities can contribute to the process by becoming designers themselves and participating directly in the task of creating an environment that is responsive to their needs. If design, broadly conceived, consists of the plans and strategies people develop in order to solve their problems and achieve their goals, then people with disabilities get more than their fair share of practice in designing, because they have more than their fair share of obstacles to overcome. A person with a disability needs to plan ahead and anticipate obstacles in most situations where people without disabilities can take for granted that they have easy and quick access to information, resources, and execution of their plans. Viewed from this perspective, people with disabilities represent a tremendous and untapped resource for designers, especially designers who are beginning to think in terms of universal design—the creation of an environment that will be readily adaptable to everyone's needs, including people with disabilities.

Conversations with people with disabilities reveal their capacity for practical problem-solving. While most of them may have a tendency to share this kind of information with each other more readily than with people who are not disabled, they are often as proud of their own resourcefulness as they are frustrated by the barriers. The following story demonstrates some of these points.

One cold and icy winter day when using my crutches, I was slowly and carefully making my way over the ice from my car to the building where I work. I had to pass close by a pick-up truck parked in a "handicapped" parking space. As I came close to the truck, the person in the driver's seat rolled down the window and started telling me about how he deals with ice using his crutches. He had installed "ice picks" into his crutches by drilling holes in the rubber safety tips and inserting barrel-type door latches into them in such a way that he could easily pull the latches in when he was about to walk on a floor, and let them out when he had to go out onto an icy street or sidewalk.

This story reveals one of the ways to begin to take advantage of the life experiences of people unfamiliar with the jargon or technicalities of a specialized discipline such as architecture. One simply needs to ask them to talk about how they have solved some of the problems associated with the activities of daily living. Interviews are increasingly being used in many different fields to collect information about life experiences that are crucial to the understanding of different perspectives, especially the perspective of people normally left out of the development process. Oral history interviews are especially well suited to the process of collecting information about life experiences from ordinary people because they are designed to place any information collected in a cultural and historical perspective. This means that the experiences described in individual interviews are being interpreted against a thoroughly researched background of a place at a specific time in history.

Therefore the professionals are not as likely to over-generalize their findings and develop ideas that are acultural or solutions that are not sufficiently related to perceived needs. Personal oral history interviews can help designers understand both the cultural meaning of disability experiences, and what suggestions people with disabilities have for solving some of their accessibility problems.

Collecting oral history interviews among people with disabilities represents a special challenge for social historians. Several studies suggest that people with disabilities respond differently to different interviewers. They are more likely to share certain kinds of information with interviewers who are themselves disabled. If the interviewer is not disabled, the information obtained must be interpreted in a different way than if the interviewer is also a person with a disability. An interviewer who is disabled may be able to elicit more statements about the barriers a disabled person experiences, the anger and frustration at the inaccessible environment, and the solutions that have been developed and put to use by the interviewee.

On the other hand, an interviewer who does not have a disability might be likely to hear more stories portraying coping and acceptance strategies that fulfill the person's need to appear well adjusted. The most widely held idea about how people with disabilities should act in order to get along in society is that they should be cheerful and positive and should make the best effort possible to adjust themselves to society and not ask for anything "extra."

Oral history interviews of and by people with disabilities would greatly enhance and strengthen the work of designers and other people involved in shaping the built environment of the future. The needs of various groups of citizens with disabilities could be worked out so they could complement instead of conflict with each other. People with disabilities would be able to describe existing barriers and rank them in order of the most frequently encountered to the least frequently encountered obstacles.

Through oral history interviews, design ideas from people with disabilities could be recognized and utilized, with credit given for their contributions in the general effort to create an accessible environment. In addition to producing suggestions as part of a design team, people with disabilities should be encouraged to become designers themselves and to work with both the professional knowledge of the field and their life experiences as citizens who happen to have disabilities. Doing so will help create the most cost-effective and efficient solutions to some of the practical problems involved in the creation of an environment that is accessible to all.

Universal Design Strategy
User Considerations in an ADA Task Force
by Joel I. Kahn

The following personal account describes one individual's experience with a corporation's attempts at complying with the ADA. The author has multiple sclerosis and has used an electric scooter since 1981. His long-term experience within the corporate environment provided valuable feedback to the task force regarding areas that needed immediate attention. This perspective is needed for any situation where processes and facilities are being analyzed and modified.

I joined the Procter & Gamble Company in Cincinnati, Ohio, in 1974 as an able-bodied mechanical engineer. In 1976 I was diagnosed with multiple sclerosis, and in 1981 I started using a scooter to be fully mobile at work. The company supported me through a career change with their standard education assistance program and assignment changes. Through the years the company met all my needs for special parking, larger offices, and reduced travel. Therefore, when the ADA Task Force was formed in 1991 by Lynwood L. Battle, I joined feeling this was yet one more step forward for the company to proactively address issues and allow all people to be as productive as possible.

The Task Force met monthly and was comprised mainly of people from human resources. My role was to provide two pieces of information: examples of where the system did and did not work for people with disabilities, and potential areas where new policies would need to be formed.

As with many large organizations, although policies were in place to meet most of the ADA requirements, sometimes the approval process was slow. For example, I work on the third floor of a four-story building where there was only one accessible washroom stall, and that was located on the first floor. There was also one other person in my extended work group who uses a wheelchair. When both of us were in the same meeting on the first floor, we had to wait for one another to use the single stall. If this stall malfunctioned, we needed to use the facilities in an adjacent building. Although one stall met the ADA guidelines, it was not efficient. It took an extended period of time to sort out who would fund additional facilities after they were approved: the general ADA project, the individual building, or our management. Throughout this process there was never any disagreement about whether to install new facilities, only a bottleneck regarding funding. This example helped the ADA Task Force to realize the need for streamlined, clearer guidelines about their practices in general, and we worked on making those improvements.

Drawing on my personal experience, I was also able to spot potential problems in advance that needed to be addressed. For example, the company's normal job interview process for new management people requires two steps: an on-campus interview followed by an on-site interview. The on-site interview usually takes up an entire day, where peers and several levels of management ask questions and share information. A problem can occur when interviewing a person on campus for a position that normally does not require travel. If the prospective employee has difficulty traveling, he/she would not be barred from the position, but the second on-site interview could be problematic. Based on my recommendations, guidelines allowing accommodations for this situation were instituted.

In a group such as the ADA Task Force, several factors combine to make input from individuals with disabilities highly useful and crucial. From my experience with the company, I knew them to be committed to doing the right things. They simply needed some perspective on how to improve things that were already fairly effective. It was always my intent to use good listening and understanding skills; I tried to understand the overall concerns before offering solutions. Finally, rather than merely trying to interpret the new guidelines, the entire team became problem solvers about meeting and exceeding economically what was required to be merely productive.

It is highly beneficial to have a "customer" of ADA policy on an ADA Task Force. Besides the insights available from this different perspective, this customer can provide a reality check to the people developing policies. The person providing this perspective needs to bring a positive attitude, understanding, and problem-solving skills to the group to have the greatest impact.

Implications for Facility Managers

4

Facilities management is one of the most challenging fields to develop recently in this country, impacting a wide range of American business, education, and public facilities. With the passage of the ADA, it is also one of the most demanding. Because it is facility managers' responsibility to oversee the interplay of the physical environment and operations, especially as it affects workers, an understanding of the ADA and the approach to universal design offered in this book is particularly vital. It will often fall to facility managers to decide the course of action to take when faced with changing demands from workers, regulators, management, the public, and the work itself.

Facility managers are hired to manage physical property so it is efficiently and safely used for its intended purpose. In the private sector, their primary function may be to ensure a profit for the facility owner. Their secondary function will then be meeting the needs of workers. While these are often concurrent, they are not necessarily so, and many owners and facility managers feel that the ADA demands an unwarranted shift in emphasis from the former to the latter. Universal design offers a means of balancing both of these demands.

In researching this book the authors found one source of ideas and information on facility design to be particularly noteworthy: James Mueller's book, *The Workplace Workbook 2.0*, is a clear, concise guide to providing reasonable accommodations in a variety of spaces. The book is organized around adaptations for 17 "functional characteristics" of disabilities. These characteristics are detailed in Mueller's essay in Chapter 5: Enabling Products.

Mueller also offers illustrations of general changes that can be made in the common workplace, such as those represented in Figure 4-1, which shows accommodations in information displays. Any facility manager who wants to understand the detailed nuts-and-bolts of accommodations should have a copy of *The Workplace Workbook 2.0* on hand.

This chapter ties together many of the conceptual threads found throughout Mueller's book. The opening essay presents an argument for how the spirit, rather than the letter, of the ADA legislation is the crucial element for true accommodation, and shows why universal design is both the conceptual and practical answer to the question of accommodation.

This is followed first by a set of guidelines created at the Iowa State University for making small businesses accessible. Next, a case study shows how Purdue University created and implemented a comprehensive ADA compliance plan. Shoshana Shamberg discusses how professionals such as occupational therapists can work with facility managers to arrive at viable solutions for accommodating individuals with disabilities. Finally, Nancy and James Canestaro present a case study of using a simulation-game to discover cultural differences between Japanese and American managers.

Universal Design Implications for Facility Management

by Timothy J. Springer, Ph.D.

The Americans with Disabilities Act has created a myriad of challenges and opportunities for facility managers. Much of the discussion surrounding the ADA has focused on the physical accommodation aspects of the legislation as expressed in the ADA Accessibility Guidelines (ADAAG). The majority of the professions concerned with devising "solutions"—architects, designers, engineers, accountants, lawyers, and so on—have focused predominantly on physical, financial, and legal issues. They have often acted in a reactive mode, fearing more potential penalties of non-compliance rather than seeking out the potential opportunities of meeting both the letter and the spirit of the law.

The ADA is, purely and simply, civil rights legislation enacted to prohibit discrimination and eliminate it by removing the barriers, physical and otherwise, that deny the "differently abled" full access to public and commercial facilities. To successfully implement the goals of the ADA, a detailed knowledge of the technical and physical aspects of the law is not as important as a committed understanding of the intent of the law. It is primarily an attitudinal question rather than one of physical change, accommodation, and

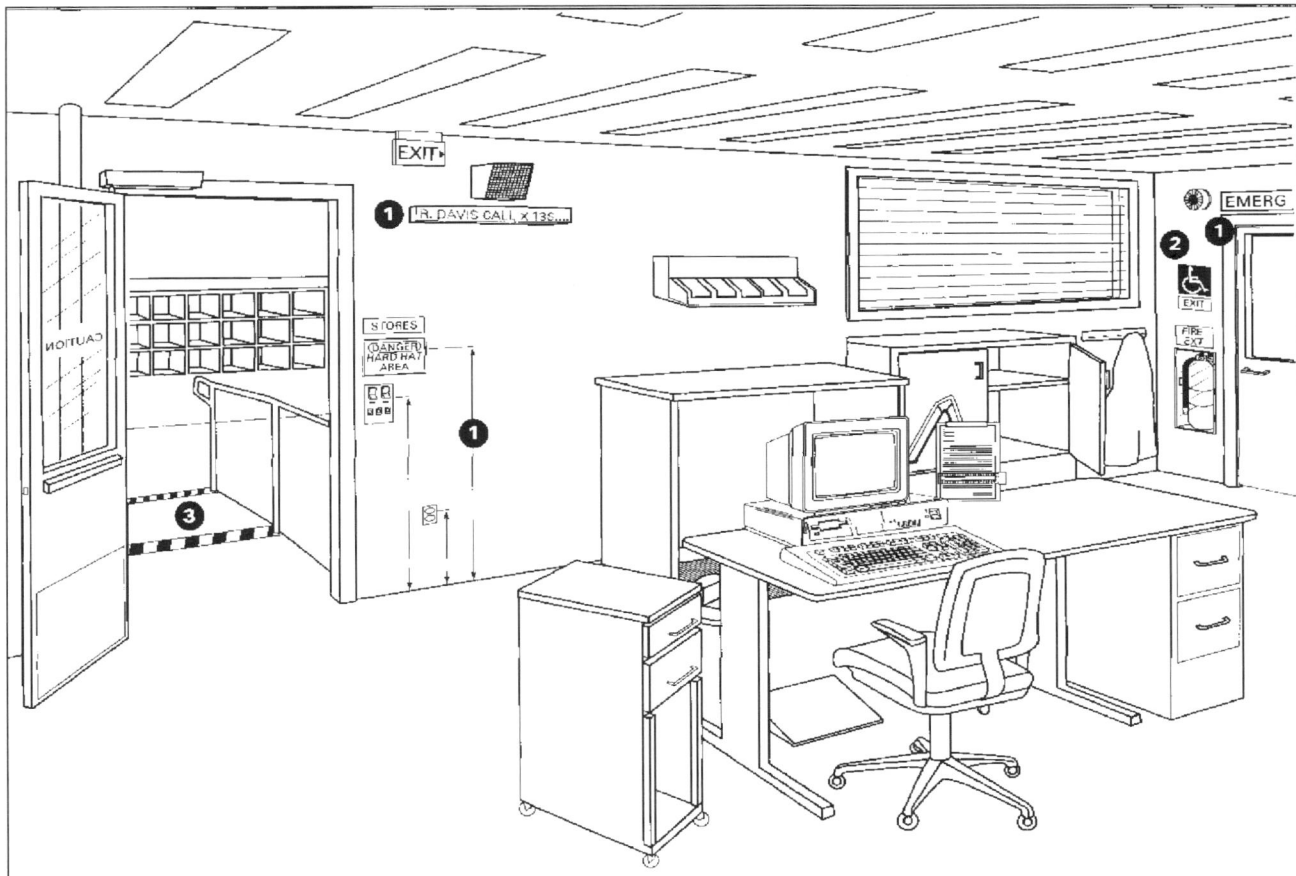

Information Displays
1. Locate signs for use with minimal peripheral vision: Most important information at center of field of vision; cluster related information, isolate unrelated information; provide redundant auditory and/or tactile information.

   Ensure adequate illumination (100–300 lux); ideal angle of illumination 45° to display.

   Make viewing angle of LCD displays as close as possible to 90°.

   Minimize glare and reflection: Use "eggshell," matte, or other nonglare surface texture.

   Contrast with surroundings (light/dark, bright/dull, smooth/textured); avoid need to differentiate among muted or pastel colors and among greens, blues, and purples.

   Use Univers, Helvetica, or similar san-serif lettering (upper and lower case preferred; exception: tactile lettering, which should be all upper case, ⅝"–2" high, raised ½", and accompanied by braille).

   Use generous spacing between letters, words, and lines; avoid underlining and borders around lettering.

   Use Arabic, rather than Roman, numerals.

   Locate room identification near door frame on latch side, 60" above floor (locate other signs as near as possible to referred item).

2. Use familiar symbols wherever possible; indicate accessible facilities/features with the appropriate symbol:

   International Symbol of Accessibility

   Amplified Telephone Symbol

   International TDD (Text Telephone) Symbol

   International Symbol of Access for Hearing Loss (indicates presence of assistive listening system)

   Symbol indicating avalability of sign language interpreter

3. Mark borders of hazardous areas with flush, contrasting visual and tactile marking strips.

4-1. An example of changes to information displays that can better accommodate all personnel (from James Mueller's *The Workplace Workbook 2.0*, pp. 14–15). *(Reprinted with permission from the Dole Foundation for Employment for People with Disabilities.)*

associated costs. Changes will have to be made; money will have to be expended. However, the long-term benefits will far outweigh the short-term costs. If the changes are approached in the spirit of "reasonable (and rightful) accommodation" for all, both those who are currently disabled and those who are "temporarily abled" will benefit.

Figures 4-2 through 4-13 show the results of the United Methodist Church's attempts to accommodate people with disabilities, including updated renderings to reflect ADAAG (the drawings are done by Jerry Ellis, AIA). It's important to understand that their efforts at accessibility have been going on for more than 20 years.

Facility management has to do with *facilitation*—how to maximize the effectiveness of the built environment for those who own it and those who use it. Implementing the ADA, and incorporating universal design as a key part of that implementation strategy, is not a question of simply compliance with a set of "minimums" as expressed in the ADAAG. It is not a cut-and-paste exercise of applying template solutions to problems, embodying an afterthought mentality to avoid potential legal hassles. For facility managers, meeting the spirit of the law involves the question, and the accompanying implementation strategies, of how one treats people. It implies using what is already known about people, their jobs, and the work environment to design the work processes properly.

Universal design is directly related to the ADA. This is understandable since both deal with issues of accommodation and people with disabilities, yet each represents a distinctly different approach to the same issue. The ADA is the most sweeping piece of civil rights legislation in recent history. As law, it is subject to challenge, interpretation, and codification in the courts. It is, by definition, a reactive approach that fosters a compliance mentality to the concepts of accommodation through "inclusive" or "ability-sensitive" design. In contrast, universal design is philosophically different from the ADA because it is both broader and proactive. According to Ronald Mace, who is credited with coining the term, *universal design* means design for people throughout their life. This is an important distinction.

The ADA attempts to deal with certain types of disabilities and recommends accommodations based on common forms of disability. The underlying premise of universal design holds that disability is a contextual state and that everyone at some point is disabled. Disability in this context is an inability to adapt to or adjust to a situation, device, or environment. Since most devices and environments are designed, universal design seeks to eliminate elements that force excessive adaptation on the part of the human occupant or user.

Implications for Facility Managers

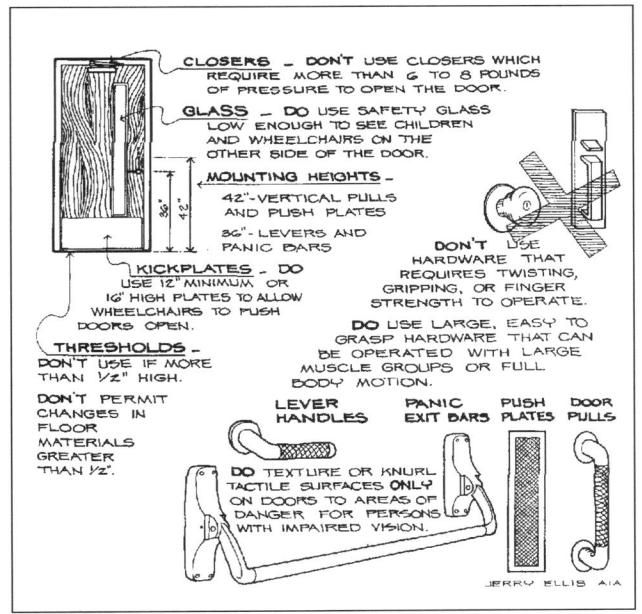

4-2. **Door hardware.** *(Figures 4-2 through 4-13 from a series on architectural barriers presented by the West Ohio Conference Committee on persons with handicapped conditions. Carolyn Knowles, Chairperson. Reprinted with permission from Jerry Ellis, Architect, various church publications, 1969–94.)*

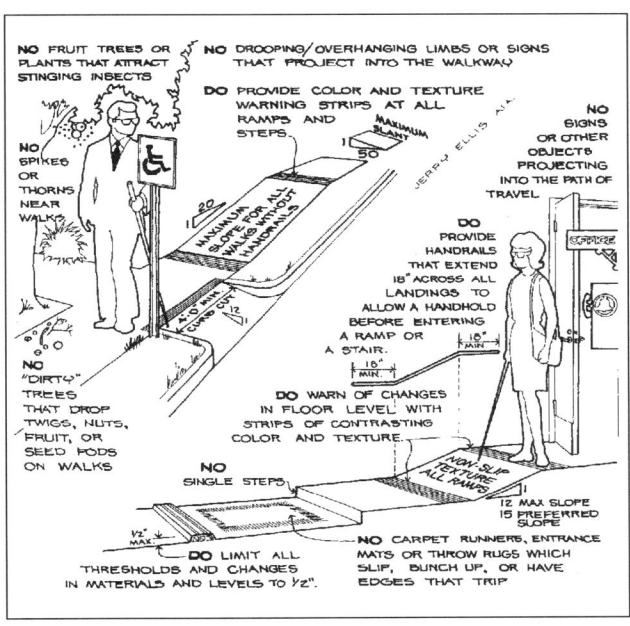

4-3. **A clear path.**

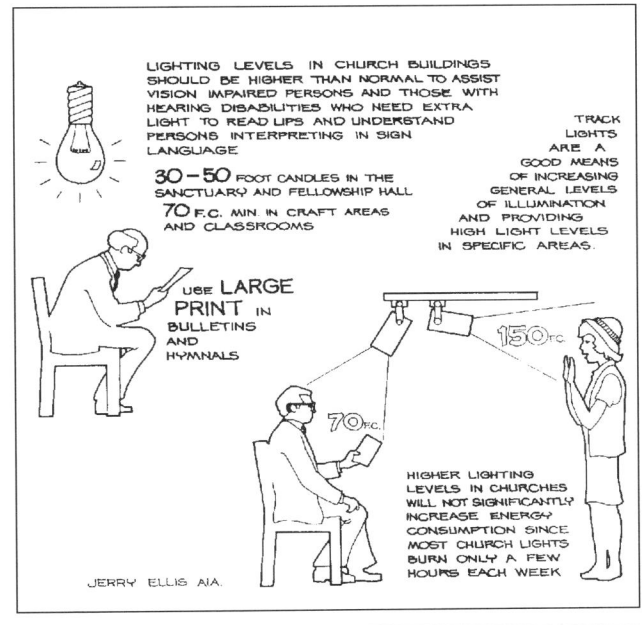

4-4. **Lighting.**

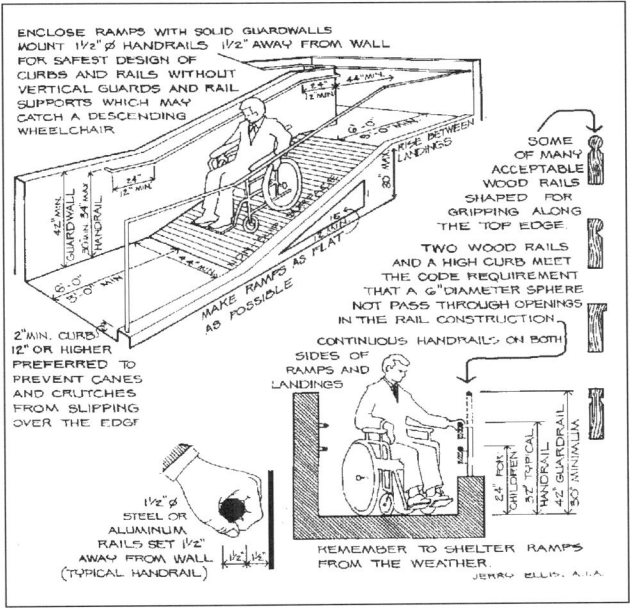

4-5. **Ramps.**

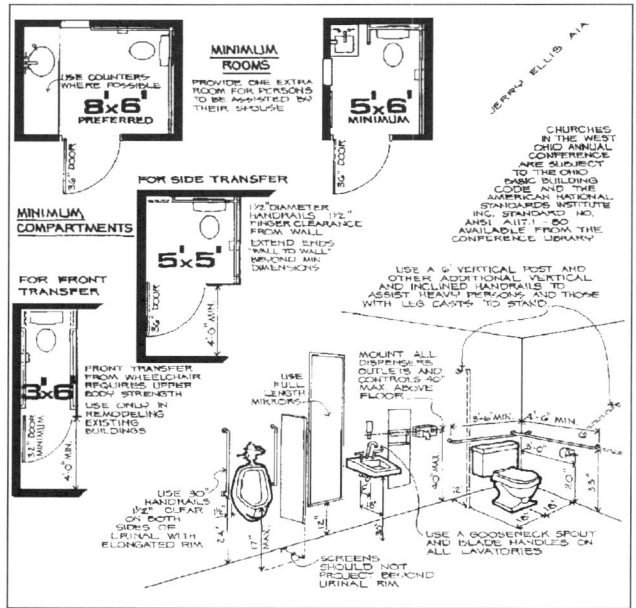

4-6. Toilet facilities.

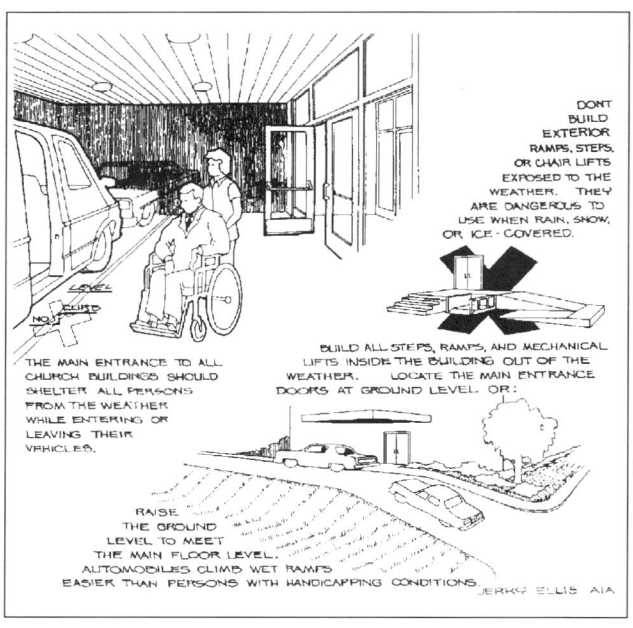

4-7. Sheltered entrance.

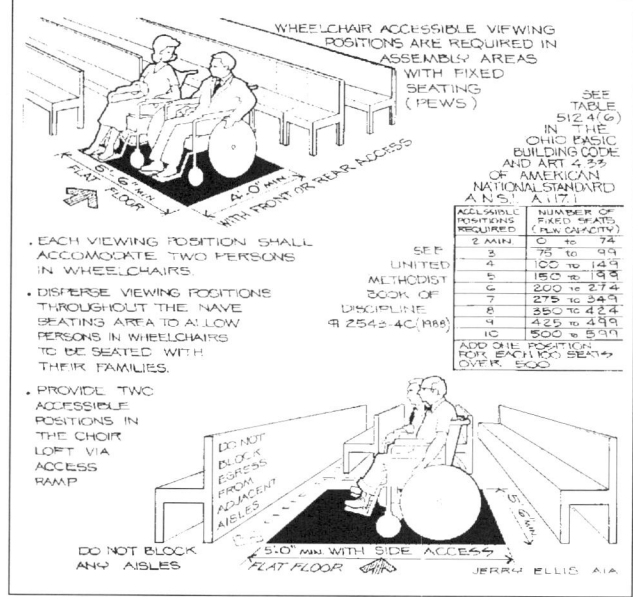

4-8. Seating.

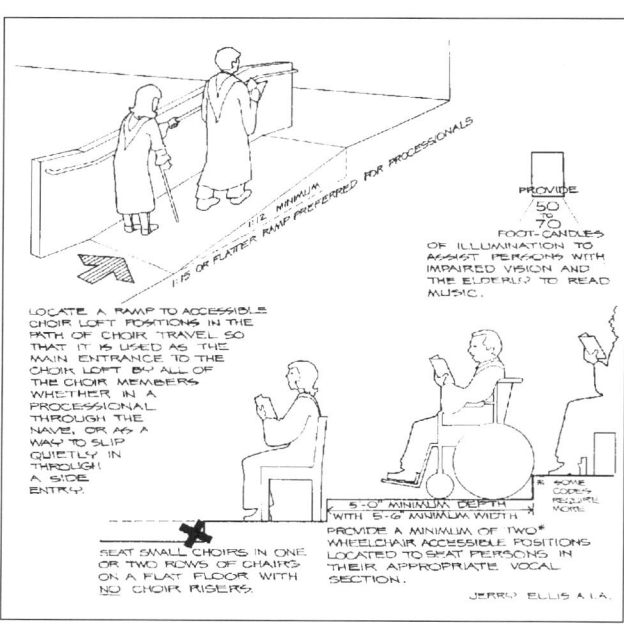

4-9. Choir lofts.

Implications for Facility Managers 77

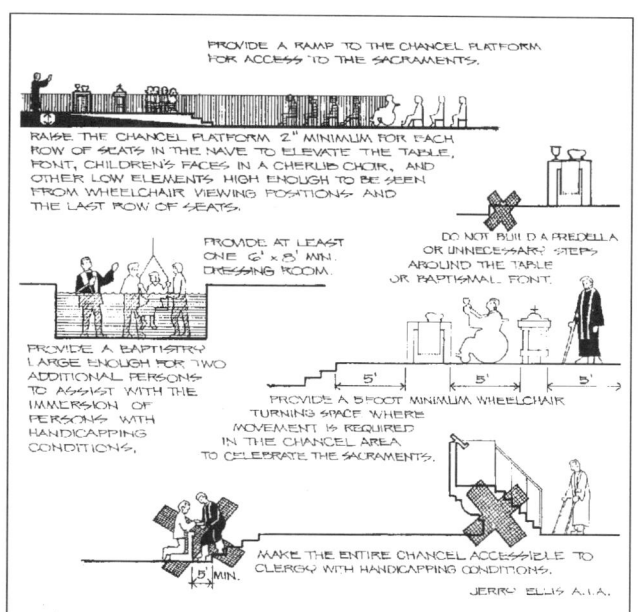

4-10. Chancel platforms.

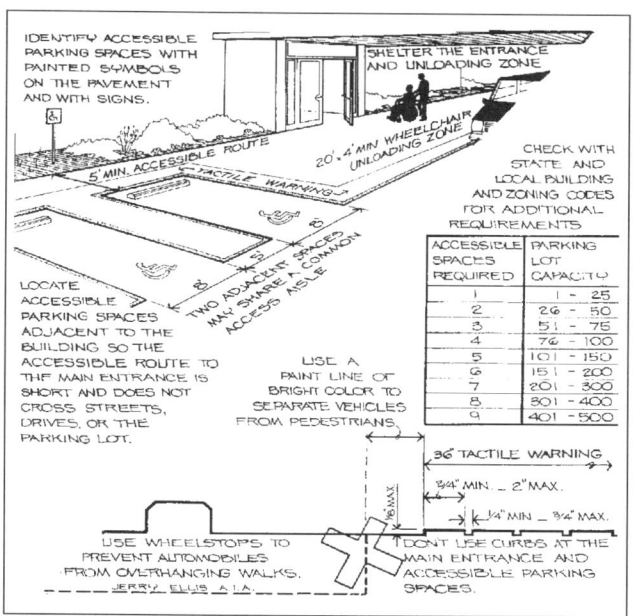

4-11. Parking.

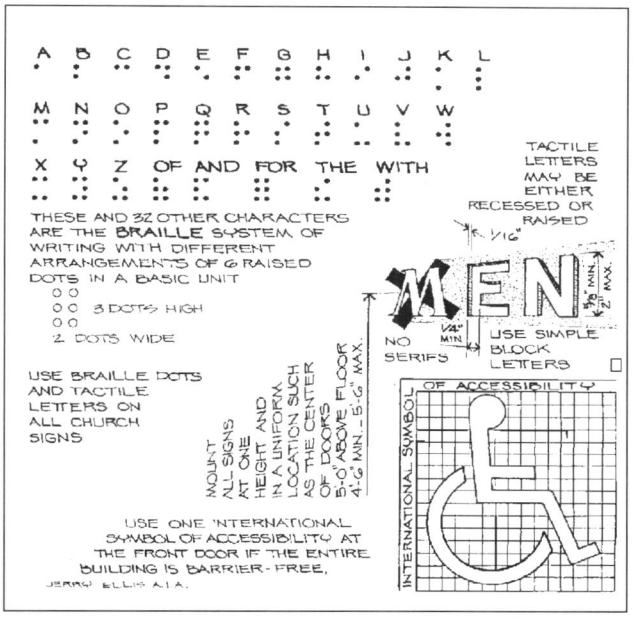

4-12. Signs.

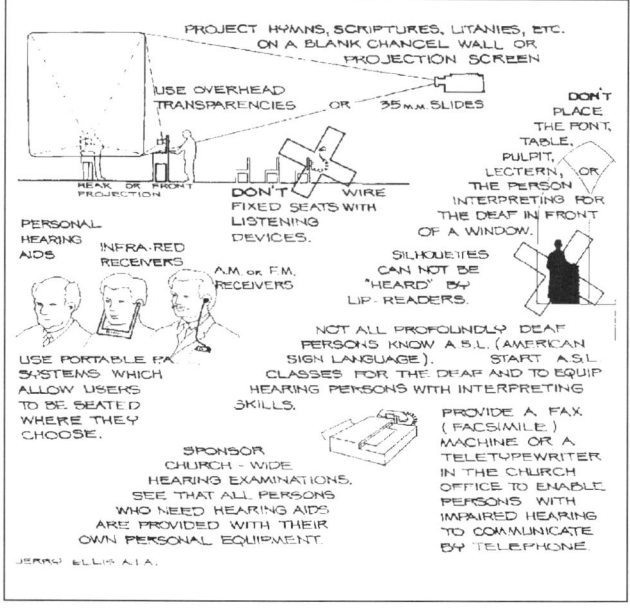

4-13. Hearing.

Disability is a continuum. We are all disabled to a greater or lesser degree at some point in time. Even Olympic athletes and other champions of physical prowess are disabled in certain situations. Those who are left-handed, pregnant, obese, wear eyeglasses, or are children belong to the "universe" of disabled people—depending upon the setting. When considered from this perspective, universal design could be said to advocate design that minimizes contextual disability for the greatest population of users.

Stephen Pheasant suggests that we "consider those individuals most people think of when they hear the term 'disabled'—the wheelchair users. These people, under most circumstances, are 'handicapped' three times over. Firstly, whatever condition put him in the wheelchair, the disabilities concerned will be handicapping in themselves. Secondly, he must operate at an eye-level that is some 16 inches lower than that of standing people, which is disadvantageous both physically and psychologically. Thirdly, he rolls around in a cumbersome, awkward, space-consuming, distinctive, and inelegant vehicle" (1988, p. 175). It is this group of users that much of the ADA is intended to accommodate. However, under certain circumstances (e.g., long, broad hallways, outdoor walkways, and so on) wheelchair users are less restricted and encumbered by their environment than are the so-called able-bodied.

Pheasant states, "It is not that the rheumatoid or back pain sufferer (i.e., disabled) needs an object that is differently designed—it is rather that the rest of us have reserves of physical adaptability that enable us to tolerate design deficiencies. Looked at in this way, many environmental adaptations or 'aids for the disabled' are only required as a consequence of faulty ergonomics" (p. 174).

Since this approach is very anthropocentric—human focused—there are certain unavoidable parallels with human factors. The discipline of human factors, or more narrowly, ergonomics, attempts to define the design requirements of devices, environments, and systems in terms of human capabilities and limitations. The goal is to make the things people use and the ways and places in which they are used as safe, easy, comfortable, and productive as possible. Human factors recognizes the value of people in human technology and human environment systems, and strives to minimize the adverse impact of design on people. Thus human factors is applied universal design.

In this context, universal design goes well beyond the ADA to address the issue of prevention as well as accommodation. Consider the contribution of design (both positive and negative) to current issues such as cumulative trauma disorders and workers' compensation costs. Universal design attempts to identify potential causes of disability as well as barriers to people with disabilities. The goal is to rectify the design environment so disabilities are *prevented.*

The challenge for facility managers is not necessarily to assess the accommodations required to serve a particular segment of the population—the so-called compliance attitude fostered by many who misinterpret the intent of the ADA. Rather, facility managers should look for ways to maximize efficiency and profitability by removing impediments to all users. Where special accommodations appear necessary, one must question the purpose of the change and the root cause of the inaccessibility.

As a simple example, consider steps leading into buildings. Steps, in general, are major contributors to slips, trips, and falls. Outdoor steps are particularly hazardous because of varied weather conditions. In northern climates, outdoor steps have associated maintenance costs of snow removal (usually by hand), and the added hazard of ice and snow. A ramp is often added to steps to increase accessibility; however, the ramp really serves only a portion of the population. Because of the angle, surface, and other considerations, it may not be appropriate for certain people (e.g., arthritis sufferers, people with walkers). A ramp also presents additional cost and maintenance concerns such as snow removal, vandalism, and damage. Several demonstration projects have shown that a different approach, that is, eliminating the steps and changing the grade of the approach walkway from the curb to the door, not only increases access but saves money, reduces safety liability, and enhances appearances if well designed and landscaped. Initial costs may be somewhat higher, but the cost of use is considerably lower. The difference between an add-on ramp and a more complete environmental solution highlights the difference between simple ADA compliance and the use of universal design. The former can be efficient: *doing things right*. The latter is effective: *doing the right things*.

The point is that few problems have only one right answer. Inside the facility, one can find many examples where universal design can yield benefits for a wide spectrum of occupants and users. Fundamentally, the focus should be on three areas—safety, communication, and wayfinding. There are many elements that can be used to affect these functions (space, light, sound, color, texture, contrast). For example, signage, an aid to wayfinding, should accommodate all users. Attention to not only the format (e.g., raised letters, braille) but to issues that will serve all users (placement, readability, content, and coding of information—color, for example) is important.

Cost is a concern of all businesses when considering universal design and/or the ADA. If viewed in the context of simple compliance with the ADA, the goal is to minimize costs by doing the minimum necessary to avoid contention. Applying universal design changes the cost consideration to one of investment. As mentioned in the step-versus-grade example, up-front costs can be somewhat higher for doing right things; however, proper understanding and application of universal design principles will yield a greater return. That is not to say that all universal design solutions must necessarily cost a great deal more than those that merely meet the letter rather than the spirit of the law. Many approaches exist that require only appropriate application and use. Spatial arrangements, such as wider corridors, can both accommodate special equipment needs (e.g., wheelchair use) and support organizational requirements (e.g., interaction spaces, informal communication). Systems furniture, for example, can accommodate a wide range of work surface height requirements with relative ease. A variety of accessory, modification, and add-on products are available at relatively low cost. Door handle levers, for example, make sense for most users in most environments and are a modest-price retrofit. Some technological fixes resolve larger design questions and make accommodation issues moot (e.g., energy controls that sense movement require very little interaction on the part of the occupant). The bottom line is that good design—universal design—is cost-effective because it considers all resources (including valuable human ones) and attempts to minimize long-term costs. This is also the goal of the facility manager.

The best criteria by which to plan and judge universal design are:

- Does the design present situations to which any people are incapable of adjusting?

- Can environmental elements be changed or removed to eliminate the challenge?

- Does the design offer alternatives—for example, stairs for those who wish to take them as well as free-access transport (e.g., lifts, elevators, and so on); different sink heights for children, wheelchair users, tall people?

There is no one right solution. Universal design as a strategy for achieving the goals of the Americans with Disabilities Act will help facility managers meet the spirit as well as the letter of the law. It's all a matter of attitude.

Universal design, with its emphasis on being supportive, adaptable, accessible, and safe to the entire range of potential users, goes far in meeting the physical concerns of the ADA. If universal design is to accomplish its intent, it is necessary to focus on removing the non-physical barriers—intentions and attitudes. These must be supplanted with the good intentions of the organization, its management, and its employees if the spirit of the law is to be achieved. This is the challenge and the opportunity for facility management.

Case Study

Accessibility for Customers: Guidelines for Making Your Small Business Accessible
by Mary H. Yearns, Ph.D., and Arvid E. Osterberg, D.Arch.

Is your business accessible to all customers? People cannot buy your goods and services unless they can get to them. Accessibility is the key to attracting new customers and keeping those you now serve.

The ADA requires all businesses to make their facilities accessible to people with disabilities. This article describes some of the major features of the ADA for small businesses and ways to improve access for customers who may have difficulty walking, hearing, or seeing.

Easy Changes

Improving accessibility need not be an overwhelming task. Changes should be *readily achievable*—easy and affordable—based on your financial resources and the nature of the modifications needed. Tax incentives are available to help with modification costs. If a change is not readily achievable, other solutions may be acceptable, as long as they are safe and they maintain the dignity of customers and employees.

Improving the accessibility of your business is a continuing responsibility. Changes that are not readily achievable now may be necessary in the future due to changes in customer demands, technology, and financial resources. The following steps are suggested to document your "good faith" effort to comply with the ADA.

- Contact resource people from local disability groups who can help with an accessibility review.

- Conduct a self-evaluation to identify accessibility problems. (Use the following list as a starting point.)

- Set priorities (note the four priorities on the list).

- Develop a long-term plan—three to five years—for improving accessibility.

- Review progress periodically.

Get More Information

Before you venture out on your own, contact other businesses to see if they would like to join efforts to improve accessibility on Main Street. Study publications and attend ADA workshops to get more information. Invite people from a local disability group to tour your businesses and identify problems. You may want to pool resources to hire an outside design consultant. Use your accessibility improvements as a marketing tool to attract new customers.

For more information about ADA requirements, contact your local extension office or the nearest Regional Disability and Business Accommodation Center at 800-949-4232 (voice and TTY/TDD). The regional center will provide free publications on a variety of ADA topics, answer technical questions over the phone or by mail, and identify local resource people or consultants who can provide on-site assistance.

Four Priorities

The following list identifies some common accessibility problems in existing buildings, listed in order of importance. Preferred solutions and other methods for improving accessibility also are identified. The list is not comprehensive. Consult state and local building codes for exact specifications. More stringent standards may apply when remodeling or building a new structure.

*Priority 1: Get Customers into Building**

Problems	Preferred Solutions	Other Solutions
Curb prevents access to pathway.	• Install curb ramp. • Cut away section of curb.	• Provide curbside or outside door service.
Steps block entrance(s) and/or entrance platform(s) are not the same height as the threshold.	• Regrade site, raise sidewalk, or build "bridge" to connect entrance with ground level. • Provide alternate path to ground level entrance. • Build ramp.	• Post sign that says "Honk for assistance." • Provide home delivery. • Install doorbell; post sign that says "Press button for customer assistance."
Threshold is too high (exceeds ½ inch) and/or is not beveled.	• Replace existing threshold with low-profile version. • Bevel existing threshold.	
Exterior door is too narrow (less than 32-inch clear opening).	• Install wider door.	

(continued on next page)

*Accessible parking must be available close to accessible entrances (see priority 4).

Problems	Preferred Solutions	Other Solutions
Strong force is needed to pull open exterior door (8.5-pound maximum force suggested).	• Install automatic door opener. • Adjust or replace closer.	
Knob or handle is difficult to grasp and use.	• Replace knobs with lever or loop handles.	
Door cannot be opened and/or reached by customer in wheelchair.	• Increase maneuvering space at front, back, and/or latch side of door. • Move obstructions away from door.	• Relocate door.

Priority 2: Make Goods and Services Accessible

Problems	Preferred Solutions	Other Solutions
Sections of building are inaccessible due to changes in floor levels.	• Install elevator or ramp. • Relocate goods and services to accessible level.	• Post sign that says "If you need assistance, please ask."
Interior doors are too narrow (less than 32-inch clear opening).	• Install wider doors. • Replace existing door hinges with offset hinges.	• Assign employees to help customers.
Interior doors require too much strength to open (more than 5-pound force).	• Adjust or replace closers.	• Bring goods or services to customers in accessible area.
Doorknobs are difficult to use.	• Replace knobs with lever or loop handles.	
Aisles and service lanes are too narrow (less than 36 inches).	• Rearrange furnishings to widen aisles.	
Doorways lack maneuvering space on one or both sides.	• Move obstructions away from doors. • Reconstruct doorways. • Remove doors.	

(continued on next page)

Problems	Preferred Solutions	Other Solutions
Maneuvering space to turn corners is lacking. (See Figure 4-14(A).)	• Rearrange furnishings to provide more turning space. • Move or eliminate walls.	
Goods on shelves are too high or too low to reach. (See Figure 4-14(C).)	• Arrange goods vertically. • Change height of shelves.	
Check-out and/or service counters are too high.	• Lower section of counter. • Provide knee space under counter.	• Supply clipboards for customers to use to fill out forms.

Priority 3: Make Rest Rooms Usable

Problems	Preferred Solutions	Other Solutions
Rest room door is too narrow (less than 32-inch clear opening.)	• Install wider door. • Replace existing door hinges with offset hinges.	
Rest room door requires too much strength to open.	• Adjust or replace closer.	
Knobs are difficult to grasp and use.	• Replace knobs with lever or loop handles.	*(continued on next page)*

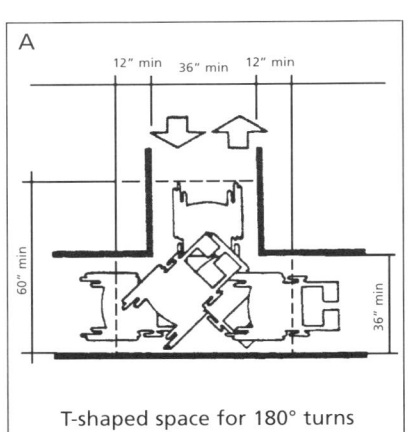
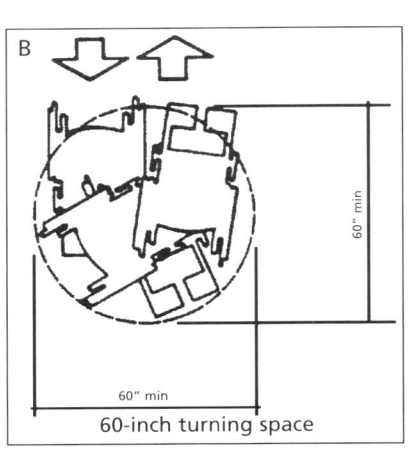
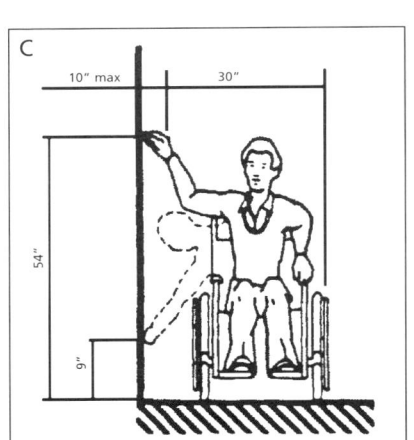

4-14. (A) and (B) Wheelchair turning space. (C) High and low side reach limit.
(Reprinted with permission from Mary H. Yearns, Ph.D.)

Problems	Preferred Solutions	Other Solutions
Entry to rest room is too small.	• Remove inner or outer vestibule door. • Make entry larger.	
Threshold is too high (exceeds ½ inch) and/or is not beveled.	• Replace existing threshold with low-profile version. • Bevel existing threshold.	
Rest room is too small and lacks maneuvering space. (See Figure 4-14(B).)	• Make rest room larger. • Move fixtures and partitions to create more open floor space.	• Remove rest room door if toilet stalls provide privacy.
Toilet compartment is too small.	• Widen toilet stall. • Install out-swinging door. • Remove partitions and install privacy lock on rest room door.	• Combine two rest rooms to create one accessible, unisex rest room.
Toilet seat is too low or too high.	• Install raised toilet seat or replace toilet.	
No grab bars in toilet stall.	• Install secure grab bars to walls behind toilet and on wall next to toilet.	
Lavatory is not accessible (top higher than 34 inches and/or bottom less than 27 inches above floor).	• Remove or alter cabinetry to provide knee space and cover pipes to prevent burns. • Lower sink. • Install new sink at lower height.	
Knob faucets are difficult to grasp.	• Replace knob faucets with electronic controls. • Replace knob faucets with wing-type lever handles or single-lever handles.	

(continued on next page)

Problems	Preferred Solutions	Other Solutions
Soap and towel dispensers are mounted too high. (See Figure 4-14(C).)	• Lower dispensers. • Install additional dispensers at lower height.	• Provide bar of soap and towels next to sink.
Mirror is too high (over 40 inches above floor).	• Lower mirror. • Replace with larger mirror.	• Add new mirror at required height.

Priority 4: Other Measures to Improve Customer Access

Problems	Preferred Solutions	Other Solutions
Vision limitations: *Obstacles protrude in pathways (more than 4 inches from wall).*	• Remove or move objects that protrude from wall.	• Provide verbal instructions and information.
Overhead objects present a hazard (less than 80-inch head room).	• Install furnishings, planters, or other cane-detectable objects underneath obstacles.	• Provide tape recording with important information.
Permanent interior signs do not have raised characters and braille.	• Mount ADA tactile signs on wall near latch side of doors to indicate rest rooms, stairs, exits, and other important information.	• Provide employee assistance.
Hearing limitations: *Fire alarm system can't be heard.*	• Install warning lights that flash when fire alarm sounds (consult fire officials).	
Public pay telephone is difficult or impossible to use.	• Install volume control on existing phone. • Modify phone to make it hearing aid compatible. • Provide TTY/TDD (telecommunication device for deaf).	• Provide sign to indicate location of nearby TTY/TDD.

(continued on next page)

Problems	Preferred Solutions	Other Solutions
Walking limitations:		
No spaces are designated for accessible parking.	• Paint parking spaces on pavement and install accessible parking signs.	• Provide curbside service. • Post sign that says "Honk for assistance."
Parking spaces are not accessible.	• Make parking spaces wider to allow access corridor for wheelchair.	• Provide home delivery.
Routes from parking area drop-off point and bus stop to building entrance are not accessible.	• Create accessible routes. • Install signs to indicate accessible routes. • Move accessible parking spaces closer to entrance.	
Water fountain is too high (spout more than 36 inches).	• Install new fountain. • Lower existing fountain.	• Install paper cup dispenser next to fountain.
Floor surfaces are slippery.	• Replace flooring with slip-resistant material.	• Treat glossy floor with slip-resistant floor wax. • Use nonslip runners or mats.
Carpeting has thick pile or is badly worn.	• Remove thick carpet padding. • Replace with low-pile, tightly woven carpet.	• Securely attach nonslip runners or mats to cover worn areas.
Stairs are not safe.	• Add or replace handrails on both sides of stairs. • Extend handrails beyond top and bottom steps. • Add extra lighting at top and bottom of stairs.	• Bring goods or services to customers in accessible area.

Source: "Accessibility for Customers: Guidelines for making your small business accessible," North Central Regional Extension Publication #535.

Case Study
Purdue University's ADA Compliance Plan
by Owen J. Cooks

Title II of the Americans with Disabilities Act required all public entities that employ 50 or more persons to have developed a transition plan by July 26, 1992, detailing the steps to be undertaken to achieve program accessibility, along with a self-evaluation examining the policies and practices to be completed by January 26, 1993. In keeping with that mandate, Purdue University set as its priority task the removal of barriers that deny individuals with disabilities an equal opportunity to share in and contribute to the vitality of university life. Although the ADA only specifically requires program accessibility and does not require that all existing spaces be made accessible, Purdue determined that *all* physical obstacles in *all* facilities should be identified. In doing so, information would become available that gives planners a better overall view of the situation, allowing a more comprehensive and long-term approach to program accessibility.

Several committees were established to oversee the various operations required to comply with the transition plan and self-evaluation. An ADA Steering Committee managed the overall project, subcommittees for the five titles were assigned, and focus groups from individual schools, departments, and areas came together to complete self-evaluations. The Transition Plan was developed through a series of facilities surveys, self-evaluations, and individual and public involvement.

Facilities Surveys

The first step was to bring together a team of university employees to conduct individual building surveys, identifying all physical barriers as determined by ADA guidelines. A detailed reference guide was compiled drawing on the ADAAG for structure and standards. Copies of this document—"Facilities Evaluation/Reference Guide to Architectural Barriers to the Disabled"—were used to train and guide the surveyors as they conducted their inspections from May 1991 through July 1992.

A summary of each identified barrier was prepared as well as a floor plan location (see Figure 4-15). All of the surveys were kept on file for reference by estimators and designers working on construction projects so that barriers in spaces being remodeled could be removed or modified to the maximum extent feasible. Each building barrier type was then assigned a cost estimate to be used for budgeting purposes, based on the average cost encountered for similar construction. The plan then required that when a barrier was determined to be an impediment to program accessibility, the change was designed and a formal cost estimate was prepared. A computerized summary of costs was assembled from all of the surveys to provide information concerning quantity and costs for compliance by both building and barrier type.

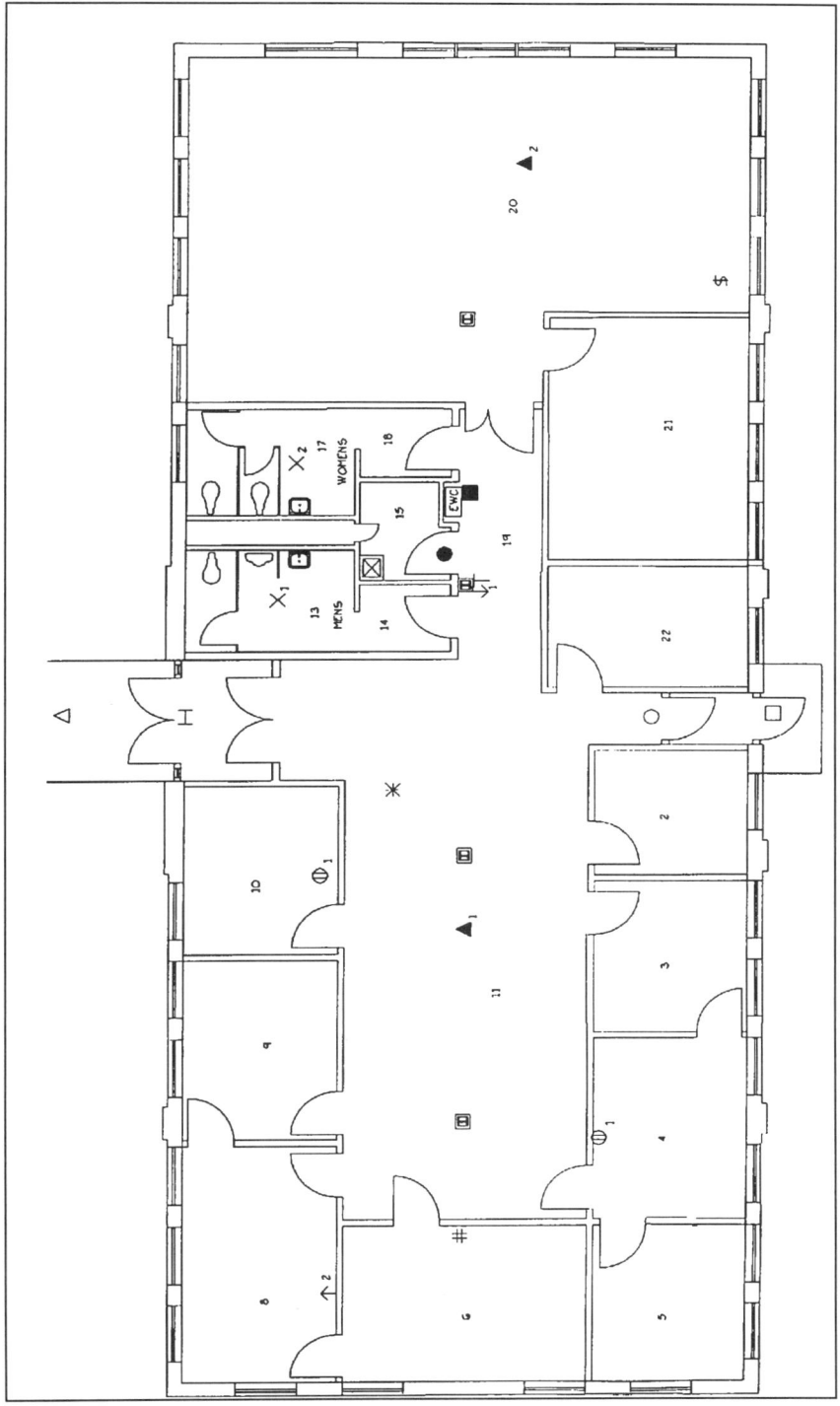

4-15. Sample Facilities Survey from Purdue's ADA Plan.
(Reprinted with permission from Owen J. Cooks, ADA Facility Coordinator, 1992, Purdue University.)

Self-Evaluations

The ADA requires that a public entity evaluate its current services, policies, and practices; determine which ones do not meet the requirements of the regulations; and proceed to make the necessary modifications. Purdue University distributed Institutional Self-Evaluation forms to all departments, which established their own focus groups and assigned individuals to complete the form. Recommendations about their findings were then forwarded by the appropriate subcommittee to the ADA Steering Committee for consideration and prioritization.

The evaluation took the form of several open-ended questions based on:

1. State policies regarding eligibility or admission criteria for program and/or services

2. State policies or procedures regarding communication, services, or programming for:

    A. Students

    B. Public

3. Comments regarding potential barriers in the present physical environment:

    A. Specific location(s)

    B. Summarize areas of concern

4. Review of information on eligibility, policies and procedures, and physical environment, and comment on the accessibility problems of programs for persons with the following disabilities:

    A. Mobility impairments

    B. Hearing impairments

    C. Vision impairments

    D. Learning disabilities

    E. Chronic illness

Step 5 was to complete a table drawing on the information from questions 1 through 4, which described:

- Tasks to complete to insure accessibility to programs, services, and activities

- Responsible person (suggested)

- Completion date (estimate/suggestion)

- Estimated cost

- Whether it is a recurring expense (i.e., equipment, alternative methods of communication, changes in policy, additional personnel, and so on)

4-16. Sample facilities survey from Purdue's ADA Plan. *(Reprinted with permission from Owen J. Cooks, ADA Facility Coordinator, 1992, Purdue University.)*

Since these forms were often completed at the department level, summary tables, were created for each school.

Individual and Public Involvement

Purdue students with physical limitations were asked to meet with campus planners and administrators to provide specific information on physical barriers they encountered and their experiences in accessibility. Four meetings were held in March 1992 grouped around specific disabilities—mobility, hearing, vision, and chronic illness. During the meetings, overall goals of the transition plan for physical barrier removal were discussed and input was requested. Both students and planners left with a better understanding of the problems and possible solutions.

Questionnaires specific to disability type were prepared and distributed at these meetings. All questionnaires requested the same general information: building identification and use (work, entertainment, study, classes, dining, living, meetings, service) and prioritization of building and area in terms of establishing accessibility. Each specific questionnaire then asked respondents to rate several items by priority and provided for comments and additions.

For hearing disabilities, the questionnaire covered:

Telephones
- Accessibility to TDDs
- Availability of volume control telephones
- Availability of hearing aid-compatible telephones

Controls and Alarms
- Strobe lights on fire alarms
- Controls in general

Elevators
- Visual controls

Assembly Areas
- Availability of assistive listening devices

Miscellaneous

For visual disabilities, the questionnaire covered:

Protrusions (concerns for objects in path of travel)
- Display cases
- Ashtray urns, mailboxes, and so on
- Other structural items
- Overhead hazards

Elevators
- Audible controls
- Raised signage and controls
- Braille signage and controls

Detectable Warnings (surface texture changes used as warnings)
- Textured door handles to hazardous rooms

- Exterior curb ramps
- Exterior ramps, stairs, and other drop-offs
- Interior ramps, stairs, and other drop-offs

Signage
- Raised for interior rooms (classrooms, offices, restrooms, and so on)
- Braille for interior rooms
- Raised for displays (maps, directories, and so on)
- Braille for displays

Stairs
- Handrail height
- Handrail extensions

- Slip-resistant step and landing surfaces
- Color contrast of step and landing surfaces

Floor Surfaces
- Gratings
- Level changes
- Slip resistance
- Color contrast

Miscellaneous

For mobility disabilities, the questionnaire covered:

Floor Surfaces
- Slip resistance
- Level changes
- Carpets
- Gratings

Ramps
- Slope
- Handrails
- Surfaces (slip resistance, and so on)

- Landing size
- Width of ramp

Doors
- Width
- Maneuvering space to open door
- Thresholds
- Hardware
- Opening force
- Automatic openers

Drinking Fountains
- Knee clearance
- Height
- Controls
- Spout location

Telephones
- Height/reach of clearance
- Maneuvering space

Seating and Tables
- Availability of wheelchair locations
- Knee space/height of tables/benches
- Reach over tables/benches

Elevators
- Interior car size
- Time to close door
- Height controls
- Handrails provided

Rest Rooms/Locker Rooms
- Space to maneuver
- Mirror height
- Dispenser height
- Lavatory height/knee space
- Lavatory controls
- Stall dimensions
- Grab bars
- Toilet height
- Urinal height
- Bathtubs
- Showers
- Lockers

Signage
- Signs for accessible entrances
- Signs for accessible rest rooms
- Directional signs to accessible entrances
- Directional signs to accessible restrooms

Controls and Alarms (light switches, outlets, and alarms)
- Reach/height of controls
- Reach/height of alarms

Sinks (in labs and other spaces besides rest rooms)
- Knee clearance/height
- Reach
- Controls

Miscellaneous
- Areas of rescue assistance in buildings
- Raised platforms/stages (needing ramps)
- Curb cuts
- Parking near accessible entrances
- Sidewalks

For chronic illness disabilities, the questionnaire first asked the respondent to identify the type of impairment, since this category covered everything from alcoholism to tuberculosis. The questions covered:

- Floor surfaces
- Ramps
- Doors
- Drinking fountains
- Telephones
- Seating and tables
- Elevators
- Rest rooms/locker rooms
- Signage
- Controls and alarms
- Sinks
- Protrusions
- Detectable warnings
- Stairs
- Environmental controls (ventilation and building temperature)

    The information from these surveys allowed planners to establish a priority list for barrier removal that was reviewed and revised at a public meeting advertised in all public media. Charts were shown to the participants that identified buildings and barriers by priority (see Figure 4-17). Then, with the group's participation, additional barriers were discussed and priorities were more clearly established.

    The group responsible for managing the self-evaluations also held five public forums to seek input on the information gathered in particular areas from the self-evaluations. Similarly, the university

4-17. Community Input Meeting Charts from Purdue's ADA Plan. *(Reprinted with permission from Owen J. Cooks, ADA Facility Coordinator, 1992, Purdue University.)*

ADA 1ST PRIORITY FACILITIES & CONCERNS									
FACILITIES	RAMPS	DOORS	FLOOR SURF.	FIXED SEAT'G	STAIRS	ELEVTR	SINKS & BENCHS	RESTRM CNTRLS	NOTES
KEY: ▒ BARRIER PROBLEM ▓ MAJOR PROBLEM								
PUBLIC								
STEWART CENTER				▒				▒	
MEMORIAL UNION		▓		▒				▒	
FREEHAFER HALL				▒			▒		
ROSS-ADE STADIUM	▓			▓					PRESS BOX
MUSIC HALL				▒		▓			
MACKEY ARENA									
AIRPORT TERMINAL									
VISITOR INFO CTR.									
BLACK CULTURAL	▓	▓				N/A		▒	
SMALLEY							▒		
MARRIED ADMIN							▒		
SERVICE								
CO-REC GYM		▓			▒	▓		▓ ▒	LOCKERS/POOL
STUDENT SERV 1									
HAWKINS									
HEALTH CENTER		▒			▒		▒		FOOD SERVICE
HOVDE HALL									
LAMBERT		▓			▒			▒	LOCKERS/POOL
YOUNG		▒			▒				

personnel office conducted an internal review of all aspects of employment from application through dismissal, and held a public meeting for input.

Making Facilities Accessible: Priorities and Methods

Based on the facility surveys, the self-evaluations, questionnaires, and meetings, barriers were placed into two categories: nonstructural and structural. Priorities were established first by individual request and second by the priority list created from the above methodology. The number one priority for the university was and continues to be meeting the needs of students and employees wanting access to a specific space. Ongoing efforts to achieve program accessibility follow the priorities set forth in the plan.

Nonstructural Barriers

The plan calls for appropriate changes to meet ADAAG standards in the following areas:

- Room signage
- Door hardware
- Telephones
- Seating and tables
- Elevator controls
- Protrusions
- Alarms
- Directional signage
- Assistive listening devices
- Power door openers
- Drinking fountains
- Counter heights
- Parking locations
- Exterior curb cuts
- Sidewalks
- Exterior projections

Structural Barriers

These are barriers that are by their nature difficult and sometimes expensive to eliminate. Alternatives allowed by the ADA include relocating a function to an accessible facility. Purdue University's plan follows the following hierarchy: relocation, renovation, and replacement.

Completion Schedule

During 1991 through 1993, Purdue University set aside over $500,000 for removal of structural and nonstructural barriers from their repair and rehabilitation funds. Additionally, the university requested $2 million from the state legislature over the years 1993 to 1995 for removal of both structural and nonstructural physical barriers. Several line item requests have also been made.

Universal Design Strategy

Occupational Therapy Accessibility, Assessment, and Consultation
by Shoshana Shamberg, OTR/L

Occupational therapists are trained to understand the dynamic interplay between the individual and the environment and to suggest modifications to maximize a person's ability to function in a particular environment. The occupational therapist evaluates the unique requirements of the individual through a comprehensive assessment that includes observation of the client's ability to perform daily activities while considering the demands of the environment and need for modification and adaptation. This includes determining the physical and cognitive skills required for self care, communication, accessibility, adaptive equipment, and occupational performance.

Occupational Therapists and the ADA

Title I: Employment

The occupational therapist offers some specific services directly related to the ADA. For Title I—Employment, the therapist:

- Conducts job site analyses to be used for developing job descriptions, identifying:
    1. The essential and marginal functions of a job
    2. Environmental, cognitive, and psychological demands
    3. Worksite modifications

- Consults with human resource personnel on how to use the functional job description as a tool during the interview process

- Conducts sensitization training for coworkers and supervisors to promote positive interaction and effective working environments for persons with disabilities

- Consults with employers to assess the occupational performance of individuals to determine their ability to perform essential functions of the job. If accommodations are needed, the occupational therapist can recommend tasks and worksite modifications and adaptations, specialized equipment, auxiliary aids, job restructuring, and scheduling.

- Assists employers in determining whether an individual poses a direct threat (one of the "defenses" offered in the ADA) and can suggest methods to minimize risks. Injury prevention programs may be implemented through occupational therapist consultation. This can include developing post-offer, job-related employee screening and evaluations for high-risk injury positions.

Title III: Public Accommodations

Occupational therapists can facilitate compliance with Title III through consultation with architects, engineers, contractors, businesses, other professionals, and consumers to determine how best to create accessible environments and programs.

Accessibility of programs, goods, and services means that public accommodations must be able to be approached, entered, and used by all people, including individuals with disabilities. If inaccessible, the occupational therapist can recommend adaptive equipment, auxiliary aids, policy changes, reasonable accommodation (including alternative methods of providing equivalent services), and environmental adaptations to remove barriers.

Accessibility is crucial to a person's ability to live independently in the community. The application of universal design principles to the construction of homes and public spaces can make those environments safer, more comfortable, and more usable for all persons. An environment should be adaptable to the changing needs of individuals.

Assessment and Applications for Specific Disabilities

Environments created using the elements of universal design are accessible, adaptable, aesthetic, and affordable. This is design that eliminates barriers and provides features that are usable by the widest range of people.

By modifying the home, tasks, and behavior, people can compensate for age-related changes in their abilities, or disabilities. The most common disabling illnesses include stroke, arthritis, multiple sclerosis, neurological illness, cancer, amputation due to diabetes or injury, respiratory disease, AIDS, and lifelong illness from birth such as mental retardation, cerebral palsy, spina bifida, and muscular dystrophy. Traumatic injuries include spinal cord injury, brain trauma, hip and limb fractures, back injuries, and hand injuries. Age-related changes also can place a person at risk for accidents and falls due to slower reactions to danger, cognitive difficulties related to memory and problem solving, limited movement, decreased agility and muscle strength, and visual and hearing loss.

The occupational therapist assesses strengths and weaknesses of the client in these areas:

- Mobility
- Use of hands for functional activity
- Body mechanics
- Balance
- Muscle strength
- Range of ability to move—reaching, pushing, pulling, bending, lifting, and so on
- Activity tolerance
- Safety and security
- Environmental obstacles/barriers and their removal
- Senses or sensory considerations—visual perception, vision, hearing, touch, smell
- Level of independence in Activities of Daily Living (ADLs)—self and occupational tasks
- Ability to communicate effectively
- Cognitive considerations—memory, impulsivity, perception, problem solving, concentration, attention span, comprehension, and so on
- Psychological considerations—stress, coping mechanisms, emotional stability, etc.
- Sociocultural issues—family support, community support services, disability organizations, professional associates, affiliates, etc.
- Caregiving requirements
- Specialized adaptive equipment

4-18. Mayline Company, Inc., offers this Vari-Task™ Workcenter as a solution to creating a comfortable work environment. It adjusts for sitting and standing.
(Reprinted with permission from Mayline Co., Inc.)

4-19. The WorkManager™ System from MicroComputer Accessories, Inc. (a Rubbermaid company), features modular components that let you put together a user-friendly office with precisely the features you need. The system offers the sophisticated features, sleek looks, and advanced ergonomics of expensive designer furniture at a fraction of the cost.
(Reprinted with permission from Rubbermaid MicroComputer Accessories, Inc.)

- Measurement of location of equipment to be installed to meet the individual requirements of the client
- General weaknesses/strengths
- Client's concerns/employer's concerns
- Medical precautions

Specific Examples of Reasonable Accommodations

A Fabric Industry Employee with Carpal Tunnel Syndrome

Ms. M. worked as a seamstress and could no longer perform a portion of the job requirements due to her carpal tunnel syndrome (CTS) symptoms. Her primary limitation was a reduced grip strength. Ms. M. could no longer push or pull the heavy fabric through the sewing machine. After research, a consultant was able to identify an automated assistive device that works in synchronization with the sewing machine to pull the fabric for Ms. M. The consultant recommended this device to company management and demonstrated that the cost for this modification was a small percentage of the annual net production of the employee.

A Secretary with Rheumatoid Arthritis of the Lower Extremity

Mr. C. had been having problems with his knees for about five years, resulting in operations that led to his use of a wheelchair for mobility. He applied for employment as a typist, passed the typing test, and was qualified for the job.

During his first day on the job Mr. C. experienced many difficulties. He found many of the older buildings to be inaccessible. The desks were of various heights, and the cabinets and typewriters

4-20. The Personal Harbor™ Workspace from Steelcase, Inc., is a 48 square foot, semi-enclosed individual work setting with a curved door developed to support the visual, acoustical, and territorial privacy needs of workers. Based on column-and-beam architecture, Personal Harbor™ Workspace provides adjustable work surfaces, shelving, marker and display services, and space for active files. It also features personally controlled lighting and ventilation and an electronic totem pole facilitating easy power access for personal CD players, radios, and other devices.

Steelcase introduced Personal Harbor™ Workspace in June 1993 after 3 years of research and development, including more than 30 person-years of real-world use. With 66 prototypes at 10 different locations throughout the United States for nearly a year, Personal Harbor™ Workspace is the most researched new product in the office furniture industry.
(Reprinted with permission from Steelcase, Inc.)

were unreachable. The "accessible" bathroom had no grab bars and the flush handle was difficult to use. The water fountain was too high, and the ramped entrance did not have handrails or a safety edge. Finally, the front door was difficult to open. Recommendations to create accessibility were provided to his employer, all of which were easily implemented.

- The middle drawer of the desk, above the knee space, was removed to allow Mr. C. to access the desk from a wheelchair.
- A small typing table was provided with access room underneath.
- Files were placed in lower file drawers within Mr. C's reach.
- Grab bars were installed around the toilet with solid blocking, and an extension was added to the existing flush lever.
- Handrails were installed on both sides of the ramp, and the door pressure was reduced.
- A cup dispenser was provided at accessible height, enabling Mr. C. to obtain water from the fountain.

All of these "reasonable accommodations" were accomplished at minimal cost and effort, and they enabled Mr. C. to perform the "essential functions" of his job.

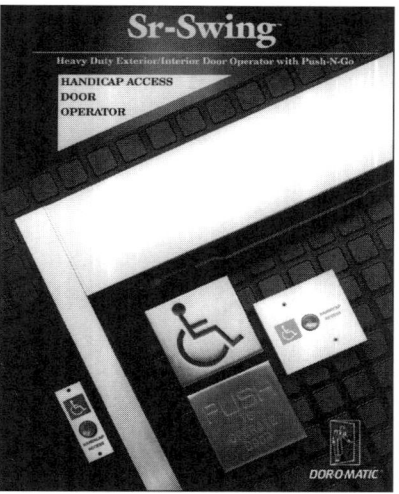

4-21. A variety of attractive devices for opening doors automatically are on the market. They meet the requirements for ADA signage and provide flexibility by allowing doors to be opened either manually or automatically. *(Reprinted with permission from Dor-O-Matic Automatic Doors.)*

Conclusion

Designing and implementing accommodations may be simple or complex, depending upon the limitations of the environment and the abilities of the individual. A Labor Department survey of employers found that 70 percent of the solutions implemented cost less than $100. The Sears Tower in Chicago, the world's tallest building, was modified to accommodate disabled employees for only $7000. Thorough assessment by a trained occupational therapist, an accessibility consultant, and the person who will function in the environment is crucial to the accurate recommendations and installation of adaptive equipment, and the removal of environmental barriers. Collaboration between occupational therapists, interior designers, architects, contractors, employers, and employees with disabilities to create accessible environments is necessary to formulate the most functional design solutions in the most cost-effective manner.

4-22. The Japanese simulated assembly line was put in place early in the game.
(Figures 4-22 through 4-27 reprinted with permission from Nancy C. Canestaro.)

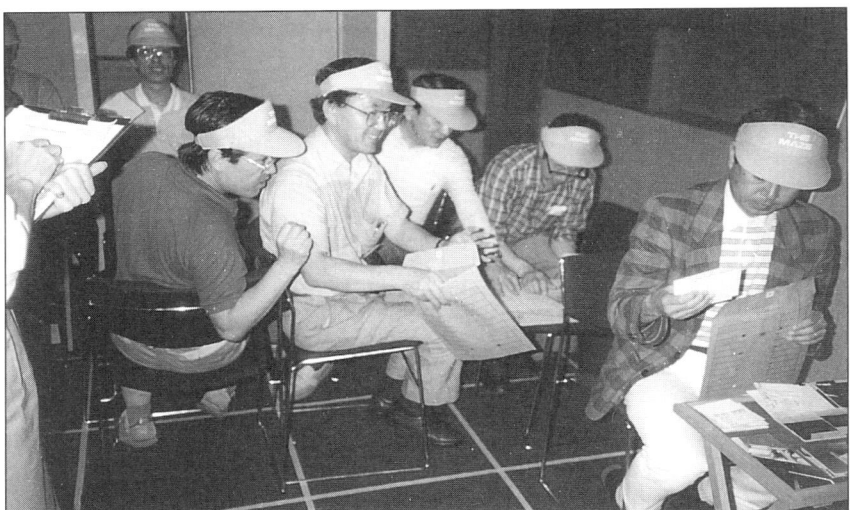

Case Study
Facility Management: A Cultural Universal Design Perspective
by Nancy C. Canestaro, Ph.D., and James C. Canestaro, AIA

Universal design is a major issue when cultural differences come into play. For the past five years, a simulation-game, "The Maze: A Facility Management Dilemma" has provided a framework to experience accessibility and issues of communication relating to Japanese and American facility managers.

"The Maze" simulates 10 years in the early life of a company producing puzzles. Time and space are condensed—10 years becomes an hour and a half, and a 20,000 square-foot office facility is condensed into a 12' x 18' space providing potential offices for approximately 60 staff.

Cultural differences may not seem to relate to universal design. However, simulations are run each summer at the Massachusetts

4-23. The Japanese CEO, backed up by his management team, plans the simulated space layout.

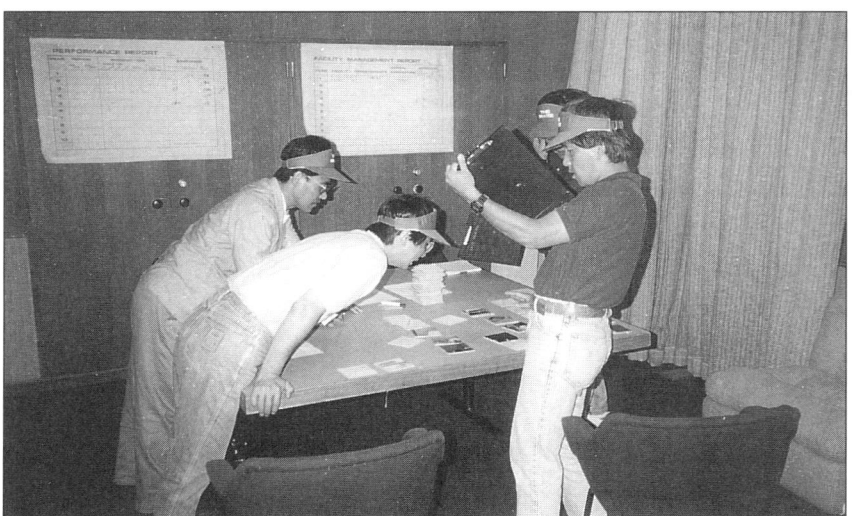

Institute of Technology with a group of Japanese International Facility Management Association members comprising a Japanese puzzle company competing for market share against an American puzzle company. It is obvious from observations of these simulations that the way these two cultures choose to work is a design issue. The following observations of cultural work patterns have remained constant for all simulation-games.

Japanese workers in the simulation tried to break down both physical and communication barriers that were limiting the flow of information and material through the assembly line they created (see Figure 4-22). Teams were quickly formed to solve problems rather than individuals striking off to address problems on their own. A decision was made at the outset on space layout by the CEO and facility manager and was implemented at once (see Figure 4-23). Very few modifications were made to the space even when problems later became apparent. The Japanese thrived on a

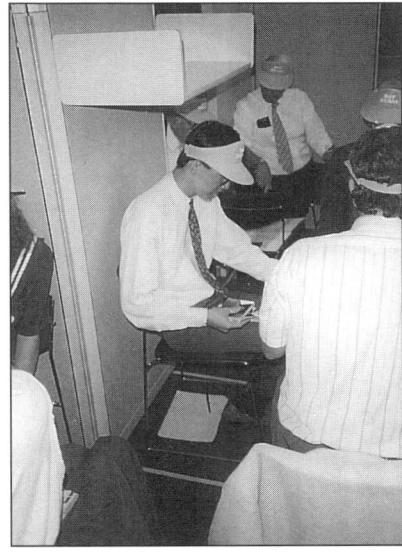

4-24. The simulated group environment supports the individual in the Japanese team.

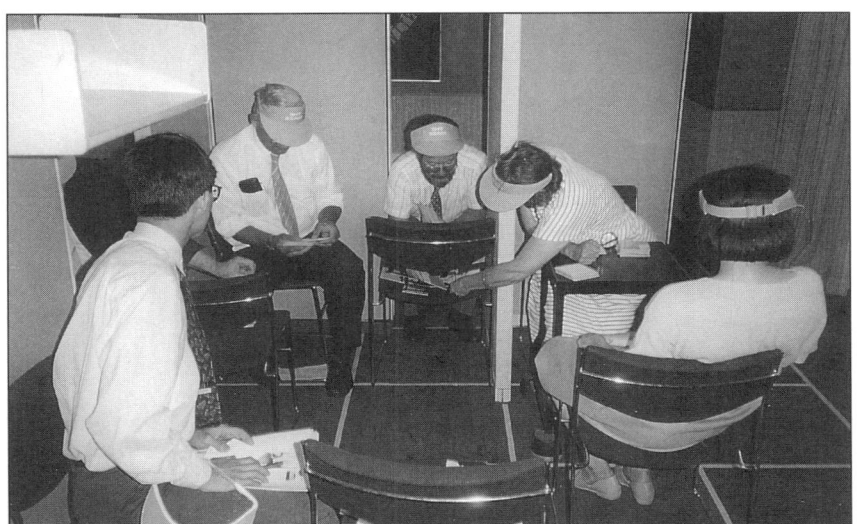

4-25. The management team is separate from workers in the American group.

4-26. The American CEO stands alone.

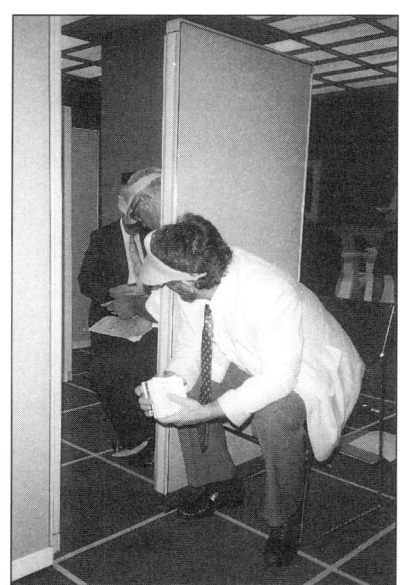

4-27. The American worker adapts to the (simulated) environment.

group environment where sound and visual stimuli were not considered a distraction to team interaction (see Figure 4-24).

The American team members, by contrast, set up physical and organizational barriers defining their territory and responsibility (see Figures 4-25 and 4-26). This resulted in limited access to critical information and a compartmentalization of the production process. Less teamwork and more individualism was apparent. It was not as critical for the Americans to see each other as they worked (see Figure 4-27), but they had no reservations about yelling to coworkers who were out of sight. The Americans preferred to be adaptable as new situations arose, and they created physical work spaces that were constantly being changed through the duration of the simulation-game.

Simulation-game experiments such as this can be used to help designers understand how people currently work in a variety of cultures and environments. It is possible, based on insights about current methods of interaction, to learn to modify the environment to foster new behavior.

Enabling Products 5

One key factor in creating supportive, adaptable, accessible, and safe environments is the products used within them. Barriers to use can exist within a product design as easily as they do in a space. The redesign of the built environment that universal design seeks also includes a reimagining of the products people use each day.

This chapter, while introducing some products for consideration for their universality, first and foremost seeks to present some guidelines for the creation of such products. The chapter also offers some case studies that reveal the process used by several companies to arrive at new, more universal designs.

James Mueller opens with a broad discussion of universal design and products. This is followed by a showcase of products that have recently been designed or introduced for use within the home, including some new prototypes from the Pratt Institute in Brooklyn, New York.

The Strategy section of this chapter consists of a short review of a customer usability laboratory operated by Whirlpool Corporation. Two case studies present a detailed look at the creation of a redesigned school lunch kit and the history of one of the first ergonomic chairs offered in America.

Products are featured throughout this book: Computer and work-related accessories are reviewed in the office chapter, while household appliances are featured extensively in "Universal Design and the Home." A mixture of interesting products is offered in

5-1. The Highline™ Lite™ PC toilet from Kohler responds to the dual issues of water conservation and accessibility. The Highline™ Lite™ PC features a 17½-inch high bowl to conform to the latest accessibility requirements and is equipped with Kohler's Pressure-Clean™ flushing system for an effective flush using just 1½ gallons of water. The toilet is suitable for both residential and commercial use.
(Figures 5-1 through 5-4 reprinted with permission from Kohler Co.)

5-2. This Lumex raised toilet seat with support arms reduces the amount of bending required.

other chapters on commercial design and marketing. In this brief introduction to universal products, the concern has been mainly on design and processes.

Universal Design Strategy
Universal Design for Products
by James L. Mueller

The Americans with Disabilities Act has reestablished the national commitment to eliminating barriers in employment, communication, access, and transportation for people with disabilities. At the same time, it has exposed a recurrent problem that has been responsible for much of the functional dependence experienced by people with disabilities. The everyday products that consumers use at work, home, school, and play are still designed and produced without consideration for the ergonomic needs of any but the most fit individuals.

Designers and manufacturers are under increasing pressure to respond to the needs of others, as their counterparts in architecture and building construction have done. They must understand that design for the ergonomic needs of both able and disabled users can result in a universal design approach that benefits all consumers.

Without the participation of designers of products, packaging, and graphics, recent public awareness and legislation can only bring people with disabilities to the brink of equality in the environment. They will be able to *access* a building, yet be unable to function independently inside it. They will be hired for jobs, yet be unable to operate the tools to get the jobs done.

The next several pages discuss why universal design is a necessary component to the integration of people with disabilities in society, and, even more importantly, show how universal design can be implemented in these fields of design.

A Growing Consumer Market

Sensitivity on the part of designers and manufacturers (most of whom are looking for new markets in order to remain competitive) toward the disabled consumer market is only now being seen. This sensitivity to designing products for all consumers (universal design) comes not only from the enforcement and passage of legislation but also from life itself. Designers and manufacturing executives have learned firsthand of the barriers inherently designed into many consumer products as they themselves become consumers with disabilities.

Long ignored and referred to as an obscure, insignificant consumer market, people with disabilities are finally receiving the attention they deserve from American businesses. Marketing and design conferences have begun to devote time to the issues surrounding disability. Print advertising and television are now marketing products (e.g., Levi's® 501® jeans, Nissan® minivans, and McDonald's® fast food) to people with disabilities by featuring them in their commercial advertisements.

However, this consumer group (people with disabilities) is far from homogeneous. It includes young people traumatically injured in sports and auto accidents, older people experiencing limitations as a natural effect of the aging process, and even includes people with chronic illnesses and workers experiencing on-the-job injuries from poorly designed jobs or workstations. It is a fact that if people live long enough they will eventually join the ranks of consumers with disabilities, making the recent focus on design for consumers with disabilities a long overdue phenomenon. More importantly, it focuses on the need to implement the concepts of universal design.

5-3. Full wheelchair accessibility is achieved with Kohler's Invitation™ countertop lavatory. The unique, loop-shaped basin positions the drain to one side at the rear of the basin and moves the faucet deck forward, creating sufficient clearance under the counter for anyone using a wheelchair, and making the faucets easier to reach. The front rim of the lavatory overhangs the edge of the countertop to bring the basin closer to the user.

Accommodating Through Universal Design and Ergonomics

People with disabilities are neither an isolated nor an insignificant group. They are, in fact, a viable, thriving, and growing segment of the American population frustrated by the reluctance of product designers and manufacturers to respond to their needs. This reluctance is based on the fear that product design for people with disabilities means designing "handicapped" products that would be unsightly, unsafe, and undesirable for "normal" consumers. What many product designers haven't realized is that generally the limitations experienced by people with disabilities are often similar to those experienced by most "normal" consumers. The difference is merely one of degree.

Accommodating physical limitations and abilities to make as many products as possible as usable as possible for as many people as possible is the purpose behind universal design. The concept dates back to the 1960s, when accessible housing was first suggested as something that would be good for everyone. Architects feared the backlash from the nondisabled community, but instead found that design for accessibility usually meant more functional design for all. (See the case study on "The Friendly Home" in Chapter 9.)

The problem since then has been to describe more fully the nuts and bolts of universal design. A new frontier has been discovered with few guidelines but with vast opportunities for creativity. Clinical literature on specific disabilities has provided the most useful information to date on the ergonomics of consumers with disabilities. The appropriate use of such information is vitally important, as improper interpretation results not in universal design but in design for people with a specific disability.

5-4. The Precedence™ bath whirlpool from Kohler is equipped with a door that swings inward for easy access to the bath. The HydroLoc™ door seal inflates automatically when the bath begins to fill with water.

Considerable effort has been invested in discovering the most common limitations shared by people with various disabilities, in order to arrive at universal ergonomic guidelines. However, such guidelines cannot include the needs of every consumer, especially those most severely limited by their disabilities. But, these guidelines can expand the ergonomic world to include a great many more consumers, including those with disabilities, while also improving the usability of products for consumers without disabilities.

Few designers have a working knowledge of the medical aspects of disabilities, and few physicians have corresponding knowledge of the process of design. This barrier in the application of medical knowledge to the development of ergonomic guidelines persisted until the establishment of the Enabler (shown in Figure 5-6). The Enabler was developed by design researchers at Syracuse University in New York for the U.S. Department of Housing and Urban Development in the 1970s. The system describes disabilities as combinations of simply defined limitations, and it has been widely adapted as a successful method of translating clinical knowledge regarding disabilities into useful guidelines for accommodation. The system has been a tool for establishing guidelines for architectural design, for modifications to vocational and educational settings, and for product and packaging design.

The Enabler system was adapted for use in *The Workplace Workbook 2.0*, an illustrated resource for job accommodation ideas. This resource uses a set of 17 functional characteristics of disabilities. These 17 characteristics are described in the following outline, along with some examples of accommodations made for these characteristics through design.

5-5. This residence hall renovation (shaded areas in the left drawing show changed areas) to provide accessibility was accomplished without making major structural changes. The costs were kept minimal by enlarging door openings, removing closet walls, moving closets, changing the bathroom configuration (sink stayed in place), moving the toilet, and replacing the tubs with roll-in showers. *(Reprinted with permission from Owens J. Cooks, ADA Facilities Coordinator, 1992, Purdue University.)*

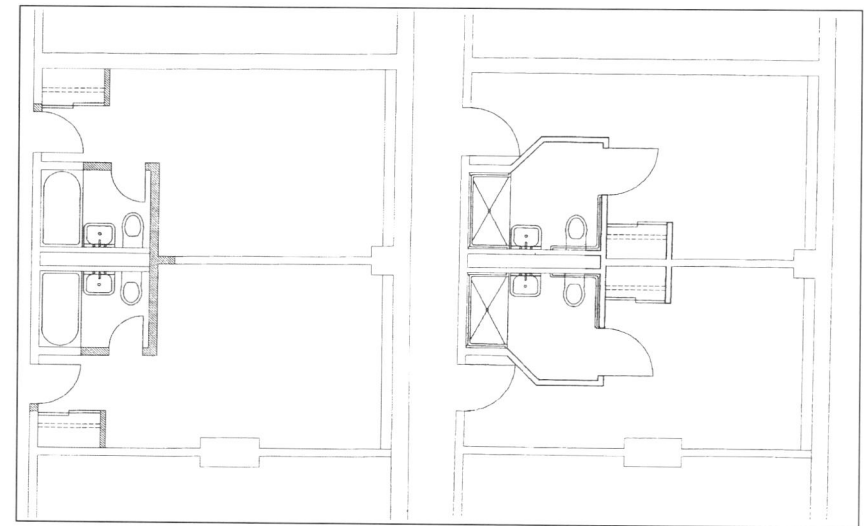

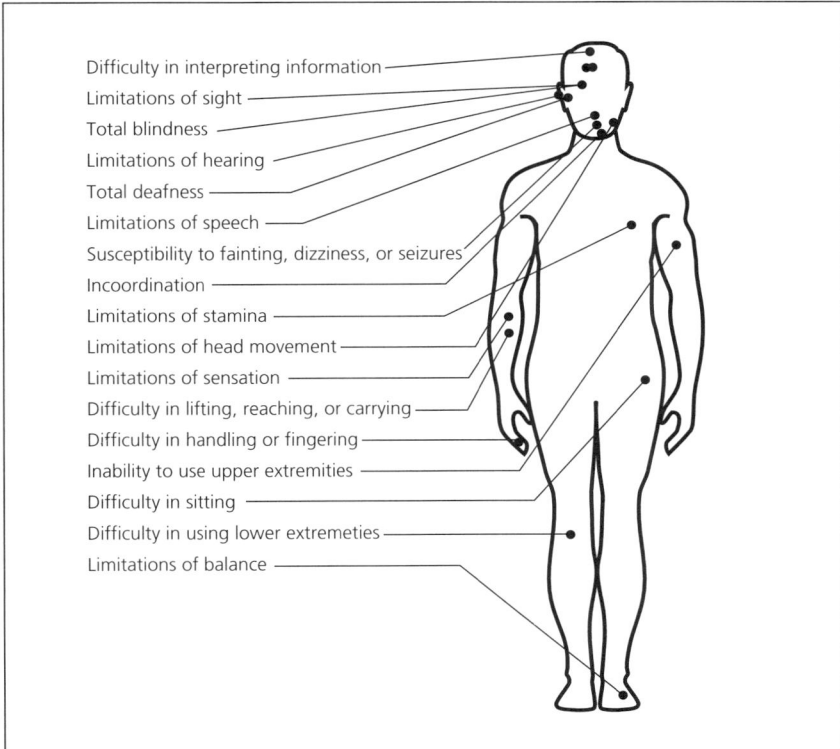

5-6. The Enabler system.

1. *Difficulty processing information:* Impaired ability to receive, interpret, remember, or act on information.

    • Use instructions that use familiar and simple symbols and words.

    • Labels and instructions should be placed as close to the referred item as possible.

    • Use interactive products that allow for reduced pace of comprehension.

    • Use conventional "mapping" (hot on left, cold on right, green means go, red means stop, and so on).

2. *Limitations of sight:* Difficulty reading newsprint-size copy, with or without corrective lenses (extends to "legal" blindness).

    • Use high-contrast and enlarged visual displays with simple symbols and words, and use increased illumination without glare.

3. *Total blindness:* Complete inability to perceive visual information.

    • Use tactile information displays with audible and tactile feedback from controls. Recent technological advances such as text-to-speech conversion and voice synthesis can be used in computers, clocks, measuring instruments, and household appliances.

4. *Limitations of hearing:* Difficulty in hearing normal speech. Problems with ambient noise.

    - Amplify audio output. Use redundant information (visual and tactile).

5. *Total deafness:* Complete inability to receive auditory signals.

    - Provide tactile and visual redundancy in information output and feedback.

6. *Limitations of speech:* Capable of only slow or indistinct speech, or capable of only nonverbal communication.

    - Minimize ambient noise that a product may generate. Minimize the need for assistance through clear labeling and instructions. Include speech amplifiers in communication products.

7. *Susceptibility to fainting, dizziness, or seizures:* Can be either spontaneous or environmentally induced by sudden loud noises or flashing lights of frequencies greater than 5 Hz.

    - Secure, nonslip support must be provided. Reliable guards on cutting edges and auto-off control features are important. Product design should also help the user avoid the need to bend down to reach or lift.

8. *Incoordination:* Limited control in placing or directing extremities.

    - Controls should minimize errors through appropriate size, separation, and actuating motion and force. Switch configuration should minimize accidental actuation.

    - Insure product durability and stability in use and provide carrying straps or loops to avoid need for firm grip. Design for use with a "closed fist" is a useful guideline.

9. *Limitations of stamina:* Fatigue, shortness of breath, or abnormally elevated blood pressure from even very mild exertion.

    - Minimize uncomfortable postures and minimize (but do not totally eliminate) need for reaching or moving in performing tasks.

10. *Limitations of head movement:* Difficulty looking up, down, or to the side. In severe cases, field of vision and upper extremity movement may be effectively limited.

    - Cluster controls, displays, and instructions within field of view.

11. *Limitations of sensation:* Impaired ability to detect heat, pain, or pressure.

    - Redundant cueing is helpful. Protect against very hot and very cold surfaces, sharp edges, and postures that concentrate pressure on limited skin surface.

12. *Difficulty in lifting, reaching, or carrying:* Impaired mobility, range of motion, or strength of upper extremities.

    - Minimize product weight and added weight and bulk of packaging; provisions for carrying and storage are also important.

13. *Difficulty in handling or fingering:* Impaired hand or finger mobility, range of motion, or strength.

    - Effective design begins with careful attention to established ergonomic guidelines. Limit activating force of controls and tools and avoid operations or grip shapes that require bending the wrist or concentrated pressures on any structure of the hand.

14. *Inability to use upper extremities:* Severe incoordination, complete paralysis, or bilateral absence of upper extremities.

    - Use electronic technology that maximizes user efficiency by minimizing user effort through computers, environmental controls, robotics, and telecommunications.

    - Flexibility and compatibility in consumer products to accommodate control through assistive technologies are vital, as is location and configuration of controls to allow alternative control inputs, such as by voice, mouthstick, or foot (see Figure 5-7).

    - Product stability in use is essential.

15. *Difficulty in sitting:* Excessive pain; limited muscle strength, range of motion, or control in turning, bending, or balance while seated.

    - Ergonomic seating design is a must. Allow space for heels beneath front edge of seat.

    - Avoid operations that require reaching up or bending down or that do not allow for regular changes in posture.

    - Some individuals will require assistive features such as a rising seat or side supports.

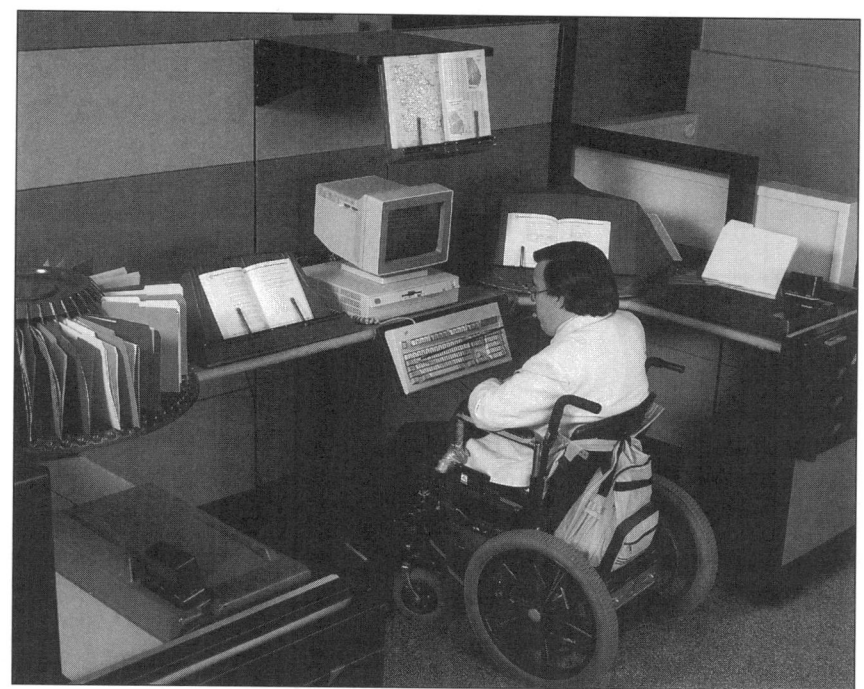

5-7. Assistive technologies, such as this mouth stick control for computer use, are vital products for accommodating people with disabilities. *(Reprinted with permission from ABLE Office, Center for Rehabilitation Technology, Inc.)*

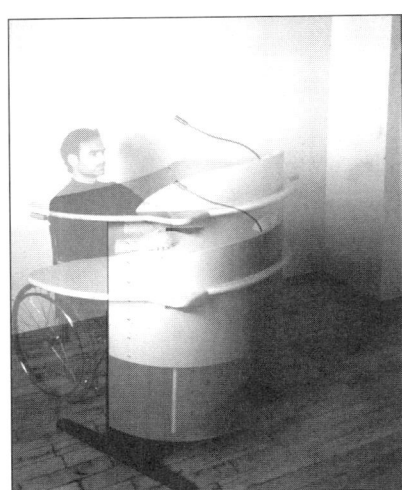

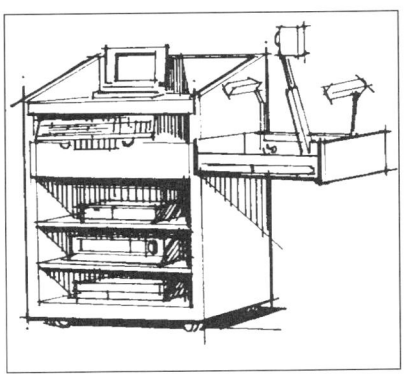

5-8. These two podiums offer two different solutions to accessibility concerns. Above is Stephen Barlow-Lawson's Biomorph™ Personal Power Podium. It is fully height-adjustable with a built-in microphone and light. It is shown here in standing and wheelchair-accessible positions. The podium below, by Egan Visual, Inc., offers flexibility and accessibility through the use of attachments that provide various levels of platforms for use standing or sitting. *(Top: Reprinted with permission from I.D./Design, New York, 1993 U.S. Patent for Work Surface Design. Bottom: Reprinted with permission from Egan Visual, Inc.)*

16. *Difficulty in using lower extremities:* Slowness of gait; difficulty kneeling, sitting down, rising, standing, walking, or climbing stairs and ladders.

    - Minimize need for mobility if possible.
    - Accommodate the use of walkers, canes, crutches, wheelchairs, and so on.

17. *Limitations of balance:* Difficulty in maintaining balance while standing or moving.

    - Floor materials and surfaces that are used for support in standing or walking must be carefully designed to avoid slipping or tripping.
    - Allow for use of mobility aids.

Meeting the Challenges of Design

People with disabilities represent one of the fastest growing consumer market segments: Currently, at least 17 percent of the American population has some form of disability. Meeting the challenges of this market means first placing a greater emphasis on ergonomics and then incorporating it and universal design guidelines into the design process. This involves a sensitivity in designing products for the potential consumer market of 43 million people with disabilities who work and live in relative independence. Some of these products may include telephones, computers, and home appliances that have particular importance not just to the disabled consumer but to everyone. Examples of podiums designed to provide flexibility and access to all users have recently appeared in the market place.

Accommodating the special needs of all consumers may be achieved through "adaptable" design, such as the membrane keyboards on microwave ovens that make cleaning easier for all consumers. However, a visually-impaired user (or one with coordination problems) may require the application of a tactile overlay to accurately set the controls. Such an overlay can be provided on request; no costly changes to a product line are needed. Appliance manufacturers such as General Electric and Whirlpool Corporation have been facilitating this and other product modifications for several years.

People with disabilities often devise unique coping skills in order to live in a world not designed for them. Some people use peripheral assistive technology to boost their functional independence skills. In this case, the usability of mass-produced products by persons with disabilities depends on the flexibility of the interface among the individual's unique functional independence skills, the assistive technology they use, and the product's functions.

People who cannot do things independently because of barriers caused by design must sometimes depend on others. This reduces productivity at work, free time at home, and opportunities in life. Promoting dependence by design, rather than promoting independence, "handicaps" all of society.

Products for the Home

Universally designed products for personal residences are beginning to appear everywhere, from specialty catalogs aimed at specific audiences to major department/hardware stores (lever handles, touch-control lighting, large-handled appliances, and grab bars, for example, are carried and displayed by many national chains). These products all stand out not because of any "institutional" look (a common detriment to including accessible products in a residence in the past), but rather because they are strikingly appealing.

A wide variety of these products are featured in Chapter 8: Universal Design in the Home, but this section presents a few that are currently on the market but under-recognized, and shows how design schools are helping create a demand for products that are universally designed.

Cutting-Edge Design

Robert Anders is a professor of design at the Pratt Institute in Brooklyn, New York. Graduate students in his courses on universal design create prototypes of products that are as diverse as they are useful.

Figure 5-9 shows a door handle/lock hardware created by student Lutz Sauvant. His description of the handle is as follows:

> The need for a universally designed method of unlocking and opening a door is readily apparent. This solution permits the user to open a door by pressing or pulling a rounded disc. The disc is placed on the front of the lever for pushing and is reversed and placed on the rear of the activating lever on the other side of the door for pulling.
>
> The key is contained within a holder that acts as a lever when the key is placed into the lock. The key holder fits into the lock for added torque. The conical-shaped keyway permits easy insertion of the key into the lock. A light-emitting material surrounds the lock and is activated by the key, assisting users in locating the lock at night.

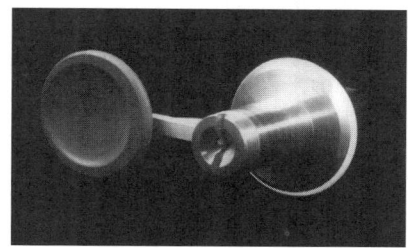

5-9. **Student designer Lutz Sauvant's Door Handle/Lock Hardware.** *(Reprinted with permission from Lutz Sauvant, Pratt Institute, student of Robert Anders.)*

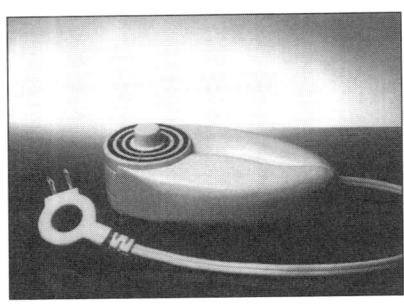

5-10. Student designer En-Bair Chang's Travel Hair Dryer. *(Reprinted with permission from En-Bair Chang, Pratt Institute, student of Robert Anders.)*

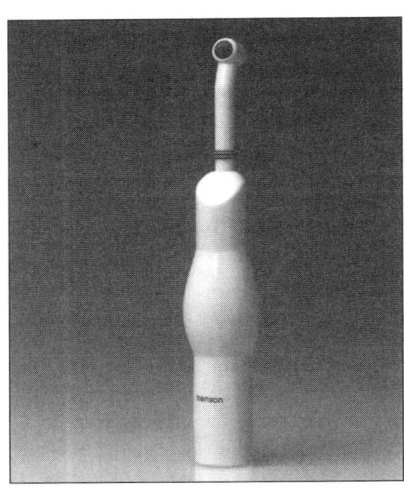

5-11. Student designer Benson Kravtin's Oral Hygiene Device. *(Reprinted with permission from Benson Kravtin, Pratt Institute, student of Robert Anders.)*

Graduate student En-Bair Chang offers a new design for a travel hair dryer (see Figure 5-10):

The concept of this hair dryer is to reduce the operating processes and arm movements. The foldable handle reduces the overall bulk of the unit and makes it easy to pack. The open shape lets the heated air easily reach around the head without undue stretching of the arm and shoulder. The electric plug snaps onto the dryer, maintaining a neat product as well as permitting the plug's removal from electric outlets by users with weak finger-grip strength.

Figure 5-11 shows a design for an oral hygiene device created by Benson Kravtin, who describes his product as "a new electric appliance for millions of people who need to clean their teeth near the gum line."

Since this is primarily a product for the older segment of the population, consideration was given to the universality of the handle and the controls. A bulb shape is provided as the primary grip, which is very comfortable for everyone and is an aid to someone with an arthritic hand. The tool can also be gripped above or below the bulb for those who like a smaller grip. The unit is turned on by pressing the head against the teeth, so there are no finger controls and no small-print instruction labels.

Finally, from Mark Zaininger comes a design for a light-grip rechargeable can opener (see Figure 5-12):

The general goal of this design problem was to analyze the process of can opening and develop a new product that maximizes the number of possible users. The new product should be easier and safer to use and be more attractive than the currently available hand-held or electric can openers.

All features that were designed into the new product to benefit a specific user group also benefit other users. For example, the auto-on/auto-off feature, which eliminates any controls or buttons, helps users who are arthritic, deaf, or blind. Single-step operation helps those with cognitive disabilities. The hidden mechanism protects children and people who are blind from injury. The tapered grip provides ease of use for both children and adults. One-hand, cordless operation helps people who are partially disabled or have the use of only one arm/hand. And the "hook and shelf" profile molds itself to a weak grip and provides the opener its distinctive look and feel, which should please all users, including those who are blind, who often identify by touched form.

These examples show how the recent and growing emphasis on universal design in universities can change the products that people use in their everyday lives. Another resource for new design ideas that meet universal design criteria is products currently in use outside of the United States that may find acceptance among the U.S. population as awareness grows about ways to more fully adapt an environment.

A New Kind of Washer/Dryer

The author first learned of this product (Figure 5-13) in conjunction with an ongoing study she is conducting on recreational vehicle (RV) lifestyles among the elderly. In the United States, that market is where the product is receiving the most attention. However, it has been available in Europe for several years and is now being marketed in the U.S. for use in small apartments, co-ops, and condominium as well as in RVs, campers, and boats.

The appliance combines a washer and dryer in one, automating the washing and drying cycles so that there is no need to transfer wet clothes from a washer to a dryer, a feature that should be noted for its usefulness to anyone with diminished strength. Not only is it space-saving; it is also labor-reducing and convenient.

5-12. Student designer Mark Zaininger's Light-Grip Rechargeable Can Opener. *(Reprinted with permission from Mark Zaininger, Pratt Institute, student of Robert Anders.)*

Personal Hygiene

Several companies (Panasonic, TOTO, and Lubidet® USA, Inc., among them) are introducing lines of personal bidets in the United States. These are products that have long been in use throughout much of the rest of the world (see Figure 5-14). Along with bathing, the ability to use the toilet independently is often the most prevalent reason for entering an assisted-living environment. (See Chapter 8 for a thorough discussion of adaptations and products available for the bathroom.)

One of the principles behind universal design is that independence should be maintained and supported as people age and change in ability. Products such as those featured here better enable individuals to remain self-sufficient as they mature, while also supporting individuals of differing abilities.

Universal Design Strategy

Using Customer Feedback for New Product Design: A Study of Appliance Controls
by Sandra S. Thurlow, Ph.D.

People who design and develop major home appliances often think differently about their products' use. They may use appliances differently than most consumers do. But it is important that

5-13. The All-in-One Combination Automatic Washer/Dryer was first introduced in the U.S. for use in recreational vehicles. Dry, dirty clothes emerge as dry, clean clothes, avoiding the transfer of heavy wet clothes to a separate dryer. *(Reprinted with permission from Water, Inc., El Segundo, CA.)*

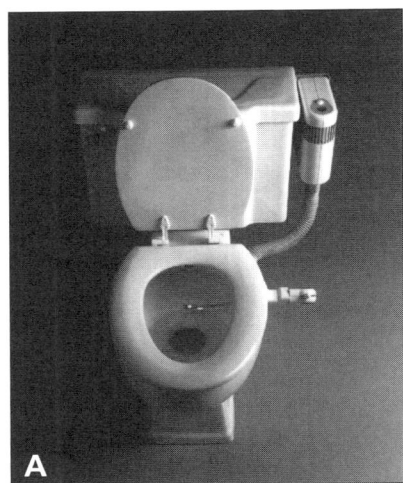

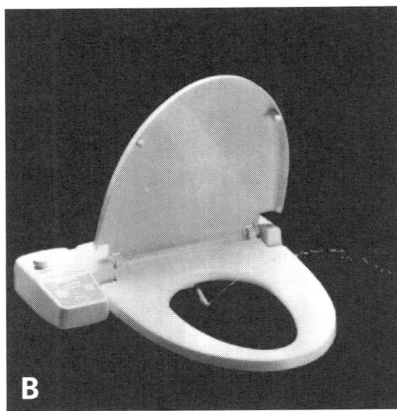

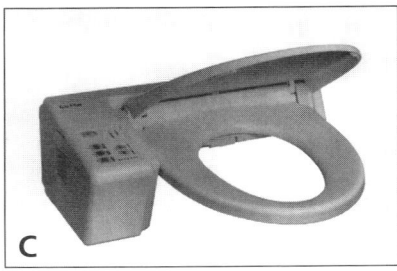

5-14. Personal hygiene systems from Lubidet®, TOTO, and Panasonic are now being introduced in the U.S.
(Reprinted with permission from Lubidet® USA, Inc.; TOTO/Kiki USA, Inc.; and Panasonic.)

they design appliances for a wide range of users, not just for themselves, whether they term this kind of design "ergonomics," "human engineering," or "universal design."

At Whirlpool Corporation, researchers are trying to increase the usability of appliances for people of various ages and capabilities. They have built a one-of-a-kind customer usability lab in their Research and Engineering Center to learn more about how people interact with appliances and appliance controls. In this lab, Whirlpool gives consumers an opportunity to interact with new appliance designs, then records and analyzes the product performance and the consumers' thoughts and attitudes to learn more about what they liked and didn't like, what worked well under normal use conditions and what didn't work so well, what they understood and what they didn't understand, and so on. This helps to create product designs that meet the needs of a wide range of people while focusing on accessibility and ease-of-use issues.

At the lab, two rooms are separated by a one-way mirror. A trained researcher takes consumers through a series of steps using prototypes of new appliances with computer simulations of the new appliance controls. In the other room, the product design team watches the consumers' interactions with the appliance, and a video recording is kept for future study. The team's goal is to better understand what consumers want and need and to design their new products accordingly.

Whirlpool recently introduced an oven control system using research from the usability lab where they had looked at many more options before production. They put people at a touch screen on a computer simulating a number of different controls, then had them go through the process of operating the oven. Whirlpool asked questions like, "Is the clock on the oven running? If you want your potatoes to be done at 6:00 PM. and it's 3:00 PM now, how would you set the controls?" Some users set the timer first, then the temperature while others did just the opposite. Whirlpool then tried to come up with a design that can accommodate as many different styles as possible.

Some of the questions the design team used to analyze different oven controls were:

- Will this control allow consumers to use the appliance the way they want to use it?

- Can the user quickly and easily correct a mistake without having to start all over again?

- Can the user change his/her mind without starting over?

- Will users be able to customize the appliance and/or controls to suit their needs?

- Does the control panel present only the necessary information when it is needed? (Too much information can be confusing.)
- Does it prevent consumers from using the oven in a clearly inappropriate or unsafe manner, such as setting the self-clean option at a broil temperature?
- Is it simple to use?

Whirlpool hoped to make the control panel self-explanatory for all potential users. The oven should do what the consumer wants it to do when he/she wants it done. An optimal design doesn't require a person to look at the instruction manual, and the key to this good design is getting a broad range of input from everyone involved early in the design process.

Case Study

Re-Creating the School Lunch Kit: Research in Universal Product Design
by Elizabeth B. N. Sanders, Sheila Zwelling, and Susan Russell

Research is perhaps the most important, but, unfortunately, also the most often neglected step in the universal design process. And participatory design—allowing the people actually affected by design decisions to play a significant role in the process—is one of the most neglected methods of doing research. The following case study shows how participatory design can be used by a research team to create a truly innovative product.

The Thermos Company, the market leader in school lunch kits, approached Fitch, Inc., a full-service business and design consultancy, to help design an ecologically-sensitive family of lunch kits. The goal was to develop something completely different from what was currently available by first delineating, and then designing for, the as-yet unrecognized needs and wants of children.

It was clear from early discussions with the Thermos Company that the lunch kit design should be based on "what kids need and want today," rather than what design team members remembered wanting when they were children. This focus on creating a product that would respond to children's *current* wants and needs—with a corresponding call to find out what those are—suggested that the design process should include a strong participatory design and research effort. Consequently, a multidisciplinary team of researchers and designers worked closely with end users to develop and test increasingly more refined versions of the lunch kit, gradually honing in on the final design.

> ## Product Design Criteria
>
> Fitch, Inc. uses the following very simple three-point checklist as a research guide for every product development project to ensure that the needs of consumers are being addressed:
>
> 1. Is the product useful?
> 2. Is the product usable?
> 3. Is the product desirable?
>
> A useful product is one that consumers need and will use. A usable product is one they can either use immediately or learn to use readily. A desirable product is one they want. A favorite pair of shoes can be useful, usable, and desirable, all at the same time. Fitch believes that for products to be successful in the 1990s, they need to meet all three of these consumer needs simultaneously.
>
> In the past, product success in the marketplace was likely if at least two of these three criteria were met. For example, many home electronic products are useful and desirable, but not very usable. The VCR is a good example, given the pervasiveness of problems reported for doing anything more than simply viewing tapes.
>
> Consider that many of the products targeted toward the aging marketplace today (a population that is growing rapidly and significantly) are useful and usable, but not very desirable—for example, bathroom fixtures with an institutional look. It appears that products developed for the general consumer marketplace have usually and primarily been driven by the need for desirability, while those developed for the aging marketplace have been driven by the need for usefulness. In the 1990s, usefulness, usability, and desirability must all be given equal emphasis and must all be addressed very early in the development process.

The team found that significant roles needed to be played by:

- The child—the primary user and the primary decision maker for a purchase
- The parent(s)—the primary purchaser, "maintainer," and (most often) "packer"
- The teacher—in whose classroom and/or lunchroom the kit is used (and abused)

The Approach

The need to combine research and design led to the formation of a strongly multidisciplinary, dynamic project team and a design process that incorporated integrative, tightly interconnected research and design. Researchers and designers worked together to make field observations, analyze data, and create and test designs.

In order to have access to children, parents, and teachers, arrangements were made with several schools and day-care centers in Columbus, Ohio (Fitch, Inc.'s headquarters). The participants were boys and girls from a variety of age groups, and they were involved throughout the development process.

The following examples of research activities describe the methods used to ensure that the lunch kit would be useful, desirable, and usable (the order is different from that listed in the "Product Design Criteria" box because of the level of involvement by the children in the actual design).

Is the Product Useful?

The first question in the three-point checklist is the most critical. If a product is not useful—that is, if consumers do not need it or will not use it—then why bother to research, design, or develop it in the first place?

Parent Survey

A written survey was sent home with participating children. The survey contained general questions concerning packing lunches, the content of children's lunches, shopping for lunch boxes, and qualities of an ideal lunch kit. The survey showed that, especially with little children, packing lunch helps parents feel connected to their children's lives at school. The emotional importance of this connection was new information for the Thermos Company. The survey also showed that children's opinions are the largest influence on lunch kit purchase—when it comes to lunch kits, parents buy what their children want.

Student Drawings

All students were asked to draw their ideal lunch kit, a sample of which is shown in Figure 5-15. Many of their drawings were elaborately detailed and annotated. Several needs (that directly influenced the subsequent design of the lunch kit) emerged from the drawings:

- Compartmentalization (i.e., everything should be in its own place)
- Personalization (i.e., ways to mark the lunch kit as their own)

Cafeteria Lunch Observation

The field research teams unobtrusively observed children during lunchtime, paying attention to what and how much children actually eat and how their lunch kits fit into the lunch experience. Written materials were prepared to provide a structure for observation; this ensured that the same kind of information was gathered by all team members while supporting the research activities of less-experienced team members.

5-15. One of the children's drawings showing an "ideal" lunch box configuration. *(Figures 5-15 through 5-17 reprinted with permission from Fitch, Inc.)*

Differences between older and younger children were quickly identified: Talking informally with the children, the team learned that the older school-age children thought the traditional hard plastic lunch boxes (that Fitch, Inc.'s client the Thermos Company currently produced) were "for babies" (many carried paper bag lunches, which, although leading to "smooshed" food, at least were acceptable by peers).

The teams also found that lunch kits were stored in a variety of spaces ranging from individually assigned shelves within a classroom to laundry baskets outside the room; this helped define size and durability requirements.

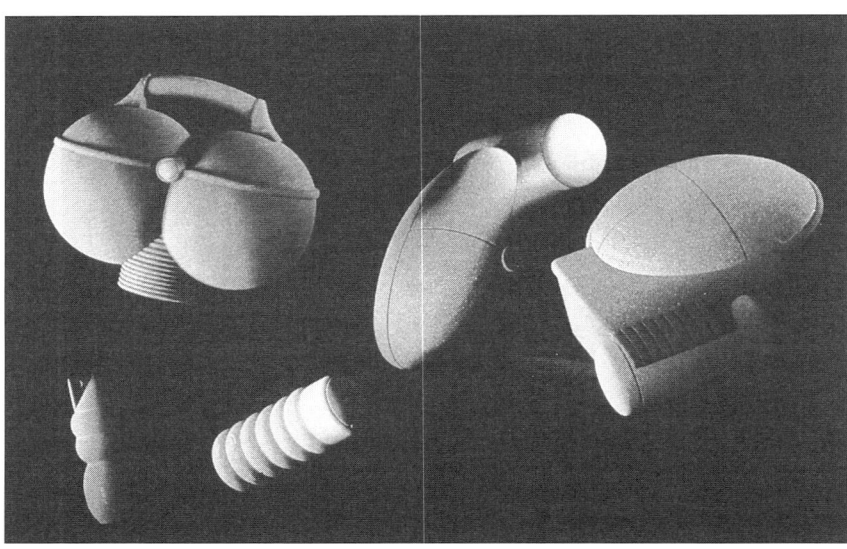

5-16. Prototypes used to measure children's reactions to various design solutions.

Is the Product Desirable?

Since the child was the primary purchase decision maker for this product, the desirability of the lunch kit to the child was critical. Fitch created multiple design concepts from the research activity in Step 1. "Desirability" research was then conducted with nine three-dimensional, non-working models (shown in Figure 5-16).

Interacting with Models

Students interacted with and evaluated the concept models. Researchers briefly described the models, trying not to bias students, then facilitated conversations about what the students did and didn't like about each concept. At the end of the discussions, students voted on which ones they liked best and which they felt were "kinda weird" (i.e., out-of-bounds, too extreme, inappropriate).

An amazing degree of consistency appeared in their evaluations of the models—two of the concepts were preferred by a majority of the students, and this preference was remarkably similar across age and sex groupings. One of the preferred concepts was the compartmentalized approach in which the compartmentalization was evident on the outside as well as inside the lunch kit.

Color Construction Kits

Color is a key characteristic of consumer products, one that can clearly influence the desirability of a product. The researchers asked students to work in small teams with 60 color chips to create color palettes for the lunch box. The colors selected were then tallied and represented on boards, showing the preferences of three groups of children: preschool, second grade, and fourth grade. The preschoolers chose mostly primary colors and very bright contrasting colors; the second-grade palette showed more "fad" colors; the fourth-grade palette showed a mixture of the primary contrasting colors and the more subtle variations chosen by the second graders. Based on these results, Fitch suggested that the color direction for the lunch kits be built from the fourth grade palette, since it represented a blend of the two younger groups. (In an alternate method of gaining information about children's color preferences, the students were asked to choose from a large array of crayon colors to color in sketches of the lunch kits. This provided further information about what kind of color relationships children prefer.)

Licensing Study

The license, or character, on a lunch box is another crucial component of desirability. The researchers created nine categories of licensing ideas and collected many examples for each category: cartoon characters, sports logos, fashion logos, TV stars, popular athletes, and so on. Conversations with the children revealed that most of the current licenses were too "young" for the school-age audience. Fitch recommended to the Thermos Company that they pursue licenses appropriate for older children, as well.

Is the Product Usable?

Usability testing with children and parents was conducted after a full-size, three-dimensional working model (i.e., capable of being opened and packed) of the lunch kit was available.

Mini-Focus Groups

Mini-focus groups were designed to test usability as well as general likes and dislikes of the lunch kit from the parents' point of view. Each group interacted with and discussed the working model and looked at existing products for comparison. Food was also provided for packing the lunch box.

Generally, parents thought the compartments Fitch had developed were too restricted, which caused some difficulty packing the lunch kit, although they became more comfortable as they worked with it. However, they said that if their children wanted the kit, that would be reason enough to buy it—regardless of their need to change their packing style.

5-17. The final lunch kit design.

Usability Testing with Children

Researchers began by showing students lunch boxes that were already on the market, encouraging them to think critically about what was available. Next, they were shown the working model and asked questions about it. Researchers then observed students interacting with the model. As with the parent mini-focus groups, the children were given food with which to pack the lunch kit.

Children responded positively to the model, especially after opening it. They were impressed with the fact that the "inside could be seen from the outside," that is, that the outside shape reflected the inner compartments. They enjoyed "playing with" the lunch kit and had no difficulty deciding how to pack it. Figure 5-17 shows the finished product in use.

Conclusion

This lunch kit was first introduced in the fall of 1992, with a "sell through" rate of 95 percent. Recently the Thermos Company added sports licenses to this line, with very good results. Without the input of actual users (mainly children in this case, but also parents and teachers), the striking design of the kit, and its success, would not have been possible. Fitch was fortunate to have the support of its client, the Thermos Company, and the cooperation of end-users—kids, parents, and teachers—allowing the team to conduct a rewarding and enjoyable research and development project.

(A longer, more detailed discussion of this project appeared in the American Center for Design's *Design Statements*, Vol. 8, No. 1, Fall 1992.)

Case Study

"discovery®" Seating and Fixtures Furniture

In Chapter 4, Timothy J. Springer shows how human factors (or ergonomics) is applied universal design. Similarly, in Chapter 6, James Postell describes the close relationship between universal design and ergonomics. Throughout the literature dealing with universal design, human factors, and ergonomics, a common thread appears in each discipline's interest in work environments, especially workstations and most especially seating. This case study looks at one of the first exercises in ergonomic chair design undertaken in America. The discovery® chair is still recognized as one of the leading examples of ergonomic seating design.

Fixtures Furniture, under the chairmanship of founder Norman Polsky, was the first U.S. manufacturer to seek out and create an ergonomic line of seating for offices. The discovery® chair was developed by their German partner firm Froescher and was marketed in Europe in the late 1970s under the trade name

"Resumo." The discovery® chair incorporates front-seat tilt and both passive and active ergonomics, along with full adjustability while seated.

The decision to establish a partnership with Froescher was made because of a shared understanding of the importance of several key elements necessary for proper seating. Good office chairs should allow work to be done in a leaning forward, upright, or leaning backward position, while the chair must also be able to adapt to the regular change between one sitting position and another during working hours—*dynamic sitting.*

Dynamic sitting (see Figure 5-18) allows body liquids to be assimilated and exchanged within the body's tissue without hindrance, thus reducing slipped disc problems and alleviating strains in the back muscles. Dynamic sitting also has a positive effect on all the muscles of the legs, back, and stomach by preventing the continual pressure in the stomach area that happens with fixed sitting. The blood and lymph circulation in the calves is also improved with dynamic sitting.

One must be able to adjust the angle of the stool when seated, and it must be so simple an operation that the user will do so regularly. The seat and back profile and the upholstery must be designed so that whatever movements and seating positions are necessary during working hours, no undue pressure points are felt.

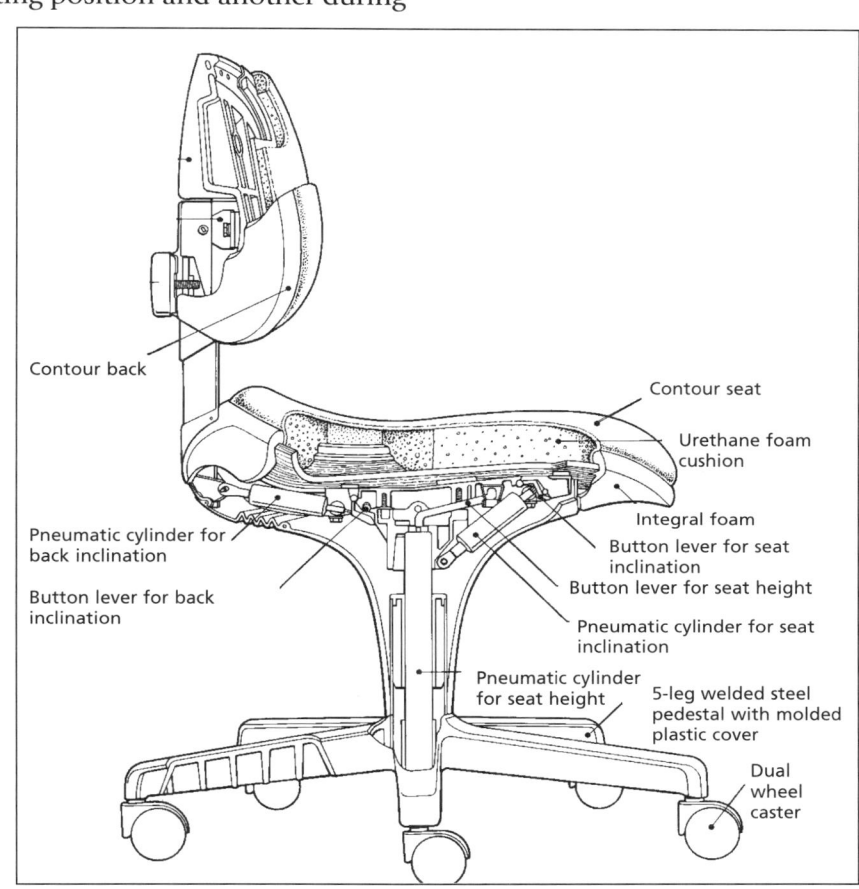

5-18. The discovery® chair offers a full range of features, including "dynamic sitting." *(Reprinted with permission from Fixtures Furniture.)*

The chair back should, when possible, encourage a slight forward curve of the spine in the small of the back but at the same time give the back a good support. When possible, this support should reach to the shoulder blades but should not impede movements of the shoulder girdle. The main supports of the stool back for the front sitting position should be found in the lower back region (lumbar-sacrum area). With the more upright sitting position the support must be in the upper lumbar area, and for the back sitting position the support should be found approximately between the shoulder blades.

This "wandering" of the point of support happens automatically because of the design of the seat back and not as a result of any adjustment to the seat back. Therefore, well-designed seats with higher back support are better than stools with smaller back rests. With the latter the support area can be altered by changing the height of the seat back. However, this is a relatively complex process and is rarely performed as it involves leaving the chair and performing a mechanical operation. Most often, smaller back chairs are either wrongly installed for the user or the back is left fixed in a middle position regardless of the sitting position of the user.

A chair that offers variations in adjustments is necessary because the individual measurements of the user must be taken into account and, depending on the type of work, height of working area, position of head to work material, and so on, the seat must be adjusted so that it aids the work and helps to bring about greater efficiency.

Fixtures led the industry in promoting ergonomic seating while supporting Dr. Marvin Dainoff's groundbreaking research on ergonomics at Miami University. From this research, the following 12 elements of ergonomic seating were developed:

1. Variety of models for various sizes and statures of people
2. Contoured padded seat and back
3. Seat height adjustment while seated
4. Lumbar support with back height adjustment and full tilt for dorsal flexing
5. Back tilt adjustment while seated
6. Seat front tilt adjustment while seated
7. All adjustments easily made while seated
8. Various static-posture settings or free-flowing dynamic-motion
9. Active ergonomic controls versus passive non-controls
10. Mechanical reliability, safety, and ergonomics by passing ANSI-BIFMA and ANSI/HFS 100 standards
11. User training to assure optimum results
12. Model is field-serviceable and backed by comprehensive manufacturer's warranty including nationwide service capability

The first discovery® chairs were modeled after the Resumo line and featured the following design elements:

- An easily accessible press-button for adjusting the overall height of the seat lies beneath the seat on the right-hand side.

- An easily accessible duo button that adjusts the angle of the back between 14° and 35° lies on the right-hand side beneath the armrest support. The duo button works in conjunction with a sliding control to allow the user to fix the back movement permanently within a chosen range of adjustment.

- Another easily accessible duo button with sliding control lies beneath the seat on the left-hand side in front of the armrest support. This control allows the seat surface itself to be adjusted for angle of incline and can be set in a fixed or range-of-motion position.

(If both duo buttons are fixed by the sliding controls, the seat can be said to be in a state of permanent motion, supporting the concept of dynamic sitting and even providing a mild form of exercise for the seated user.)

- The seating area and back are well upholstered with an optimal shape. Central column springs cushion away extra weight when the stool is in use. In all positions the user is free of pressure points in either the seating area or back. Seat height can be adjusted to leg length, thus removing unnecessary pressure behind the knee.

- Body weight is spread over the whole seating area. The lower part of the stool back is slightly convex, the middle part concave, and the top part convex again, which supports the natural curves of the spine. Movement of the shoulder joints and shoulder blades is unimpeded, as is sideways movement.

The discovery® line now includes five different models, which fit the needs of a variety of work types (see Figure 5-19):

- *discovery® original*—offers three seat widths and five back heights in three frame finish colors. The independent front seat and back tilts can be pneumatically fixed inclinations for static-posture settings or free-flow dynamic-motion for manager or intensive task or multi-shift operators.

- *discovery® adjustable*—fully adjustable, with easy-grip paddles for three adjustment controls with visible graphic instructions. T and loop arms are individually adjustable in height and width.

- *discovery® economy*—same features as discovery adjustable, available with two optional arm styles.

- *discovery® passive plus*—features passive ergonomics including knee tilt motion plus front seat inclination.

- *discovery® flair*—similar to passive plus with a new sculptured concept and uniquely shaped back and arms.

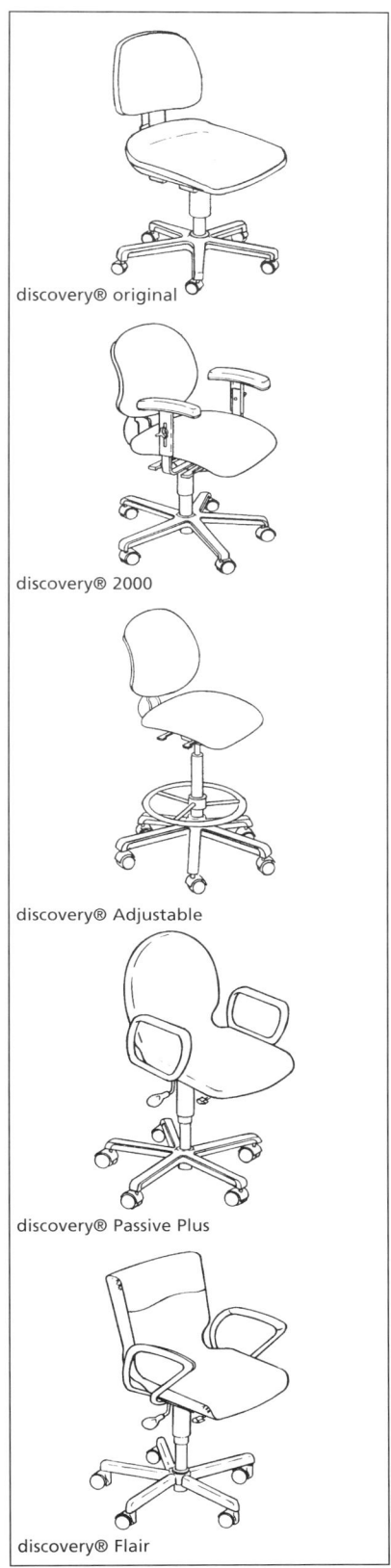

5-19. Features of the discovery® line of seating. *(Reprinted with permission from Fixtures Furniture.)*

Case Study

Seating Posture Theories:
A Research Approach to Ergonomic Chair Design
by Johan Ullman, M.D.

In this article, Dr. Ullman (of Gothenburg, Sweden) takes a global approach to the creation of the ultimate seating environment. Dr. Ullman has researched all major theories related to seating postures and chair design and has designed an office chair that provides a comprehensive solution to the problems created by each of the seating posture theories he describes.

The design of most working chairs in general use today is based on the classical right-angled sitting position. Recently the theories upon which this design is based have begun to be questioned, and several alternative theories and formulas for "the perfect sitting position" have been advanced. The following presents an analysis of the various theories, as well as opinions about the advantages and disadvantages of proposed solutions to the problem.

The Classical So-Called Perfect Sitting Position (Sitting at Attention)

This sitting position (see Figure 5-20) has been described in many textbooks during recent decades. It is generally considered to be the correct position in the ergonomic information distributed by many government agencies and forms the theoretical basis for the systems of rules after which most chairs today are being designed and manufactured.

Laboratory studies measuring disk pressure in the lumbar region appear, in theory, to justify the use of this position. The pressure seems to be greater when one sits with a hunched back than when the curvature of the spine is held in place with a lumbar support.

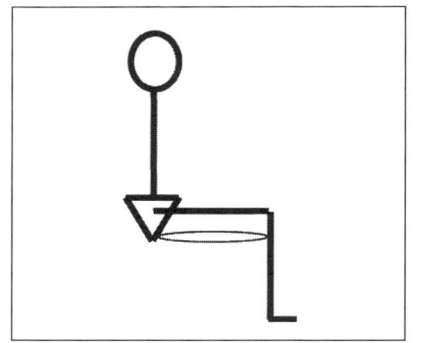

5-20. The so-called perfect sitting position. *(Figures 5-20 through 5-33 reprinted with permission from Johan Ullman, M.D.)*

Advantages
The position is easy to teach, and the theory is easy to describe using two-dimensional models or drawings. It is simple to design furniture that adheres to this theory.

Disadvantages
People rarely, if ever, use this sitting position spontaneously. It is very hard to "perform" this position for more than a couple of minutes. Whenever a person tries to hold this position, the usual result is that the lumbar region straightens out by itself, causing the entire back to hunch and the center of gravity of the head to move to a position in front of the skeletal structures which normally support it—the atlanto-occipital joints (see Figure 5-21).

It is now generally accepted that the head in this position will cause fatigue of the neck muscles, which can lead to musculoskeletal disorder and chronic pain in the neck and upper back region.

Swelling in the legs is experienced by people of short stature when seated on the flat surface of these seats at a normal work table since their feet normally don't reach the floor, causing their lower legs to hang. This can cause a compression of the blood vessels on the back of the thighs closest to the knees where vessels and nerves are not protected by as much muscle tissue as can be found farther up on the thighs.

Compensating for this fault with footrests leads to fixed sitting positions that are harmful as they further decrease the spontaneous movements of the legs.

5-21. What actually happens when one tries to maintain the "perfect" position.

Explanation

One reason why no one voluntarily assumes this position is because the hamstring muscles become so tensed that the individual consciously—or the body unconsciously—reacts to protect itself from the resultant static tension. This is done by sliding forward away from the backrest, thus allowing the pelvis to tip backward and straightening the lumbar lordosis at the same time as the tension in the hamstring muscles is relieved.

Another possible explanation is that the quadriceps muscles are relaxed when sitting in the right-angled position. These muscles originate above the axis of movement of the pelvis and, when stretched, can help to tip the pelvis forward. In addition, defenders of the right-angled sitting position neglect the fact that, when seated at a desk, most people transfer a portion of their body weight to the desk by leaning on it with their forearms.

The Danish Model

Sitting high up on a seat that slopes forward has been observed on Italian murals dating from the 15th century and in Egypt in 1500 B.C. A Danish surgeon, A. C. Mandal, caused a renaissance in this mode of sitting when, some 20 years ago, he published his monograph, "Homo Sedens—the sitting man." According to this model, one should sit on a flat surface that slopes forward and is placed high enough over the floor so that the lower legs are in a vertical position, allowing the feet to be planted on the floor supporting the body (see Figure 5-22). Adherents of this model usually claim that the working surface should also slope (10–15°) toward the sitting person. Even this has been illustrated on the ancient murals mentioned previously.

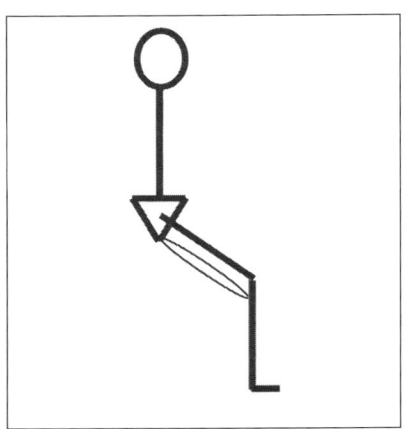

5-22. The Danish model for sitting suggests that a higher, sloped sitting surface is best.

Advantages

This model's advantage is that the angle between the thighs and trunk is wider so that the hamstring muscles' tendency to tip the pelvis backward is less than it is when sitting on a horizontal seat positioned at the height of the backs of the knees. It thus becomes easier to resume or maintain lumbar lordosis 7, or curvature of the spine, by activating the extensor muscles in this part of the back.

Disadvantages

Since the hamstring muscles are, in this position, in theory just as long as in the right-angled sitting position, and their tendency to tip the pelvis backward is still present, the extensor muscles of the lumbar region must constantly be activated to compensate for this tendency and to keep the back in its balanced position and in shape. This means that the individual must learn a new behavior pattern and, at least at the outset, must be constantly thinking about how to sit.

Moreover, this position is difficult to combine with other positions that the individual spontaneously attempts to assume. In certain types of school desks attributed to Mandal, a special foot plate has been added to make it possible to assume the right-angled position.

Hydrostatic Pressure

Plethysmograph measurements have demonstrated an increased swelling tendency in the feet and lower legs. This can result in discomfort in older people and even in young, healthy people in some cases. Inactivity in the lower legs and the small unconscious muscle movements that constantly occur in normal sitting can also lead to an increase in swelling in the lower legs.

Individual Adaptation

The Danish model requires that the height of both table and chair be carefully adjusted to fit the individual user. This must be done within an even broader scope than is necessary when sitting in the traditional manner. In principle, should a person change from high-heeled to low-heeled shoes, the height of both table and chair would need to be readjusted.

Mandal recommends seat heights that vary between 20 inches and 32 inches and table heights between 28 inches and 40 inches for individuals who are between 52 inches and 80 inches tall. This is based on experiments performed using seats and tables in which the height could be changed. It is interesting to note that the graphs for the preferred heights were directly proportional to how tall the individual was. This indicates that individuals of greatly varying heights all seem to prefer the same difference in level between chair and work surface. The preferred difference was between 8½ inches and 11 inches. This proved to be approximately 10 percent of the person's height.

Explanation

The Danish model has not won approval (with the possible exception of schools) because there are so many practical problems involved in adjusting table and chair heights that are not present in more traditional furniture. In addition, persons of different heights cannot use the same workplace without extensive readjustment. Furthermore, this position is not comfortable for any length of time.

The Norwegian Model

Just as in the Danish model, the Norwegian model also means sitting on a sloping plane. The difference is that sliding forward is prevented by a knee support (see Figure 5-23). The position is described as a semi-kneeling position. Peter Opsvik, the inventor, together with several Norwegian manufacturers of knee support chairs, usually claim that sitting on one is like sitting on a horse. This comparison is not quite accurate since a person sitting on horseback, at least in Europe, assumes a position where angles are greater both in the hip and knee joints and body weight is distributed differently. When sitting "correctly" on horseback, both the pelvis and the os ischium are, in principle, on a horizontal plane and the thighs rest on a sloping surface. Only the weight of the feet and lower legs are supported by the stirrups, and the knees are not used in any way to transfer body weight over to the horse.

5-23. The Norwegian model for sitting suggests a sloping plane, but also provides a knee support.

Advantages

A noticeable advantage of the knee support chair is that the hamstring muscles are allowed to relax, thus almost completely eliminating their tendency to rotate the pelvis backward. Both back and pelvis spontaneously assume a balanced position.

Disadvantages

In most knee support chairs one is more or less forced to assume the balanced sitting position. Recently, however, models have appeared that include a back support. Adherents say that one should use the knee support chair in combination with an ordinary chair so one can vary positions. But one obvious disadvantage of the knee support chair is that many people feel trapped by the knee support. A fairly common complaint is discomfort from the pressure on the knees.

Cartilage in the joints receives its nourishment by diffusion via the liquid in the joints, and since cartilage is living tissue, symptoms of arthrosis arise when it ages. The more a knee is flexed, the smaller are surfaces of contact in the joint and the higher the pressure on the surfaces. One may thus ask what the effect of the daily application of pressure to the bent knees will be.

Explanation
Many knee chairs have been sold due to the immediate relief from pressure that occurs when users experience the relaxed feeling brought about by balanced sitting. This is especially so for people who suffer from back and neck pain. But the chair is subsequently not used by people because the opportunity to change position is limited and causes people to experience knee pain and feel trapped.

The Swiss Model
Swiss professor Etienne Grandjean, like Dr. Mandal, was interested in finding out how people wanted to sit. He found that many people working at computers preferred to sit leaning back with a high chair back for support (see Figure 5-24).

Advantages
When using a correctly designed chair back, a certain portion of the trunk weight can be transferred to the chair back, thus reducing the weight pressing downward on the lumbar region. In addition, this sitting position provides a wider thigh-pelvis angle than the classical right-angled position does. It appears that a wider thigh-pelvis angle reduces the load on the back as well as the pressure on the disks in the lumbar region.

Disadvantages
When the angle of the leaning becomes sufficiently great, the head assumes a position where the sternocleidomastoid muscles must contract in order to hold the head up. This can be counteracted by using a correctly designed and positioned neck support. However, normal work at a desk is difficult to carry out seated in this way.

Explanation
Most people spontaneously choose the leaning back position for activities such as watching TV or when seated in a cinema—activities that don't require the use of the arms to any great extent. Desk

5-24. The Swiss model for sitting provides for leaning back with a high chair back for support.

work is generally not done in this position because when one is engaged in writing, one almost always seeks support for the entire forearm as far up as the olecranon or point of the elbow. Also, when one is leaning back, both head and eyes are positioned too far away from the work to be convenient.

The Standing Model

In recent times a new hypothesis has been put forth that claims that man was not built for sitting. This has led to the development and installation of standing workplaces in offices (see Figure 5-25).

Advantages
In a standing workplace people move about much more, and some of the strain on the neck and back that occurs in the sitting position is eliminated.

Disadvantages
Disadvantages associated with standing at work are easily recognized by anyone who has been forced to stand for long periods with no chance of sitting down. Common complaints are swollen feet, tiredness in the lower limbs, back pain, and shoulder-neck problems.

5-25. The standing model does away with sitting for long periods and is used in some workstations.

Explanation
Swelling of the feet and lower legs when standing still can be explained in part by an increase in hydrostatic pressure and in part by a lack of muscular activity.

Apparent Exceptions

If, without considering the various theories that have been put forth, one takes the time to observe how people actually choose to sit in different situations, one can easily discern a number of notable exceptions. An analysis of these positions from a biomechanical standpoint leads one to a certain number of conclusions.

The "Sack of Potatoes" Slouch
This condition is characterized by being seated with a bent lower back and the buttocks moved so far forward that the upper back is supported by that portion of the chair designed to support the lumbar region (see Figure 5-26).

Why sit in this position? "Because it is comfortable," is the excuse one gets from the party caught slouching in this manner. The object is to find support for the apex of the scapulae in order

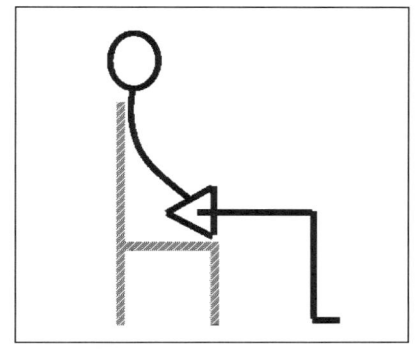

5-26. Many people actually find themselves sitting in this "sack of potatoes" position for its comfort.

to transfer the weight of arms and shoulders to the back of the chair. Thus the load is taken off the muscles supporting these skeletal structures—the levator scapulae and the m. trapezius, for instance.

Tilting Backward

What happens when we tilt back on a chair? The farther back we lean, the greater the portion of our trunk weight, shoulders, and arms that is transferred to the back of the chair (see Figure 5-27). The limiting factors are partly psychological and partly due to the fact that the center of gravity for both chair and body must lie somewhere between the rear legs of the chair and the feet of the seated individual. Also, the farther back one leans, the more effort is required to support the weight of the sitter's head.

5-27. We also choose to lean our chairs back to reposition our body weight.

Tilting Forward

This position, most commonly seen in schoolchildren, is characterized by moving the center of gravity forward. This causes the chair to rest on the front legs and the weight of the sitter to be distributed to the table via the forearms and to the floor through the front legs of the chair and through the feet of the sitter, which tend to be positioned under the chair (see Figure 5-28).

5-28. Sometimes we lean forward so that the chair rests on the front legs and some of our weight is distributed through our forearms.

The Conversational Position

This is the position one often takes at the dinner table after the dishes have been removed. Without tilting the chair, one usually assumes a seated position where the lower legs are folded back under the chair, toes on the floor, often with the feet crossed one over the other, elbows resting on the table edge, and the shoulder line forward over the vertical line of the forearms on the edge of the table (see Figure 5-29). Here the forearms are sometimes kept on top of each other, and sometimes one or both arms are used to support the head by placing the chin in the palm.

5-29. Another familiar position is found among persons holding conversations.

The Writing Desk Position

The normal seated position one assumes when writing is not one that fits in with the various theories about the "perfect sitting position." It is, in fact, normal for a person to sit with the center of gravity of the trunk positioned in front of the os ischii (seat bone), the shoulder line above the edge of the table (or even farther forward), often with the feet tucked back under the chair. Almost without exception the entire forearm up to the elbow is resting on the table (see Figure 5-30). In this position, the weight of the arms and shoulders, and sometimes part of the trunk, is transferred to the table. What is almost never seen, however, is someone with their arms resting on the arms of the chair when writing.

Feet On the Table

Whenever the knee joints are straight and the hamstring muscles are stretched, the pelvis tends to tilt backward. For comfort, the trunk must be leaning backward. This means that sitting with the feet up on the table almost always requires support for the upper back and, preferably, even the head as well (see Figure 5-31). Whenever these conditions can be met, this is a popular variant because it implies a great departure from the positions one normally assumes while working seated.

Free, Unfettered Sitting

No one has ever willingly conformed to the traditional models; if we assume that the information received via the senses is relevant, it would perhaps be wiser to sit comfortably than to sit correctly according to one of the different formulas for the "perfect sitting position." No one willingly remains in the same position for long periods of time. Judging from man's natural spontaneous behavior, constantly changing one's sitting position is preferred.

The Ullman chair (see Figure 5-32) was introduced in Sweden in 1986 and is based on the premise that the more sitting positions one has access to, the shorter time one remains in any one of them. This assumes that moving between the various positions is so easy that one doesn't need to think about the fact that one is switching.

With the Ullman chair one can assume a balanced sitting position whereby the pelvis rests on the os ischii on a horizontal surface while the thighs angle downward, resting on a sloping surface. Since the pelvis rests on a horizontal surface, it is possible to fold the lower legs back under the chair without sliding off. This makes it possible to relax the hamstring muscles so that the pelvis may tilt upward to approximately the position it assumes when standing or on horseback. Sitting on a chair with a flat forward sloping seat like the Danish model and folding the legs backward under the chair will cause one to slide off.

The back of the Ullman chair is designed to give optimal support to both back and shoulders when leaning back. Observations of how people, despite a "proper upbringing," often slouch like a "sack of potatoes" has led to a chair back design where people can rest their shoulder blades.

Our shoulder blades are almost entirely held in place by muscles—actually by those very muscles that most often are the source of upper back pain. What is more, the entire weight of the arms is

5-30. This figure shows the "writing desk" position, which almost always requires that the entire forearm rest on the writing surface.

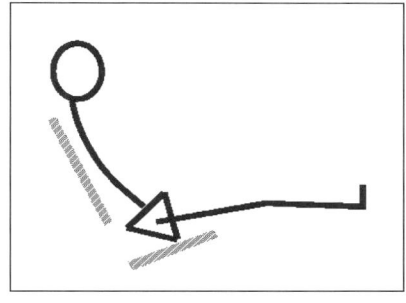

5-31. This position is often found in situations where one is relaxing or enjoying an activity.

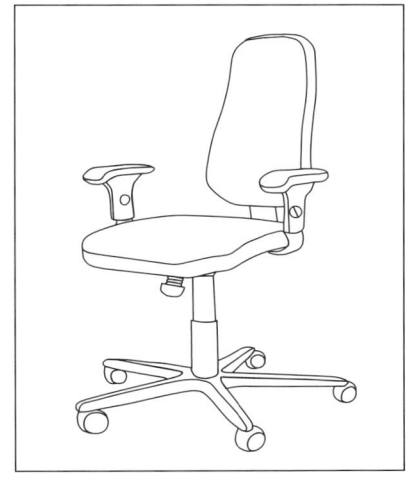

5-32. The Ullman chair, designed by Johan Ullman, M.D.

5-33. The "perfect" chair will allow for all of these positions.

supported by the shoulder blades via the shoulder joints. The Ullman chair has therefore been designed to support the weight of both arms and shoulders through the shoulder blades.

This is possible thanks to a design where the entire seat and back of the chair rock backward as far as needed to permit the transfer of the weight without disturbing the balance of the head. If one were to rock too far back, the sternocleidomastoid muscles would have to contract in order to prevent the head from falling backward.

Advantages

The Ullman chair allows the seated person to assume all the positions described above. Without touching any adjustment levers, one can switch among the positions described above as the balanced position, the classical position, and the Swiss model. People of body height ranging from 56 inches to 82 inches can be comfortable on the same chair and can, if necessary, get a decent work position at a work desk 28 inches to 29 inches high.

Disadvantages

Some people report an immediate feeling of sliding forward when trying the chair. This feeling disappears within minutes, or hours at most. Others have reported discomfort from the seat before they were used to actually sitting on their seat bones, but this feeling disappears within a few days.

The chair has adjustments for depth of seating and resistance to tilting according to the user's height and weight. Despite the fact that these adjustments need only be made once and the instructions are printed on the back support of the chair, many times even ergonomists have neglected to carry out these simple but necessary tasks (see Figure 5-33).

Universal Design in the Office

6

Of all the environments affected by the ADA, the one most universally impacted is the office. Typically, the spaces we work in are at least in part open to the public and thus covered with the public accommodation section. And, of course, the employment provisions are directly related to the office.

The majority of the areas focused on in this book are relevant to accommodation within the office. Chapters on facilities management, enabling products, and public and commercial environments all connect to office-based universal design. And the Techniques and Strategies described in this book can be utilized throughout the work world.

Consequently, this chapter opens with a more global, theoretical discussion of the features that make up a universally designed office. James Postell seeks to define "quality" as the term relates to the interplay between worker, work, and environment. In the process, he arrives at an "ecology" that fulfills our description of universal design.

The chapter then moves into a more detailed focus by examining current technology, specifically the use of computers in a safe and productive manner. Diane Davis describes several leading-edge products and discusses proper design of the environments within which they are used. Next Cindy Paulson-Schiefelbein reports on an issue that has received far too little attention—chemical sensitivities—and presents alternative materials and treatments currently available that reduce the harmful effects of common chemicals. Finally, Franklin Becker and his colleagues at Cornell University look at office design and management around the world. Their case study offers some exciting possibilities for change in the American work environment.

The Universal Office
by James Postell

Historically, little attention has been paid to providing a work environment that can serve *all* the needs of a company, including maintaining corporate identity and increasing worker safety, satisfaction, and productivity while facing financial realities. This is now changing. Universal design presents a critical approach to rethinking conventional solutions for office design by drawing on a knowledge of ergonomics and human factors, as well as information on special needs groups, changing technology, and changing work styles.

If a person is unable to perform a task due to physical constraints in the workplace, is unable to interact with others due to barriers or physical limitations, or experiences a loss of self-worth due to a lack of control over the immediate environment, then there is a design problem that needs to be addressed.

Two interrelated theories—*ergonomics* and *proxemics*—are useful to universal design since they can help the designer understand how an environment that adapts to the individual can be better created. Ergonomics is the study of people's reactions and behaviors in relation to their work. The general aim of such study is adapting work conditions to the physiological and psychological nature of human beings and optimizing the fit between people and machines relative to their needs and activities. This results in the most important principle of ergonomics: fitting the task to the human being. From this concept, new furniture systems are developed, new equipment and machines for the office are created, and new workstation configurations are conceived.

Proxemics is the study of the personal, cultural, and spatial needs of humans and their interactions with the environment—the spatial relationships between people and things relative to activity, purpose, culture, and time. Design activities that affect proxemics include lighting strategies, spatial organizations, and workstation layouts. These components directly affect personal interaction, communication, and territorial definition within the workplace.

The physical office environment is an integration of building systems (structural, electrical, spatial) and furniture systems (desk and work surfaces, seating, storage, and accessory products); equipment and machines (computer, monitor, keyboard, mouse and pad, telephone, typewriter, pencil sharpener, calculator, and so on); lighting specifications; indoor air quality; climate control; acoustics; and material, chemical, and finish quality. These elements are each discussed in detail in "The Office Ecosystem" section of this chapter.

It is important to consider less tangible, or tacit, contributions to office design: management, personal interaction and communication, behavioral response, degree of self-control over one's microenvironment, and environmental stress. Although these conceptual aspects receive academic and scholarly attention, the general public (including many professionals) is most attuned to the visual and tangible. But both aspects are necessary for a complete understanding of universal design in the office environment.

The Tacit Office Environment

Tacit features of a workplace can be broadly grouped into considerations of:

- Health, safety, and welfare issues
- Psychological and behavioral aspects of design
- Personal control

Health, Safety, and Welfare Issues

The health, safety, and welfare of workers are crucial concerns within an office design. This area encompasses a wide range of factors—from short-term physical concerns to long-term psychological effects. Definitions of health, safety, and welfare are currently expanding to include a greater emphasis on long-term issues of health maintenance, well being, and personal growth. The ADA and the American National Standards Institute/Human Factors Society 100 Act of 1988 (see ANSI/HFS 100-1988) are examples of legislative action that consider long-term issues.

Creating a healthy, safe office environment can be facilitated by asking:

- Does the office environment (at minimum) meet existing federal, state, and local health and safety standards?
- Do the design and spatial layout of the furniture and equipment systems promote ease of use for as many people as possible?
- Are access and egress designed with safety in mind?
- Are the work areas and surrounding environments safe for all existing employees at all times?
- Are fatigue, discomfort, or stress evident in the users (or are they expressed as problems on surveys or questionnaires)?
- Are there excessive repetitive or functional activities that might lead to repetitive motion strain (RMS)?
- Does the environment provide individual climate, acoustic, light, and air quality controls?

ANSI/HFS 100-1988

Enacted in 1988 and overturned by the Superior Court of California after only a year in legislation, the American National Standards Institute/Human Factors Society 100 Act (ANSI/HFS 100—limited to the city of San Francisco) was written for individuals working in a video display terminal (VDT) work environment. The ordinance mandated companies to provide their employees working at VDT workstations more than four hours a day with the following:

- Pneumatic seating—height adjustment ranging between 16 inches and 20.5 inches.
- Arm-, wrist-, and footrests when requested by any operator who routinely performs repetitive keystrokes
- Angle and height-of-back adjustment and seat-depth adjustment on chairs
- Document holders with angle and height adjustments upon request as appropriate
- Seat rake (angle between seat back and seat pan) fixed back: angle shall be 90° or more; adjustable back: range shall include some part of the range from 90° to 105°
- Minimal seat width of seat cushions at least 18.2 inches measured at the spindle center and measured to the edge of the seat, not to the edge of the fabric
- Footrest of at least 2 inches in height for those using a keyboard if they are unable to place their feet flat on the floor
- Special lighting
- Rest breaks
- Noise reduction
- Appropriate lighting for VDT use (proper window treatments, antiglare screens, and other measures to ensure visual comfort)
- Employee education and training on furniture systems

While this ordinance was in effect, it was applicable to all businesses, private or public.

Psychological and Behavioral Aspects of Office Design

Maintaining psychological and behavioral health among workers in an office environment is obviously important. Unfortunately, acceptable levels of privacy for individuals, aesthetic preferences, and successful interaction strategies are difficult to measure or define. Nonetheless, people must be able to negotiate with their environment and with others in that environment.

The designer must thoughtfully address the following:
- Do the overall qualitative aspects of the workplace (character and ambiance) support the image and personality of the users?

- Do workspaces promote privacy, allowing one to concentrate while also providing the opportunity for occasional distraction?

- Is there flexibility in occupying individual workstations?

- Are there facilities for small and large group gatherings?

- Do conference spaces promote interaction, allowing one to be both part of a group and an individual?

Communication and Productivity

Planning strategies throughout the late 1960s led to radical departures from the norm in the physical layout of office interiors in order to optimize communication and productivity. Such departures are evident in the work of the German Quickborner Team, a design firm responsible for many innovative office space plans. It may well have been the absence of formal training and involvement with interior design and architectural professionals that made it possible to conceive such fresh proposals: "Let us play in a green field," they said, meaning a nonrestrictive open space with no set boundaries or limitations. Personnel would continue to be placed at workstations strictly grouped according to working needs for easy communication; rarely was space planning executed on a grid. Their planning schemes looked simple, but were actually highly organized around a series of rules and concepts related to openness, lighting, communication, interaction, participation, and revision. The solutions they offered were arrived at by raising and answering these questions:

- Does the design facilitate personal communication at a variety of psychological and physical levels and through a variety of means and techniques?

- Are important patterns of daily communication reinforced by the spatial layout of the office and design of the objects, furnishings, and equipment within the work environment?

- Is there space available for confidential conversation? For public interaction?

A more recent trend in office planning is seen in "shared offices"—a space allocation practice in which single individuals are not assigned a desk, workstation, or office for their exclusive use. Shared offices can reduce costs, improve flexibility, and maintain effectiveness for people who often are out of the office. This is a relatively new concept adopted by Shimuzu Institute of Technology's Planning Department and the San Francisco offices of Anderson Consulting. Typically, shared offices include an initial investment of portable phones and laptop computers, but they often pay for themselves within the first year from space savings. This is an example of universal design wherein the same size "footprint" (a plan for an individual workstation) is capable of housing different furniture and equipment components depending on specific job functions and work styles. This plan may include flexible furnishing adaptable to different users, including those with a variety of disabilities. The case study later in this chapter describes several innovative office configurations.

Stress

Stress is a body's response to the demands placed on it. Sources for stress can be physical and/or psychological. Short-term stress generally refers to temporary annoyances or physical discomfort. A small amount of it is healthy, but long-term psychological stress can eventually lead to a number of ailments including headaches, cardiovascular disease, ulcers, digestive problems, skin rashes, and nervous disorders.

Access, egress, and wayfinding throughout the office environment are some of the elements of space planning that affect a person's level of stress, anxiety, and effectiveness (Shumaker, 1982). The psychological stress and discomfort attributed to poor access through and egress into or out of the workplace is magnified for those who are visually impaired or otherwise disabled.

Job stress—working in extreme physical or psychological conditions, handling too much information in too little time, poor employee relations, and a lack of control over one's workplace (furniture, lighting, acoustic, and climate control adjustment)—can lead to a number of job-related illnesses. This degraded quality in the office is as costly to firms as it is to individuals. For example, cardiovascular disease, widely believed to be stress related, accounted for $11 billion of lost output to industry in a single year in the United States.

Recently, several U.S. businesses have introduced policies that seek to reduce stress through "life management." These include workplace amenities designed to promote psychological well-being, such as child care, flex time, on-site banking facilities, and exercise facilities. Other related concerns for employee well-being are increased participation, empowerment, and opportunities for personal growth.

Personal Control

Some degree of control over one's work schedule, physical workplace, and work order can significantly increase an employee's sense of well being. Research performed by Karasek (1981) indicates that the people most at risk for cardiovascular disease are those in high-demand, low-control situations. Clerical or other static-oriented, fixed-task production jobs are activities wherein employees have little control over their work environment or their work schedule and are often under great pressure to perform.

Personal control over one's work environment is enhanced by universal design features (adaptable and adjustable furnishings). While it is important to design the physical environment efficiently, it is equally important to design a degree of flexibility into the office environment in order to allow employees the necessary freedom to assert personal control. Ideally, all employees should be involved in the programming and design development stages of any new office design or major renovation project, thus increasing their sense of participation, worth, and control over the environment.

One office configuration will not suit everyone or every type of organization. In addition, the office ecology is dynamic—ever changing—in terms of its social organization and the technology employed by the users. Therefore, it is important to consider whether:

- The work environment allows people to influence, alter, or otherwise affect their micro-environment

- The physical components (e.g., furniture, equipment, air-handling systems, and electronic systems) allow for expansion or reorganization

The Physical Office Environment

Worker satisfaction and overall office quality can be significantly improved when designers visualize the office workplace as a large and expanded *ecosystem*. Within this ecosystem are a measurable number of physical systems that affect office design: building and furniture systems, indoor air quality and material toxicity, lighting, and acoustics.

Building and Furniture Systems

Building systems include structural, mechanical, electric power (including expansion), physical security, egress and access (including number and location of elevators), lighting, ceiling, flooring, wall systems, information systems (computerization and interconnection), floor-to-ceiling heights, and usable floor area. Furniture systems include seating, desks, tables, storage (for occupant, equipment, and files), movable partition and panel systems, portable equipment, accessories, and machines.

Surprisingly, the bulk of the total office system investment is not in these physical systems; rather, it is the salaries of employees themselves. A recent study by the BOSTI group revealed that over

COMMON WORKPLACE REQUIREMENT

Please rate common workplace on each of the characteristics below. First indicate your satisfaction with each one, and fill the number corresponding to your answer in the left side box. Then rate how important each one of the characteristics is to you, and fill your answer in the right side box. If you have some specific reason or explanation about your rating, please put your comments on the last column of each question.

1. Dissatisfied
2. Somewhat Dissatisfied
3. Neutral
4. Somewhat Satisfied
5. Satisfied

1. Not Important
2. Hardly Important
3. Neutral
4. Somewhat Important
5. Very Important

Physical Settings
Satisfaction | Importance | Comments

☐ 1. Overall workspace size ☐
☐ 2. Shape of workspace ☐
☐ 3. Density of people ☐
☐ 4. Location of workplace on the floor ☐
☐ 5. Quality of lighting ☐
☐ 6. Quality of air conditioning ☐
☐ 7. Color of floor covering ☐
☐ 8. Color of overall furniture ☐
☐ 9. Noise level at workplace ☐
☐ 10. Overall image (color, atmosphere) ☐
☐ 11. Overall environment (comfort) ☐

Communication on the Floor
Satisfaction | Importance | Comments

☐ 12. Number of meeting spaces ☐
☐ 13. Size of meeting space ☐
☐ 14. Privacy of meeting space ☐
☐ 15. Location of meeting space ☐
☐ 16. Furniture of meeting space ☐
☐ 17. Visibility to coworkers ☐

6-1. (A) An example of a post-occupancy evaluation form. Adapted from *The Total Workplace* by Frank Becker, pp. 269–270. *(Reprinted with permission from Frank Becker, The Total Workplace.)*

a 10-year period the cost of hiring and maintaining personnel was estimated to be more than 13 times the cost of constructing, enclosing, operating, wiring, and equipping an office. A relatively small increase of investment in the physical systems may go far toward improving the overall health, safety, and welfare of the workers.

Evaluating building systems requires a great deal of reliable data. Simply understanding a building's physical attributes (such as size and power capacity) is not enough. Franklin Becker, in his book *The Total Workplace*, offers several classifications that are useful in assessing building performances. In nearly every case, the idea of formalizing building evaluations is organized around concepts and formats employed by post-occupancy evaluations (POEs). There are several types of POEs presented, the most common of which are:

- Customized (individually tailored)
- Standardized (uniformly applied)
- Mixed (standard components mixed and modified)

Custom POEs are constructed by individual researchers and are tailored to specific circumstances of the building and its occupants. They provide information on how well the completed building meets the needs of the occupants in relation to their personal work environment. But the adequacy of the building systems in terms of maintenance, repair, and operating costs, and the effect of the building form on organizational and group functioning and other organizational objectives, tend to be neglected.

Standardized POEs allow for comparisons with other buildings, organizations, and time periods. The voluntary standards organization, American Society for Testing and Materials, is now constructing a standardized battery of valid and reliable tools that will be publicly available to anyone doing a POE. The charts in

Figure 6-1(A) and 6-1(B) illustrate the questions and format of standardized POEs.

Building appraisal methods are not panaceas for all building-related decisions. They are, however, useful diagnostic tools that, through their structure and organization, allow individuals to keep track of the many subsystems in an office building.

Indoor Air Quality

Indoor air quality is the impact of interior contamination in the air people breathe and its subsequent effect on human wellness and productivity. Indoor air pollutants are often overlooked in office design, yet they affect people in a number of ways. The Environmental Protection Agency (EPA) estimates that problems of indoor air quality may be detrimentally affecting the health and productivity of an estimated 20–35 percent of U.S. white-collar workers, representing an annual loss in income or productivity of $60 billion (Hedge et al., 1989). Also, a growing number of individuals are reporting environmental sensitivities toward air quality and material finishes (see next section, as well as "Chemical Sensitivities" later in this chapter). Such sensitivities are recognized as a disability under the ADA and may therefore require accommodations from employers.

There are three general classifications of air pollutants of which designers need to be aware:

- Gas (carbon dioxide, carbon monoxide) and vapors from volatile organic compounds given off by equipment and materials made of almost any synthetic product in a confined space, (e.g., plastics, fibers, coatings, and cleaning chemicals including chlorides, formaldehydes, and hydrocarbons)

- Inert particles of dust, ash, and microscopic inorganic material

---

PERSONAL WORKPLACE REQUIREMENT

Please rate your personal workplace on each of the characteristics below. First indicate your satisfaction with each one, and fill the number corresponding to your answer in the left side box. Then rate how important each one of the characteristics is to you, and fill your answer in the right side box. If you have some specific reason or explanation about your rating, please put your comments on the last column of each question.

1. Dissatisfied	1. Not Important
2. Somewhat Dissatisfied	2. Hardly Important
3. Neutral	3. Neutral
4. Somewhat Satisfied	4. Somewhat Important
5. Satisfied	5. Very Important

Satisfaction   Importance   Comments

☐ 1. Location of your workspace ☐
☐ 2. Arrangement of furniture ☐
☐ 3. Amount of work surface ☐
☐ 4. Function of furniture ☐
☐ 5. Amount of storage for work materials ☐
☐ 6. Function of storage ☐
☐ 7. Display area for graphic materials ☐
☐ 8. Style of furniture ☐
☐ 9. Color of furniture ☐
☐ 10. Comfort of chair ☐
☐ 11. Degree of privacy ☐
☐ 12. Suitability to your work ☐
☐ 13. Opportunity to personalize workplace ☐
☐ 14. Image of workplace ☐
☐ 15. Overall satisfaction with workplace ☐

16. What do you like most about your current personal workplace?

17. What do you like least about your currrent personal workplace?

6-1. (B) An example of a post-occupancy evaluation form. Adapted from *The Total Workplace* by Frank Becker, pp. 269–270. *(Reprinted with permission from Frank Becker,* The Total Workplace.*)*

- Microorganisms such as fungal growth, harmful bacteria, and viruses nourished by normal humidity and temperature, often causing undesirable odors (implicated as the major contaminant in 40 percent of sick buildings)

A fourth source of air pollutants is attributed to people: Individuals bring to the workplace germs, body odors, fragrances, and a significant amount of carbon dioxide emitted through breathing.

The American Society of Heating, Refrigeration, and Air Conditioning Engineers defines acceptable indoor air quality as "air in which there are no known contaminants at harmful concentrations as determined by cognizant authorities and with which a substantial majority (80 percent or more) of the people exposed do not express dissatisfaction." This definition leaves a lot to be desired since it allows for 20 percent or more of the people affected to express dissatisfaction.

A more useful definition has been offered by the World Health Organization: "the physical and chemical nature of indoor air, as delivered to the breathing zone of the building occupants, which produces a complete state of mental, physical, and social well being of the occupants, not merely the absence of disease and infirmity."

Given that indoor air quality needs to be considered in our designs, designers should be aware that there are three generally accepted ways to control pollutants and maintain air quality in office environments:

- Eliminate pollutants at the source.

- Remove pollutants near the source or where they accumulate.

- Dilute indoor air with large volumes of clean fresh air.

Material, Chemical, and Finish Toxicity

Material toxicity can be prevented and/or alleviated through programming, specification of material and finishes, and a carefully planned design and construction process. Designers should be aware of the needs of allergic and chemically sensitive users in the early stages of design. Designers also need to be aware of the volatile organic compounds emitted by material agents such as paint, varnishes, fabrics, wall, floor, and ceiling coverings, and be aware of materials containing lead, arsenic, heavy metals, tin, mercury, and zinc. They should also recognize that:

- Carpets are breeding grounds for dust mites, which have been implicated in sick building syndrome.

- Ceiling tiles and furniture partitions can shed mineral fibers and other particles.

- Solvents, new products, and furnishings may continue to give off a significant amount of gas for up to nine months; these emissions can contain chlorides, formaldehydes, and hydrocarbons and are leading causes of building-related illnesses.

- Some plastic laminants used in desk and table designs are microscopically porous, causing long-term wear on clothing and skin; a new laminant "silque," produced and marketed by Steelcase, is designed to help alleviate long-term abrasion.

- Fume-generating equipment, photocopiers, and print machines can and often do cause headaches, dizziness, and short-term illnesses.

- Insulation, gypsum board, door glue, and a host of other building materials are toxic to some people.

Another problem for both equipment and workers is static. Static charge buildup has been linked to outbreaks of skin problems, including skin irritation and facial rashes (Stellman and Henifin, 1983). Though the evidence is not conclusive, specifying antistatic carpeting may represent an important protective measure for both machines and operators. (See "Chemical Sensitivities" later in this chapter for a thorough review of ways to alleviate material toxicity.)

Lighting

Lighting is considered to be the most important component in a healthy office environment. The more scientific information designers have about light, the clearer the link becomes between lighting design, health, and productivity. In the last decade, researchers have devoted increased attention to lighting and its effect upon VDTs and the workplace:

- The American Society of Interior Designers has found that 68 percent of employees complain about the light in their offices.

- A Silicon Valley study pointed out that 79 percent of VDT users want better lighting.

The degree of dissatisfaction with lighting in many of today's offices is difficult to ignore. The National Lighting Bureau notes the following benefits of healthful lighting:

- Greater productivity
- Error rate reduction
- Better quality control
- Reduced absenteeism
- Effective mood setting
- Improved employee morale

Although lighting is clearly important in the office environment, it usually accounts for less than 1 percent of operating expenses. A 1986 study by the Building Owners and Managers Association (BOMA) determined that the annual cost for a typical office was $164.60 per square foot. Of this total, $130.00 went to wages and salaries, $18.00 for space, $8.60 for services and supplies, $7.00 for furniture and equipment, and only $1.00 for lighting.

Most workspaces are illuminated using general fluorescent lighting. A large portion of these workspaces use parabolic baffled direct downlighting, which generally produces glare. There is much debate on how to properly light the office environment. However, there is some agreement about the need for low-level, even light throughout an area in which electronic tasks are performed. The problem in good office lighting design is to accommodate the need for low-level, even light while providing specific task-oriented lighting where and when necessary. There is a definite trend toward the use of indirect uplighting accompanied by controllable task lighting for writing, reading, and typing. This lighting may be incorporated into the furnishings, independently suspended, or mounted on the ceiling.

A major study performed at the University of Colorado at Boulder by D. L. Dilaura and R. G. Mistrick and sponsored by Peerless Electric Company compared a parabolic louvre direct lighting system with two indirect systems for the VDT workplace. They found a three-to-one preference for the two indirect systems, which produced less glare on VDT screens, walls, ceiling, and other workplace surfaces. Workers also felt that the indirect uplighting produced a more pleasant, comfortable environment.

Measured footcandles taken at similar worksurface levels can be calibrated to the same reading, but there is typically a perception of less light in the indirect system. Lensed-indirect uplighting has been shown to improve visual surroundings and promote satisfaction and productivity of computer users (Hedge et al., 1989). Augmenting the indirect overhead lighting system with individually controllable lighting (including both task and ambient lighting) enables personal control of the workspace and consequently helps to promote wellness by design.

Recent studies indicate that people are more comfortable with lighting when they know where it is coming from. If office workers are unable to distinguish fixtures or determine the source of lighting in their environment, they may feel disoriented and not be able to detect whether or not the lights are on. Therefore many manufacturers of indirect uplighting luminaires have designed their fixtures with baffled under-openings so employees can determine the source of light. These baffled under-openings also help to combat the high contrast created by the silhouette of the fixture against the ceiling.

Reflectance (reflected light) in the office environment is also an important consideration in lighting research. According to a noted lighting designer, reflectance values not only influence footcandle levels but also illuminance (which is measured brightness), which is what people actually see. Reflectance is directly related to how people perceive light and should be considered when designing an office interior.

The Illuminating Engineering Society recommends the following reflectances throughout the office environment:

Ceilings	70–80%
Walls	25–50%
Floors	10–20%
Panels	25–45%
Desktops	20–50%

Designers must also carefully assess whether to provide natural daylight in the workplace. Daylight can provide orientation—a connection to the outdoor world—and is an important psychological component in office design, but it is one that must be handled with care. Direct glare on VDT screens is a common problem created by direct light from windows. Try to keep lighting contrasts within a 3:1 ratio. For example, if there are approximately 10,000 footcandles of light coming from an exterior window into a room lit by approximately 30 footcandles, the lighting difference between the two sources would cause glare, eye fatigue, and discomfort. Diane Davis's section "Universal Design in the Computer Environment" offers several solutions to lighting problems in typical offices.

Acoustics

The acoustic atmosphere of any office is the result of several factors:

- The ceiling with its lighting: Light fixtures can reflect and reverberate sound even though the other ceiling panels are sound absorbent.

- The ballasts for fluorescent lamps

- Windows (outdoor noise)

- Air-handling components (intake, ducts, compressors, fans, generators)

- Office machines and equipment, both in use or idle

- People

There are many conventional ways to control unwanted sound in the office:

- Use of screens and acoustical panels
- Use of carpet, draperies, and wall coverings
- Sound-masking techniques (white noise, pink noise)

The level of sound in an office should be kept low, but not too low. If it is too low the space becomes acoustically "dead" and everyone can hear everyone else's conversations. If this happens, "white-noise" or sound masking may be used. Masking is generally attained by a generator producing mixed, unintelligible sounds across the sound spectrum.

Conclusion

All elements of an office environment change over time; some changes occur more often and more rapidly than others. The history of the office has been characterized by intermittent reevaluations about work and ways to do it. It is in the twentieth century that the changes have been greatest, with processes and products evolving radically during the past 50 years. Machines and equipment have become smaller and lighter; seating and work surfaces have become more adjustable and synthetic in their material construction. Every new piece of technological innovation changes the way people work. This in turn changes the way people think about their jobs, and eventually changes the structure and organization of a firm...even its image. The United States seems to be experiencing waves of change that profoundly affect today's workplaces. It is generally clear that designers need to be aware of the following trends:

- The globalization of markets (multicultural and multinational corporations)
- Decentralization into more flexible, product-oriented business units
- More mixing of office-work and product-work in places that look like "workshops;" more research, testing, and development in offices
- More frequent organizational restructuring
- More genuine recognition of the value of employee individuality
- A maturing and aging workforce (impacting environmental and product design in response to the natural changes in vision, smell, hearing, stamina, upper body dexterity, and mobility of an aging workforce)
- Accelerated insistence on speed and quantity of information necessary for decision-making

These are all significant shifts in the industrial climate of the U.S. Design professionals need to consider the design ramifications of these developments while maintaining a keen interest in ensuring universal design within office environments.

Products made for the office environment are also becoming more and more complicated as the work environment itself becomes more complicated. Technology and the office environment have negatively affected people's vision, hands, wrists, arms, and neck and back areas. A large matrix of complex systems, machines, and equipment must be rethought to fit well with today's activities. The introduction of VDTs has caused a radical transformation in the traditional concepts of ergonomics, resulting in a considerable change in office working conditions and the spatial quality of the workplace. Diane Davis's piece on computers in the work environment speaks directly to these concerns.

Universal Design Strategy
Universal Design for the Computer Environment
by Diane Davis

Many areas of the computer work environment can either positively or negatively impact office workers. Although substantial investments in computers have been made throughout the 1980s and into the 1990s, anticipated increases in white-collar productivity have not been evident. According to a Rutgers University Occupational Safety Officer, part of the reason for these disappointing productivity rates has been due to the incorrect use of computers—which leads to personal injury and pain at work. This has ultimately resulted in decreased productivity, higher absenteeism, and increased health costs.

An appropriately designed computer workstation can not only increase productivity, but can also open work opportunities to persons with disabilities who formerly could not be a part of a workforce using computers. However, in order to achieve improved productivity and more universal accessibility, *disabling* work environments need to become *enabling* ones. Manufacturers of computer-related products, ergonomists, and designers are developing new products and directives on using computers in a healthy manner. Products that maximize adjustability allow each user to exert greater control over the work environment. This type of control appears to be a critical factor in worker satisfaction and health.

As component products of the computer environment become more adjustable and flexible, the design of the total environment must also be changed. For example, the positive benefits provided by an ergonomic chair can be negated by an inappropriately placed keyboard pad, by an inappropriately tilted work surface, or by

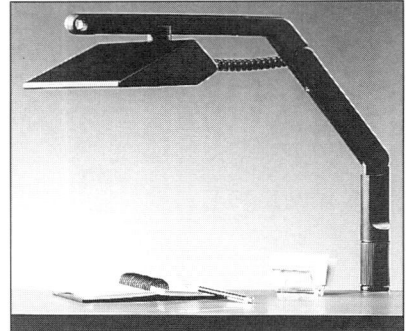

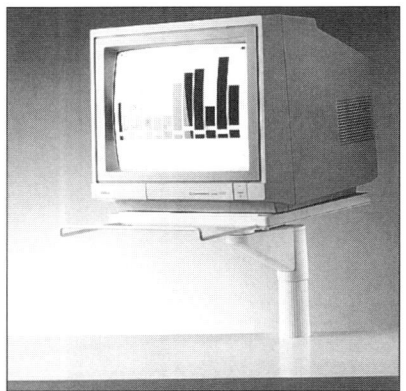

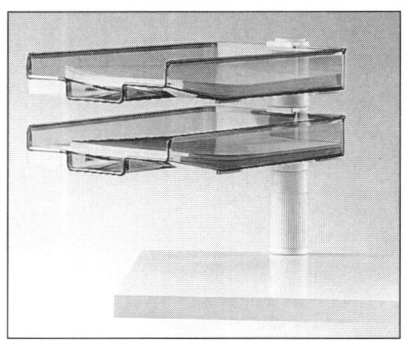

6-2. H'A'FELE America Company's desk lamp uses an energy-saving light source and highly polished anodized asymmetric reflector to ensure excellent illumination, without shadows in any position. The monitor stand is a rotating platform designed to provide the viewer with full control of angle and distance. The letter trays are real desktop liberators that speed up any job. Papers can be placed out of the way, suspended above the work surface on two or more levels. Trays can be swung round their axis effortlessly. *(Reprinted with permission from H'A'FELE.)*

monitor glare. The best designed environment won't be of any help if users can't easily make furniture adjustments or don't take the recommended rest breaks.

This section presents current health/safety recommendations, enabling products designed to minimize accidental injury related to computer use, and enabling features for people with disabilities, with the product information grouped by the physical disability it enables.

Recommendations and Aids for the Reduction of Eyestrain

In some cases, eyestrain may simply be due to vision defects that are correctable with glasses or lenses (Hembree, 1990). On the other hand, individuals who spend a great deal of time in front of a monitor may suffer from eyestrain as a result of screen glare. Many individuals find that special glasses corrected for the VDT distance are only helpful if prolonged computer work is necessary.

Back pain can be an additional problem to eyestrain in conditions where glare or lighting are problems. Screen reflections tend to make users bend forward to read the screen, causing static loading in the back muscles. Ways of dealing with the problems of screen glare and lighting include:

- Controlling window glare
- Adjusting screen angle
- Angling monitor screens
- Using antiglare screens and filters
- Using appropriate overhead lighting
- Optimally placing written copy

Window Glare

It is preferable to place the VDT screen perpendicular to the window in order to minimize glare (i.e., the user's line of sight is parallel to the windowpane). If the user faces a window while seated at the terminal, intense light in the field of view may wash out the character images cast on the retina, thereby reducing visibility and increasing eyestrain (Hembree, 1990). If the VDT faces the window (user's back toward window), window light and images can reflect in the screen, also impacting visibility and contributing to eyestrain. Monitor glare can be checked by looking for face or image reflections when seated in front before turning the computer on. Often the glare can be reduced by angling or tilting the monitor or by placing a visor of black construction paper around the top and/or sides of the monitor (Dainoff and Dainoff, 1992).

Flexible window treatment can also help to minimize window light fluctuations caused by weather or seasonal changes; transparent blinds or transparent roller shades can be lowered when needed and drawn when not. Using a combination of transparent shades and vertical blinds is an alternative that allows for a great deal of flexibility. Using several small segments of window treatment rather than fewer larger segments also allows for greater flexibility in controlling light fluctuations from windows.

Tilted, Recessed Screens

Several companies have produced computer desks that recess the VDT below the work surface at a fixed angle. This solution frees up more of the workspace surface and minimizes screen glare. However, it does not provide individual flexibility in the angle of tilt and the distance from eye to screen.

If one is selecting tilted, recessed-screen furniture, it is important to make sure that the angle and screen distance fall within ergonomic recommendations. Dainoff and Dainoff (1992) recommend that the operator's line of sight be kept between 10° and 20° below the horizontal to minimize excessive head angles. Some users, especially those with bifocals, may go lower, to around 30°. A range of 15 inches to 25 inches is recommended as optimal eye-to-screen distances. Ideally, the head should be held straight and should not be tilted up or down.

Not all recessed monitor systems have an adequate work surface for mouse or digitizer input devices. If mousing or digitizing is important, be sure the selected system has mouse or digitizing pad support with adjustable horizontal and vertical positioning that is within an immediate reach zone.

Antiglare Screens and Filters

The April 1993 issue of *Modern Office Technology* indicates that while most monitors come with screen glass that reduces glare from office lighting, there are also antiglare coatings available for monitor screens used in especially bright office light or in direct sunlight. These antiglare surfaces reduce monitor glare in most lighting conditions, and some are equipped with static discharge wires that help reduce the amount of dust and dirt attracted to the screen surface, thereby alleviating another cause of eyestrain and fatigue.

Filters placed in front of VDT screens can also aid in controlling reflections. There are several types of filters: neutral density filters, micro-mesh filters, and circular polarizing filters. Neutral density filters reduce diffuse reflections from the screen phosphor by filtering light as it passes through the filter on the way to the screen, and again as reflected light is passed back through the filter toward the operator. However, this type of filter does not effectively control specular reflections from the glass surface of the screen. Specular reflections can be reduced by etching the surface of glass or by coating it. Micro-mesh and circular polarizing filters help control both specular and diffuse reflections. The honeycomb mesh of nylon fibers in the micro-mesh filters prevents wide-angle ambient light from passing through to the screen. However, this type of filter diminishes the on-screen legibility of characters when they are viewed at an angle. The circular polarizing filters block light in a fashion similar to polarizing sunglasses and polarizing camera lenses.

Appropriate Overhead Lighting

The Rutgers Environmental Health and Safety Office indicates that a combination of indirect lighting and task lighting creates the best lighting environment. It recommends:

- Using several small, low-intensity fixtures rather than a few large, high-intensity fixtures

- Using a mixture of indirect light fixtures that diffuse light and direct light fixtures with parabolic louvers that concentrate light

- Increasing brightness around the area of the glare source

- Using adjustable lighting controls to control brightness

- Using low-gloss paper

- Painting offending surfaces with a flat or semigloss paint to matte the surface finish

- Removing highly polished, shiny objects that may reflect in the monitor

- Following Illuminating Engineering Society lighting levels

- Positioning fluorescent light tubes parallel to operator's line of sight, but making sure that light fixtures are not to the front or directly overhead

- Keeping the screen clean at all times

Designing adjustability in lighting levels with individual control over levels around the work area can also provide necessary flexibility for eye contrast differentials with aging eyes (for more information on the characteristics of aging eyes, see Joseph Koncelik's article in Chapter 9—Marketing Universal Design).

Copy Placement

Awkward placement of written copy can increase eyestrain as well as neck strain. To eliminate refocusing of the eyes between copy and screen, copy should ideally be placed at the same viewing distance and in the same plane as the monitor (Dainoff and Dainoff, 1992). Some document holders, like those produced by Proformix™ of Whitehorse, New Jersey, have a surface with a concave curvature designed to conform to the natural curvature of focal distances. This curvature helps to eliminate the possibility of glare on material positioned on the document holder. There are numerous copyholders on the market in a variety of price ranges.

Aids for the Reduction of Hand, Back, Arm, and Neck Injuries

As the number of repetitive stress injuries grows and litigation against computer manufacturers and employers increases, creative product solutions to these problems are entering the marketplace. Many of these products seek to aid workers harmed by computer work as well as individuals with disabilities. As with many enabling products, flexibility is a critical factor in meeting diverse needs. (For a detailed listing of computer resources for individuals with disabilities, see "Apple Computer Resources..." and "Solutions..." in Chapter 10—Resources.) A wide variety of enabling products focus on addressing hand, back, arm, and neck injuries, along with other disabilities. These products include:

- Adjustable keyboards
- Head- and mouth-controlled input devices
- Voice input devices
- Tilting keyboard and mouse pad supports
- Adjustable workstation heights
- Palm and wrist rests
- Ergonomic seating
- Adjustable armrests
- Footrests
- Adjustable monitor placement
- Telephone aids
- Copy stands

6-3. The Graphic File provides a means of filing and indexing assessment materials of all sizes in a neat, space-saving, vertical format. *(Reprinted with permission from Logan Graphic Products, Inc.)*

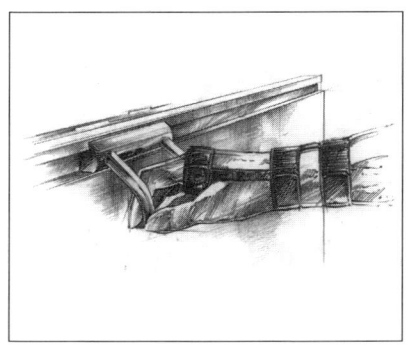

6-4. Meridian's enhanced access pull (offered in two styles) is the first and only pull designed specifically to meet or exceed ADA requirements for persons with upper extremity disabilities or ergonomic challenges. Both styles require no more than 6 pounds of distal strength to open a 150-pound loaded drawer from any functional angle. *(Reprinted with permission from Meridian, Inc.)*

Adjustable Keyboards

The traditional geometric shape of the keyboard, the QWERTY layout of keys, and the upward slope of the keyboard are carryovers from typewriter design. The QWERTY keyboard layout was purposely designed to slow typing speed so that mechanical jamming of manual typewriter keys could be avoided. Now that high-speed keyboard input is no longer a problem, there have been proposals for keyboards with alternative layouts. These have not been readily accepted, though, because of the massive amount of retraining that would be made necessary.

Fortunately, many alternatives are being proposed to deal with problems created by the shape, slope, and touch mechanics of the traditional computer keyboards which are inherent sources of hand and wrist fatigue. This fatigue is attributed to the rectangular keyboard shape and slope, which requires positioning the fingers parallel to the keyboard, thereby angling the wrist (ulnar abduction). Maintaining this posture for long periods of time increases the likelihood of cramping or other muscular disorders (Dainoff and Dainoff, 1986). Unlike the typewriter, which forces workers to pause for carriage return and paper insertion, the computer allows for nonstop keyboard stroking. Also, typewriter key strikes were cushioned by a slight spring-like action, while computer key strikes hit a hard, unforgiving base (Horowitz, 1992).

In addition, manufacturers are developing products with critical keyboard features that can assist people with cerebral palsy, muscular dystrophy, and arthritis, as well as quadriplegics who use head wands. These products include variable key sensitivity and the flexibility to place the keyboards perpendicular rather than parallel to fingers or wands.

The appropriate posture for minimizing repeated strain on wrists requires the following conditions (Dainoff and Dainoff, 1992):

- Forearms are parallel to the floor.
- Wrists are held flat.
- Keys are hit with a light touch.
- Arms and shoulders are relaxed with upper arms hanging vertically from shoulders, and wrists are held flat when typing.
- Elbows are not angled out to the side.

Products such as split and modified keyboards, wrist rests, special armrests, and tiltable keyboard pads have been developed to meet the above requirements and to achieve maximum adjustability and proper positioning of wrists, arms, elbows, neck, and shoulders.

A split keyboard developed by Grandjean allows for the right and left sides of the keyboard to be angled at 25° in their respective directions. The entire keyboard is then angled at 10° (DeWitt, 1992). Similarly, the Apple Adjustable Keyboard™ features a split alphanumeric keyboard that allows adjustment of the left- and right-hand sections up to a 30° angle. Detachable palm rests provide a flat surface to rest hands when not typing, and adjustable feet allow for flexibility in slope of the keyboard. The TONY™ keyboard, designed by Anthony Hodges of Mountain View, California, is hinged in the middle between the *g* and *h* so that the hands are positioned in a more natural thumbs-up position (DeWitt, 1992).

Another very flexible split keyboard on the market (and a prizewinner of the 1992 Johns Hopkins Search) is the Comfort™ Keyboard System by Health Care Keyboard Company, Inc., of Menomonee Falls, Wisconsin (see Figure 6-5). The Comfort™ Keyboard is broken into three parts (the right and left segments of the traditional keypad plus a numeric keypad) that can be independently raised, lowered, and rotated into an infinite number of positions to suit a variety of individual needs. The segments of the board can also be repositioned; the number pad can be placed in the middle or on the left for data entry. This flexibility in adjustment allows for individualized control that provides maximum comfort and accessibility when used with hands or a wand. The stickykeys feature eliminates the need for an operator using only one hand or a wand to press two keys at once. The slowkeys and bouncekeys features adjust the response time and pressure of keys. These features are especially helpful to people with spasticity or tremors. For those people with contractions/contractures (limits in joint range of motion), arthritis, spasticity, or tremors, the repeatkeys feature allows for modification of the response time for repeating functions.

BackCare Corporation of Chicago has a keyboard, the FlexPro™, that allows for angular and rotational adjustability of the QWERTY segment of the keyboard (as shown in Figure 6-6). This keyboard also features built-in adjustable hand rest pads.

A keyboard by Kinesis Corp. of Bellevue, Washington, recesses keys into two saucer-size wells about a hand's width from each other, and relocates hard-to-reach function keys, allowing for greater wrist support (DeWitt, 1992).

The DataHand® by Industrial Innovations of Scottsdale, Arizona, has replaced the conventional keyboard altogether and developed two padded hand rests and finger wells. Each finger can activate five different characters by pressing forward, backward, left, right, or straight down (DeWitt, 1992).

6-5. The Comfort™ Keyboard System from Health Care Keyboard Company, Inc., offers a very flexible split keyboard. *(Reprinted with permission from Health Care Keyboard Company, Inc.)*

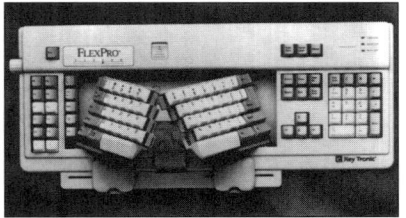

6-6. The FlexPro™ keyboard from BackCare Corporation of Chicago allows for angular and rotational adjustability. *(Reprinted with permission from the BackCare Corporation, Chicago, Illinois, FlexPro™ keyboard by Keytronic® Corp.)*

Head- and Mouth-Controlled Input Devices

A major enabling product for individuals who are unable to use their hands but have good head control has been developed by Prentke Romich Company of Wooster, Ohio. HeadMaster™ makes computer work accessible for those with high-level spinal cord injuries, closed-head injuries, and other disabilities that impair the use of upper extremities. The product consists of an ultrasound signal transmitted from a small box placed on top of the computer monitor and an operator's headset with sensors that measure the relative strength of the ultrasound signal and the physical tilt of the user's head. As users turn, raise, or lower their heads, the mouse cursor follows the action on the monitor screen. Mouse button action is achieved with a puff switch that is inserted into either side of the user's headset and mouth. The HeadMaster™ also works for individuals with physical or neurological deficits who must work with their heads in asymmetric postures. No special software is required, and the HeadMaster™ can be used on both Macintosh and DOS platforms.

Other software has been designed to be used with HeadMaster™. Prentke Romich Company has special software programs that generate an image of a keyboard on the monitor. Users can then point to the keyboard characters on the screen and activate them with a puff on the mouth tube.

For computer-aided design (CAD) functions, AbiliCAD™—also a headmaster/puff switch system—has been developed by Abilitech, Inc., of Thief River Falls, Minnesota. AbiliCAD™ has been used in a CAD training program jointly sponsored by the MultiResource Centers, Inc. (a nonprofit human services agency), the Minneapolis Rehabilitation Center, Thief River Falls Technical College, and Abilitech, Inc.

Voice Input Devices

Voice-controlled input devices are also available. IBM programmer Frank McKiel was a prizewinner in Johns Hopkins' 1992 Search with his talking mouse that generates musical tones, filtered noise, sound effects, and synthesized speech to provide users with audio feedback as they move a pointer over the windows, control, and other graphical computer features (Wagner, 1992).

Tilting Keyboard and Mouse Pad Supports

Several manufacturers of computer furniture have designed flexible keyboard supports that allow for positioning the keyboard at a positive or negative angle. Ergonomists believe that the critical position for arm-wrist-hand alignment on a keyboard is a straight line parallel to the slope of the keyboard (Hedge, 1992). If the wrists are flexed upward or downward during accelerated hand movements like keyboarding, there is a greater risk of carpal tunnel syndrome (CTS) injuries due to an increase of pressure and tension on the tendons. This means that if an individual is using an ergonomic chair in a position that tilts slightly backward from a 90° angle, then the keyboard pad support should be angled slightly upward to maintain this straight alignment. If the seated position is perpendicular to the floor or slightly forward, then the keyboard pad should be angled downward to maintain the correct alignment. This is an excellent example of an instance where the chair and computer desk selection must be integrated.

Mousepad supports should also slope in the same direction as the keyboard pad and should be placed within an immediate reach zone so that shoulder abduction, elbow rotation, and ulnar-radial deviation are minimized. Most often mouse pads are placed too high and too far to the right or left of the keyboard for maximum safety and comfort. For maximum flexibility, a mouse pad support should have adjustable horizontal and vertical positioning so that it can be placed within the immediate reach zone and at an appropriate height.

Adjustable Workstation Heights

Workstation height needs to be flexible and individually controlled. A noted occupational safety officer observed that a high work surface might cause workers to hunch their shoulders and hold their arms sloping upward away from their bodies. Conversely, if the work surface is too low, the worker will be forced to bend over, potentially causing neck and lower-back pain. There are many adjustable workstations on the market. Ease of adjustability and keyboard surface tilt are important considerations in product selection.

Palm and Wrist Rests

Many manufacturers have developed palm/wrist rests designed to reduce risk of developing repetitive strain injury (RSI) problems. Palm/wrist rests should follow the same inclined plane as the keyboard support does. The rest should be sufficiently broad to avoid pressure or pinch points as well as soft to firm but not rigid. Some rests are padded while others feature a firm surface that is textured enough to promote air circulation. The textured surface allows perspiration to evaporate, thereby reducing the risk of developing dermatitis attributed to soft wrist rests. If a rest is not needed because the keyboard position is low, at least 2 inches of table surface should be available for resting the palms or wrists (Dainoff and Dainoff, 1992).

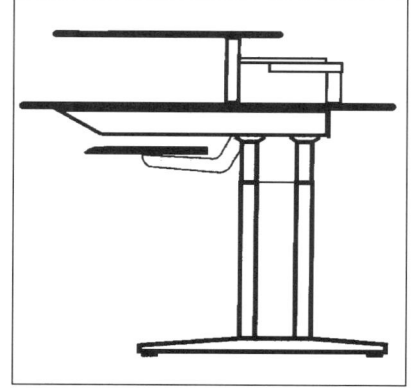

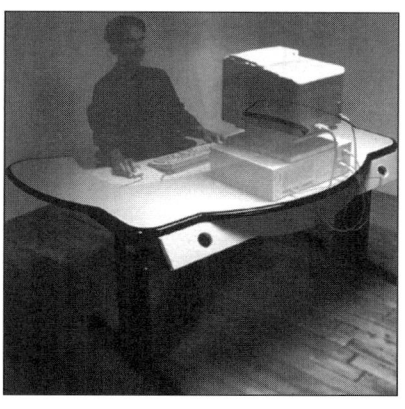

6-7. Industrial designer Stephen Barlow-Lawson devised a conceptual scheme called Biomorph™ to better design furniture to fit people "as they really are." His Biomorph™ desk is the result of his attempt to show how a system can accommodate the natural curves of the human body and subsequently enhance the quality of a worker's life and productivity. It's constructed of a new, solid-surface material, Gibralter™, made by Wilsonart. *(Reprinted with permission from I.D./Design, New York, 1993 U.S. Patent for Work Surface Design.)*

6-8. Equa™ chairs from Herman Miller, Inc., were designed by Bill Stumpf and Don Chadwick to provide a chair appropriate for people of all shapes and sizes. The low back, split-pad Equa™ workchair's unique achievement is its shell's patented shape and material. Once you've made a few quick adjustments for seat height, tilt tension, and arm height, the shell takes over. With no conscious effort from you, different areas of the shell flex and adjust naturally, maintaining support through each movement. For example, when you lean back, the "knee-tilt" mechanism keeps your feet flat on the floor and relieves thighs of extra pressure. *(Reprinted with permission from ©Herman Miller, Inc., 1984.)*

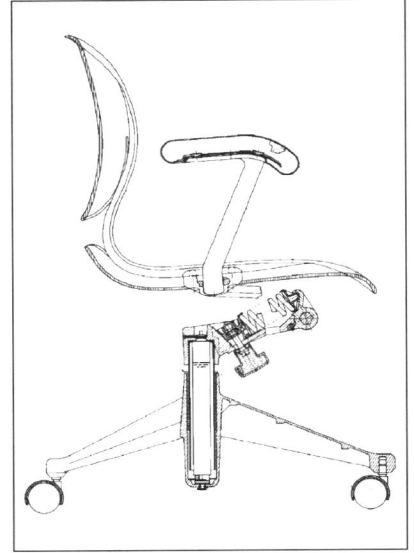

6-9. (Left) The GRAHL Ergomatic 2 Hugger has a patented dual-back that offers support in any position, elbow support with padded disc, and a six-star base that increases stability and anti-tilting without increasing the base diameter. *(Reprinted with permission from GRAHL Office Ergonomics.)*

6-10. (Right) The GRAHL Xellence Duo-Seat has a split seat that allows the left and right sides of the seat to be adjusted individually. *(Reprinted with permission from GRAHL Office Ergonomics.)*

Ergonomic Seating

Flexible, ergonomic seating is a critical feature in the enabling computer environment. In Chapter 5, the case study on the discovery® chair provided specific requirements for effective seating design. Hector Serber, president of the American Ergonomics Corporation in Sausalito, California, has designed a less traditional chair to rectify some of the constraints brought about in seating design due to assumptions regarding posture alignment and support (see Figure 6-11). Serber's Ergomax® 1700 (see Figure 6-12) offers:

- Continuous balanced motion, which eliminates dangerous excessive lumbar bending while performing reclining, erect, and forward-leaning tasks. The triple action lever independently controls the chair height, torso support tile, and friction brake.

- The torso support cushion provides an anatomic contour formed to the lumbar/thoracic "S" curve with wraparound lumbar support, and has an integrated armrest.

- Lumbar height operation with an easy grip, pull-knob

- Lumbar depth operation controlled by screw knob

- Continuous balanced motion seat with anatomic contour formed to buttocks and thighs with side bolsters and inner pommel

- Chair height that adjusts from 16 inches to 21 inches (floor to top of seat) by pneumatic lift

- Five-star base with hooded twin wheels

- Stock upholstery that is an olefin-based wear- and stain-resistant fabric

- Leg rest anatomically contours to shins and rotates 360°

- Neck rest formed to the nape of the neck/head with a push-button height adjustment

- Computer armrest contoured to the forearm

6-11. The Ergomax® 1700 allows seating in traditional and front-support postures. *(Figures 6-11 through 6-13 reprinted with permission from American Ergonomics Corporation; Ergomax® designed by Hector Serber.)*

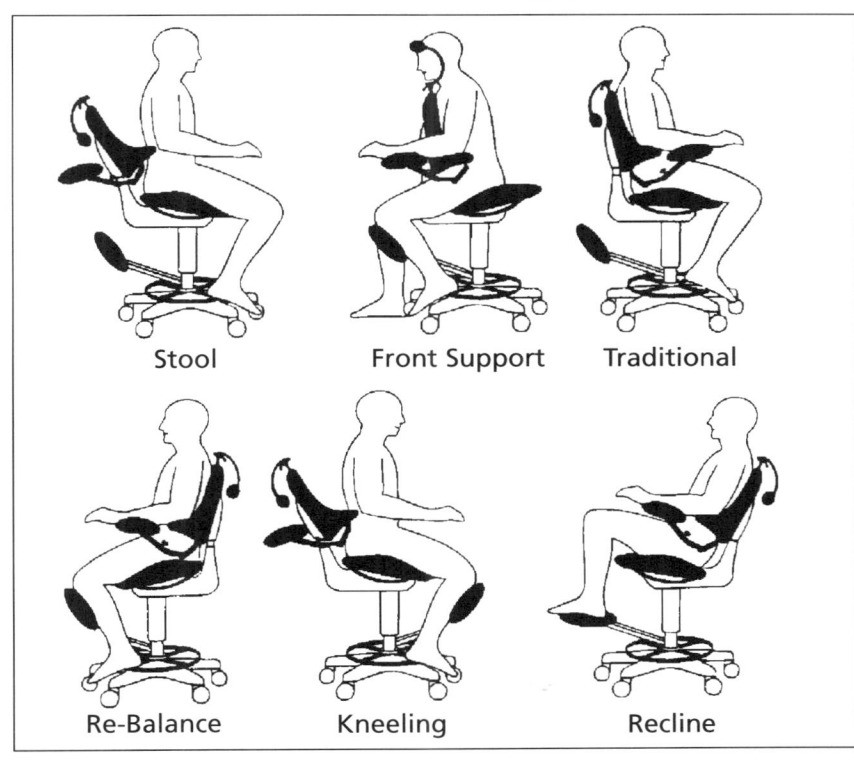

6-12. Diagram of the Ergomax® 1700.

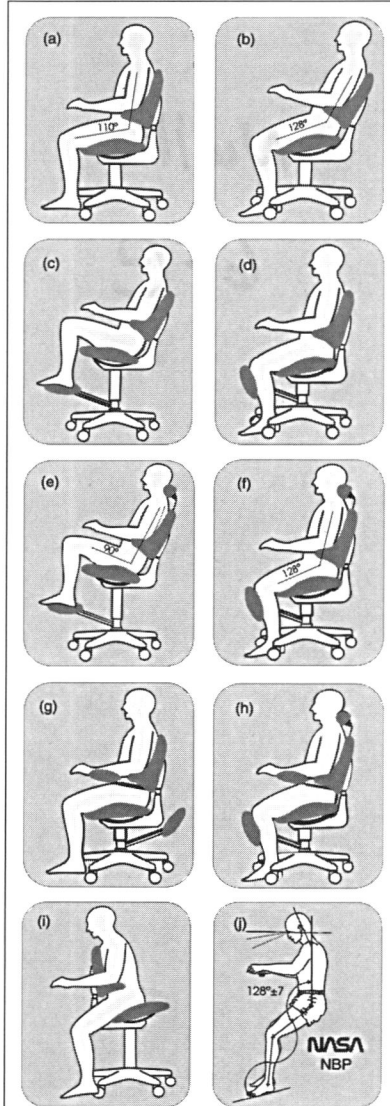

6-13. Ergomax® System of Postural Support (SPS).

Traditional Postures (a)

SPS begins by offering traditional, recline, and front support postures. It is fully adjustable to the user and to standard work stations.

Neutral Body Posture (b and j)

The NASA Neutral Body Posture (NBP), the most relaxed state for the body, is easily maintained by the Ergomax®. In reclining, re-balance, and front support, the seat-to-back angle can reach 128°, relieving body weight for a relaxed, restful, supported posture.

Leg Rest Postures (c and d)

All models 1100 and up have a leg rest that swivels and adjusts. It expands postures to one more level of support, adding re-balance plus reclining with leg support to the SPS. The leg rest also adds stability to the lower body to provide anti-slouch posture for additional comfort.

Head Rest/Neck Rest (e and f)

The neck rest adjusts for height and length and is contoured for nesting in the nape of the neck to hold the weight of the head comfortably while relieving tension and fatigue in the neck and shoulders.

Articulating Computer Arms (g and h)

The computer arms glide smoothly with the hands from side to side. They adjust to accommodate various typing styles and keyboard heights. They relieve stress and fatigue in the upper back, shoulders and arms, and reduce the risk of carpal tunnel syndrome.

Front Support Postures (i)

All models can accommodate a fully supported front support posture for lengthy forward-leaning tasks, such as microsurgery and lab work, that require full concentration and more precise support. This also eliminates low back stress and fatigue for safety and comfort in forward tasks.

Adjustable Armrests

If chairs with armrests are specified for the computer work space, it is very important that the height and angle of the rests be adjustable. Static armrests that are too high force the operator to raise the shoulders and arms, and they angle the elbows outward.

Some seating provides articulated forearm supports as part of the chair. Another option is articulating forearm supports, attachable to any work surface, developed by BackCare Corporation (see Figure 6-14). Articulated arm supports allow the user smooth-gliding, uninterrupted moveability. This device supports the weight of the arms so that the user does not need to rest that weight on the wrists or palms, and thereby maintains the wrists in a neutral, straight-line position.

6-14. BackCare Corporation offers a line of articulating forearm supports that can be attached to any work surface. *(Reprinted with permission from BackCare Corporation, Chicago.)*

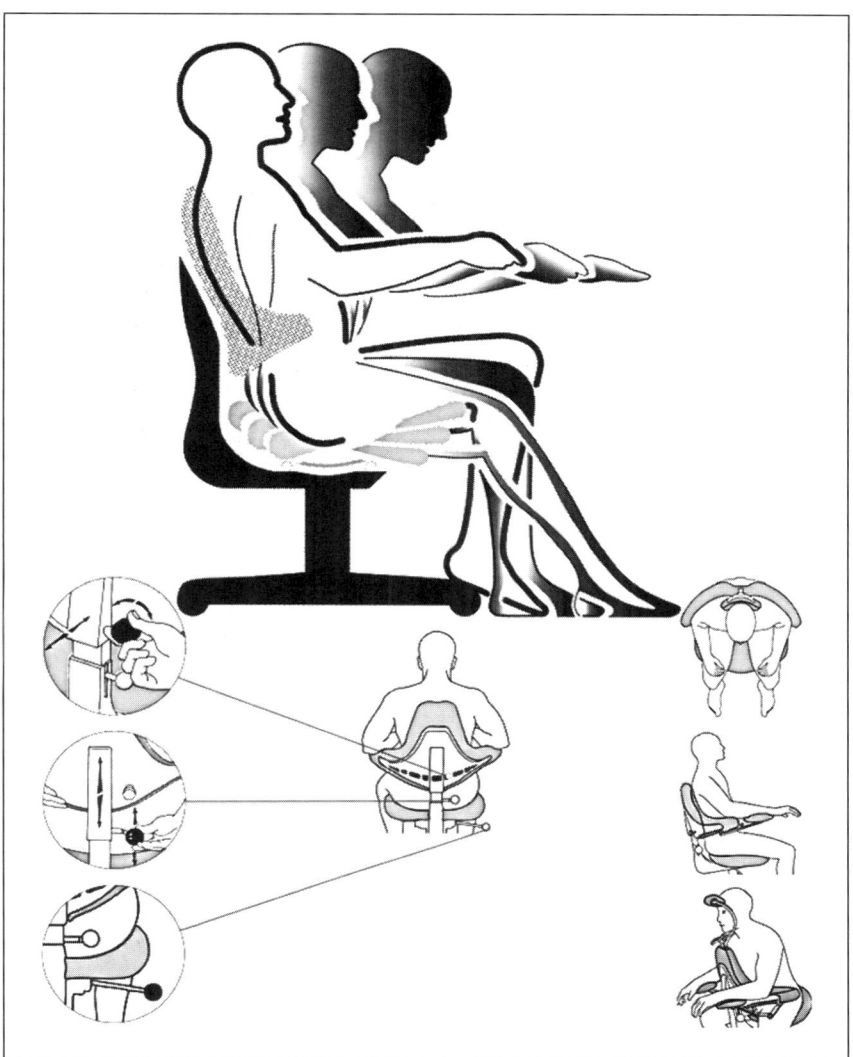

6-15. The Ergomax® chair offers (from top to bottom): (1) Lumbar Depth Adjustment, for increasing lumbar support for healthful spinal alignment; (2) Lumbar Height Adjustment, for optimal individual back support and comfort with minimum effort; and (3) a Triple Action Control Lever, for independent seat and back adjustability. *(Reprinted with permission from American Ergonomics Corporation; Ergomax® designed by Hector Serber.)*

Footrests

Most ergonomic recommendations require that lower legs be vertical and that feet be flat on the floor or some type of resting surface. Since the ergonomically safe work environment (chair height, work surface height, and so on) may require the chair to be too high to place the feet flat, footrests become an important component. Footrest formats can vary: Some are flat, some are angled from 10° to 30°, and some have a concave surface. The type of shoes worn by the user (flat-heeled or high-heeled) should be factored into the choice of footrest style. It is important to keep in mind that only the part of the footrest nearest to the chair augments popliteal height (the part of the leg behind the knee); the rest simply raises or lowers the toes (Dainoff and Dainoff, 1986).

Adjustable Monitor Placement

The device for supporting the monitor (whether split table support, adjustable stand, clamp on support, or stackable boxes) should allow for flexibility in angle, viewing distance, and monitor height, especially if the workstation is used by more than one person. The monitor should be placed about an arm's length from the body or as far away as one can comfortably read the screen.

Monitor vertical placement should allow for the user's head to be held straight with chin neither pointing down nor up. This vertical flexibility is important in accommodating users with bifocals, trifocals, or reading glasses (Dainoff and Dainoff, 1992).

There are many split-level, adjustable tables and monitor stands on the market. Where adjustable tables or monitor stands are not used, stacking trays like the stackABLE™ Monitor Risers produced by Able Ergonomics Corporation of San Diego can be used. These are a series of interlocking, stacking trays that allow monitors to be elevated in 1 inch increments. Paper or file folders can also be placed in the trays.

Telephone Aids

Keyboarding while talking on the telephone creates strain for the neck and shoulders over prolonged periods of time. Speakerphones or headsets allow the head and shoulders to maintain proper positioning while the user does both tasks simultaneously.

Copy Stands

Copy placement can positively or negatively affect posture and neck strain; laying copy flat on the desk encourages the user to lean forward, twist, or side bend the torso and/or neck, thereby creating a potential for neck and back strain. Document holders should allow for copy to be placed on the same plane as the monitor. If the user views the copy more than the monitor, the copy should be placed directly in front of the user with the monitor placed off to the side. Some holders can be moved up, down, and sideways because they are attached to the workstation by means of an adjustable arm, while others are designed to be placed directly in front of the operator. Built-in task lights, magnifying line guides, and a foot pedal control for moving the line guide electrically are also available features on some holders (Dainoff and Dainoff, 1992).

Aids for Noise Reduction

Computer noise can be a problem in environments where many computers are being used in one room, for example, in teaching and training facilities. Low-height acoustical panels (like those used in open office systems) placed behind the computer desks or between rows of back-to-back computers can reduce noise without reducing visibility. Sound-masking systems can be used in areas where open office systems do not provide sufficient noise reduction.

Protection from Electromagnetic Radiation

There has been concern that exposure to radiation emitted from VDTs can increase the risk of cataracts, reproductive problems (birth defects, miscarriages, spontaneous abortions), and facial skin rashes. According to William Murray, Chief of the Radiation Section of the National Institute for Occupational Safety and Health, Division of Biomedical and Behavioral Science, there is no scientific evidence that the above problems are directly related to radiation exposure from VDTs (1985). As yet there are no national or international standards for worker exposure to electromagnetic radiation (EMR) from monitors. While many experts agree with Murray and feel that radiation levels emitted from VDTs are not large enough to present a health hazard (Dainoff and Dainoff, 1992), some companies are looking closely at Sweden's national safety and testing bureau's recommendations on establishing allowable levels of EMR exposure and are producing monitors that follow these guidelines (April, 1993, *Modern Office Technology*).

In the meantime, many computer users are taking a "prudent avoidance" approach by maintaining a 4- to 5-foot clear space behind VDTs. This is based on the observation that the strength of the EMR field changes from the front to the back of the display, with EMR levels being acceptably low at 3 feet in front of the VDT and 4 to 5 foot at the back of the VDT (Krimmer, 1991).

Universal Design Strategy
Chemical Sensitivities
by Cindy Paulson-Schiefelbein, M.A., OTR

Chemical sensitivities and indoor air pollution are not specifically addressed by the ADA, but they are important factors in offices, public buildings, and private residences. Over the last several decades, in the push toward energy-efficient buildings, little recognition or thought was given to the "soup" of chemicals that could be outgassed from commonly used building and decorating materials. Products such as plywoods, fiber and chipboards, hardboard, wall and floor coverings, cabinet surfaces and laminates, furniture, window coverings, and upholstery fabric can all emit toxic substances from the formaldehyde or other petrochemicals from which they are made or treated. Gas appliances can also be offenders.

Recently there has been a growing awareness of the concept of the "sick building" syndrome, though most of medical science still does not officially recognize the area of chemical and environmental allergies or sensitivities. For those who are only too aware of the physical and emotional reactions one can experience when exposed to various substances or chemicals (reactions can include headaches, nausea, insomnia, skin rashes, respiratory problems, severe joint pain, anxiety and depression, and so on), one recognizes the need for solutions.

By making some broad suggestions of substitute products for the chemically sensitive and providing names of companies that sell them, as well as some names of consulting services, this section begins to lead the way to better health and more responsible design and manufacture.

The following table identifies problem substances traditionally used in construction and home decoration and presents some general solutions to the hazards they create. However, further study and inquiry may need to be made before a workable solution is found for a specific sensitivities—even some of the "natural" products are quite odorous until completely dry or cured, and natural fibers can be grown with pesticides, which may remain as residue. (The suggestions, names, and references are only a starting point for further investigation; it's always best to self-test a product under typical working or living conditions.)

Where does the consumer begin to locate these products? Appendix A provides a listing of several companies and resources. If none of the resources can provide all the needed products, they may be able to refer one to another company or resource. Some of the companies deal in only one type of product; others provide a variety of products from building materials to cleaning products and cosmetics.

Common Chemical Concerns

Problem	Solution
Wood Products: plywood, particle, chip and hardboard; paneling (formaldehyde outgassing)	Use solid wood or exterior grade plywood that's been sealed with a vapor barrier; steel beam; non-toxic tilt-up concrete slabs; or rammed earth construction.
Subfloor: particle board or plywood made with formaldehyde	Use formaldehyde-free subfloor (Wonderboard, Homasote 440, or Carpetboard); or seal with vapor barrier.
Floors and Coverings: carpet and rugs (made of toxic synthetics, and/or treated with toxic substances for stain protection)	Use carpet sealers, untreated natural fiber carpet (fibers grown without pesticides), wood flooring or tile; non-toxic cement; or natural linoleum (Forbo).
Vinyl Floor Covering: petrochemicals and plasticizers	Use natural or ceramic floor tiles (commercial grade recommended for large areas), and non-toxic cement.
Wood Floor Finishes: solvents and sealers	Use natural finishes and provide adequate ventilation and drying time.
Wall Surfaces and Coverings: vinyl wallpaper (plasticizer outgassing); glues (formaldehyde, fungicide, or mildewcide); drywall joint compound (preservatives, formaldehyde, and mildewcides)	Use wall coverings of paper, linen, or metallic foil; use low-toxic glues or wheatpaste glue; or use low-toxic joint compounds.
Adhesives (used in flooring installation): formaldehyde, hydrocarbon solvents, and reactive chemicals	Use water-based or natural adhesives.
Tile Set and Grout: preservatives	Use portland thinset and grout without preservatives.
Paints, Stains, and Finishes: oil-based and alkyd products contain hydrocarbon solvents; water-based paints may contain biocides and solvents	Use low- or non-toxic products that are water-based and don't contain mildewcides and fungicides.
Wood Preservatives: fungicides and mildewcides	Use low-toxic or natural wood preservatives and naturally rot-resistant woods (redwood, cedar, cypress).
Adhesives and Glues: toxic hydrocarbon solvents	Use natural and non-toxic glues.

Problem (continued)
Furniture: plywood and particle board with formaldehyde

Fabrics: formaldehyde, plasticizers, fungicide, and so on, for stain and wrinkle resistance

Solution (continued)
Use solid wood furniture, metal, or natural materials (bamboo, wicker, rattan, and so on).

Use untreated natural fiber fabrics. Washable fabrics can be soaked in hot water and laundered several times to remove the stain-resistant finish and biocides.

(Adapted from Alvarez)

Case Study
Cornell University's International Facility Management Program
by Franklin Becker and William Sims

Rapidly changing demands on office environments have elevated the position of the facility manager and facility management teams in both large and small corporations. Their decisions on space planning, furnishings, and management policies are increasingly important as the complexity of the office and work environment grows. The following study addresses the relationship between research and facility management issues.

In the autumn of 1989, the Cornell University International Facility Management Research Program was initiated under the theme "Managing Space Efficiently." The program's purpose was to respond to the following five factors that were transforming facilities into a major management issue in many large organizations:

- Increasing cost of space
- Rising space requirements
- Changing employee expectations
- Dynamic organizations
- New information technologies

The major goals of the research were to systematically investigate how different types of facility innovations affect organizational performance and to achieve a better understanding of the nature of organizational and technological changes required to effectively support selected facility innovations. Emphasis was placed on studying successful cases, from which effective solutions could be learned.

Comparative case studies using a combination of interviews, surveys, observations, and archival data were selected because they offered the best chance of understanding the dynamic interplay of different factors. Using this general approach, three specific studies were jointly selected by the Cornell team and consortium members:

1. Shared Office Case Studies
2. Universal Footprint Case Studies
3. Approaches to Portfolio Management Case Studies

This study discusses the first two of these, offering detailed examples of each along with some general conclusions for use in facility management.

Shared Office Studies

Space allocation practices involving no individually assigned desks, workstations, or offices have proven successful from a financial, employee satisfaction, and productivity viewpoint. Most successful were approaches that were productivity-driven rather than cost-driven, and that were designed from the ground up as integrated systems that considered information technology, management, and policy needs as much as physical design and layout. In most cases employees rated their own performance as being about the same or slightly better than when they had personally assigned offices. When combined with substantial space savings, this data suggests that shared offices can be highly cost-effective.

Universal Footprint Studies

Reducing the number of workstations or offices to three or less was effective in reducing the costs and disruption of relocations (or churn) while still maintaining generally high levels of employee satisfaction. A critical success factor is that the same size footprint must be capable of housing (and used to house) different furniture and equipment components, depending on specific job functions and workstyles. Supervisors were initially more resistant to the idea than professionals and support staff, but over time these management levels accepted the system because of its organizational benefits.

General Conclusions

At both a macro level (asset and portfolio management) and a micro level (space planning and allocation), firms are experimenting with new approaches that challenge the status quo. The use of differences in the amount and type of space and furnishings to reflect status and to reward performance is giving way to a concern for providing employees with the tools they need to get their job done—wherever and whenever that makes most sense. Facilities are being developed and managed with a much greater concern for their effect on costs and productivity. The best approaches to managing space efficiently balance, consciously and formally, the need to reduce costs with the need to enhance employee effectiveness. The data from these studies indicates that new approaches to portfolio management and space planning, including non-territorial offices and the use of a universal footprint, are meeting the twin challenges of reducing costs and maintaining, if not improving, productivity. The following examples show the methodology and findings.

Non-Territorial Office: Field Sales Office, Helsinki, Finland

Helsinki is the sales headquarters for an American-owned multinational computer company. The overall size of the headquarters office staff is approximately 600 people, about 450 of whom use some form of the non-territorial office. The following description concerns the original installation of a non-territorial office for field sales staff on a single floor of a leased building a few hundred meters from the headquarters building. The "Postscript" section describes how the concept has been applied throughout the headquarters building to a variety of different groups. In understanding this site, it is important to realize that the Finland office is far removed not only from its American home office, but also from its European headquarters offices. The country area manager is widely known as a maverick and a high risk-taker. His company has regularly been among the most profitable both in Finland and among the parent company's many different country locations. Innovation and risk-taking are central to this firm's, and especially this site's, corporate culture. Sales staff are motivated by and assessed against the ultimate performance measure for this type of work: sales and profits.

Goals
- Increase profitability; meet or exceed sales targets.
- Enhance all forms of communication, creating an innovative workplace that is fun to work in and that facilitates teamwork.
- Incidentally, reduce occupancy costs.

System Description
This site illustrates superbly the idea of a highly interdependent ecological system shaped by the desire to integrate new developments in information technology, management structures and styles, and interior design. It reflects the critical role senior management plays in significant innovation, and the impossibility of understanding the system by looking at only its constituent parts. The intent of

management was to stimulate informal communication and more teamwork by removing panels and walls, thereby creating the likelihood that people would both sit next to and talk to different people as they occupied different unassigned work areas. Thus the non-territorial aspect of this case evolved from the goal of stimulating informal communication and teamwork, not from cost-cutting.

Physical Design

The floor plan (see Figure 6-16) and the photo (see Figure 6-17) show the original free-address installation. (The idea was subsequently implemented, albeit with less extreme furniture, throughout the headquarters building for all users who spent 60–70 percent of their time out of the office.) The system's salient physical characteristics are a complete open plan (with the exception of a glass-enclosed conference room); a wide range of work settings and furniture including residential style sofas, reclining easy chairs, and an outdoor swing set; large, colorful wall murals; and a small, centrally-located but visible kitchen with stand-up break areas.

Storage

Each staff person has one assigned rolling file pedestal. These are "parked" in assigned spots beneath cordless phone chargers located near the entrance to the office. The maximum distance between the desks and "parking lot" is

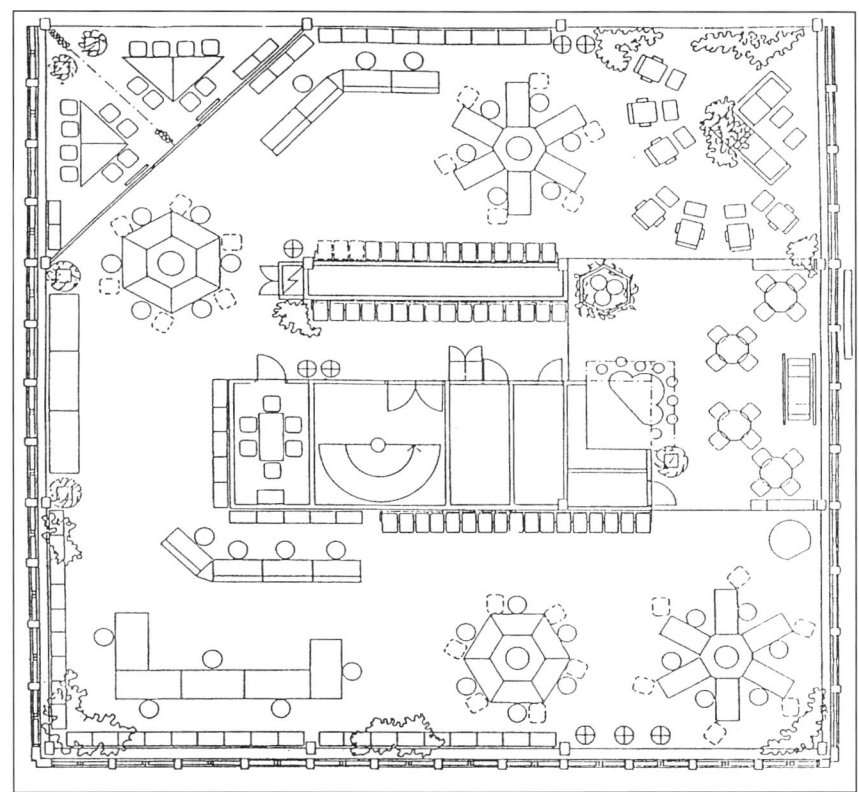

6-16. Non-territorial, free access floor plan.

6-17. Informal, lounge-type work areas. *(Figures 6-17 through 6-21 reprinted with permission from the Cornell University International Facility Management Program.)*

approximately 75 to 100 feet. Centralized storage for reference materials and manuals is provided in the form of free-standing, rolling, circular shelf systems that rotate so materials are accessible to the 4 to 5 desks surrounding it. There are a number of these free-standing circular files located throughout the office; they are maintained and updated by one of the support staff to ensure that all materials are current and correct. The firm also has a sophisticated electronic-mail, messaging, and administrative system that eliminates considerable paperwork.

Technical Support

This site has one of the largest installations of cordless telephones in the world. It also has ordinary telephones for some outbound calls (for security and sound quality reasons). The cordless phones work for 10 to 12 hours before recharging and have a range of 262 to 934 feet, depending on the model. Fifty percent of the sales staff also have mobile telephones that can be portable or permanently fixed in their cars. (The same mobile telephone system is used throughout Scandinavia, the Netherlands, and Switzerland.) Terminals are located throughout the office for logging onto the network. (This electronic network houses all functions including travel itineraries, customer documents, and telephone directories. The terminal is a major step toward a true paperless office.) Over 50 percent of the employees also have terminals at home, all of which are supplied by the company (about 300 total) and are directly connected to the company's network. The country area manager strongly believes that a high technology company should use and make available to its staff the best and latest in high technology equipment that can enhance productivity; he views the cost of this technology as quite modest in relation to the sales volume generated through its use.

Administrative Support

Staff are free to come in and out of the office as needed to work at home, on the road, or at client offices. Employees are allowed to reorganize furniture and equipment to meet task requirements: The only stipulation is to check and work with others to insure that the changes do not undermine others' work effectiveness. The order administration staff answer any calls not received on portable phones, and they help with follow-through calls to customers, generating pricing information, placing orders for delivery, and so on.

Use Policies

Employees can use any unused desk or work area at any time; managers have no special office accommodation. If a phone call is not answered, it is forwarded to the administration staff and a message is left on a bulletin board. The bulletin board is also used to let others in the office know when a person is out; times for his/her return are indicated in a box with that person's initials marked on it. The boards are placed in central, highly-visible areas.

Implementation Process

The country area manager selected and empowered three innovative, risk-taking managers to develop a new approach to space planning. This management team mobilized all the other staff. The entire process was guided by a few inviolable rules set by the country area manager: no panels (because they inhibited communication); non-assigned offices (fewer desks than people) to promote more contact among staff who sit next to different people on different days; reduced storage; and more use of electronic media. For the original project no budget was set; the project leaders were told to get what they needed to do the job. However, the goal was very clear: to meet or exceed sales targets. The project was driven from the beginning by a focus on productivity, not cost-cutting.

Initially, several different outside architects were hired to assist on the project, but all were unable to break the mold of conventional office planning. In the end, the group itself planned the layout and selected the furniture after doing detailed analyses of work patterns. The project was not publicized until it became a (successful) reality. Being in a remote location reduced corporate scrutiny and control during the process, as did being a highly profitable subsidiary.

Cost Implications

Only limited cost data were available. Occupancy requirements went from about 46 to 52 square feet per person to 26 to 33 square feet per person—a space savings of about 60 percent.

Employee Response

Employee response to the non-territorial offices throughout the headquarters site has generally been positive. The original non-territorial workplace became a highly distinctive, fun place to work: Employees reported feeling a sense of freedom and a strong group identity and team feeling; respondents indicated that having the right equipment, especially the cordless telephones and the latest computers, contributed significantly to increased work effectiveness and satisfaction with the overall system. Rank and file staff also received a lot of positive publicity in Finnish media.

The staff commented that the open plan and varied seating locations increased informal communication, thus reducing scheduled meetings and leading to a much better understanding of the overall group's activities. Group managers reported that less time was needed for formal job training because new staff could learn easily by listening, questioning, and watching their experienced temporary neighbors in the office. The company also reported less turnover (from a company-wide average of 9 to 3 percent in the first year).

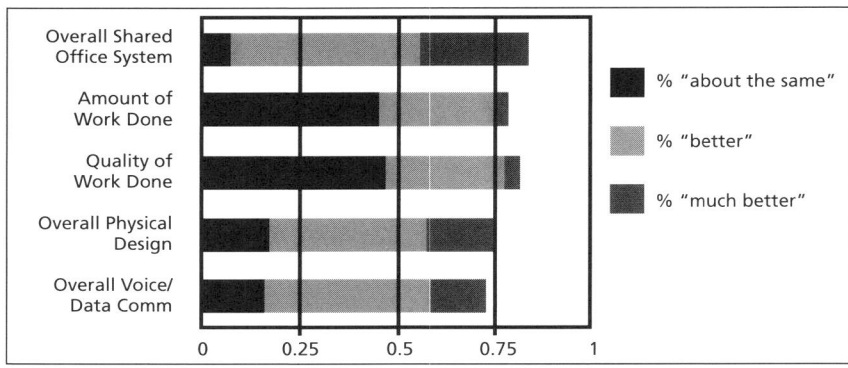

6-18. Initial implementation, work effectiveness—frequency of responses of "same" or "better."

Figure 6-18 shows data collected several years after the initial project completion for a sample of occupants located in the original office installation. The space was virtually unchanged from its original state, but the occupants were different. About 70 percent of the respondents rated the non-territorial office as "better" or "much better" than their previous office accommodation. The amount and quality of work done was rated as "about the same" as under the previous form of office accommodation. As was true of other sites, the opportunity to display personal items was not rated as high; but neither was its importance. Access to files and reference materials was rated as important, however, and almost 50 percent of the respondents felt that this aspect of the office had become worse as a result of the new office planning approach.

Conclusions and Lessons Learned

Access to files and reference materials was an inconvenience, even with wide use of cordless telephones and distributed shared filing. For some workers, not having materials right at hand was considered annoying, despite the fact that these materials might only be a few feet or seconds away from their desk. Cordless phones made it possible to keep contact with someone while going to reference materials or files, but the technology—at least at that point—did not totally alleviate staff concerns about access to reference materials and files.

This site underscores the importance of a clear and strong top management mandate for risk-taking and change, and a willingness to put the right people for a particular job in top management positions, regardless of their formal education or title. It is also a brilliant example of developing a corporate image and identity around a distinctive design that evolved from a desire to change a typical corporate image of bland "professionalism." However, it is important to underscore the fact that the data comparing the original and subsequent non-territorial installations suggest that the rather extreme design of the original office was useful for generating widespread positive publicity, but the data also indicated that the extreme design was not necessary to create the generally positive response among staff.

Postscript

This company's first implementation of the free address office occurred on the second story of a two-story speculative office building a few hundred meters from the headquarters building. The concept was subsequently carried into the headquarters building in a series of projects involving different departments. The key princples carried over (i.e., unassigned desks, no panels, reduced storage), but with each project the furniture became more conventional (because budgets were set). The remarkable outcome, in terms of typical corporate practice almost anywhere in the world, is that each department's area looks distinct: different furniture, different layout, different ways of working. There is no attempt here to create a unified design image. The focus now is on the facility management group working directly with staff and (more recently) an outside design firm that is comfortable with high levels of staff involvement and limited design control in creating a work setting that supports how each particular group works best.

Universal Footprint Office:
Insurance Headquarters, Hartford, Connecticut

Headquartered in Hartford, Connecticut, this is one of America's largest general insurance companies. Its home office facilities are housed in a number of large facilities, including both the original headquarters office and a new building linked to it that was built about 10 years ago. Rising costs and the need to become much more efficient have led this company to look for new approaches to space planning and design that reduce costs, especially those associated with relocations, which in one year cost over $3 million. Until quite recently, the company was very formal and hierarchically-oriented, but it is now seeking to become more team-oriented and to adopt a flatter organizational structure.

Goals

- Reduce cost, time, and disruption of relocations (churn).

- Provide greater equity in space allocation: few status differentials.

- Provide needed environmental support for different job funtions.

- Provide additional areas to meet in groups or teams.

- Provide better, more organized file storage in the workstation.
- Allow more light and views for rank and file staff.

System Description

The primary difference between the new universal design and the system it replaced is that the new approach basically eliminated the use of different workstation and office sizes to reflect differences in status. The new design replaced the old workstations with two basic footprints. The way in which cabling, conferencing, and offices were organized was intended to reinforce both new management concepts (e.g., flatter organization, more egalitarian, more teamwork) and to compensate for the loss of some space (i.e., smaller management offices) with more conference and meeting rooms.

Physical Design

Figure 6-19 shows the plan of the universal footprint. Managers and directors moved from 150 square foot offices on the perimeter to 120 square foot enclosed offices on the interior (see Figure 6-20). All other employees (supervisors and lower) moved to 60 square foot workstations near the windows (see Figure 6-21). Vice presidents and the CEO still have large enclosed offices on the building's perimeter.

Some of the space saved by the smaller universal footprint was used to provide both more conference space and what were called "Oases." These were deliberately designed as permanent (but not fully enclosed) rooms that would be difficult and expensive to change or remove. The intent was to reduce the likelihood that as soon as additional space was needed for offices, the interaction space would be eliminated (essentially, because it was viewed as a luxury rather than a critical functional element). While workstations along the power spine (see "Technical Support") can technically be made different sizes simply by moving panels perpendicular to the spine, they are in fact the same size. However, the kind of furniture or function of each module varies with the job function (e.g., a drafting table can fit in a module that in another location is a standard L-shaped work station).

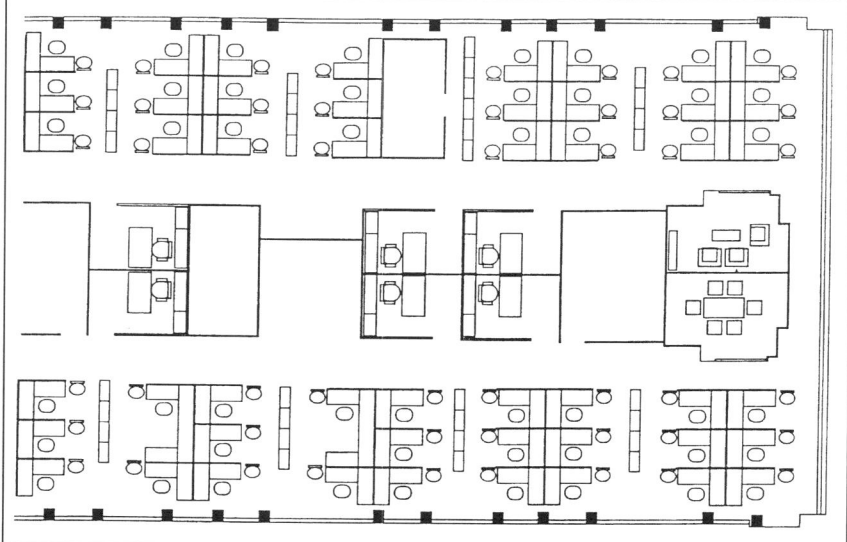

6-19. Universal footprint floor plan.

Similarly, the space between the spines can be used for different furniture and work functions, depending on what is needed for a particular group.

Technical Support

The office layout is based on a "spine" concept; that is, a module is established with a low "spine wall" containing power, data, and communication lines and leaving circulation corridors fixed to provide an overall space organizing principle. Workstations are located along this fixed spine. Cabling is fed through electrified panels along the spine, coming up from the floor. All workstations are wired identically, and all of the company's on-line systems are available at all desks.

Storage

Storage for each employee is provided at the workstation in the form of overhead binder bins hung off of the workstation panels. In addition, shared storage is provided in the center of work areas (between two service spines) whenever needed.

Administrative Support

No special administrative support is needed for this form of space allocation.

6-20. Standing universal footprint office for higher level managers.

6-21. Standard universal workstation footprint.

Use Policies

Staff have no choice in workstation footprint size. They can, however, request different furniture components for their workstation from a single line of systems furniture. Most recently the opportunity to "customize" one's own workstation footprint includes the ability to select ergonomic accessories from a catalog of products developed by the company for its own use.

Implementation Process

The adoption of the universal plan is part of a large-scale ($2 million) renovation of the corporate headquarters. This company has used formal employee surveys and post-occupancy evaluation methods for many years. In addition, for this project, the company created several full-scale mock-ups and asked staff to work in them. The mock-up was of the total environment, including sound masking, lighting, and HVAC systems as well as over 100 workstations in two different buildings. It cost $1 million to set up and was in place for 3 months. This turned out to save the company money in the long run because contractors bid much more accurately knowing exactly what the installation would be like. By the end, the company also felt very confident about what would and would not work.

Staff were asked to provide verbal feedback and to complete a survey. While individual employees provided feedback through surveys and interviews, employees were represented in the actual decision process by executives on a tenant working group throughout the process. In this sense, the process was top-down. The feedback from the staff and the cost data were presented to senior management, who then approved the proposed plans.

Cost Implications

The cost savings attributed to the universal footprint were estimated at somewhere between $300,000 to $1,000,000 annually. This savings came from the fact that workstations do not have to be reconfigured or modified each time an organizational change occurs, a new staff person is added, or someone is promoted. The time for relocating an individual was reduced to one hour, essentially a "shopping cart move" in which the only things physically moved are the person's files and personal belongings.

Employee Response

In interviews the employees reported that the aspects of the universal plan they liked most were the privacy; the availability of the oases; greater storage capacity; a cleaner, more pleasant environment closer to windows and natural light; the more professional appearance of the office; and the opportunity to hang pictures and other materials on the panels. Most of the expressed dissatisfaction came from supervisors and managers, the highest level staff occupying open workstations. A number of staff at this level felt the workstations did not provide adequate privacy, were not large enough to hold meetings with 3 to 6 people, and undermined morale because the same size office did not communicate differences in status.

The survey data show that ratings of the universal plan indicated that on average this approach was considered slightly "better" than the previous office accommodation. Approximately 90 percent of the respondents felt the universal plan was about the same or better than previous office accommodation; and, of this figure, 25 to 40 percent felt the system was "better" or "much better." Seventy-five percent of the respondents reported that the new approach was "about the same" or "better" in terms of individual morale and in terms of how the offices reflected how the company valued individuals. The new office accommodations were especially successful in terms of overall design, and were an improvement in access to work materials, number of work surfaces, and display of personal items.

Conclusions and Lessons Learned

The universal plan was generally well-received by rank and file staff. In fact, they benefited directly in the form of new furniture and better and more storage. Most dissatisfied were supervisors and middle level managers who lost some of the traditional status perquisites. It is important to note that implementing the universal plan is likely to be much less threatening than implementing the non-territorial office. The universal plan simply challenges the status quo to a lesser degree. At the same time, it makes for a more equitable distribution of space and provides for additional group and functional areas. It does not actually reduce the overall space requirement significantly since its primary cost savings comes from reduced costs of relocating offices; that is, moving people is far cheaper and faster than moving panels and other furniture. The service spine concept provides a strong organizing principle but also allow for flexibility, both in how modules are used along the spine and in what kind of furniture and work functions are accommodated in the areas between the spines. In effect the universal footprint, as implemented here, simultaneously limits diversity (in terms of status distinctions) and enhances it (through the opportunity it provides to staff to customize the workspace within the footprint, by selecting furniture elements and ergonomic products). The combination of increased satisfaction with the new office footprints, combined with significant cost savings due to lower relocation costs, makes this an attractive alternative for organizations who currently have generous space standards and/or a work environment that could benefit from a more functional and thoughtful design.

Conclusions

These studies reveal a pattern of much more conscious, deliberate thinking within organizations about the role facilities play in the organizations and how that role can best be served during a time of diminishing resources and rising expectations. Cutting across all the cases studied (a total of 14) is a new willingness to challenge conventional practices. This willingness to question the status quo includes such things as eliminating the use of office size and furnishings to reflect differences in status and rank, redefining the nature of facility quality, embracing a genuine concern for the end-user—now seen as a customer whose needs must be understood and met, and genuinely involving rank and file employees in the planning and design process. The customer orientation found in all of the case study sites is not a minor shift in attitude; it reflects a profoundly different way of doing business for these organizations. It is reshaping the definition of quality in buildings.

In general, significant innovation requires new ways of managing; the greater the innovation, the greater the shift in management approach required. In no case was it possible, or desirable, to try to understand the success or failure of a particular facility approach in terms of its constituent elements. Good facility design requires a systems or ecological view from the beginning; this means considering the nature of technology, management style and organizational practices, use policies, facility design, and work practices as interdependent components. The system is not likely to prosper, or even survive, unless all of these factors are working in harmony.

Design in Public and Commercial Environments

7

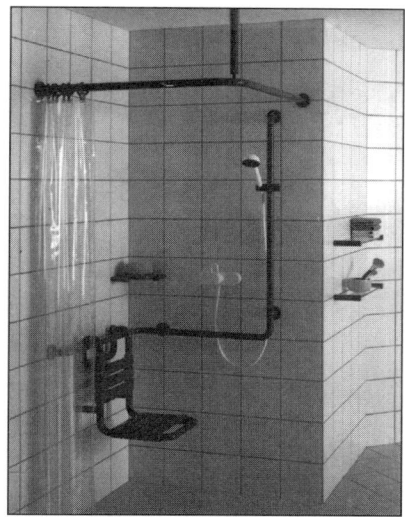

7-1. HEWI, Inc., manufactures a variety of seats, grab bars and other bathroom accessories for universal access in commercial and residential settings. Seats for showers and tubs are free standing, wall mounted with a fold-up feature, or hanging on a rail or inside a bathtub. *(Reprinted with permission from HEWI, Inc.)*

Public and commercial environments have been heavily impacted by the passage of the ADA. As noted in Chapter 1, virtually every place of business and every public building must be made accessible to individuals with disabilities. The cost for meeting this requirement can often seem daunting, especially for places with limited resources. However, as pointed out throughout this book, there are methods for making accommodations that are not overly expensive, and the returns on investment are high in terms of increased service to a neglected and changing population.

The case studies and strategies offered in this chapter cover a wide spectrum of public and commercial environments. Each is an example of how research can be applied to ADA compliance and universal design through comprehensive team activity. This is the theme of Kerry Nelson's theoretical essay "Defining and Designing Public Spaces." Henry Sanoff's case study of a child development facility uses a team approach in a very complex environment and shows the importance of end-user feedback throughout the design process.

Bradley Knopp and Joseph Maxwell describe a universal design approach taken in the creation of an air terminal, including wayfinding mechanisms and the redesigning of seating elements to better serve the entire population of air travelers. Anne Seltz discusses the need for increased focus on the acoustic environment and includes numerous examples of accommodation from her years of experience as an audiologist interested in the designed world.

Alan Wier provides a case study of high-speed railcar design from the standpoint of ADA compliance and reveals how student

7-2. The Interlude lavatory from Kohler permits full wheelchair accessibility and convenient countertop installation for commercial and residential use. The lavatory basin slopes to the rear, positioning the drain out of the way of a wheelchair user's legs. Interlude has an attractive half-round shape and a straight front that permits forward positioning of the lavatory in the countertop for easy reach (pictured here with Kohler's Touchless™ faucet). *(Reprinted with permission from Kohler Co.)*

teams (in this case from Industrial Design) can work together to create universal designs that far surpass the letter of the law. Finally, Susan Zavotka describes one restaurant's efforts to reach full accessibility despite having finished major reconstruction prior to the ADA's implementation. In doing so, she reveals how many relatively simple and inexpensive changes can be made that significantly improve access and use in commercial facilities.

Universal Design Strategy
Defining and Designing Public Places
by Kerry A. Nelson, ASID, IDEC

When one initially thinks about the term "public place," parks and plazas, post offices and courtrooms, libraries and schools may come to mind. But public places, as defined in the ADA, also encompass entities of public accommodation such as social service agencies, retail stores, banks, professional businesses, hotels, motels, restaurants, and theaters. All have one thing in common—service to the public—yet each functions differently, depending on the type and means of service provided.

Additionally, each public space possesses macro, middle, and micro environments—separate scales that interlock to form the whole. The *macro* environment includes the largest scale considerations, such as site and building access, the architectural envelope, horizontal and vertical circulation, and spaces for the general public's use. The *micro* environment involves the smallest scale considerations, private or individual spaces, and also specific areas such as storage rooms, rest rooms, an employee workstation, or a barrier-free parking space. The *middle* environment, as the name implies, falls in between the largest public and smallest private spaces. It might include secondary access corridors, an employees' lounge, an interactive holiday display in a retail store, or a private conference facility within a hotel.

The boundaries among these three sub-environments are difficult to define, since they often overlap. However, an understanding of the interdependency of the three is fundamental to the design of public places. The success of a design project is determined by the cohesive interaction of all of its parts. A failure of the design within any of these sub-environments can result in an unsuccessful public place. The macro, middle, and micro environments must combine to form the entity and must unify to support its intended purpose of public accommodation, as any design's content must support its intent.

The Design Process for the Built Environment

Any design process, including one that strives for a more universal design, can be divided into the following three stages of activity:

- Defining and analyzing the problem
- Solving the problem and communicating the solution
- Actualizing and evaluating the solution

Each of these stages can be further subdivided into phases, which, when followed sequentially with intuition and infused creativity, should result in a valid and appropriate design:

Define Problem	Design Statement: Who, What, Where?
	Research and Gather Information
	Write Up/Diagram the Program
Solve Problem	Conceptualization
	Schematic Design
	Design Development
Actualize Solution	Documentation
	Implementation
	Post-Occupancy Evaluation (POE)

The universal design process outlined in Chapter 3 shows that of these phases, attention must be devoted to improved definition of the problem through thorough research and user input. The process also requires actualizing a universal solution through the use of POEs. Finally, the entire process can be facilitated by using a team approach.

The Team Approach to Universal Design

Typically, the creative design of a commercial or public place project will involve many specialists: engineers, architects, landscape architects, interior designers, consultants, and contractors. Each specialist represents a discipline that often overlaps in scope with another. The territorial boundaries of specializations can often be hazy, resulting in the creation of incompatible solutions or areas of concern left unattended. Errors and gaps allow for design failures to occur in the interactive flow of the macro, middle, and micro environments. To maintain fluidity among the sub-environments, it is important that, in the design of public places, a team approach be employed with a high level of communication and coordination among the players.

To illustrate the importance of a cooperative effort, consider an icon of American culture: the shopping center or mall. In the broadest sense of the macro environment, potential users must be alerted to its existence. Advertising agencies and graphic designers might be retained to mount campaigns and create signage to lure and alert customers to the site. Site and building access is required for both vehicular and pedestrian traffic to get customers safely inside, which falls within the purview of the urban planners, engineers, architects, and environmental and landscape designers. Within the building, users must be provided with all of the stimuli possible to promote them to circulate, shop, and spend both time and money; this becomes the creative responsibilities of engineers, architects, lighting and interior designers, visual display artists, and an array of other consultants.

The middle environment in this case might be considered the department and specialty stores, public toilet facilities, telephone and water fountain areas, or food service establishments. It might also be considered the circulation within the selling floor of a retail shop and the cash/wrap counter where customers make their purchases. So the middle environment might be within the realm of responsibilities for just about everyone on the project, from engineers to store owners, architects to salespeople, and interior designers to subcontractors. Similarly, the micro environment could encompass the contents of atrium planters, dressing rooms, managers' offices, individual toilet stalls, or the other side of the above-mentioned cash/wrap counter from the salesperson's perspective, and again could be influenced by any of the disciplines.

If a cooperative effort among design team members is employed, it is highly likely that a good design, providing smooth transitions from the macro through to the micro environment, will be created.

Case Study
Redesigning a Child Development Center
by Henry Sanoff, Ph.D., AIA

The successful design of a complex public space such as a child development facility requires the integration of research and programming strategies. In the following case study, Professor Sanoff describes a collaborative design process that combines the following components: design research, design participation, and design development.

This case study describes how research findings can be integrated into a design process. The techniques described are based on the results of personal experiences in designing and programming child development facilities. Earlier experience suggests the need for a new approach that can engage the architect and the client/user group in a process that links children's developmental needs to facility requirements. Strategies are described that engage parents, teachers, and administrators in collaboration with the architect during the initial stages of design. This process has produced teachers with new capabilities in playroom planning and organization, as well as an understanding of the way in which architects make decisions. Although the example described is a campus child development facility, the techniques can be generalized for other types of facilities as well. The concept of the non-paying client is integral to the process. For programming purposes, people who use the building are the clients of the architect, whether or not they pay for services. Reference to the user as the non-paying client then attaches greater significance to the importance of user contributions, and to a more binding relationship between the paying and non-paying client.

Programming and design consultation were requested by the planning group of a proposed 75-child facility and training center for Wake Community College's Child Development Program in North Carolina. They contacted Henry Sanoff, Director, Community Development Group, North Carolina State University, for design assistance. Since this facility was intended as a demonstration site for the county, the department head and client representative, the teaching staff, and the educational consultants to the program were anxious to follow a planning process in which research findings, their expertise, and educational philosophy would be linked to design decisions.

The Design Process

Three major components of the collaborative design process are *design research*, *design participation*, and *design development*. These components precede production, construction, and evaluation. In this model, programming represents the synthesis between design research and design participation. This collaborative design process is a departure from traditional programming approaches since the client, the non-paying client, and the architect are directly involved in all decision-making stages. Furthermore, the stages described as design research and design participation subsume what is normally referred to as facility programming. This distinction enables the identification of discrete activities for each stage and clarifies the difference between information received from secondary sources, such as surveys and data bases, and from primary sources, such as direct, face-to-face involvement.

Typically, institutional client groups planning a child development center initiate a formal needs assessment that includes the following steps:

1. Campus survey of student child care needs
2. Surveys of campus child care centers
3. Site visits to child care facilities

4. Consultation with child care experts
5. Departmental planning

The above steps constitute the *design research* phase of the collaborative design process. The design research phase included a needs assessment, visits to other child development centers, and the establishment of educational goals, which included desired staff-child ratios and other factors inherent in a high-quality center. Although typically initiated by the client, the architect can often provide guidelines for more systematic fact-finding procedures. Surveys and visits to existing facilities, if properly organized, can reveal valuable insights into their functions, since casual visits frequently reveal only obvious results.

Design Participation

During this stage of the process, background research findings are integrated into the activity analysis. Accompanying the area requirement for usable activity space for each child is the need for well-defined areas limited to one learning activity, with clear boundaries from circulation space and from other activity areas. Well-defined activity areas or centers may be created with surrounding partitions, storage cabinets, changes in floor levels and surface materials, or other visual elements that suggest boundaries. Spatially well-defined areas support social interaction, cooperative behavior, and exploratory behavior, and they also prevent ongoing play from being disrupted by intruders. Running and chasing activities are common in classrooms where boundaries are not well defined. Conversely, well-defined activity centers, with clear boundaries from circulation space and from other activity areas, and with some visual or acoustic separation, decrease classroom interruptions and contribute to an increase in attention spans of the children. This implies that activity centers within the classroom require a high degree of spatial definition. The design task thus requires the development of a building program that can spatially respond to the developmental goals of the teachers of young children, as well as to goals identified in child development literature.

Modeling the Playroom

Since the playroom is the basic spatial unit of a children's center, prior familiarity with its organization can enable teachers to enter into a productive dialogue with the architect. Playroom modeling is an activity developed for a teachers' workshop that allows participants to manipulate fixed and movable playroom elements in order to achieve the desired developmental objectives. Working in teams of three people each, teachers are asked to design a playroom for a specific age group, such as infants or toddlers. Materials including cardboard, wood blocks, Styrofoam, construction paper, and plastic are provided along with instructions to the teachers for measuring and cutting the materials needed to construct a three-dimensional model (see Figure 7-3).

The model making is preceded by an exercise where developmental objectives and corresponding activity areas for specific age groups are discussed and agreed upon by each team. Model results are discussed by participants; playrooms are then joined together to resemble a building for different age groups. At this juncture, issues of playroom adjacencies, building flow, and locations of services are discussed by participants in an exercise that lasts for 4 hours.

Playroom modeling is an effective method for preparing the client group to actively and constructively participate in planning a child development center.

7-3. **Playroom planning workshop.** *(Figures 7-3 through 7-9 reprinted with permission from Henry Sanoff, Department of Architecture, NCSU.)*

Recording Activity Data

Planning the center began with focusing on the child as the basic unit of development. Next, the design participation phase involved the collection of behavioral data relating to each activity in which infants, toddlers, and preschoolers would be engaged. The activity center was the conceptual framework used for the design of the facility. The teaching staff of the child development training program identified the developmental objectives for each activity center by age group and the specific (or "molecular") activities that would occur in the activity center (see Figure 7-4 for one example).

The water play area, for example—the objectives of which were sensory and perceptual acuity, concept formation, and eye-hand coordination—would include such molecular activities as pouring, measuring, mixing, and floating objects, all of which are related to the primary activity. Activity data sheets were prepared to record the relevant activity information that served as a program and resource for future decisions. The data sheets provided a format where specific equipment needs could also be identified for future purchasing.

7-4. Activity center data sheet.

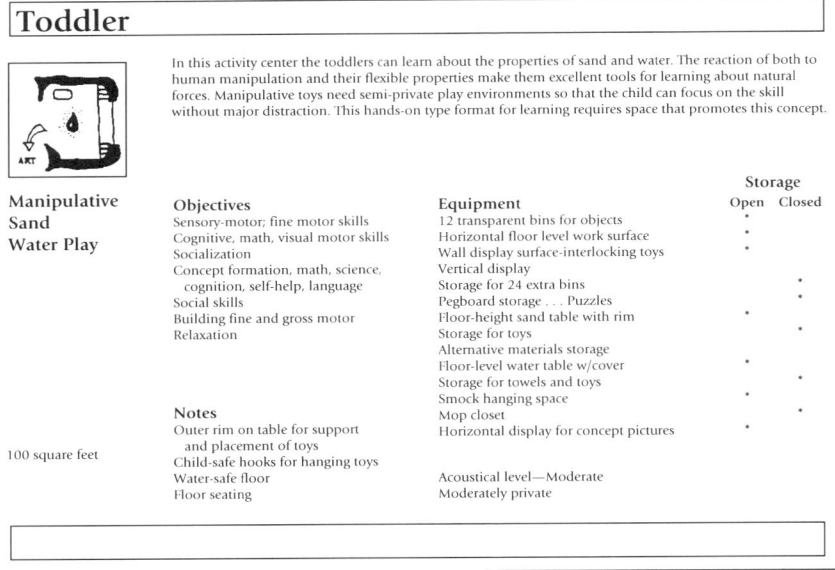

Spatial Planning

Since the planning of a child development facility also reflects a particular ideology about child development, a space planning exercise was developed to engage the teaching staff in decisions related to playroom layout. Since a planning guide of 50 square feet of usable space per child limited the number of activity centers that could be included in a playroom, scenarios were written by teachers about a typical child's day. The constraints encouraged the teaching staff to use trade-offs effectively since they were required to decide which activity centers were most important for various age groups. Graphic symbols corresponding to each activity center (as shown in Figure 7-5) enabled the manipulation of children's movement patterns in the playroom and was the first step in providing environmental information to foster the development of mental images. Spatially organizing activity centers on a "game board" corresponding to a playroom permitted the determination of which centers were to be fixed and which flexible. The spatial layout process required teachers to consider planning concepts, adjacency requirements, circulation, and

7-5. Teachers' arrangement of a toddler playroom using spatial symbols.

visual and acoustic privacy between activity centers. Most of all, the process reinforced the concept of activity centers.

The teachers worked through a playroom layout by manipulating activity symbols for each age group. They outlined the flow process from entering the facility, greeting the staff, removing coats in the cubby area, and moving to various activity centers. When planning the infant room, the teachers identified the diaper change area as the focal point, with surveillance to all other activity areas. To avoid the clustering of unsightly cribs, the teachers proposed decentralizing the sleeping activity into several crib alcoves. This process entailed small group discussions that required consensus in all decisions. When agreement was reached, the symbols were fastened to the base to constitute a record of the group's decisions.

Cardboard scale models of each playroom, with movable walls and furniture, were then constructed by the designer that corresponded with the flow patterns in the diagrams developed by the teachers (see Figure 7-6). This stage of the process permitted the teaching staff to visualize the three-dimensional implications of their decisions. Schematic models of the playrooms limited the amount of information presented at one time, conveying only the most significant issues in order to minimize information overload. Teachers could reconsider earlier decisions, particularly when they saw conflicts arise that were not easily predicted in the two-dimensional diagrams. Although circulation between activity centers was considered in the development of the activity symbol diagrams, the scale model conveyed the need to establish clear boundaries between centers to prevent distraction, while permitting the teacher an unobstructed view of all children's play areas. The scale models included information not shown on the activity diagrams, such as furniture and equipment, but the movable pieces were easily manipulated by the teachers as they referred to the activity data sheets.

When the teachers reached agreement about the best playroom arrangement, form diagrams were developed by

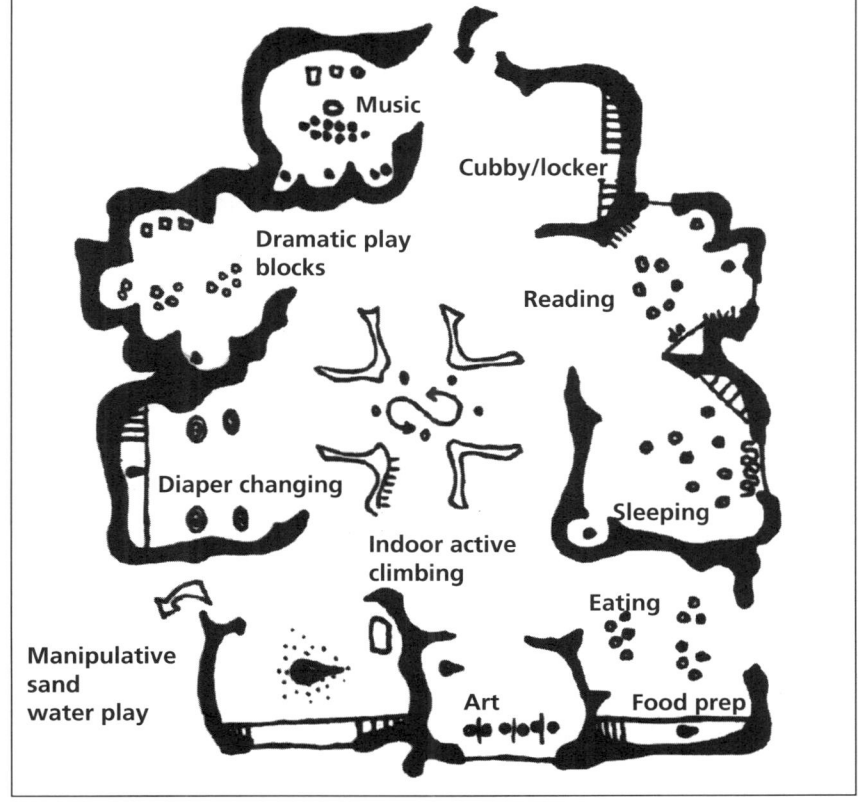

7-6. Form diagram of toddler playroom developed by designers.

7-7. Model of toddler playroom corresponding to spatial diagram.

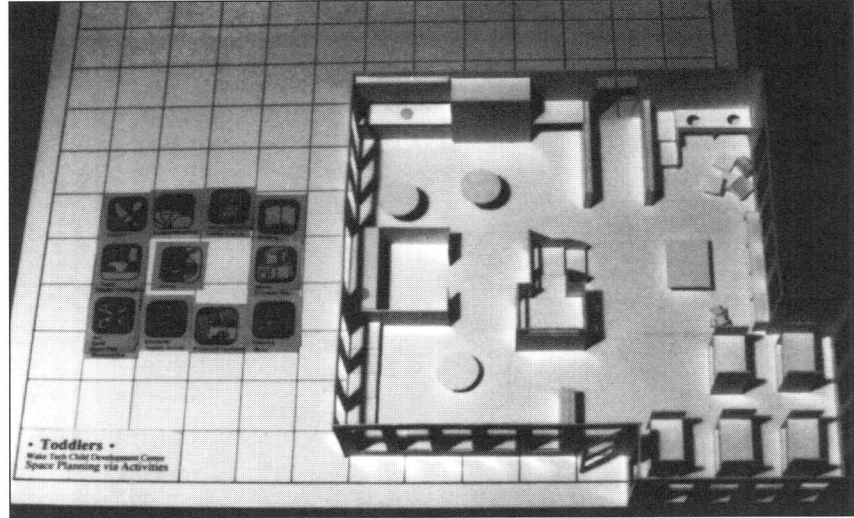

the designer, elaborating on their spatial decisions (see Figure 7-7). These diagrams combined activity centers into playrooms for different age groups. The diagrams allowed teachers to gain an understanding of "conceptual relationships." Teachers were thus better able to visualize how educational objectives could be enhanced through the design of playrooms.

Design Criteria

The results of the participatory exercises helped to generate design criteria and modify the requirements of the building program. Several statements were developed to describe the fundamental environmental characteristics of an effective child development center:

> The environment must be comfortable and inviting for children and adults. It should reflect an atmosphere conducive to children's growth. Materials and equipment should be easily accessible to children in order to encourage independence and self-esteem. An effective means of organizing the environment is to develop interest centers where the playroom is divided into areas that focus on specific activities. It is advisable that quieter activity areas be placed in close proximity in order to promote a quiet atmosphere. Activity areas demand visual clarity and well-defined limits if children are expected to interpret cues on appropriate areas for certain types of play. A quality playroom would include the following activity areas:
>
> - Creative expression/art
> - Literature/language art
> - Dramatic play/housekeeping
> - Block building

- Self-image, personal hygiene
- Science and exploration
- Cooking
- Water play
- Carpentry
- Manipulative play
- Music and movement

More specific guidelines that influenced the final solution included:

- Protected outdoor play area adjacent to each playroom
- Southern orientation for playroom and adjacent outdoor area

7-8. Interior view of "street" connecting all playrooms.

Facility Design

The teaching staff was involved in organizing the building components into a facility design using graphic symbols that corresponded to the major areas, such as playrooms, kitchen, offices, corridors, and lobby area. Age group adjacencies were considered, with opportunities for different age groups to have visual contact with each other. This was achieved in many ways, including low windows in each playroom for children to look into an adjacent room. The planning concept that emerged from the discussions was that of a "central spine" from which playrooms would be connected. The spine would be more than a corridor, yet similar to a street, where parents, teachers, and visitors could look into the playrooms and observe children's activities (see Figures 7-8 and 7-9). To emphasize the street concept, the area was filled with daylight through the use of overhead skylights. Each of the playrooms would have a central spine leading to a covered outdoor play area. Spatially well-defined activity centers were located on either side of the playroom spine. These playrooms included fixed areas for art and water play, and centers that could change their focus at the discretion of the teacher. The phrase "spatially well-defined centers" implies the need to be distinctly different from adjacent centers. This differentiation was characterized by physical features such as partially surrounding dividers or storage units, implied boundaries through the use of columns, changes in floor level or ceiling height, changes in floor covering, and changes in light levels. Learning materials, furniture, and equipment also contributed to the distinctiveness of the activity centers.

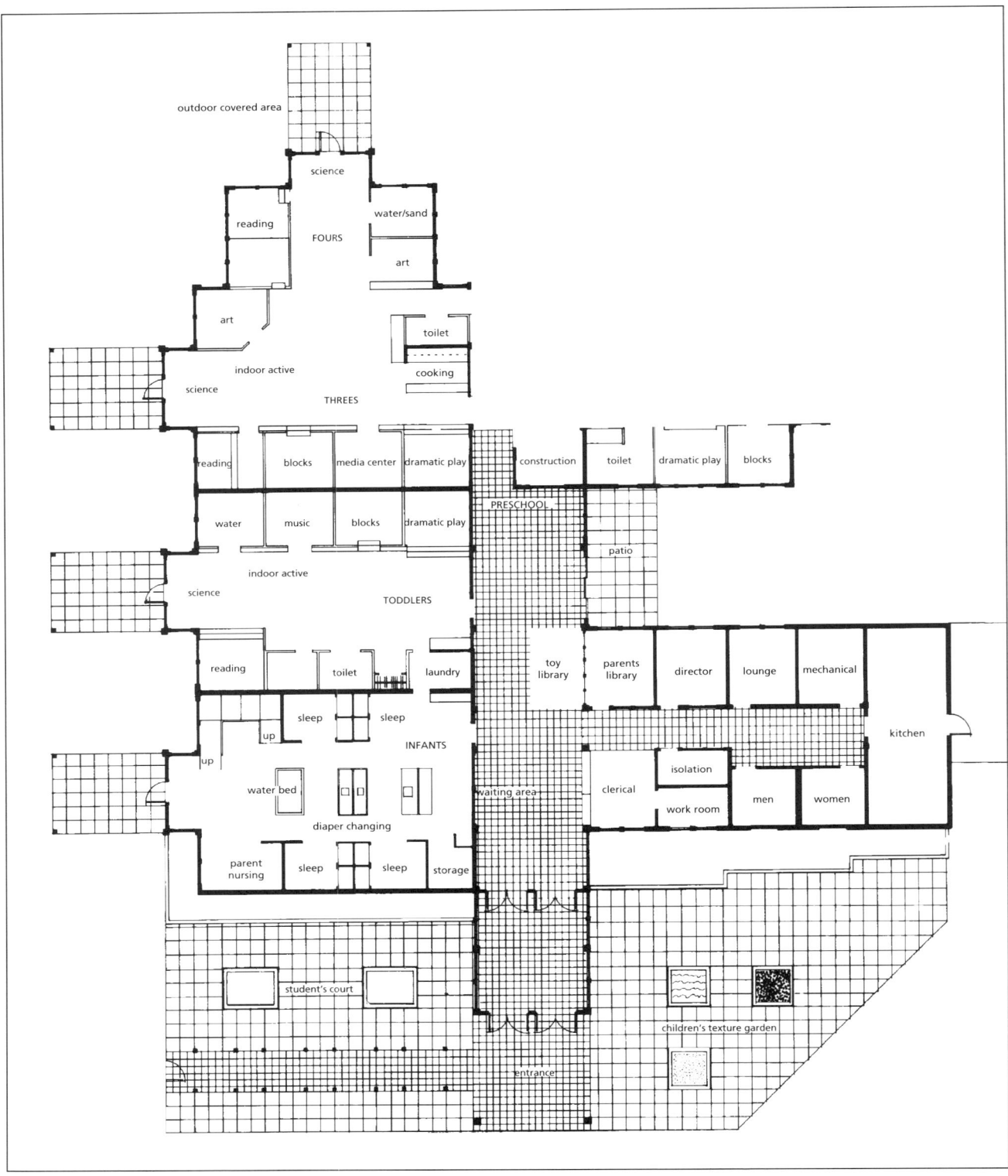

7-9. Floor plan of children's center.

Teachers' Response to the Process

The diagrams and scale models provided a clear sequential procedure to which all decisions could be traced and subsequently modified. The teachers, however, had some difficulty comprehending the consequences of many spatial decisions. While they were able to follow the process of playroom organization, they had difficulty visualizing the implications of alternative playroom arrangements; continual reference to scale models and perspective drawings helped the teachers substantially in contributing their expertise to the design of the building. Teachers remarked that this process provided them with a better understanding of the principles of spatial planning and the role of the architect. They experienced the "ripple effect," where minor changes in adjacency relationships manifested themselves into major revisions in the spatial layout of the playroom, or the building. This diagnostic procedure of examining flow processes and linking objectives to activity centers enabled teachers to develop a conceptual understanding of playroom and building layout principles.

Conclusion

The interaction between the teachers and the designer described in this project is clearly a departure from the traditional approach to facility development. Conventional practice usually denies the expertise of the user (the non-paying client) and their involvement in design decision making. Traditional designers also focus on the formal and visual issues and give less attention to the behavioral factors that may equally influence the form of the building. Facility designers typically consider defining relationships between playrooms and other areas, disadvantaging the teaching staff because of their inability to comprehend floor plans and the consequences of spatial decisions. The teachers' expertise occurs at the level of the children's behavioral interactions within the playroom, a factor that is usually considered only after occupancy of the facility.

A structured process was provided to enable child development professionals to lend their expertise to the initial programming stages of the design process. Use of activity data sheets, activity symbols, and form diagrams permitted the designer to integrate knowledge about children's behavior and their requirements into a format that was conducive to making space planning decisions. Integrating the expertise of the staff in this structured process established clear linkages between child development goals and the types of places where these goals could be fulfilled. The teaching staff's continual involvement in the building design process encouraged the exchange of ideas and concepts with the designer, which increased the staff's ability to act as effective design team members. The active part of the process usually terminates with the schematic design of the children's center, which has resulted from the team's involvement.

The effectiveness of a collaborative process is contingent upon the involvement of the architect from the inception of the project. When the architect is an integral part of the process, the building design proposals are clearly understood by the user/client group of teaching staff, parents, and administrators. On those occasions when the program is completed prior to the architect being commissioned for the project, significant communication problems can occur between the user group and the architect. In this instance, the architect of record was appointed by the college administration after the program and preliminary design had been completed by the consulting design team. Although considerable effort was made by the design team and teaching staff to explain the rationale for the design decisions, the architect could not easily comprehend the nuances of the proposed design solution. Similarly, the architects' drawings were not understood by the teaching staff, since they were prepared for construction purposes. This created difficulty in the working relations with the client because the architect often urged quick approval to expedite the process.

The language of the program should reflect the concepts developed by the teaching staff and conveyed in terms of educational goals and children's activities. The language of the architect—the floor plans and elevations—is the interpretation of verbal concepts and is often unintelligible to the user group, especially if it is not developed simultaneously with the program. The implications of these experiences are that ownership in the design process, achieved through active involvement in design decisions, permits the user/non-paying client to exercise free and informed choice. The separation of the programming and design stages not only limits participation of a wide range of experts, but also jeopardizes the ability of the product to fulfill the expectations of the program.

Acknowledgment

The success of this project is due to Joan Sanoff, Department Head, Early Childhood Development, Wake Technical Community College, who participated in the programming and design development phases. Thanks are also due to James Utley for his design work.

Case Study
Airport Interior Design: An Integrated Approach
by Bradley A. Knopp, the HTM Group, and Joseph A. Maxwell, Joseph A. Maxwell Industrial Design

An environment as complicated as an airport terminal requires special emphasis on communication and wayfinding as well as on proper use of signage. The case study that follows shows how preliminary and ongoing research, development of evaluation tools, evaluation of use patterns, and the actual design of furniture and signage must all be integrated to create a successful environment for use by large groups of individuals.

Airport passenger terminals have grown considerably from the simple shelters constructed 70 years ago. Their future growth will depend upon their success in maintaining an equilibrium among diverse passenger, airline, and operator interests as these interests expand and evolve within a truly globalized air transport system. Since the "accommodation of diversity" lies at the very heart of universal design, the fortunes of any given airport terminal may well be determined by the success with which universal design principles are applied to ongoing program development. This case study (1) describes an integrated design approach that facilitates the application of universal design principles to every interior design element in an airport terminal, and (2) presents a new seating concept as a way of illustrating the type of design innovation fostered by an integrated approach to airport interior design.

The ideas and methods presented in this study are the result of intensive design research originally undertaken to assist the Hillsborough County (Florida) Aviation Authority in designing Tampa International Airport's award-winning Landside Terminal. The concepts developed were then applied to the Airside A Terminal now under development. The coincident progress of Tampa's ADA Compliance Program expanded the scope of the Airside A work and also prompted Landside designers and developers to review that terminal's ability to meet the human, environmental, and economic challenges facing all major airports today.

The Social Challenge: Meeting Human Needs

Although no one would question that airports serve people, this self-evident assertion has often been ignored in the final design of airport interiors. Confusing or lengthy traffic routes, cramped lining-up or seating space, harsh reflective light and sound, poor orientation cues, and related problems ignore basic physical and psychological needs, thereby making air terminals stressful, irritating places.

Many of these needs are obvious: Airport visitors don't want to walk long distances or travel any distance in a direction they are not certain they should go; crowding is stressful, as is seating that forces people to look directly at one another (or else turn deliberately away to avoid doing so). Time is critical to most visitors, so no one wants to hunt for rest rooms, concessions, or flight information displays. Nor does anyone want to leave his/her intended route, or stop, to scrutinize signage that is unintelligible at a glance. No one wants to move through an area where deteriorating finishes or obtrusive maintenance and repair pose safety hazards, and everyone wants clean rest rooms. To respond to these needs, the interior design must be more than efficient; it must be hospitable, as well.

Special Needs and the Americans with Disabilities Act (ADA)

The needs mentioned above are shared by all people. There are a great many more human needs that, although not universal, are critical to an ever-increasing number of people traveling through, or working in, air terminals. For instance, fixture heights and walking distances are formidable obstacles for children even when they are quite convenient for able-bodied adults. Signage, warning devices, and information displays that are readily intelligible to young visitors may be undetectable or illegible to older ones. Similarly, the elderly cannot bend as low or reach as high as they might once have done to select food or other merchandise. The very young and the very old frequently require assistance when using the rest room.

Furthermore, interior design elements that prove to be merely fatiguing or annoying, but accessible, to the young and the elderly may be entirely inaccessible to people of all ages with disabilities. The implicit exclusion of people with disabilities from public facilities such as air terminals has finally elicited a comprehensive legislative response in the form of the Americans with Disabilities Act. As provided under Title II of the ADA, "Nondiscrimination on the Basis of Disability in State and Local Government Services" (28 CFR Part 35), persons with disabilities can no longer be denied "full and equal enjoyment of goods, services, facilities, privileges, advantages, and accommodations."

The challenges that the ADA requirements pose to airport interior design are both immediate and profound. For example, a given design element (drinking fountain, telephone, merchandise, or storage shelf) cannot facilitate wheelchair access, yet prohibit access or use by anyone other than a wheelchair user. Nor can accessible elements be provided for visitors, yet denied to people with disabilities who work in the air terminal. "Full and equal enjoyment" also means that accessible pathways and seating must be integrated with public-use pathways and seating, and not pushed to remote corners of the interior space. Maintainability and structural integrity become even more critical design values under ADA guidelines, since an accessible design element that is broken or inoperable no longer complies with the provision for "full use and access by people with disabilities." The ADA's mandate for a "barrier-free environment" extends beyond architectural design to cover wayfinding and communications systems to ensure that a building is sensorially, as well as physically, accessible.

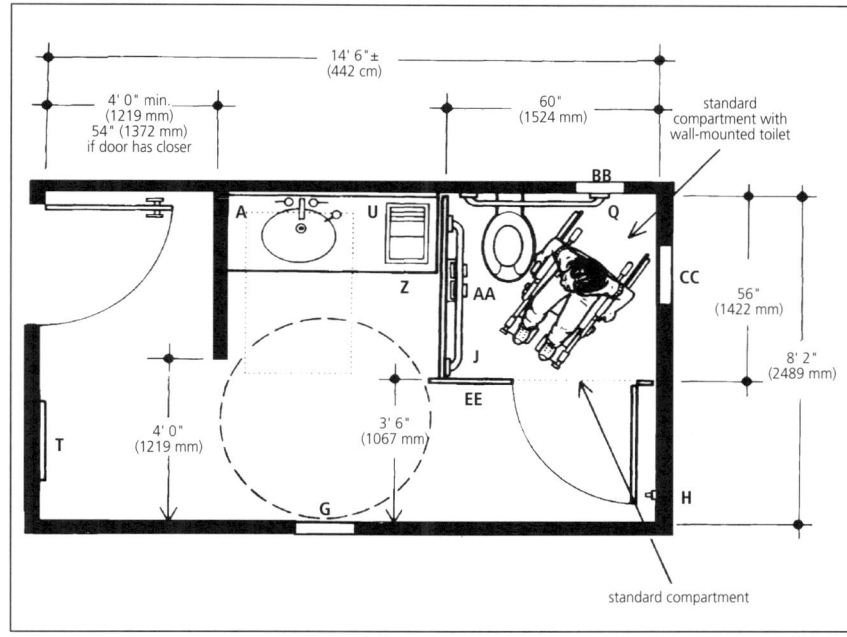

7-10. Small public washrooms require one standard 60-inch wide toilet compartment because it is the most universally usable. Minimum 60-inch diameter or T-shaped turning spaces are also required, as well as a barrier-free lavatory, accessories, and access aisles that meet ADAAG specifications. Entry doors should swing into vestibules, not directly into corridors, access aisles, or clear floor spaces required by lavatories and other washroom equipment.
(Reprinted with permission from Barrier-Free Washroom Planning Guide, Alan Gettelman, ed., 1993, Bobrick Washroom Equipment, Inc.)

Environmental and Economic Demands

Because the air terminal serves people, it must also serve the world outside the facility. The interior design must therefore meet environmental as well as human demands. After all, an airport terminal gains little by providing a congenial setting for visitors if it also poses a health risk to its service people or fouls neighboring communities with its wastes. The likelihood of future environmental legislation similar in scope to the ADA also makes environmentally-responsible design a cost-effective and life-affirming initiative. An environmentally-responsible approach to airport interior design encompasses the building's structure and the various colors, finishes, materials, and furnishings used within it. The basic structure should be designed for easy expansion and modification to ensure that it has a very long and useful life. Finishes used in interior spaces should have the longest possible lifecycles and cause the least possible harm to the air, water, and soil.

Since air terminals are businesses, it is clear that their operations must be economical both to the airlines and to airport owners/operators. Considerations of cost and economy cannot, however, be divorced from the human and environmental imperatives discussed previously. An attractive, congenial setting will also prove to be a cost-effective one, because people will want to visit, shop, and eat there. Likewise, the use of durable, soil-resistant finishes is both environmentally sound and cost-effective because cleaning, repair, and replacement add to the waste stream as well as to the design unit's lifecycle cost. By contrast, a design unit that features a lower initial cost but must soon be discarded because of wear or an inability to adapt with changes in the surrounding interior space violates all three imperatives: People are inconvenienced when that unit is sealed off, ripped out, or otherwise removed from use; the environment bears the burden when that unit is discarded; and the "low" initial cost becomes weighted with maintenance, removal, and replacement costs. For a facility intended for long-term service to its clients, there must be no short-term design.

Meeting the Demands: The Principles of Durability, Adaptability, and Convenience

An increasing sensitivity to human, environmental, and economic demands is changing the face of commercial aviation in this country. Airport interior design must move with this change in the direction of universal design, toward design solutions directed at a far greater percentage of people than heretofore attempted. Moreover, each universal design solution should solve more than one problem; it should address, for instance, cost-effectiveness and human needs at the same time. In this sense, "universal" applies to the comprehensiveness of the design approach as well as to the wide accessibility of the product designed. (There will, of course, always be someone with a combination of severe physical, sensory, and cognitive impairments who will not be able to access or use the design.) But a piecemeal, reactive approach that attempts special designs for each major design unit to accommodate each one of the immense varieties of disabilities or combinations of disabilities invariably ends up satisfying no one's demands. The same holds true with respect to environmental and economic demands: Universal design evolves from a careful balancing of diverse factors and constraints.

Universal design requires an integrated approach to the demands facing the nation's airports. From the preceding discussions of these demands, three principles emerge that demonstrate the interrelatedness of human, environmental, and economic imperatives and point to a design approach capable of integrating them all. Careful and continual attention to these three principles—*durability, adaptability,* and *convenience*—ensures that design development moves toward the desired goals of universal accessibility and use.

Durability

Durability includes not only structural integrity but also aesthetic longevity. A given design unit must maintain a high appearance level for a very long time; its styling should never look dated, and its colors and finishes must resist soiling and wear as much as possible as well as mask whatever soiling and wear is inevitable. Moreover, these colors and finishes should be available for years to come. In short, *durability* encompasses any aspect of design that affects the useful life cycle of a design element.

Adaptability

Changes in airline operations, business activity, aesthetic concepts, the seasons—all of these combine to create an ironic "constant state of transition" at air terminals. Interior design units must be easily modified, expanded, adjusted, or extended as necessary to accommodate this continual state of flux. *Adaptability* also means that a modified or relocated design element should still be compatible with the surrounding space. From the perspective of design as problem-solving, an adaptable design is a solution that solves more than one problem. From a human factors perspective, an adaptable design accommodates the different manners in which a wide variety of users are accustomed to performing a given task. This includes the multitude of substitutions or coping skills developed by persons to compensate for deficits in one or more areas of physical, sensory, or cognitive functioning.

Convenience

As used in the Tampa International Airport design research, *convenience* embraces both functionality and aesthetics. Included under this principle are design unit safety and ease of installation, cleaning, and repair, in addition to the ease of use and wide accessibility typically associated with the term. Design features generally described as providing comfort or amenability also serve the principle of convenience, since they make easier whatever activity the user is engaged in—whether it is a long wait in hold room seating or a short pause beside the concessions area.

Applying the Principles: The Airside A Design Evaluation Guide

The principles of durability, adaptability, and convenience form the basis for an integrated approach to interior design. Principles alone do not, however, produce an effective working design. Rather, the gap from an integrated design approach to final design integrity is bridged by a qualified design team who applies these principles at every stage in design development. They are the ones who must perform the careful balancing of diverse considerations so crucial to achieving universal design.

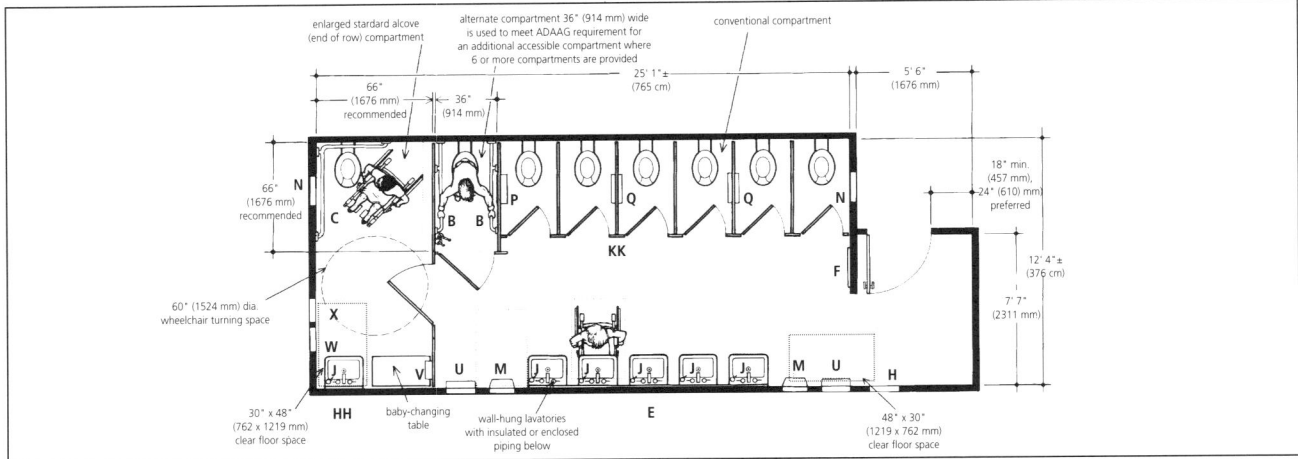

7-11. Plan for a women's washroom with a single-door entry from Bobrick Washroom Equipment. Universal design features meet or exceed ADAAG specifications. *(Reprinted with permission from* Barrier-Free Washroom Planning Guide, *Alan Gettelman, ed., 1993, Bobrick Washroom Equipment, Inc.)*

One of the tools developed to assist the Airside A design team in applying the aforementioned principles was an Interior Design Evaluation Guide. Originally based on the design successes and failures observed at major U.S. airports over the past 20 years, the Evaluation Guide itself proved quite adaptable in incorporating ADA-related criteria (including UFAS and ADAAG recommendations) as they were developed.

In this guide each interior design element in Airside A is evaluated with respect to the principals of universal design discussed previously. The guide is organized into 18 sections, many of which are further divided into subsections. Each section begins with an introduction to the design element to be evaluated along with a discussion of any special considerations. Following this introduction is an Evaluation Checklist in which the relevant design criteria are expressed as questions requiring simple "Yes" or "No" responses. The questions are constructed so that a "Yes" response indicates that the desired criterion has been incorporated into the unit's design. Designs, therefore, should be developed so as to receive as many "Yes" responses as possible. Space for comments is provided at the end of each question. Because the Evaluation Checklists express actual design criteria, they are intended for consultation throughout the design process, and not just as a way of rating completed plans.

A list of the sections found in the Evaluation Guide is provided below. The example following the list is representative of the depth of questions covered in each section.

1. Overall layout
   - Overall layout
   - Pathways
   - Doors and gates

2. Hold room areas
   - Hold room areas—general
   - Hold room seating system
   - Hold room areas—specific gates
3. Seating units
4. Smoking areas
5. Rest rooms
   - Men's rest rooms
   - Women's rest rooms
   - Companion rest room
6. Concession Areas
   - Concessions—general
   - Concessions—signage
   - Concessions—news and gifts
   - Concessions—food and beverage
7. Cleaning system
8. Floor finishes
9. Carpets
10. Wall finishes
11. Ceilings
12. Lighting
    - Lighting—general
    - Lighting—specific types
13. Ticket check-in counters
14. Ash/trash units
15. Public telephones
16. Drinking fountains
17. Elevators
18. Communications
    - Communications—general
    - Communications—signage
    - Communications—alarm devices
    - Communications—flight information displays

Example—Section 18: Communications

Under ADA guidelines, communications systems that are ineffective for those with physical, sensory, or cognitive/language impairments are "barriers" to people with disabilities and must be removed just as structural barriers must be eliminated. Whereas effective communication is important in any public facility, the very nature of commercial aviation makes the timely and effective transmission of flight schedules, operational changes, hazardous conditions, and similar information of utmost importance to all terminal visitors. No design accent or amenity is appreciated by someone who does not know where it is or how to use it, or who is just plain lost. True hospitality, in this case, must involve timely and unambiguous communications from Airside A to its guests. This total communications approach must include an appropriate theoretical framework for understanding how people acquire and represent navigational and other environmental information.

To address all the various types of communications systems used in the terminal, three specific Evaluation Checklists are included in this section, together with a list of general criteria that all forms of communication should fulfill.

Evaluation Checklist: Communications Systems—General

1. Does the design of the Airside interior presently accommodate, or will it accommodate in the near future, the installation and use of the following auxiliary aids and services that are intended to make communication with people with disabilities as effective as communication with others?

    - Videotext displays?

    - Telephone handset amplifiers?

    - Open- and closed-captioning?

    - Audio-description services?

    - Secondary auditory programs?

    - Tactile maps and guides?

    - Assistive listening systems (e.g., induction-loop, FM, and infrared transmitters)?

    - Audible signage?

    - Multimodal information centers?

2. Are public-address systems provided that transmit announcements clearly without excessive volume in any one area?

3. Do the public-address systems feature automated announcement sequencing to prevent announcements from being interrupted or lost completely by pages or other messages?

4. Do the public-address systems feature adequate high-frequency response to improve speech discrimination by people with hearing impairments?

5. Are the public-address systems located as close as possible to hold room seating to ensure optimum high-frequency response (i.e., through proximity to the auditor) without the need for excessive volume?

6. Are both active and passive measures employed at Airside to reduce ambient noise levels that compromise the intelligibility of audible information?

Evaluation Checklist: Communications—Signage

1. Are signs unambiguous and limited in number to avoid confusion?

2. Is signage consistently placed so it can be readily located by persons with vision deficits?

3. Are directional and informational cues coherent throughout the facility?

4. Are orientation guides readable from far away by people walking (or being transported) quickly from a number of different directions?

5. Are color coding or other visual cues used to assist in area identification and orientation?

6. Can information be conveyed equally well to those unable to distinguish colors?

7. Can menu boards be read by those with vision impairments?

8. Is signage in compliance with the following ADA guidelines concerning optimal legibility?

    - Character width-to-height ratio between 3:5 and 1:1?
    - Stroke width-to-height ratio between 1:5 and 1:10?
    - High contrast between characters and background?
    - Characters and background in eggshell gloss, matte, or other nonglare finish?
    - Sans serif print fonts used?
    - Wall signs at 60 inches above floor have characters and symbols on signs raised at least $\frac{1}{32}$ inch?
    - Nonglare illumination for backlit signs?

Evaluation Checklist: Communications—Alarm Devices

1. Do alarms and other detectable warnings meet the following ADA performance specifications?

    - Audible alarms exceed prevailing sound level in room or space by 15 dbA?

    - Visual alarms feature a xenon strobe type or equivalent?

    - Color of visual alarm clear or nominal white (i.e., unfiltered or clear filtered white light)?

    - Minimum intensity of 75 candela for visual alarm?

    - Maximum pulse duration of visual alarm is 0.2 seconds, with maximum duty cycle of 40 percent?

    - Minimum flash rate of 1 Hz, maximum of 3 Hz?

2. Are visual signal appliances provided in rest rooms, hallways, lobbies, and any other areas for common use?

3. Are visual signal appliances detectable from all parts of a general usage area?

Evaluation Checklist: Communications—Flight Information Displays

Are the flight information displays:

1. Located so that they can be easily read from a wheelchair?

2. Located on gate level?

3. Visible when entering the gate level?

4. Readable by those with vision impairments?

5. Readable by someone on the move?

6. Located so that those who line up to read them do not block traffic flow?

7. Linked so that flight information is fed back to displays at the Shuttle Lobby in the Landside Terminal?

8. Is the following information for a given gate provided electronically at that gate:

    - Air carrier?

    - Flight number?

    - Time of departure?

    - Boarding in progress?

New Directions in Seating Design

The development of an integrated approach to airport interior design confirmed what had been suspected among certain design circles for many years previously: namely, that the conventional approach to interior design as "fixtures, finishings, and furnishings" is unequal to the social, environmental, and economic challenges confronting the airports of the future. In very few design elements was this more apparent than in the case of hold room seating layout. Upon application of the three universal design principles of durability, adaptability, and convenience, the Airside A design team developed the following list of seating layout criteria.

Durability

1. Design must provide adequate seating for years to come.
2. Tabletops must resist damage and be easy to replace when damage occurs.

Adaptability

1. Design should pose no line or other traffic problems when flight delays or other conditions change hold room occupancy.
2. Seating should be easily added, removed, and reconfigured to conform to changes in hold room area.

Convenience

1. Seating design must provide ready access to all varieties of terminal visitors (including people with disabilities) and their luggage.
2. It must offer "natural" seat selection; it must not force strangers into proximity with one another.
3. Ashtrays and trash disposal receptacles should be incorporated into seating areas.
4. Seating must not block cleaning and maintenance of carpet.
5. Seating must facilitate conversation and social cohesion among families and larger groups.
6. Every seat should have direct access to a circulation area.
7. No person should be seated where someone is looking at the back of his or her neck, or directly across from someone else.
8. Conversational arrangements must allow access and placement for wheelchairs.

No more than a cursory review of the typical tandem seating layouts was needed to see that what has become the status quo in airport hold room seating does not meet the wide range of human and facility needs now facing the commercial aviation industry. To fulfill the seating layout criteria listed previously, industrial designer Joseph A. Maxwell developed a patented cluster layout that establishes a relaxed, conversational setting while facilitating the cleaning and maintenance of adjacent areas (see Figures 7-12 and 7-13).

Compared with the standard tandem seating featured in the nation's airports, the cluster seating arrangement offers the following advantages:

1. The arrangements are conducive to conversation.
2. Every seat is an excellent seat, with two arms and a table.
3. Any seat can be reached without climbing over people and bags.
4. There is room for wheelchairs in every seating group.
5. There is full access for people with disabilities.
6. Any seat can be made into a smoking seat.
7. A table for every seat reduces floor cleaning costs.
8. The plinth table base and cantilevered seats simplify cleaning.
9. There is ample room to store carry-on items without taking up seating or circulation space.
10. The seating arrangement does not create tripping hazards.
11. There is room for free movement and stretching.
12. No one looks directly at another person; seats are not placed tightly back to back.
13. Seating is less stressful and more comfortable.
14. Layout is more interesting; it fits into circular motif.

Cluster seating's sole disadvantage is that it is so far unproved except in the Landside Terminal at Tampa International Airport. It has also been argued that tandem seating would yield greater seating densities per given area if people were forced to crowd into every available tandem seat. This contention, however, is insupportable for two reasons (1) the current trend toward greater cross-utilization of common hold room areas minimizes whatever spatial advantage tight rows of tandem seating may have over cluster arrangements; (2) airport travelers typically occupy slightly over half of the available tandem hold room seating at any one time. This actual, as opposed to theoretical, seating-density yield was determined from two tandem-seating utilization studies conducted at Tampa International Airport and Charlotte (North Carolina) International Airport.

In these studies, researchers observed the seat selection and utilization behavior of nearly 1000 airport travelers over several days at each facility, ascertaining that nearly 90 percent of these travelers come to an airport singly or in pairs. Over 35 percent of all the people observed in both studies placed something in the seat next to them. Lone travelers select their seats with space around them. In uncrowded areas, where there are plenty of seats available, groups of two and three do the same, spreading themselves over the entire seating area. Larger groups tend to split up and sit across from each other, making two smaller groups.

As hold room areas become crowded, most of there remaining available seats are in singles and pairs. Late-arriving groups of more than two people often cannot find space where all can sit together, leading some group members to sit while the rest stand or go elsewhere (e.g., concessions, cocktail lounge, and so on). This holds equally true for lone passengers or anyone with lots of carry-on items; those persons stand or go elsewhere rather than occupy a seat they feel is unacceptable. One simple fact confirmed in these studies of U.S. airports is that people do not want to crowd or be crowded by others they do not know.

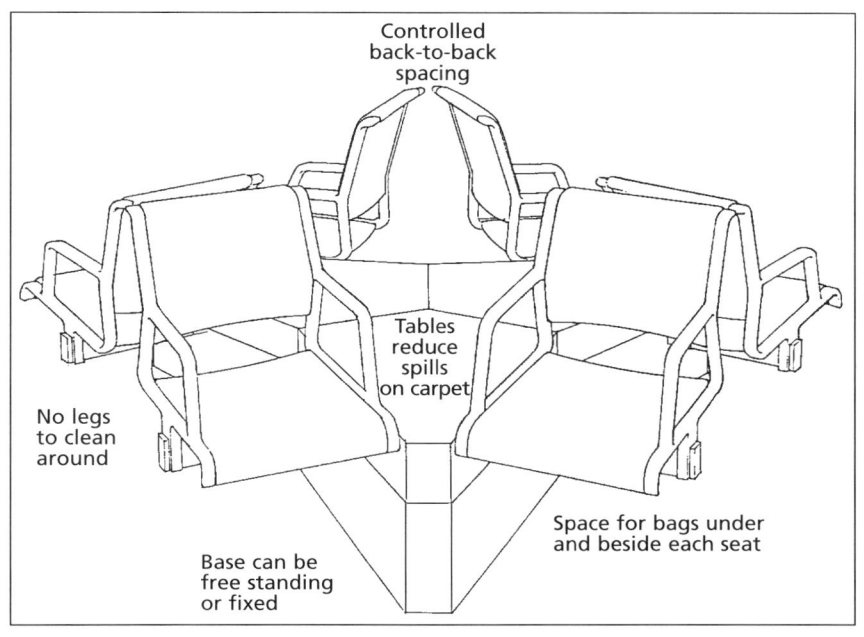

7-12. Cluster seating element (general representation).
(Reprinted with permission from Joseph A. Maxwell, Industrial Design.)

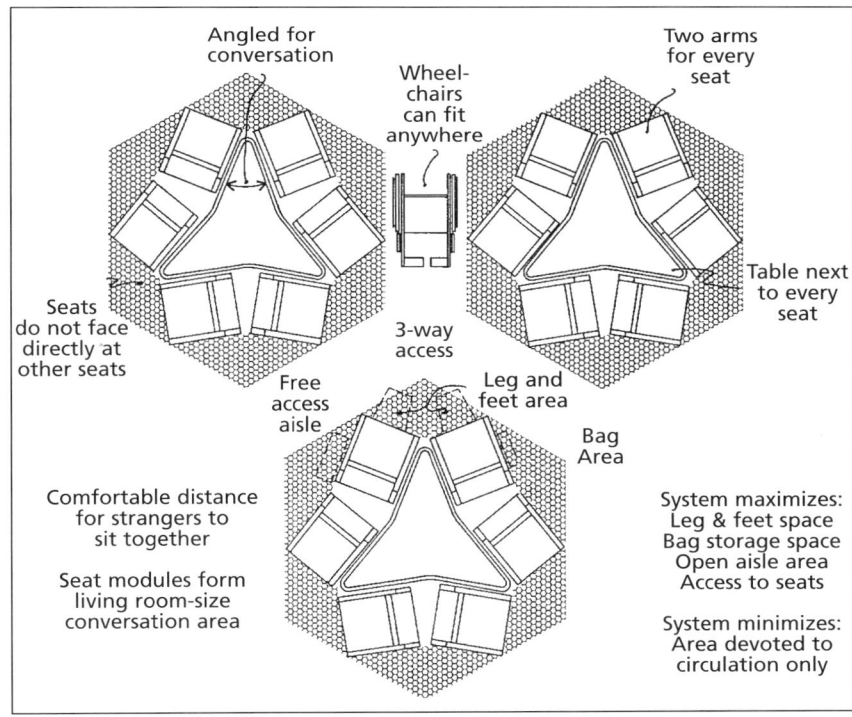

7-13. Cluster seating layout.
(Reprinted with permission from Joseph A. Maxwell, Industrial Design.)

Multiple analyses of the data from both the Tampa and Charlotte studies, and also from subsequent inquiries at additional airports, yielded the same figure—59 percent—as the maximum occupancy rate for the tandem seating arrangement. Comparing this figure with the 75–80 percent occupancy assumed in required seating formulae developed for the airport industry, it becomes clear that to realize such estimates, airport management are left with only the following options:

1. Force people to crowd into every available tandem seat, as in sold-out theater shows.
2. Add more tandem seating.
3. Find an alternative seating layout that increases the number of desirable seats.

The unattractiveness of the first option is obvious; the second option is hardly less so, since additional rows of tandem seating would take up space reserved for deplaning aisles, lining-up areas, and so on. The most acceptable way to seat the greatest number of people in a given space is to use a seating layout that works with, not against, people's natural seat-selection habits. The cluster arrangement provides just such a layout, as evidenced in a special trial installation conducted at Tampa International Airport after the seating utilization study there was completed.

In this test, a seating mock-up was installed in Tampa's Airside F terminal. For several days, the tandem seats in the mock-up area were videotaped for 2.5 hours each during the two peak periods of each day. The tandem seats were then replaced by cluster seating units featuring the same seat elements as those used on the tandem bases. This mock-up was videotaped during the same time periods, for the same number of days as for the tandem seating mock-up.

Utilization of the tandem seats was the same as observed in the formal study. The cluster seating, however, filled to 100 percent as the area became crowded. In fact, the cluster seating mock-up was so well received that it is still in place. The videotape recorded wheelchairs being moved through these areas during active periods, and people were also observed putting their baggage in the space provided, rather than on a seat.

Conversational groups of seating have been used in the public areas at Tampa International Airport for 20 years, and their success has been well proven. People tend to be friendlier, and they speak to strangers. The tensions of travel are reduced, and long waits seem shorter. In addition, access and use are increased for a variety of individuals, including the young, the elderly, and those with disabilities. It is time that these attributes become a common element in all the nation's airports, large or small.

Universal Design Strategy
Design for Acoustic Environments
by Anne E. Seltz, M.A., CCC-A

As apparent from the previous case study, communication is a crucial area in public environments. A multitude of products have appeared on the market to better enable individuals with hearing disabilities to take part in the services offered by commercial and public entities. Also, the design of environments that reduce noise while enhancing communication and comfort has been heavily focused on in recent years. In this section, Anne Seltz presents an audiologist's viewpoint of the areas that need the most attention in accommodating people with hearing disabilities, and also offers a number of examples from her own experience.

People's basic listening abilities change over time: Ears change; central auditory systems change. These changes cause softer sounds to be unheard and complex sounds to be distorted. Natural maturation of the human body causes most of these changes. But some changes are caused by damaging noise and toxic chemicals in the environment. Cigarettes, alcohol, diseases, medication, and familial tendencies also affect how a person's hearing/listening system works at various ages.

Designers need not be concerned with the causes of hearing loss. However, they do need to know that each person's hearing ability will change by varying degrees over time. As people age, they hear fewer softer sounds and speech begins to sound distorted in noise. While some spaces are dedicated to a specific population, such as senior housing where usually 50 percent of the residents will have significant hearing loss, most spaces are designed to accommodate the full range of human beings.

Difficult, noisy, listening environments include a car with a window down, a restaurant with no carpeting, a home or small office with window air conditioners and printer fans, overhead pink noise or music, or a reverberant large space. Noisy places are not just manufacturing places. Noisy places are everywhere.

Wherever human beings work, reside, or play, they communicate; information comes to them and goes from them. Environments must enable the communication process. When designers, planners, and facility managers attend to acoustic environments, signage, and alarm systems, they have the opportunity to offset the effect of hearing loss. Then everyone using the space—those with normal hearing as well as people who are hearing impaired—will benefit by functioning more comfortably and accurately.

Most persons born deaf (less than 1 percent of the general population and less than 10 percent of all persons with hearing loss) can advocate for their special needs because they're often a member of a deaf advocacy group. Usually this group clearly identifies its needs and knows the solutions needed in various settings. The designer needs to consult such groups because they are quite knowledgeable.

However, the majority of persons with some degree of hearing loss, those whose working and living environments require some alteration or preplanning, are often unaware of how to manage their personal listening problems or how to effectively change or design their acoustic environments; they may even be unaware of their listening problem. Almost all persons with mild and moderate hearing losses—90 percent of all people with hearing loss—enjoyed normal hearing at one time. Their hearing loss came on gradually, usually in mature adulthood. They rarely identify themselves as having a disability, and few belong to any advocacy group. For example, many adults with hearing loss:

- Have never asked for professional assessment
- Do not know about reverberation or sound absorption
- Are unfamiliar with amplified phones

Many adults with hearing impairments who could benefit from personal hearing aid usage, personal FM systems, assistive listening devices, and adaptations of their acoustic environment have never explored these options. They don't know where to start, and few health care professionals encourage them to learn.

Why, then, should designers and planners attend to the needs of people with hearing disabilities, when they're not asking for help?

- Because it makes economic sense. Their hearing loss does cause them difficulty in many environments. Persons who can communicate effectively are more productive and content.

- Because it makes legal sense. People with hearing loss will soon be demanding the accommodations required by law.

- Because any work done to improve communication within an environment will benefit all current and future users of that space.

The strongest reason for attending to the needs of people with hearing disabilities is the universal design reason: Whatever is done to solve their listening problems will enhance the communication abilities of every other person in the space. The solutions developed will benefit all future space users and can be used in the design and planning of spaces and acoustic environments for many future facilities. Eventually everyone will be able to enjoy spaces and communicate well in them.

Commercial Spaces

A 20-year-old who could eavesdrop on every conversation within a 20-foot radius in a noisy restaurant, at age 60 can barely understand the person sitting across the table in the same environment. And that 60-year-old blames the restaurant, unaware that the problem is due to his diminishing hearing systems, and he is therefore unable to ask for reasonable changes from the restaurant. So he simply does not return.

If that restaurant wants to serve customers of all ages (and considering the aging of society, this would be a good idea), it needs to change the acoustic environment to reduce the overall noise by using sound-absorbing materials and making listening comfortable at most tables for most of its customers.

Similarly, theaters can provide unobtrusive, assistive listening devices, either infrared or FM systems, so that more people can have access to what is being said on the stage or in the film.

Senior Housing

Much has been written about senior housing design, yet many such units remain inadequate for the communication needs of the residents. It is not uncommon to have a communal dining room that is so noisy (reverberative) that people rarely talk with each other. And, since most residents are hearing impaired and not all use personal hearing aids, TVs are usually loud enough to boom out into hallways and through walls, floors, and ceilings.

In emergencies, that TV volume may drown out any alarm in the hall: A rap on a door is often an inadequate alerting system, and smoke detectors are often not loud enough for some people who are hard of hearing and for anyone who is deaf.

The solutions here are to ensure that sound transfer is less possible between walls and floors. Public dining spaces should be sound treated to achieve low reverberation. Emergency communication systems are available that use flashing lights, low-pitched horns, bed shakers, and so on. Wireless personal devices can also be used that receive coded signals for smoke detectors, doorbells, phones, and so on.

The Traveling Nun

Sister C., age 45, is a consultant on grieving and women's mental health issues. She has moderate to severe hearing loss. Sister C. visits many poor communities and facilities, setting up support groups, conducting individual counseling sessions, and holding meetings. Sister C. is like many professionals who offer services in environments they cannot control or design ahead of time.

7-14. This architectural plan for an accessible sanctuary was designed by John M. Scott, AIA, and Richard M. Takach, ASID, of Largo, Florida. They are members of the Interfaith Forum on Religion, Art, and Architecture (IFRAA) of Washington, D.C. Specific features are as follows: (A) Covered pathways leading to portico and other buildings. (B) Entry area, narthex, with glass walls and space for overflow seating or for assembling participants in processional. (C) Wheelchair- accessible cabinets and pamphlet racks. (D) Men's rest room with wheelchair-accessible facilities. (E) Wheelchair-accessible water cooler or water fountain. (F) Women's rest room with wheelchair-accessible facilities. (G) Choir robing room. (H) Nave, main seating area for approximately 350 people. (I) Vesting sacristy. (J) Choir area with ramps to all levels. (K) Wheelchair locations within the main seating area and choir area. (L) Sanctuary/chancel, with ramp access to each level, including areas for individual readings. (M) Access ramps with a slope of 1-inch height:12-inch length. (N) Parent's/bride's preparation room. (O) Work sacristy. *(Reprinted with permission from Richard Takach, ASID, Liturgical Designer.)*

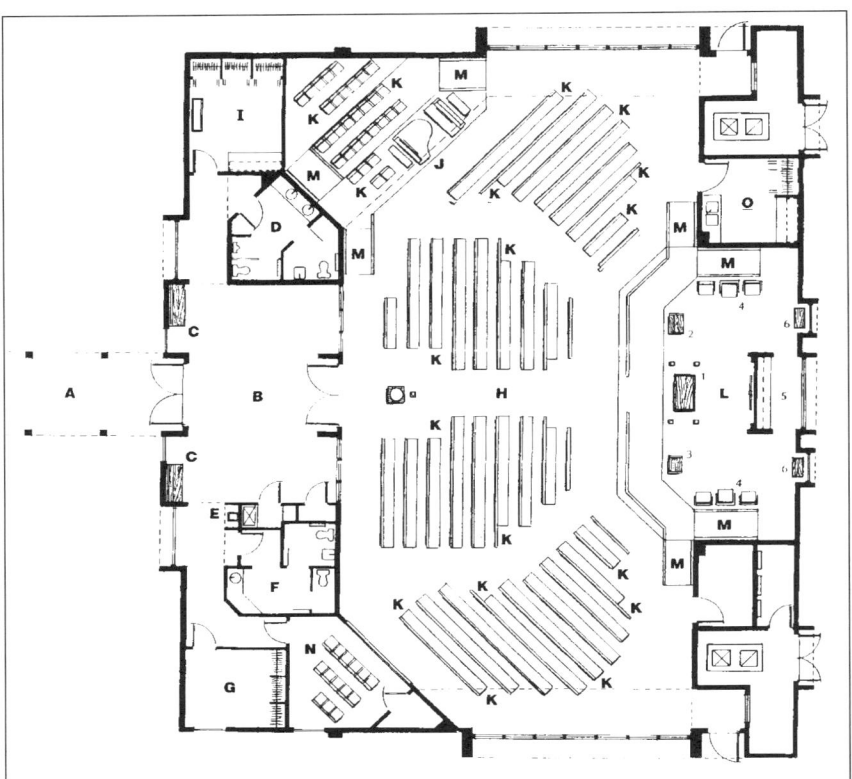

However, the proper design of facilities and spaces can better enable this flexible lifestyle. She has minimal trouble in a one-on-one situation where her excellent hearing aids are most effective. But her group effectiveness is often dependent on the room acoustics, the loudspeaker system, and the surrounding noise.

Sister C. can use portable amplification systems, personal FM systems, or loop systems, but if environments in general were better designed, her work would be much more spontaneous and effective. And, since the work that she does affects a number of others, such changes would benefit everyone involved. Sister C. would also feel much more valued if environments were built that better considered her needs.

A Parish Minister

C.B. is a minister with moderate hearing loss who, at age 38, is in the demanding role of parish minister. Her duties include not just preaching and private counseling (both of which can tolerate a fair amount of hearing loss), but also meetings, church dinners, visits to nursing homes and private homes, committee work, and talking with troubled persons who often mumble. Personal hearing aids help tremendously, but C.B. still suffers from difficult acoustic environments.

Churches are exempt from the ADA, but they're not exempt from common sense. If C.B. works very long in difficult listening situations, she is exhausted much of the time. She needs to avoid premature burnout. Perpetuating her competency is of value to her parishioners, so her working environments need to be altered and redesigned. What helps C.B. will ultimately help all her parishioners, especially the many older members who share this disability.

School Environments

Each year schools face variable populations, varying time schedules, varying curriculum, and variable use of support staff. Teachers sometimes have a home-base room from which they teach, but they often carry their materials with them and move each hour. When teachers are stable, students move; when students are stable, teachers move. Acoustic environments may need to be different for an art class than for a German class—listening requirements and teaching styles will be quite different.

Both teachers and students can be hearing disabled or deaf. Therefore, the flexible school district will want to design or retrofit their facilities to meet the broadest range of students and staff; modifications might include wireless systems, acoustic treatment of rooms, reduction of reverberation, redundant alarm/emergency systems, creative loudspeaker announcements using both loudspeakers and room-based computer network systems, or E-mail. Buddy systems are also needed to add to the redundancy in the systems.

These alterations will serve not only students who are partially hearing and deaf, but also any student who happened to be on a field trip that hour, or was sick, or in the bathroom; the student who is hyperactive; the staff needing more visual information for clarity; or those whose room was so noisy during announcements that the message was incomprehensible.

An architect was once asked why so little attention was paid to acoustics. He had just finished designing a new high school for a district where the superintendent was the sole determiner of building criteria. The architect was not allowed to interview staff members or students. The superintendent's main interest was having an impressive looking gymnasium. The results? Space that ignored many needs of the learning student body and the teaching staff.

Conclusions

The days of pre-OSHA noise-induced hearing loss are perhaps over. Gone are the 50-year-old farmers with irreversible hearing loss from noisy machinery, the 19th-century blacksmith who was always made deaf from his work, the dentist with major hearing loss from using high speed drills, the junior skeet champion who could not enter medical school because hearing loss prevented him from ever using a stethoscope.

Noise still exists, but the environments that prevent this verbal society from communicating comfortably and accurately have much more impact on people. This is the next horizon in sound management that will help everyone.

Case Study
The ADA and High-Speed Railcar Interiors: Creating Equal Access for All Travelers
by Alan P. Wier

In this case study, professor Alan Wier describes a class exercise that focused on the transportation requirements of the ADA. Student designers worked in teams to apply a variety of innovative research techniques to develop full-scale mock-ups, scale models, floor plans, and supportive products for high-speed railcars. Such railcars are presently used in many parts of Europe, and they offer a solution to the transportation needs of many American cities.

Applying the ADA to public railcar design and rail transportation systems presents a significant challenge for practitioners of universal design. The challenge comes from both the law and the physical environment of railcars. The following case study provides a brief overview of the relevant ADA law and describes efforts to study and address railcar redesign.

The Challenge of the Law

There is a compromise strategy (developed to allow for cost-effective compliance in the face of rapidly changing technology) built into the ADA that presents a challenge in and of itself: While the ADA provides landmark direction for equal access to architectural environments, it sidesteps and delays action for equal access to the public rail system. Provisions within the ADA protect the public rail transportation system from immediate or significant compliance. Commuter railcars are specifically excluded from compliance with the ADA. Existing rail stations do not have to be compliant with the accessibility provisions of the ADA until 2011. Meanwhile, every business open to the public should have been accessible by January 26, 1992, and faces immediate potential liability for noncompliance.

In all fairness, it should be stated that the ADA does address some accessibility issues within railcars—primarily for people with physical disabilities, and most specifically, for people using wheelchairs. The ADA requires wheelchair accessibility from the railcar entrance to a holding space within the railcar. If the traveler wants a meal, the ADA requires that they have access to the passenger car adjacent to the dining car. Obviously this scenario leaves a great deal undiscussed. For example, how do wheelchair users get to the adjacent railcar if they do not board the train directly into that car, or how do they get their meals, and how do they eat their meals with the dignity afforded passengers in the dining car?

The law at present simply does not provide equal access protection within the public rail system and railcar environments. Within the current environment of public travel (especially long distance travel), public rail travel comes in a distant fourth after air, car, and bus in terms of usage. As a result, railcars within the United States at present may be considered by many as an insignificant issue for the ADA. However, this shows very short-term thinking, without consideration of trends currently developing. There is an increasing need and demand for dependable medium-distance travel that could be filled by an effective rail system.

The Challenge from the Physical Environment

Consider that railcars are really long, narrow tubes, about 10 feet wide, 10 feet high, and 100 feet long. As with aircraft and boats, floor area is at a premium. Any space given over to circulation decreases fare revenue and creates some undeniably significant problems within the current physical design of railcars. However, a solution to the problem is to start fresh with a new generation of railcars—high-speed rail.

High-speed rail travel represents an important step in increasing travel efficiency and reducing pollution in the United States. To investigate the application of universal design in these railcars, beyond basic ADA requirements, six teams of design students were formed under the guidance of professors Alan Wier and Reinhart Butter. The student team project was conducted jointly between interior space and product design majors in the Department of Industrial Design of the Ohio State University. During the 10-week project, students developed equal access goals and objectives and examined their impact on railcar interior performance and utilization of space.

Defining the Problem

Based on projections of travelers and their needs, student teams identified problems, goals, and objectives for business and family travelers, and for providing refreshments for all travelers. In each case the teams developed objectives for the use of space, comfort, and service.

For the business traveler, the basic objective was to create a productive and comfortable environment for individual work as well as for small group meeting areas, phone and data links, and storage compartments (see Figure 7-15). For family travelers, the basic objective was to create an environment that supported family

7-15. Student design of meeting area in high-speed railcar.
(Figures 7-15 through 7-17 reprinted with permission from Alan Wier.)

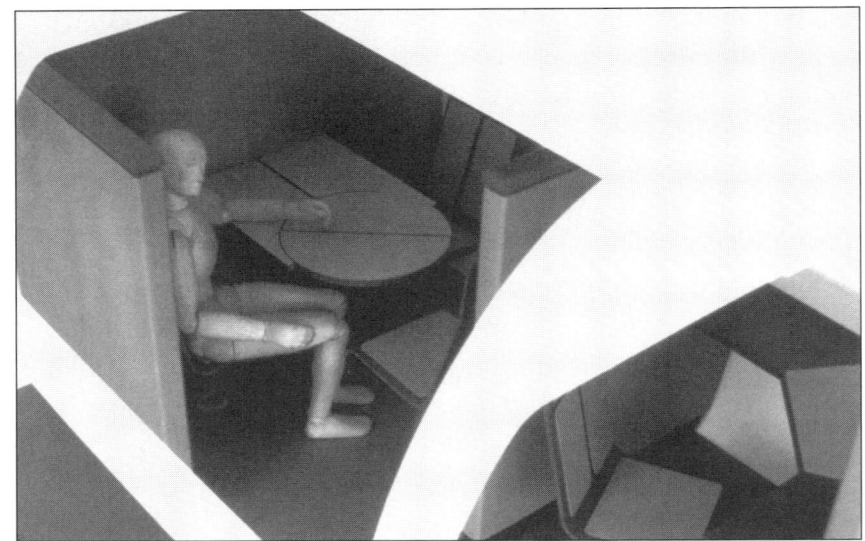

7-16. Student design of family area in high-speed railcar.

7-17. Student design of common eating area in high-speed railcar.

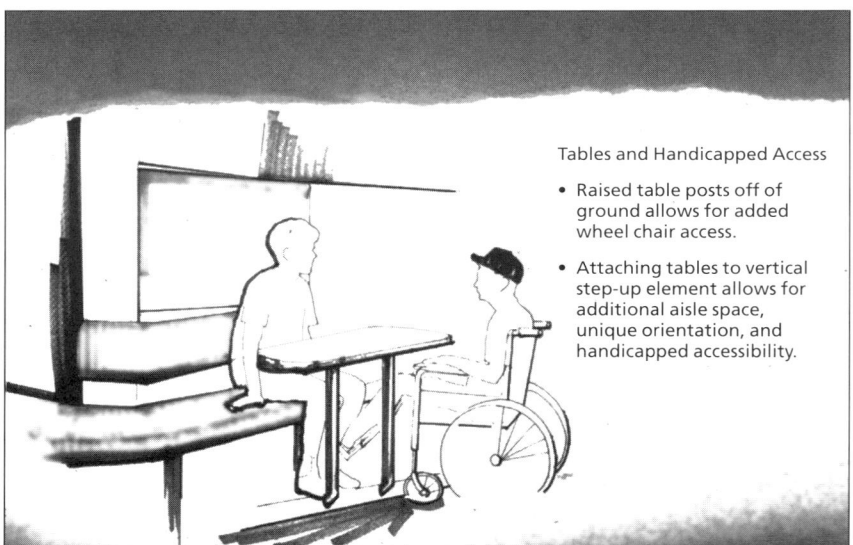

Tables and Handicapped Access

- Raised table posts off of ground allows for added wheel chair access.
- Attaching tables to vertical step-up element allows for additional aisle space, unique orientation, and handicapped accessibility.

interaction, including design for a range of age groups, child care and security, and the control of noise and disruption (see Figure 7-16).

For traveler refreshments, the basic objective was to create an environment that gave access to food and drink, fostered personal and social interaction, and provided visual relief (see Figure 7-17).

ADA Issues in Railcars

Students identified problems of equal access for individuals with physical, visual, and hearing disabilities in each of the railcar types. They also considered the needs of older individuals. The general issues covered are:

- Movement through the entire railcar
- Signage and identification
- Operation of passenger-accessible systems
- Washrooms
- Service for the very young and the elderly

For the business traveler, students focused on accessibility to private work areas, meeting areas, and storage. Seating mobility and circulation are vital for both the private work and the meeting areas. Storage design must consider passenger reach to and into the compartment, as well as operation of the compartment hatch.

For the family traveler, students focused on child care, entertainment, and washrooms. Flexibility of seating and surfaces is a vital consideration in child care and entertainment areas. Adjustability, reach, and ease of movement are vital considerations within washrooms.

For refreshments, students focused on accessibility to food service and social interaction areas. Circulation space, reach, and operation of equipment are the important considerations in the food service area. Space, access, and operation of equipment are the concerns within the social interaction areas.

Procedure

Each team followed a procedure of research, problem definition, concept development, and design development during the 10-week period. A variety of research topics were examined. Passenger demographics were determined; relevant laws and regulations were reviewed; trains were ridden; and child care, food service, and business sites were visited. From the resulting information, the teams developed goals and objectives to address the universal design issues.

The decision was made to use an existing high-speed railcar shell for the designs. After review of several European high-speed railcars, the German InterCity Express (ICE) railcar was selected. The plans were quickly and graciously supplied by the German Federal Railway Design Center. Within this shell the teams developed ideas for the three types of railcars: business, family, and refreshment. Scale plans were developed and refined. To get a clear sense of the railcar space, the teams then built an 8-foot section mock-up of the railcar in full scale. The teams were thus able to study and test their concepts in the full-scale mock-up, even conducting usability testing with individuals using wheelchairs. Once the concepts were selected, each team prepared a detailed 1:5 scale mock-up model along with plans, evaluations, and perspective views.

Conclusions

Each team discovered methods to address the integration of ADA equal-access issues and universal design into high-speed railcar design. Of particular concern was circulation within specialized spaces such as washrooms, meeting spaces, child care areas, and food service centers.

Circulation and corridor widths are directly affected by the railcar width and rail gauge. Since high-speed rail requires new track and an isolated operation route, the opportunity exists to widen the rail gauge and the railcar. Although it is not necessary that corridors be wide enough for wheelchair accessibility in all cars, it is necessary in parts of business cars with meeting rooms, parts of the family cars, and parts of the refreshment cars. Equally important is the consideration of door-opening widths between adjacent railcars (especially between the refreshment car and adjacent passenger cars) and into washrooms.

Case Study
One Restaurant's Efforts at ADA Compliance
by Susan Zavotka, Ph.D., and Jillianne Pfeifer

The owners of the Monk Restaurant in Bexley, Ohio (a suburb of Columbus), had completed a remodeling project during the year before the ADA became effective. They had attempted to make the restaurant accessible for people with disabilities and were interested in finding out whether they were in compliance with the ADA guidelines, even though the remodeling was not covered by the law.

The design team conducted a two-day analysis of the site, and Figure 7-18 graphically shows areas of compliance and noncompliance. Areas in gray on the floor plan are in compliance, and included:

- *Accessible routes:* Both exterior and interior access routes are within the required guidelines. Sloped curbs are provided where needed. Doors meet minimum width clearance and have appropriate hardware.

- *Main dining room:* Ground floor dining meets the 5 percent of total seating requirement. However, the restaurant needs a management plan to insure that accessible tables are available for those who need them. Due to limited space, construction of ramps to two other dining areas on separate levels was determined to be unreasonable.

- *Bar/lounge:* Tables in the bar areas are accessible and meet the 5 percent of total seating requirement.

- *Bathroom area:* Areas on the floor plan that are shaded and numbered to match the following key were found to be not in compliance with the ADA, and included:

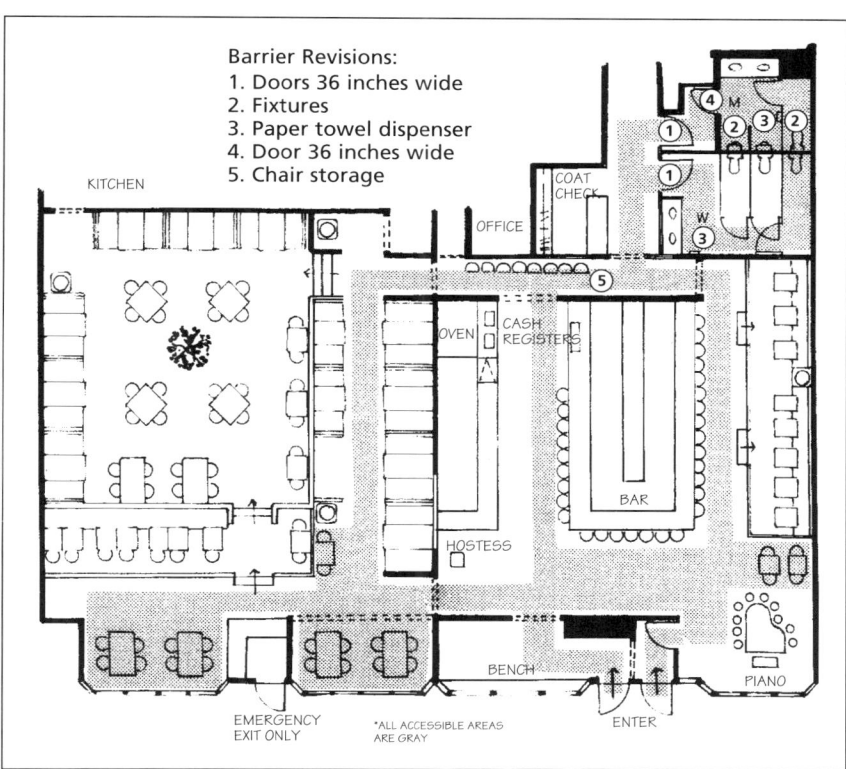

7-18. Floor plan of the Monk Restaurant showing areas of compliance and non-compliance. *(Drawing by Dara Baldrige, Jillian Pfeiffer, and Susan Zovotka, researchers. Reprinted with permission from proprietors Jack Cory and Edward Miller.)*

1. Bathroom doors need the International Symbol for Accessibility.

2. Flush controls for the urinals in the men's bathroom are 52 inches from the floor. This is 8 inches above the maximum allowable height. *Recommendation:* Move urinals to a lower height. Estimated cost = $300.

3. Paper towel dispensers are 57 inches above the floor. The required height is 40 inches. *Recommendation:* Move existing dispensers to required height. This could be accomplished in-house with negligible expense.

4. Clear floor space between the two entrance doors to the men's bathroom is inadequate. *Recommendation:* Remove the second door at no expense.

5. Chairs stacked in hallway leading to the bathrooms prohibit access. *Recommendation:* Store chairs elsewhere.

This case study shows that ADA guidelines can be readily met in many existing facilities. In this instance the restaurant had attempted to remodel in an accessible manner prior to the ADA's enactment. Consequently, changes to meet the current requirements were relatively minor.

Case Study

Camden Yards Ballpark: A State-of-the-Art Facility for Accessibility
by John P. S. Salmen, AIA

Widely acclaimed for its architectural beauty and urban placement, the new Orioles Park at Camden Yards in Baltimore, Maryland, has also been hailed for its accessible design that meets the requirements of the Americans with Disabilities Act. Nationally-known architects Hellmuth, Obata, and Kassabaum (HOK) designed the facility to include 426 "Camden seats" for people who use wheelchairs (see Figure 7-19). These special seats are located in nearly every level of the stadium at every price range.

Design time and effort to create the special seats were donated by representatives of the Volunteers for Medical Engineering, the Maryland Stadium Authority, and Governor William Donald Schaefer's Accessibility Task Force. Kim Beasley, a task force member and director of architecture for Paralyzed Veterans of America (PVA), drew the sketch for the seat, which was built by the American Seating Company. PVA has since been granted a patent on the seat. Other recreational facilities including the Superdome in Louisiana, the Oregon Arena Project, and a minor league stadium are using the seat or plan to use it.

Because the seat folds up and pivots to one side to accommodate people with disabilities, the design is really universal. Beasley notes that the design concept went far beyond the letter and intent of the law because wheelchair users can sit with everyone else.

While the Camden seats cost about $230 more than the standard $67 seats, accessibility requirements didn't make much of a dent in the total cost of the $250-million park. The design goal was to consider accessibility guidelines under the ADA, but also to make the stadium comfortable for all baseball fans, not just those who use wheelchairs. Ramps and handrails make moving about the stadium easier for ambulatory people as well.

In addition to the seats, which represent about 1 percent of the park's total 46,620 seats, the stadium has gradual-incline ramps, braille signs, and an FM broadcast station that allows people with hearing

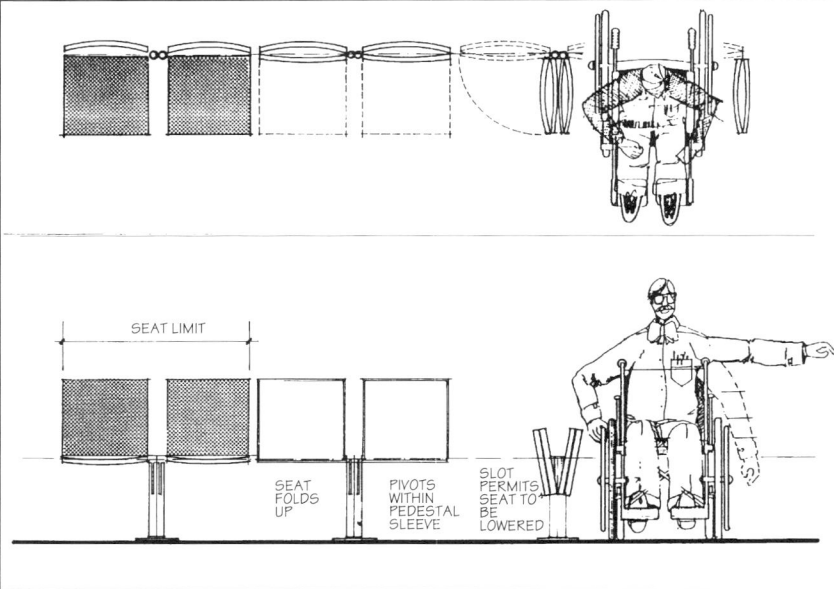

7-19. Drawing of Kim Beasley's accessible seating design for Orioles Park. *(Reprinted with permission from John Salmen, President, Universal Designers and Consultants. Drawing by Kim Beasley.)*

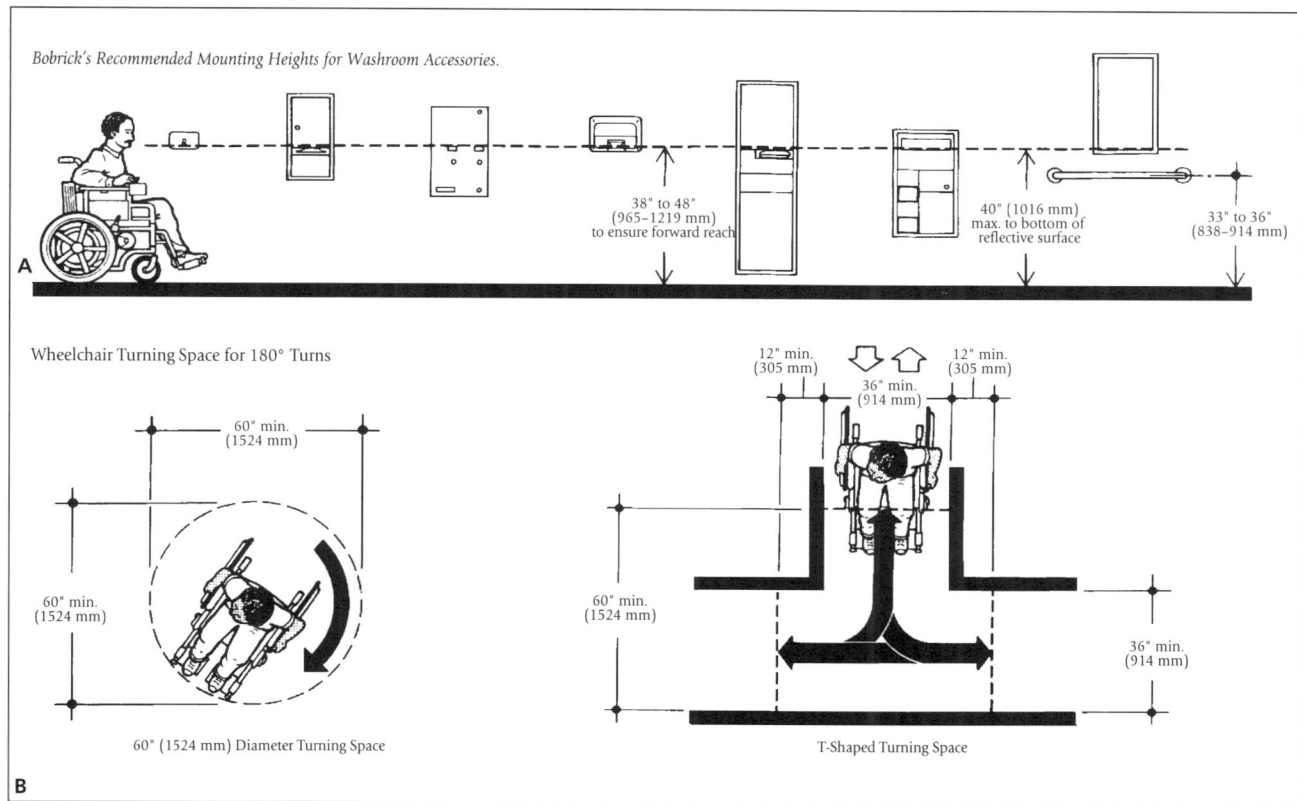

impairments to follow the game. Other accessibility features include wide corridors and elevators; accessible ticket windows, rest rooms, telephones, and concession stands; public announcements shown on a giant television screen for fans with impaired hearing; and wheelchair access to the playing field.

With forethought and planning, stadiums and other, similar facilities can have a distinctive style and flair and still be accessible to people with disabilities. The alternative is to retrofit facilities in a piecemeal fashion, which can inflate costs and damage the aesthetic appeal.

7-20. Space for people in wheelchairs is a fundamental design consideration. By utilizing a wheelchair perspective, you can also accommodate a person using a walker, cane, or crutches. Bobrick Washroom Equipment, Inc., provides the mounting heights shown in (A) for washroom accessories, and (B) for wheelchair turning space. *(Reprinted with permission from* Barrier-Free Washroom Planning Guide, *Alan Gettelman, ed., 1993, Bobrick Washroom Equipment, Inc.)*

Universal Design in the Home

8

Although the Americans with Disabilities Act has no legal bearing on single-family residences, the spirit of the law, as previous chapters have discussed, speaks directly to how people design, arrange, and live in their houses. There are several laws governing accessible housing. The most recent of these is the Fair Housing Amendments Act of 1988, which affects new construction of buildings with four or more units ready for occupancy after March 13, 1991. Among other general requirements, all elevator-accessed units and ground floor units in non-elevator buildings must have accessible light switches and electrical outlets, reinforced bathroom walls to allow installation of grab bars, and kitchens and bathrooms usable by people in wheelchairs. Such legislation for accessible housing in specific cases points to the need for the design community to provide universal design for everyone.

Perhaps no other environment so readily reflects the underlying principle of universal design and the ADA: The environment should adapt to fit people, not vice versa. When you think about "home," it is that fit that most readily comes to mind; home is where you are surrounded by the possessions you most value and enjoy, organized in a spatial arrangement that best reflects your personality and desires. Housing, however, has never really been designed to support the wide range of human beings that exists. If at some point your body changes because of accident, illness, or simple aging, then normal houses become less like homes and more like obstacle courses.

8-1. This "Idea" kitchen from Whirlpool was the first in a series used to highlight universal design features. The room view photo shows the use of accented flooring to delineate obstacles, large space and good traffic pattern for accessibility, and D-shaped handles. Specific features (left to right below the overview) are as follows: (1) Additional counter-height flexibility is achieved by the use of pull-out boards, and the down-draft exhaust system on the cooktop eliminates the need for hard-to-reach overhead venting. (2) The lazy Susan base cabinet provides easy access to corner storage, and the corner "appliance garage" allows convenient, out-of-sight storage. (3) The pull-out cutting-board drawer provides a landing pad for hot items coming from the adjacent wall ovens. (4) The under-cabinet microwave placement with adjacent landing pad pull-out board is very accessible.

(Figures 8-1 through 8-3 reprinted with permission from Whirlpool Corpiation.)

Another reason for creating more universal housing is one that is seldom considered: Inaccessible housing isolates individuals with disabilities, subtly segregating them from the mainstream. Even if an individual's own home has been adapted for his or her use, if friends and relatives live in inaccessible environments, there is little room for the type of socialization most people take for granted. This point is argued eloquently by Eleanor Smith, who convinced the Atlanta, Georgia, branch of Habitat for Humanity to make all of their new homes more universal. Her grassroots organization, Concrete Change, lobbies for basic access to every new house, including 32 inch wide doors and one no-step entrance (1993). Ms. Smith stresses the primacy of these two features, while acknowledging the need for a more encompassing universal design throughout the house. She also makes a strong case for such basic access being extremely reasonable since in most cases it can be accomplished at no added expense (and almost always for less than $400) by more fully utilizing the natural terrain and grading to the best advantage.

It's important to remember that most people are only temporarily able-bodied. Nearly all people will experience limits to dexterity, sight, hearing, and their senses of touch, taste, and smell. Therefore, homes must be designed with universal features so that families will not be disrupted or uprooted because of sudden disability or the natural effects of aging.

A home should allow for each individual's uniqueness, and universal design offers the platform from which adaptations can be made to support that uniqueness throughout the lifespan. The 21st century will find many Americans not only living in their homes but working there too, thus design principles fundamental to the workplace will also be applicable to spaces within the home. Requirements for accessibility and adaptability will need to be transferred to home construction and design.

Some general suggestions for universal residential design in new construction or major renovations include:

- Doorways with at least 32-inch clear access
- Level or ramped living spaces
- Powder room, or full bath, with 32-inch clear doors and wheelchair maneuverability on every level
- Room on main living level that can be converted into a bedroom (multi-level homes)
- Staircases that can accommodate a lift, or space for a home elevator (multi-level homes)

However, it is not just builders, designers, architects, and product manufacturers who are responsible for enabling or blocking

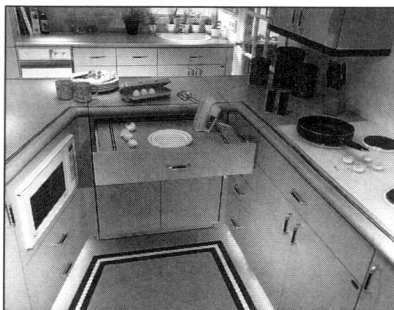

8-2. This second version of a total universal design kitchen from Whirlpool features contrasting floor demarcations and contrasting D-shaped door pulls, a variety of counter heights, and a combination work/eating area in the center of the room. Specific features (left to right below the overview) are as follows: (1) The cutting board pull-out drawer directly under the microwave is an important safety feature, protecting against dropping heavy items. (2) Side-by-side refrigerator-freezer with water and ice source in door, hot water tap and flexible wand faucet in the sink. (3) Floor-level lighting, lower microwave placement, and removable cabinet unit with a pull-out mix center. The glass-top range features staggered heating elements and convenient front location for controls.

universal environments. People are psychologically most comfortable with the familiar; they want to continue to experience life in similar ways—especially within their homes. But there's a danger to this, and within that danger is a pressing reason for approaching universal design in the home as a priority.

In a recent study of elderly individuals confronted with new disabilities, Bettye Rose Connell and Jon A. Sanford describe what happens when people with a lifetime of habits and experiences are confronted with physical limitations. They studied a group of retirees in the Atlanta area with a variety of disabilities encountered late in their lives—disabilities ranging from paralysis of the legs to loss of sight. These individuals all lived in single-family houses, and many had already received some counseling from local disability agencies.

The researchers administered questionnaires that solicited the retirees' self-evaluations of their ability to perform routine household tasks: washing dishes, collecting the mail, using various appliances, regulating temperature through adjusting windows and thermostats, and so on. The authors followed up on the questionnaire by observing and videotaping how the tasks were actually being performed.

A striking observation was the degree of difficulty the subjects displayed in performing even the most fundamental everyday tasks, including opening doors and windows, maneuvering through the house, and wayfinding, with a concomitant inability to recognize and report on their limitations. Many subjects reported that they were quite capable of acting independently, when in fact they were almost completely dependent upon a spouse or relative for support of these activities.

To a large degree these activities could have been conducted independently given relatively minor and inexpensive changes to the subjects' environments. However, in almost every case, home adaptations and behavioral changes had already been suggested but not followed. The individuals stubbornly refused to change either their homes or their methods of operation.

What is to be made of this? Recall from Chapter 2 that Lorraine Hyatt cites reticence to change as one problem encountered in trying to instill independence in the elderly; but in Chapter 3 recall how successful the San Diego Center for the Blind has been in reaching and reteaching low-vision elderly clientele. Two things are apparent:

1. Individuals do not know about and accept the behavioral and environmental adaptations that could facilitate an independent lifestyle in the face of changing physical capabilities.

2. Home environments have not been created with adaptability in mind.

8-3. This most recent universal design kitchen from Whirlpool offers variety in cabinet height and raised dishwasher placement, open base-cabinet beneath sink, and side-by-side refrigerator-freezer.

The need for such adaptability—and for making it the norm—is the focus of this chapter.

Underlying the call for universal design in the home is the belief that homes should be able to change gracefully to meet changing needs. To this end, the essays within this chapter serve as guides to creating fully adaptable and supportive universal homes.

Universal Design Strategy
Applying Universal Design Philosophy to Housing Design
by Lois J. Moore, M.S., and Edward R. Ostrander, Ph.D.

The philosophy of universal design holds great promise for improving housing design. A home must support the needs of individuals with widely different physical capabilities, in a wide range of activities, over long periods of time. Differences in physical capabilities may be due to age, temporary illnesses and injuries, or other circumstances that are a normal part of the life course. A resident with a permanent disability is only different from other residents in the duration and specifics of his or her limitation. A home designed with the universal design philosophy would meet the functional requirements of all these residents at once. Thus, universal design has the potential to enhance the quality of people's daily lives and save them the future financial and emotional expense of moving or making major renovations.

At present, success in pursuing universal design is hampered by a lack of accessible, well thought out, research-based design requirements for a wide range of physical capabilities. But even if designers had ready access to such information, refining their designs to meet the needs of everyone would not be a simple task.

The requirements of different people will sometimes conflict so completely that a universal design solution cannot be found. Sometimes the cost of the universal solution will be prohibitive. Those who espouse the universal design philosophy must be willing to prioritize the needs of different user groups and work hard to find the closest approximation to a universal design.

The Americans with Disabilities Act and Universal Housing Design

The ADA is a bold step toward universal design. It is significant first, because it has defined a set of design requirements for a previously neglected segment of the population and made them readily accessible to the design community; and second, it has legislated the priority that must be given to these functional requirements in designing public accommodations and commercial facilities. Every designer in this country must now develop and apply a "functionality mind-set"—an ever-present awareness that their designs must meet the functional requirements of certain disabilities. At minimum this mind-set will motivate designers to design public accommodations and commercial facilities to meet the needs of people who use wheelchairs, but many may also take on the larger challenge of universal design for all environments and all physical capabilities.

As designers accept this challenge, design researchers must progress in developing design requirements for many specific physical limitations (e.g., hearing problems, use of a walker, use of crutches) and many functional spaces (e.g., bedrooms, living rooms, garages) that are not yet well understood. Further, they must publish such information in places that are familiar and accessible to designers. An extensive search of gerontological design research publications (Moore & Ostrander, 1992) for housing design recommendations for ambulant older adults (the majority of the over-65 population) revealed that many publications that purport to present housing design guidelines for the physical limitations of older adults, in fact, focused on design guidelines for wheelchair users, leaving large gaps in the existing knowledge of how to design for ambulant older adults. Those who believe in and design for the universal design philosophy must realize that although the design requirements of wheelchair users are well represented in the ADA and in design research literature, there are many other physical capabilities that must be considered in creating truly universal design. Legislators wisely limited the ADA to public accommodations and commercial facilities, recognizing that in environments such as housing, the needs of people who use wheelchairs might not always take priority over the needs of those with different capabilities.

Applying Universal Design Philosophy to the Residential Kitchen

Every physical limitation, whether a normal part of the life course, normal variation in the size of the adult population, or the result of a disabling condition, has different design requirements. As one learns more about the physical capabilities of different people, one will also identify some conflicts between design requirements that make the goal of universal design so challenging. The following are examples of such conflicts in the domain of residential kitchen design.

Safety Conflicts

Safety is a particularly important criteria for universal design because an unsafe environment can lead to accidents that can result in physical disability or even death. When deciding where to locate potentially dangerous kitchen design features, one encounters several conflicts in the design requirements of different potential residents:

- *Location of electrical outlets:* Electrical outlets located at the front of the kitchen counter are much easier for short adults and wheelchair users to reach (Goldsmith, 1984; Raschko, 1982). But this location is more accessible to children than the usual back-of-the-counter location. It is also more dangerous for ambulant adults who may become entangled with appliance cords hanging off the counter.

- *Location of stove controls:* Controls at the back of a stove reduce the chance of injuries to small children by making the controls inaccessible. But controls at the front of a stove reduce the chance of injuries to adults whose clothing may catch on fire when they reach over a hot burner (Schumacher & Cranz, 1975; Uniform Federal Accessibility Standards, 1984). Front controls are also accessible to those using wheelchairs (Goldsmith, 1984; Olson, 1990). Some designers compromise by providing stove controls at the front of the stove that require a degree of manual dexterity that children are presumed not to possess. However, this solution creates a problem for those adults with severe arthritis in their hands, who also lack manual dexterity.

- *Location of microwave oven:* A microwave/range hood combination locates the microwave oven above the cooktop in a position that is safely out of the reach of children and that is in a convenient location for healthy adults. However, it is inaccessible to those who need to work from a seated position, and it increases the chance that frail adults will spill a pan of

8-4. This kitchen from Granberg International offers a variety of counter and cabinet heights and configurations. *(Reprinted with permission from Granberg Superior Systems, Inc.)*

hot food down over themselves (43.25-inch maximum comfortable reach per Goldsmith, 1984).

- *Location of kitchen shelving:* Kitchen shelves designed for easy access by a wheelchair user also insure that everything will be easily accessible to children, including items such as cleaning products that must be stored out of their reach.

Supportiveness Conflicts

Universal design is also supportive of the physical abilities of all residents. Some examples of the conflicts that must be resolved in designing a universally supportive kitchen are:

- *Kitchen counter height:* Ideal counter height is based on the user's elbow height and the requirements of the task (Grandjean, 1973). Thus a compromise must be made in order to accommodate people of different heights (who may be working together) or the same person performing different cooking tasks (see Figure 8-4).

- *Type of refrigerator:* Side-by-side refrigerator/freezers are best for those who use a wheelchair (Olson, 1989); however, they can be more difficult for ambulant older adults with mobility problems to use because the second door is an obstacle between the refrigerator and the adjacent counter.

- *Clear door openings:* The ADA allows doors to have clear openings of 32 inches for wheelchair users (DOJ, 1991). However, 36-inch-wide doors provide easier access to those who use crutches and walkers (Goldsmith, 1984; Kira, 1960).

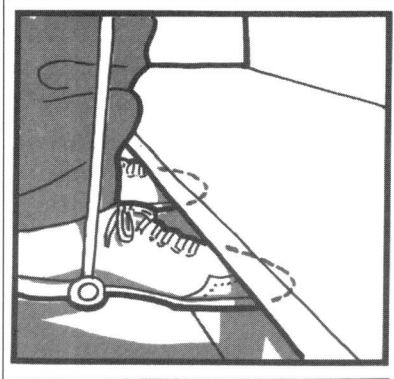

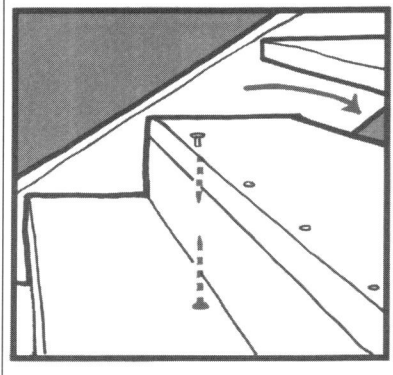

8-5. Open risers (found on many exterior wooden stairs) are a real hazard to most people because of their tripping potential, but one can easily close them off with pieces of wood. *(Reprinted with permission from AARP. Drawings from* The Doable Renewable Home: Making Your Home Fit Your Needs, *by John P. S. Salmen, AIA.)*

Conclusion

These examples should make it clear that simply applying ADA design requirements to housing will not result in universal housing design. A large proportion of the design recommendations in the ADA and its more comprehensive and housing-oriented predecessor, the Uniform Federal Accessibility Standards (1984), is for wheelchair users. The housing designer needs to integrate design recommendations for wheelchair users with design recommendations for infants, young children, teenagers, and adults of all ages and abilities. Where a truly *universal* design solution cannot be found, priorities must be established among different user groups to guide design decision making. Universal design is a challenge even in the absence of budgetary, aesthetic, structural, and other important considerations. Nevertheless, the process of recognizing conflicts and creatively resolving them should lead to better housing design than would be achieved if such conflicts were overlooked.

Some of the Best Things are Free and Easy

The American Association of Retired Persons is a remarkably good resource for information on home adaptations. Two of their publications offer illustrated guidelines to making simple yet effective changes in the home for the creation of supportive, safe environments.

The Doable Renewable Home: Making Your Home Fit Your Needs, by John P. S. Salmen, AIA, is a short booklet that has been around since 1985. Salmen provides suggestions for improving exterior and interior access and for modifying stairs, doors, controls, and storage facilities, as well as more wholesale remodeling of kitchens and baths (the two most troubling rooms for most individuals with disabilities). The book covers the needs of individuals with visual, auditory, and mobility difficulties. Figure 8-5 shows a representative illustration.

The Perfect Fit: Creative Ideas for a Safe & Livable Home by Jon Pynoos, Ph.D., and Evelyn Cohen, M.A., is a 1992 work that uses before-and-after fictional case studies to help the reader understand how relatively simple changes in the home can lead to safer and more enjoyable living. The booklet covers entry to the home, living rooms, kitchens, stairways, bathrooms, and bedroom modifications. The use of cartoons and checklists makes for an interesting and easy-to-follow yet informative read. Figure 8-6 shows a representative illustration.

Both publications are available free of charge from: AARP Fulfillment, 601 E Street, NW, Washington, DC 20049, (202) 434-6030.

8-6. BEFORE. Now that her husband has retired, Mrs. Allegro has found they spend more time at home. Her husband has noticed he's had difficulty reading and getting up from some of the furniture. Mrs. Allegro has decided to make some changes so the living room is more functional and comfortable. She knows that much of what she sees in decorating magazines looks good but isn't practical, especially for older adults. What changes would make the Allegros' living room more functional? *(Reprinted with permission from AARP. Drawings from* The Perfect Fit: Creative Ideas for a Safe and Livable Home, *by Jon Pynoos and Evelyn Cohen.)*

AFTER. (1) Furniture: Select couches and chairs that have arms and are not too deep or too low. (2) Tables: Select tables of appropriate height. (3) Lighting: Provide additional lighting where reading and other activities take place. Position lighting for best illumination. (4) Passageways: Provide clear passageways by eliminating excess or oversized furniture and objects. (5) Trailing wires: Remove trailing wires where people walk by adding a phone jack or cordless phone. All wires should be kept out of circulation path. (6) Blinds: Add adjustable blinds or other window covering to regulate glare. (7) Books: Read more interesting books.

Case Study

The Bartlett Independent Living Laboratory
by DeVonna L. Cervantes and Margaret J. Weber, Ph.D.

The Bartlett Laboratory, located on the Oklahoma State University campus, is a model environment for barrier-free living. The laboratory, also known as Independence Hall, is housed in a former home management residence. It was renovated in the late 1980s with a major grant from the Pete Bartlett family, to fulfill a dream of a demonstration unit for continuing education and research that would provide a model for a user-friendly environment for all individuals, regardless of age or ability.

The major purpose of the laboratory is to allow all individuals throughout the lifespan to function at their maximum potential. The laboratory/residence is a functional environment that offers accessibility and independence with the least amount of resistance. The three-bedroom residence presently serves a wheelchair-assisted graduate student and supports her ability to function more easily in the university environment. The house has also served as a model home for other students with various disabilities.

One important feature of the design involved the renovation of an older residence by subtly incorporating many aspects of universal design. Many of the barrier-free features are so unobtrusive that they must be pointed out to visitors. This aspect of the design helps overcome the stigma that barrier-free design is only for those with special needs. (Figure 8-7 presents a floor plan of the facility and shows many of the universal features.)

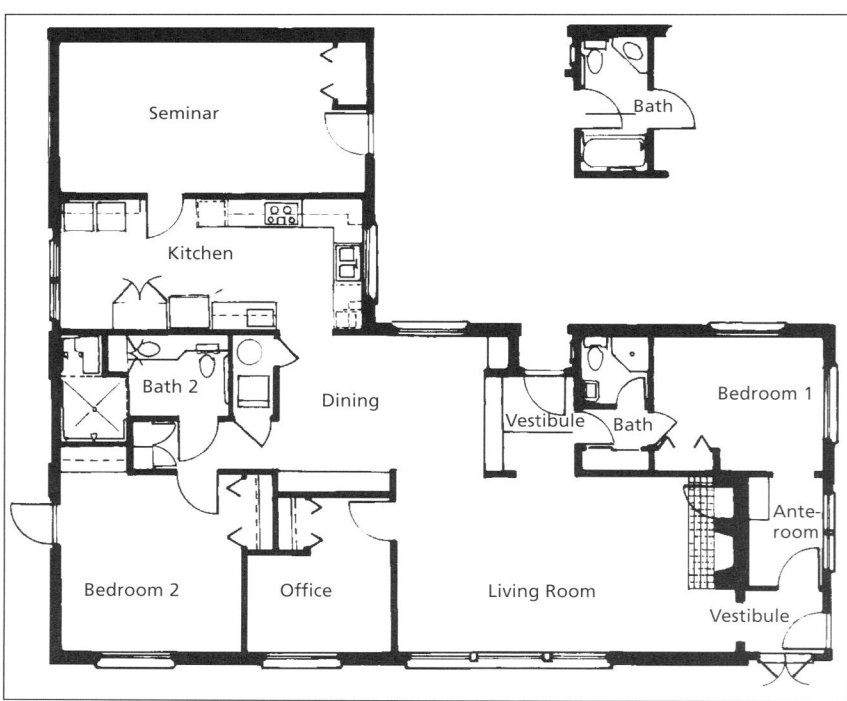

8-7. Floor plan of the Bartlett Laboratory. *(Reprinted with permission from DeVonna L. Cervantes and Margaret J. Weber, Ph.D. Drawing by Dara Baldrige.)*

The Bartlett Lab includes over 100 structural features and technological devices aimed at helping older people and persons with disabilities live independently in environments of their choosing. The laboratory demonstrates how an existing home can be modified, or a new home designed, to meet the needs of older people or persons with disabilities. Structural features include but are not limited to the following:

Ramps and curb cuts	Low thresholds
Environmental control systems	Side-opening oven door
Wide doorways and halls	(Kitchen location) front-loading washer
Roll-in showers (Bath 2)	Easy-opening doors and windows
Motorized window treatments	Transfer shower
Lifts	Sophisticated alarm systems
Adjustable-height work centers	Pull-out shelves

The Bartlett Independent Living Laboratory has the comprehensive goal of helping all individuals function at a high level of ease, independence, and comfort. The universal design features allow all individuals to function easily and efficiently, regardless of age or ability, providing a model environment for aging comfortably in one's own home.

Universal Design Strategy

The Universal Kitchen
by Carol V. Dagwell, Ph.D.

The kitchen is one of the most challenging residential spaces to design for both aesthetic pleasure and function accessibility for users of a variety of ages and abilities. This study examines the concepts relative to the design of the universal kitchen in terms of its location and space, kitchen work centers, counter heights, storage, lighting and electrical issues, hardware, and controls.

Location and Space

The first consideration in the design of the universal kitchen is its location within the floor plan of the dwelling. Of primary concern is adjacency to both the entrance (where groceries and supplies enter the house) and the eating area (to facilitate the serving of meals). As cooking becomes more social in nature, adjacency and/or openness to living areas of the house, both indoors and outdoors, becomes more desirable.

The universal kitchen must incorporate enough space to allow use of the kitchen by an individual who may require some type of assistive device such as a walker, wheelchair, motorized scooter, or crutches. A universal kitchen should also provide enough space to accommodate multiple users, a lifestyle option or necessity for many of today's households. The two primary areas that must be considered in order to provide this space are the entrance or access to the kitchen itself and the clearances between opposing cabinetry and appliances. Criteria for doors and entrances into the kitchen are the same as for those in other accessible spaces (see ANSI, 1992).

A clearance of 60 inches between opposing appliances or cabinets is most desirable as it provides for ease of maneuverability using assistive devices. Some standards for accessibility (ANSI 117.1, 1992, for example) allow for a T-turn with arms at least 36 inches wide and a length of 60 inches. Under any conditions, a clear floor space of 30" x 48", either parallel or perpendicular to the appliance or counter, must be allowed in front of all appliances, counters, and storage. Provision of generous clearances is especially important in kitchens incorporating an island or peninsula, as the inappropriate placement of these features can effectively negate the entire basis of the universal kitchen concept. Also, note that simply enlarging the kick space from 3 inches to 6 inches or 9 inches will allow one to cut overall dimensions.

Four Common Work Center Arrangements

Some work centers are easier for certain people to use than others. If the existing work station is not appropriate for use by the family, the descriptions below suggest ways you can modify the design to make it more appropriate. However, unless the limitation is only temporary (such as broken leg), the best solution may be to redesign the kitchen to use a more suitable work center.

U-Shaped Work Center

Appropriate:
- Provides room to maneuver wheelchair
- Provides room for two people to work
- Reduces kitchen traffic flow problems
- Reduces risk of bumping into appliances

Inappropriate for:
- People who have difficulty maneuvering or seeing across wide open areas, such as people with walkers, crutches, or low vision

To adapt a U-shaped work center for their use, place appliances closer together to shorten the work triangle.

(continued on next page)

L-Shaped Work Center

Appropriate:
- Provides room for kitchen traffic to flow through the room without interfering with work triangle
- Provides ample room for storage next to each workstation
- Provides sufficient room for two people or a wheelchair

Inappropriate for:
- People who have difficulty maneuvering or seeing across wide open areas, such as people with walkers, crutches, or low vision

To adapt an L-shape work center for their use, place a cooking work station closer to the corner of the L.

Island and Peninsular Work Centers

Appropriate:
- Shortens work triangle for easy use by people with low vision, walkers, or crutches.

Inappropriate:
- Open appliance doors may partially block aisle space needed for wheelchair.

To adapt a work center for use with a wheelchair, move the island/peninsula further away from the main wall to increase aisle space.

Corridor and Pullman Work Centers

Corridor work centers put appliances across an aisleway from each other. Pullman work centers place all appliances along the same wall.

Appropriate:
- Shortens work triangle for easy use by people with low vision, walkers, or crutches.*

Inappropriate:
- Open appliance doors may partially block aisle space needed for wheelchair.

To adapt a work center for a wheelchair, widen aisle space.

*Note: The distance between the sink and appliances can make these work centers tiring to maneuver when using crutches, a walker, or a wheelchair. Shortening the distance will help eliminate inefficiencies.

Recommended Work Triangle Dimensions

	Standard	Wheelchair	Walker/Crutches
Total distance connecting refrigerator, range and sink	12'–22'	14'–24'	10'–12'
Refrigerator to sink	4'–7'	6'–9'	2'–5'
Sink to range	4'–6'	6'–8'	2'–4'
Range to refrigerator	4'–9'	6'–11'	2'–7'

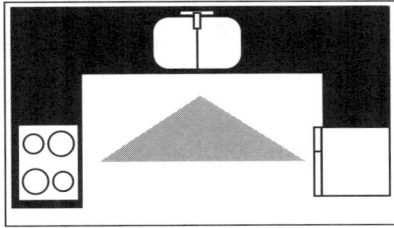

8-8(A). U-shaped work center.
(Reprinted with permission from Whirlpool Corporation.)

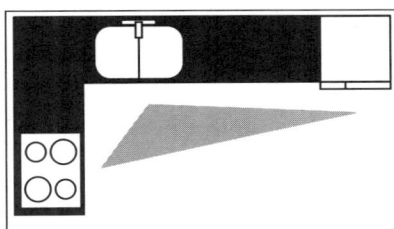

8-8(B). L-shaped work center.

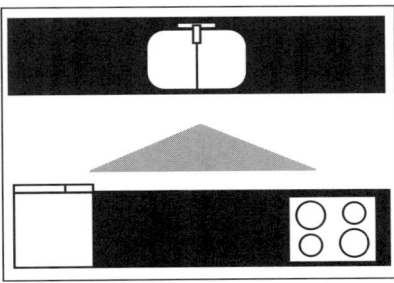

8-8(C). Island and peninsular work centers.

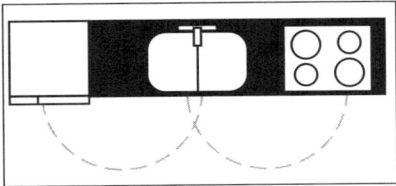

8-8(D). Corridor and pullman work centers.

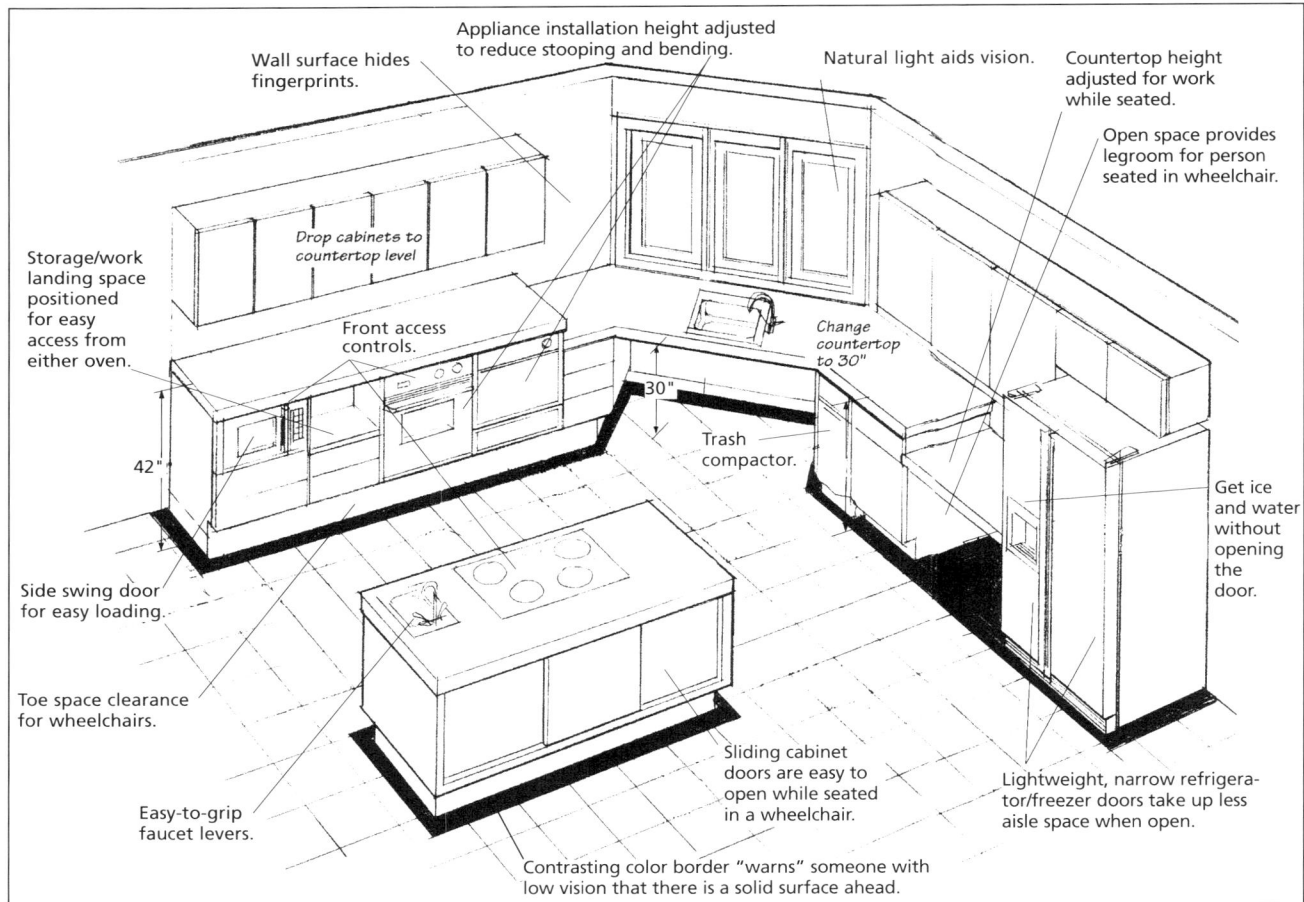

8-9. Workstation arrangement with appliances and storage in place. *(Reprinted with permission from Whirlpool Corporation.)*

Work Centers and Counter Heights

The conventional approach to the design of kitchens focuses on five centers related to the food preparation process: refrigerator, mix and/or preparation, sink, cook, and serve (see Figure 8-8). A right-to-left sequence is generally preferred, although this may be reversed when the cook is known to be left-handed or when architectural constraints prohibit a right-to-left order. The important point is for the centers to be in the order listed so that the food preparation process is facilitated. This is simply good universal design that helps to create a safe work environment.

An additional consideration in the design and layout of the universal kitchen is the height of the work surfaces at each of the centers. The customary standardization of all counter heights at 36 inches does not allow for comfortable use by seated users, shorter or taller people, people with neck or back problems, or children. In order to provide work surfaces at suitable heights for these users, some of the surfaces must be adjustable or the kitchen must include countertops at several heights (see Figure 8-9).

Since side-by-side refrigerators provide both types of cold food storage at all heights, they are the best choice in the universal kitchen. The refrigerator should be located so both doors open to a full 180°

with space for a lateral approach by seated users. Door ice and water dispensers make this type of refrigerator even more convenient.

The mix and preparation center should be either adjustable in height or permanently lowered to a height comfortable for seated users. Permanently lowered work surfaces can be achieved through provision of a mix center, desk area, or eating area (peninsula, island, and so on)—all areas usually built at lower heights. Pull-out cutting boards, drawers equipped with cut-outs to hold various sizes of mixing bowls, and pull-out or fold-down tables are other methods of providing a variety of heights of work surfaces.

Convenient, comfortable access to the sink center is essential in the universal kitchen, just as it is in conventional kitchens, because of the many food preparation and clean-up activities that take place there. If the primary cook is seated, the sink area may be made adjustable in height (*Barrier Free Environments*, 1991) or may be permanently lowered with open knee space below (Figure 8-10). In either case, the sink should be no more than 6½ inches in depth, with a rear drain and pipes that are insulated or covered with a panel to prevent burns (a panel is preferred for both safety and aesthetic reasons; see Figure 8-11). An instant hot water dispenser operated by a lever located at the sink is a great convenience for those with limited abilities.

Two appliances normally located at the sink center, the garbage disposal and the dishwasher, present problems when the sink and surrounding countertop are lowered and open

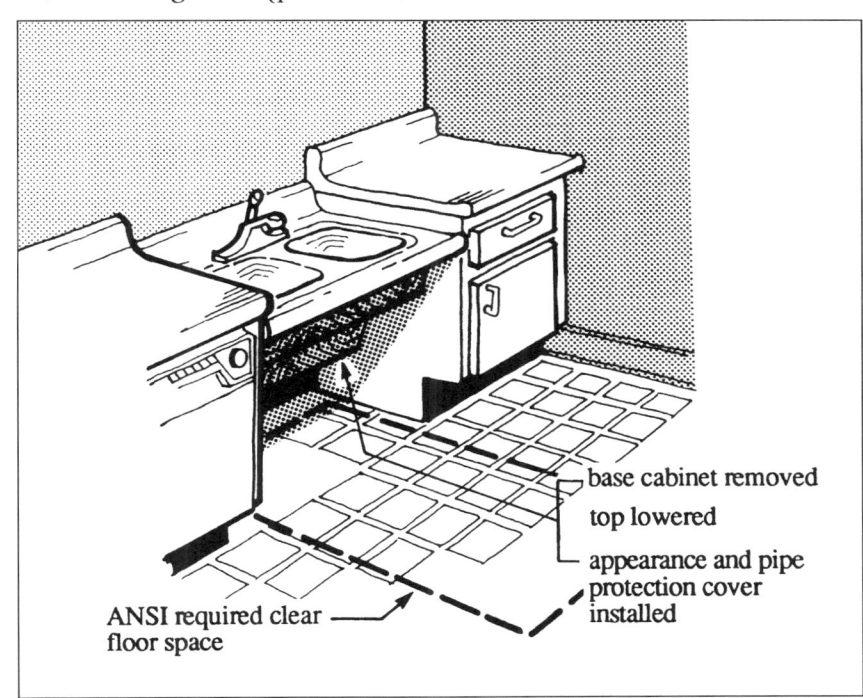

8-10. Placement of adjustable sink in a lowered counter position with base cabinet removed.

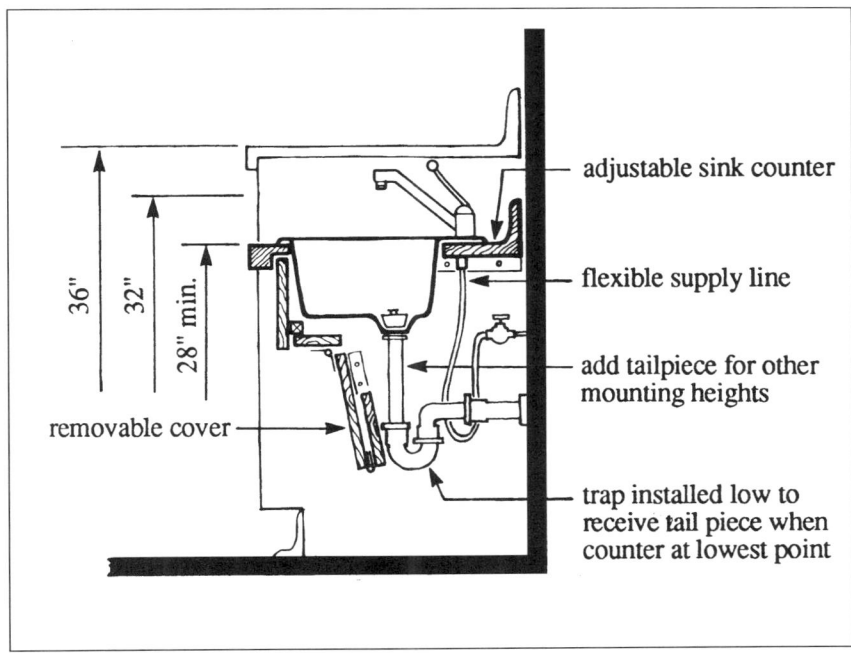

8-11. Side view of adjustable sink with base cabinet removed and appearance and pipe protection cover installed.

knee space is provided below the sink. The garbage disposal restricts access to the sink when installed with a single-bowl sink, but may be installed under one bowl of a two-bowl sink and enclosed in a standard base cabinet. Knee space is provided under the second bowl and adjacent countertop to achieve an opening of at least 30 inches in width. In environmentally conscious households, the garbage disposal may be replaced by a composting bin located immediately adjacent to the open space under the sink (Koontz and Dagwell, 1994). Another alternative is to use a separate garbage disposal sink that sits at the back corner of the sink (available from Kohler and others).

The problem created by the dishwasher (which should be front-loading in design) is that it is available only in heights that finish to 36 inches to conform to standardized kitchen counter heights. When the dishwasher is placed adjacent to a lowered sink area, care must be taken to provide enough lowered work surface so that the user's elbows do not bump the higher side of the dishwasher.

An alternative solution (and one that shows a good example of choice) to the problems created in the sink center by the garbage disposal and dishwasher, and one that also meets the lifestyle consideration of multiple cooks, is to install a secondary sink center. The primary sink center can then be at conventional height and contain both the dishwasher and garbage disposal. A secondary sink, in a lowered counter (with knee space below and pipe protection), can then be available for seated users, children, or another cook and, with the addition of a microwave oven, can form the basis of a second cooking station (Koontz and Dagwell, 1994).

The provision of a separate cooktop and oven in preference to a standard range not only provides greater flexibility and accessibility, but also accommodates two or more cooks with greater ease. Cooktops with burners arranged in a straight line or staggered format enhance safety by reducing or eliminating the need to reach across the front burners to attend to food cooking on the rear burners. Controls for the cooktop unit should be along the side or front for better accessibility.

Design of the cooktop area with open knee space below will allow easier access to the cooking elements by a seated user. The safety of this arrangement is sometimes questioned—the potential for spills on the cooktop overflowing into the lap of the user is obvious. Consequently, some individuals may prefer a cooktop placed with a base cabinet and space provided for a lateral approach to the cooking elements. In this case, the straight line configuration of burners would provide the highest level of both accessibility and safety.

Ovens with side-hinged doors (currently manufactured by Gaggenau and Frigidaire) provide the greatest ease of access for both the standing and seated user. For these ovens, ANSI (1992) suggests that a pull-out shelf be located immediately under the oven.

A microwave oven can be of great assistance to persons with reduced abilities. The location of the microwave should be determined on the basis of its most frequent type of use. It may be placed on the countertop or above the countertop on a microwave oven shelf, or it may be installed below counter height. Installation of the microwave with the controls at an accessible height (no greater than 48 inches above the floor) assumes special importance with the realization that the microwave is often used by children on an independent basis.

For the serving center to meet the needs of the universal kitchen, space for a lateral approach using a wheelchair or scooter should be provided along with storage features that enhance accessibility. Also, it is helpful to provide a continuous surface from the preparation/cooking-to-serving area to allow people with limited strength to slide dishes, pots, and so on from one area to the next (see Figure 8-12).

Storage

Sufficient, well-designed, and properly located storage is essential to the success of any kitchen. The universal kitchen demands a consideration of ease of access to storage.

Traditional base cabinets with fixed shelves make access to storage difficult even for the ambulant, able-bodied user. Improved access to storage in base cabinets may be achieved by specification of units with drawers and pull-out shelves or trays (with a lip on the front to prevent items from sliding off). Corner base units become more effective and accessible when provided with swing-out shelf units or revolving shelves. Visibility in wall units is enhanced by the use of either wire or clear plastic shelves (Liebrock with Behar, 1993).

In a conventional kitchen, some of the most easily accessed vertical space, the space between the base cabinet units and the wall cabinets, is usually left empty. Some of this space may be designed for use in the universal kitchen through the following means: a shallow shelf (8 inches in depth, wall mounted), a portable U-shaped shelf that rests on the countertop, or appliance garages.

Adequate pantry storage for food items is important in any kitchen design, but it is even more critical in the universal kitchen as persons with limited abilities often prefer to minimize grocery shopping trips by keeping larger quantities of food on hand. Walk-in pantries should be avoided as they generally do not provide adequate maneuvering space for a person using assistive devices. Shallow closets with bi-fold doors provide an alternative that is easily accessible

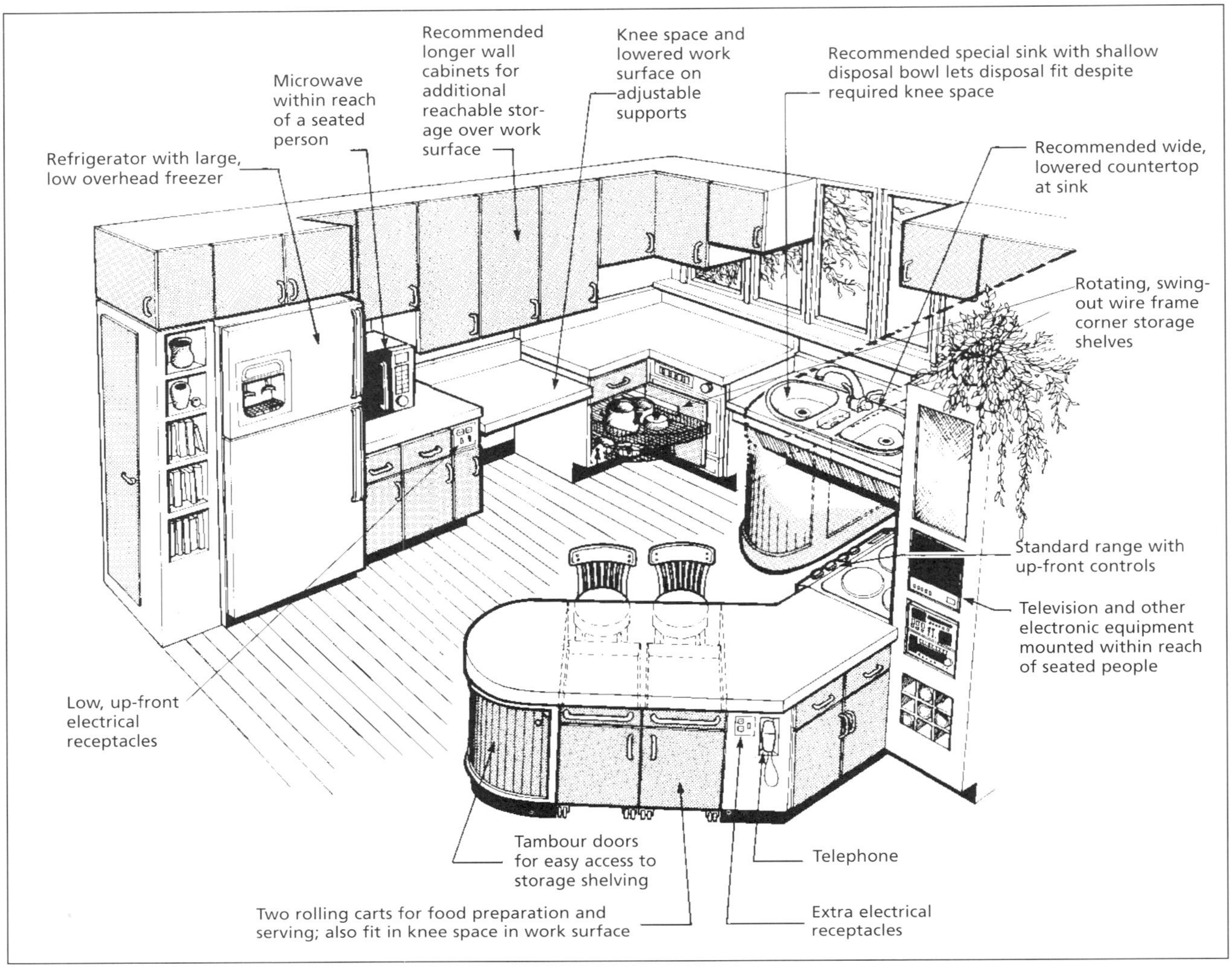

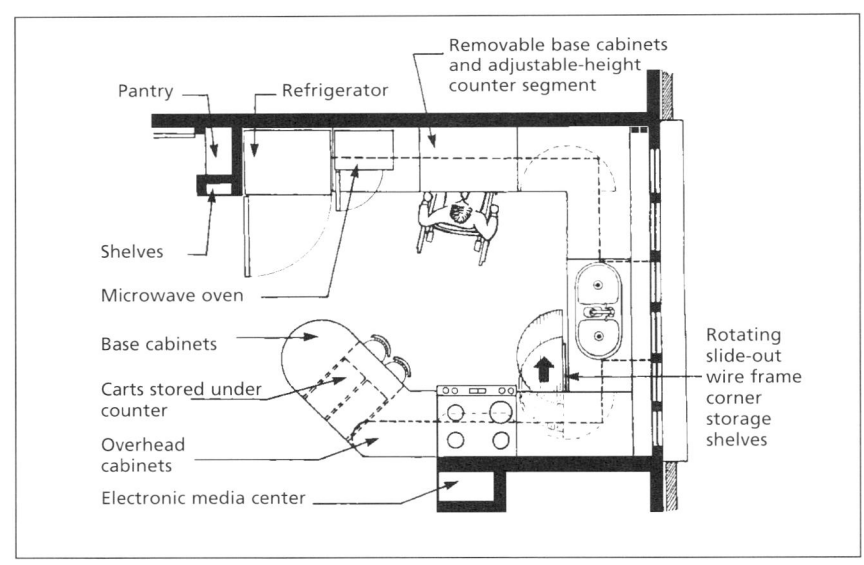

8-12. Perspective and floor plan views of an elaborate kitchen with adaptable features.

for most persons. A second suitable alternative for pantry storage is the full-height or pull-out pantry units available from many manufacturers of kitchen cabinetry. These units capitalize on the underutilized but accessible space between the base and wall cabinetry.

Lighting and Electrical Concerns

In a universal kitchen design, lighting assumes greater importance because the aging eye needs more illumination to perform effectively. Installation of rheostats and flexible lighting controls allows individual users to adjust the lighting to their particular needs.

The usual recommendation for ambient lighting in the kitchen is 25–50 footcandles, while task lighting should be 50–100 footcandles (Kaufman, 1987). When elderly or low-vision users of the kitchen are present, it is desirable to provide both ambient and task lighting at the upper ends of the suggested ranges. Switching should be carefully planned so that controls are located near the lights they operate.

Switches and receptacles that are usually placed on the wall at the rear of the countertop may need to be relocated to a panel on the front of the base cabinet unit in order to accommodate seated users or children. This may be done by replacing a drawer unit with a panel designed for the necessary switch and receptacle plates. In households where young children are present, receptacle covers should be used at all times to ensure the children's safety. Another alternative for making receptacles accessible for a seated cook is the use of a power strip with an extension cord (Null, 1987). In addition, Raschko (1982) recommends that all receptacles in a kitchen designed for elderly or disabled users be equipped with ground fault circuit interrupters.

Controls and Hardware

Faucets in the universal kitchen should be controlled by a single lever for greatest ease in use. In addition, a spray attachment on a long hose (separate or part of the faucet head) eliminates much lifting and carrying of heavy pans.

Controls for ovens and burner units are easier to operate if they are of the blade, extended-blade, or small-lever type, according to *Barrier-Free Environments* (1991). Knobs that audibly click into operating position are helpful for users with reduced visual abilities. Many microwave ovens are controlled by touch panels that are operated relatively easily by most users, including those with mobility limitations. For low-vision users, several manufacturers of kitchen appliances make available, at no charge, braille or raised letter panels to add to the control area of both these and other

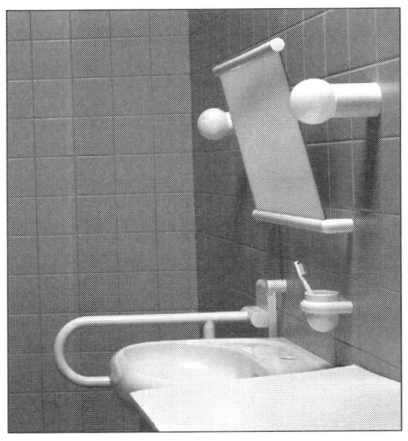

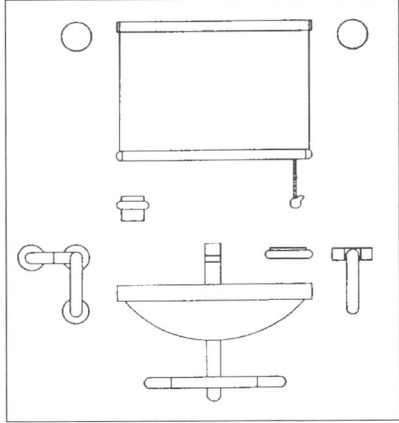

8-13. This bathroom shows HEWI's adjustable mirror that tilts to a 30° angle, light fixtures, tumbler with holder, and fold-up support bar. The accompanying diagram also shows the use of a drain guard. *(Reprinted with permission from HEWI, Inc.)*

types of appliances. All appliance controls and switches should be located no more than 48 inches above the floor.

Hardware on cabinetry units should be selected so that operation is possible with a minimum of strength and gripping ability. This is best accomplished by selecting hardware in a D or loop shape. Knobs and recessed pulls and handles should be avoided.

Additional Concerns for Low-Vision Users

A common hazard to the low-vision user in a standard kitchen is the use of swinging doors on wall cabinets. Safer choices are to use open shelves; wall cabinets with sliding doors; or doors that are counter-balanced so that they open up, out of the way, and then close down very easily.

Utilization of the concept of value contrast can also facilitate use of kitchens by those with limited vision. A light-value countertop contrasted with a dark-value backsplash and countertop front edge facilitates perception of the beginning and end of the countertop space (Null, 1988). This concept can also be applied in terms of the floor material and cabinetry or wall color so that the delineation of the edge where the two planes meet is clearer.

Additional Resources

As the market for products that enhance accessibility continues to expand, new products and additional resources for product information are constantly becoming available to assist the designer. Useful references currently include the *Directory of Accessible Building Products* (1992) and *Sweet's Accessible Building Products* (1992).

Universal Design Strategy
Universal Bath Design
by Joan M. Eisenberg

Until recently the bathroom in the United States has been truly the "Necessary Room" and nothing more except for the very wealthy users. Indoor plumbing with a tub, water closet, and lavatory in one room was not an option for even the wealthy until the early 1900s; the modern bathroom did not emerge into general housing until the 1920s. At that time, well-designed spaces were not high priorities for architects and builders, so Americans still have the 5' x 7' bathroom that currently challenges so many when they are remodeling. As the population has become more sophisticated, bathroom requirements have changed. Today, most new buildings have at minimum a family bath, a master bath, and, in most cases, a powder room.

Function and universal design as it relates to the bathroom can be divided into two categories: *safety* and *accessibility/comfort*. In order to help designers provide safe and accessible bathrooms, the National Kitchen and Bath Association has established 27 rules of bathroom design. These rules are merely the starting place for exceptional universal design, but they require the creative input of involved designers.

1. A clear walkway of at least 32 inches must be provided at all entrances to the bathroom.

2. No doors may interfere with fixtures.

3. A mechanical ventilation system must be included in the plan.

4. Ground fault circuit interrupters must be specified on all receptacles. No switches may be within 60 inches of any water source. All light fixtures above tub/shower units must be moisture-proof special-purpose fixtures.

5. If floor space exists between two fixtures, at least 6 inches of the space should be provided for cleaning.

6. At least 21 inches of clear walkway space should exist in front of the lavatory.

7. The minimum clearance from the lavatory centerline to any side wall is 15 inches.

8. The minimum clearance between two bowls in the lavatory center is 30 inches, centerline to centerline.

9. The minimum clearance from the center of the toilet to any obstruction, fixture, or equipment on either side of the toilet is 15 inches.

10. At least 21 inches of clear walkway space must exist in front of the toilet. (Note, however, that ANSI requires 48 inches and a wheelchair width of 26 inches to 28 inches.)

11. The toilet paper holder should be installed within reach of the person seated on the toilet. The ideal location is slightly in front of the edge of the toilet bowl, the center of which is 26 inches above the finished floor.

8-14. Accessibility gets a stylish new look in Kohler's newest products for the bath. The Precedence™ bath whirlpool features a watertight door that provides easy access to the bathtub, and it also features (not visible here) a seat that can be used for bathing or showering and can be folded up to become a backrest. Also shown is the new Invitation™ countertop lavatory, designed with a drain to one side at the rear of the basin to provide wheelchair clearance under the counter; and the Highline™ Lite™ PC toilet. *(Reprinted with permission from Kohler Co.)*

8-15. The versatile MasterShower™ tower from Kohler features multiple water functions to create a stimulating and fun showering environment. MasterShower™ tower features an overhead sheet flow spout for a drenching rinse, two adjustable body sprays, and a three-way showerhead. Any two of the MasterShower™ tower's functions can be used in combination. Function selection can be easily switched back and forth on a solid state 10 push-button panel. *(Reprinted with permission from Kohler Co.)*

12. The minimum clearance from the center of the bidet to any obstruction, fixture, or equipment on either side of the bidet is 15 inches.

13. At least 21 inches of clear walkway space should exist in front of the bidet. (See note to #10.)

14. Storage for soap and towels should be installed within reach of the person seated on the bidet.

15. No more than one step should lead to the tub. The step must be at least 10 inches deep and must not exceed 7¼ inches in height. (Note that it is better to avoid steps if at all possible, and if they must be used, grab bars should be in place to facilitate safe entry and exit.)

16. Bathtub faucetry should be accessible from outside the tub.

17. Whirlpool motor access, if necessary, is included in plan.

18. At least one grab bar is installed to facilitate bathtub or shower entry.

19. The minimum usable shower interior dimension is 32" x 32".

20. A bench or footrest should be installed within the shower enclosure.

21. A minimum clear walkway of 21 inches should exist in front of the tub/shower. (See note to #10.)

22. The shower door swings into the bathroom.

23. All shower heads are protected by pressure balance/temperature regulators or temperature-limiting devices.

24. All flooring is of slip-resistant material.

25. Storage must be provided in the plan, including counter/shelf space around the lavatory, grooming equipment storage, convenient shampoo/soap storage in shower/tub area, and hanging space for bathroom linens.

26. Heating system must be provided.

27. General and task lighting must be provided.

Safety

When designing and specifying products for bathrooms, it is the designer's responsibility to address safety before beauty. It is known that 25 percent of all accidents and 3 percent of all fatalities that occur in the home take place in the bathroom. Some of the hazards include falls, electric shock, scalding, broken glass, poisoning, and door swings.

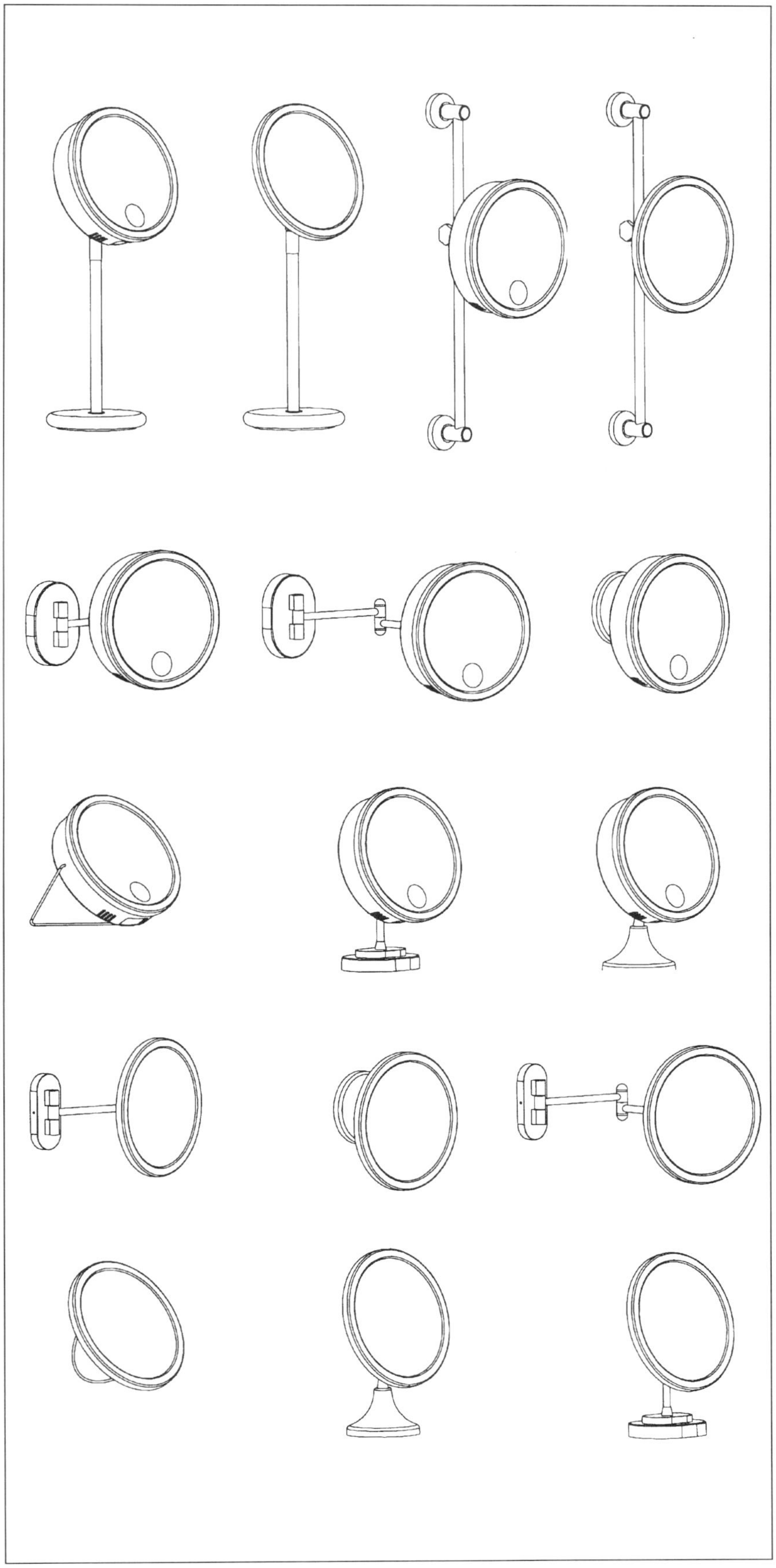

Universal Design in the Home 243

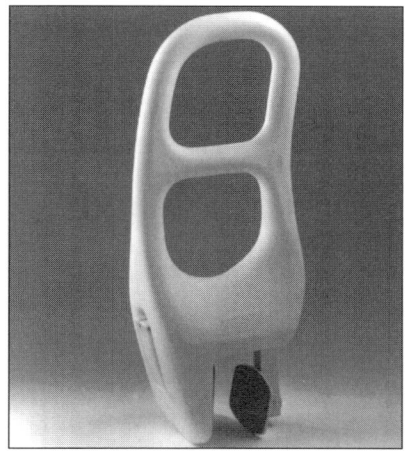

8-16. The Lumex Tub-Guard® Tall bathtub rail is a convenient and attractive product for ensuring a safe entry and exit from any bathtub.
(Reprinted with permission from Lumex.)

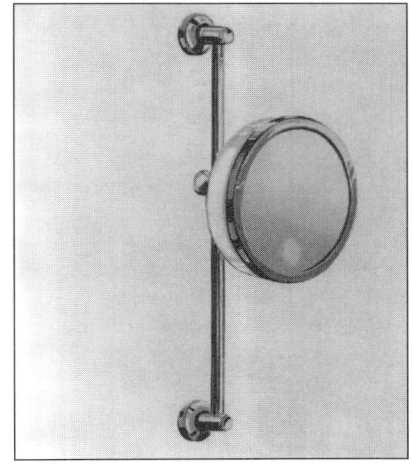

8-17. Versatile grooming accessories from BACI® by Remcraft have built-in lights, magnification to accommodate varying levels of vision, and a range of flexibility in mounting.
(Reprinted with permission from Remcraft: BACI.)

Slippery surfaces—on the floor and in tubs and showers—are a major cause of accidents. Shiny tile and polished marble should be avoided. Throw rugs—even those with slip-resistant backing—can cause a fall if tripped over. Bathroom carpet, although generally believed to be the least sanitary flooring, can provide a warm, slip-resistant flooring if installed properly. Most tub and formed shower manufacturers offer nonslip surfaces in at least some, if not all, of their units. If unavailable, the next best thing is for the client to use a rubber mat or "place and press" rubberized flowers. For site-built showers, be sure to specify a small (no more than 2" x 2") nonslip tile for the base. To further prevent a fall, grab bars should be installed in all tubs and showers. Once thought to be only for the elderly or for people with disabilities, grab bars have been proven to enhance everyone's safety. Note that grab bars must be able to support a 300-pound static load (see Figure 8-18).

The National Electric Code requires that, in any room where there is a combination of high humidity, water, and electricity, the electric circuits must be protected with ground fault circuit interrupters. These help prevent electric shock. Many local governments have passed plumbing codes that require pressure and temperature balanced tub and shower controls to prevent burns from scalding water and falls caused by "shower shock." These are all single-handle configurations. Specifications should include only tempered glass or shatterproof plastic glazing on all glass areas to protect against broken glass.

Finally, in terms of safety, consider the way the door swings. Most bathroom doors swing in so as not to block hall traffic. However, if someone falls in a bathroom (especially one that is small), they may block the door, preventing entry. Also, in small spaces, open drawers from vanities can block the door from opening.

8-18. Four possible universal bathroom floor plans.
(Reprinted with permission from Center for Accessible Housing.)

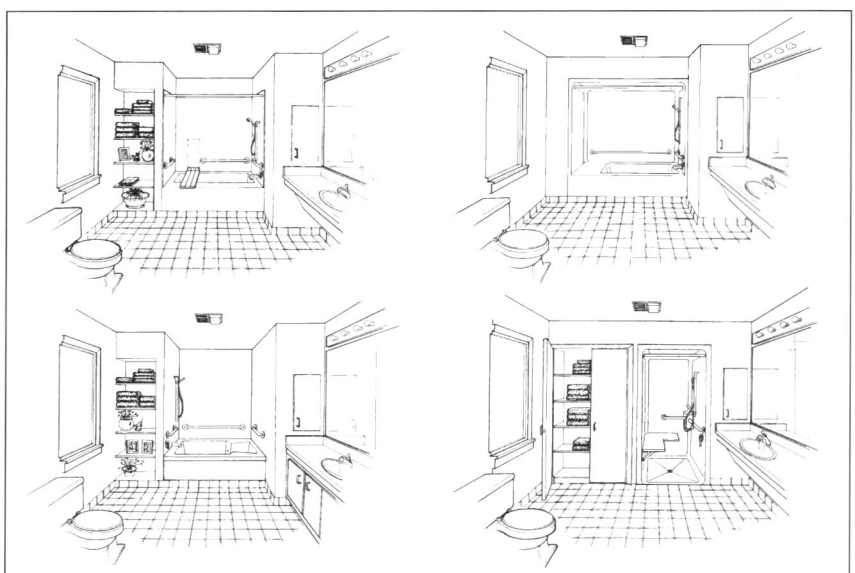

If swinging the door out is not an option, then try to have it swing against a blank wall or in front of the tub. Definitely avoid having it open into the water closet or lavatory.

Doors within the bathroom itself must also be considered for accessibility and safety. Shower doors that open out into the room or sliding doors are an essential safety feature. When using sliding doors, triple-panel sliders or accordion doors allow maximum access to the space. In a compartmentalized bathroom, door swings for the various compartments will have major impact on the room design.

Accessibility/Comfort

It wasn't until 1976, when Alexander Kira wrote *The Bathroom*, that people started thinking in terms of comfort in bathrooms. The most obvious example is the height of the standard vanity. How did this uncomfortable standard come into being? Washstands were approximately 30 inches to 32 inches high, with a wash basin sitting on top, creating an upper measurement of 34 inches to 36 inches, which is almost ideal for most adults. Somewhere in the translation to indoor plumbing, instead of raising the washstand around the basin, the basin was dropped into the stand. Nearly everyone can be made more comfortable by raising the vanity height. Other areas where height could affect the comfort of the user are the water closet, shower head, towel bars, soap dishes, and toilet tissue holders.

Adequate lighting is critical to a well-planned bathroom. A variety of types of lighting on separate switches and dimmers for incandescent or halogen lights should be designed into all bathrooms. General room lighting is the first area of concern and can easily be achieved in many aesthetically pleasing ways. Task lighting should include lighting for the tub and shower as well as for the vanity and water closet areas. An adjustable, lit, magnifying mirror should be included so that anyone with visual impairment can comfortably use the vanity without having to be a contortionist.

Conclusion

Safe, accessible, functional, comfortable, and aesthetically pleasing spaces to live in; homes that will change with people as they change so that individuals will not have to leave if injured or disabled—these are the goals of residential universal design.

Case Study
Residential Redesign for Accessibility
by Lee Meyer

The following case study describes two design projects that architect Lee Meyer undertook to provide accessibility for wheelchair users. In each example, the changes made were relatively inexpensive and added to the overall value of the residence.

Many people are beginning to ask for accommodations in their existing homes to allow greater independence for themselves or for family members who are disabled. Architects and designers are the primary source of information for these individuals.

Project 1: Three-Bedroom Rambler

The clients owned a three-bedroom rambler house and had a limited budget from which to draw. They have two adult sons, both of whom use wheelchairs. Their main request was for better access to bedrooms and bathrooms. Figure 8-19 shows the solutions described below.

Access to the sons' bedrooms was improved by repositioning the doors at 90° angles to each other. This change required the installation of a header to replace the bearing wall.

The hall bathroom and master bedroom bathroom were combined. The stool remained in the same position, and a large corner shower was constructed in the same area as the master bedroom shower. The door to the master bedroom was retained, providing secondary access for the parents.

The linen closet was removed and a new 3-foot doorway was installed into the bath, while the vanity cabinet and sink were realigned along the hallway wall to provide better access to the stool. Bath linens were stored in the vanity. The sink portion of the vanity was constructed cantilevered so that wheelchair access at the sink could be maintained. Plumbing changes were kept to a minimum, primarily involving the removal of existing fixtures.

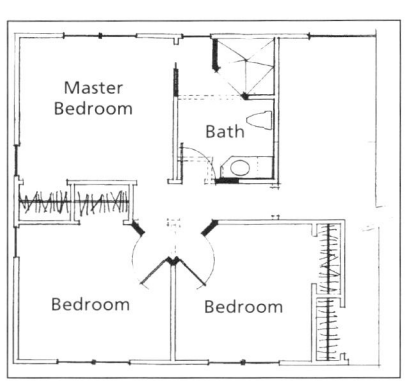

8-19. Floor plan of redesigned three-bedroom rambler for wheelchair accessibility.
(Reprinted with permission from Lee Meyer.)

Project 2: Townhouse

The client for the second project was an adult male who used a wheelchair. His main concern was to achieve better access on the second floor, bedroom level, while maintaining an unmodified appearance for future resale purposes. Figure 8-20 shows the solutions described herein.

A residential elevator was installed in an existing hoistway since the units in the townhouse development were planned with space for residential elevators, connecting all four levels of the structure within each unit.

The door at the bottom of the third floor stairs was eliminated, and one step was removed and a winder added. Doors to the office and guest bedroom were realigned in order to provide access to the office. Both doors had been 2 feet wide, and they were replaced with doors of 3-foot widths. The realignment also provided a turn-around space at the end of the corridor.

In the master bathroom, a whirlpool tub and bidet were removed, and a large drive-in shower was constructed. The toilet was repositioned, and the wall between the bath and dressing area was removed. The two-sink vanity was removed, and a single-sink vanity was installed with knee space at the sink and with drawer storage at each side for medical supplies and personal items.

The door to the walk-in closet was removed, and a 4-foot cased opening was installed. Low rods were installed on each side of the closet, with an Elfa™ basket storage system installed below the window for foldable items. A pocket door was installed in the bathroom, and a 3-foot door was placed at the entrance to the master bedroom.

Changes throughout the balance of the townhouse were minimal: The island in the kitchen was reconstructed to create a lower eating/work surface; the microwave oven was located in a base cabinet, immediately below the countertop, and a pull-out breadboard on roller extensions was installed below the microwave as both a landing surface for hot items and a cutting surface accessible to the chair. The toe-kick and raised bottom of the sink cabinet were eliminated to provide drive-up access to the sink. A bar sink was added at the lower level of the island. Finally, a washer and dryer were placed in the basement laundry. The front-loading washer and the dryer both featured front controls.

The client remained in the townhouse for three years following the renovation. The new owners had been seeking a luxury townhouse that could be used by an elderly parent with mobility problems.

Case Study

An Innovative Home Renovation: Making Use of a Residential Elevator
by Betty Jones

One means of designing an accessible home is often overlooked, that is, installing an elevator for safe and easy access to various levels of the residence. At first glance, adding an elevator seems extravagant. However, prices for purchase and installation are frequently no higher than the cost of building a stairway, and technology has improved to the point where home elevators are virtually maintenance free.

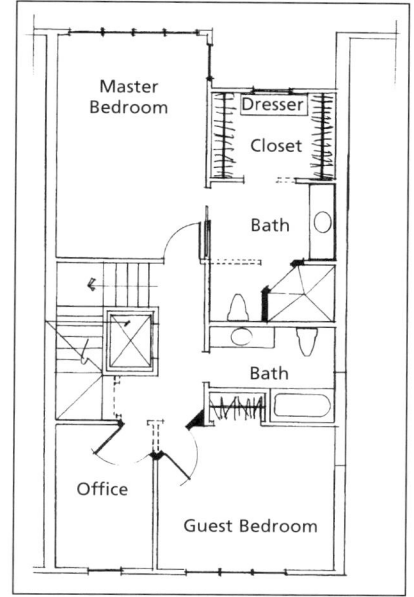

8-20. Floor plan of redesigned townhouse for wheelchair accessibility. *(Reprinted with permission from Lee Meyer.)*

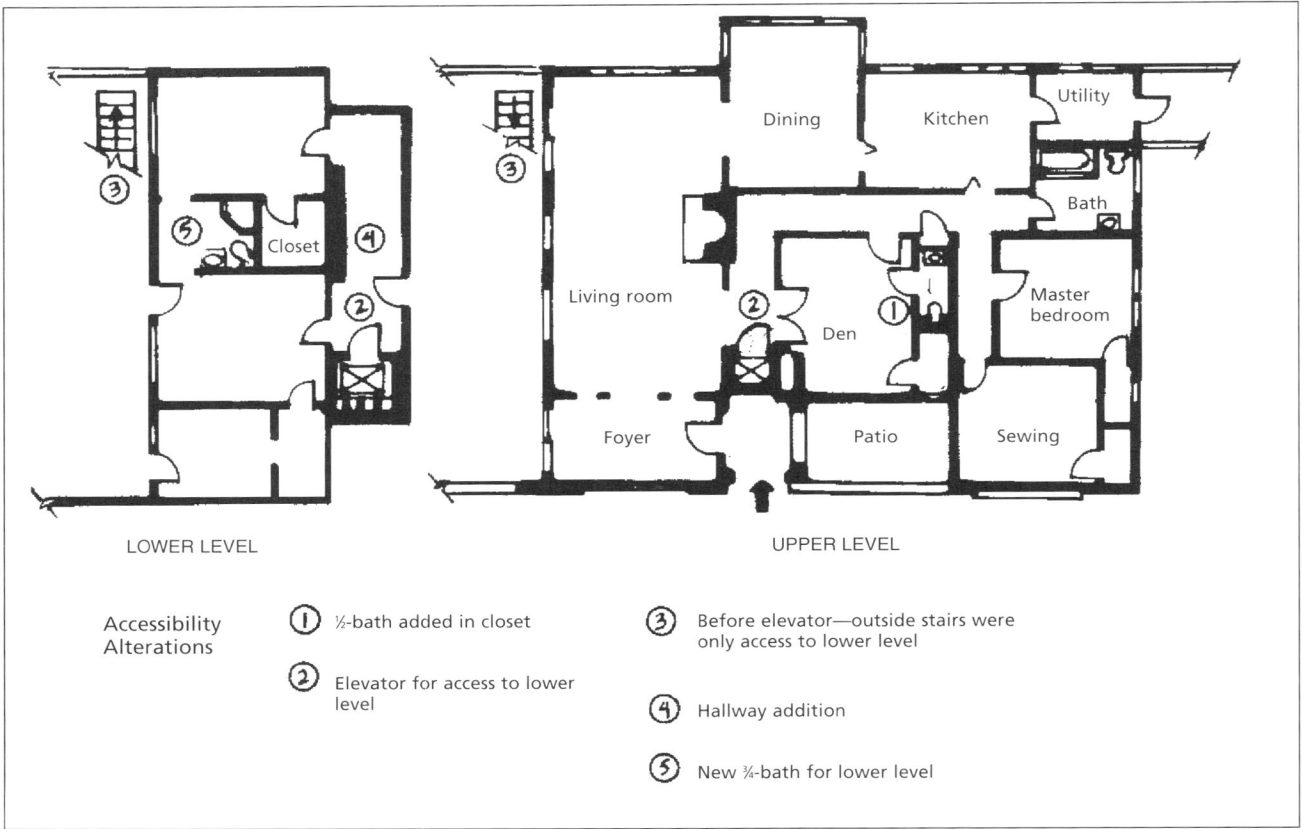

8-21. Plan for renovation of a private residence with a home elevator added.
(Figures 8-21 through 8-23 reprinted with permission from Elizabeth and Robert Tillman.)

Robert and Elizabeth Tillman of San Diego, California, were looking ahead to the time when Elizabeth's mother would need to live with them in their home. They needed to provide access to a downstairs area of the house, and provide a living space in that area to include a bedroom, closet, and bathroom (see Figure 8-21). They also wanted to maintain the integrity of the space where an elevator might be located, and so decided to install it in an existing closet and replace lost closet space somewhere else. Finally, the Tillmans needed to convert a second upstairs closet into a bathroom since they hosted large parties and needed a second bathroom on the main floor.

At the time they made their decision to have the renovation done, the Tillman's home had a downstairs space that was virtually unused, except for storage and Elizabeth's craft projects. However, the only entrance to the downstairs was by an outside wooden stairway—not very accessible to an older person. There was adequate space for a bedroom and closet to be created by simply fixing up existing rooms, but the furnace room had to be moved and a new furnace installed to create space for the downstairs bathroom. An entrance hallway was added downstairs off of the elevator landing, allowing entry to both the apartment and the existing craft room.

Universal Design in the Home 249

8-22. Elevator shown with entrance closed and open. Notice how the entryway blends into the room.

8-23. Closet added next to elevator entryway, allowing increased storage with little loss of space.

8-24. The Automated Closet Carousel™ from White Home Products, Inc., provides ample capacity, convenience, and accessibility while solving the universal problem of storage efficiency.
(Reprinted with permission from White Home Products, Inc.)

The elevator installed in the upstairs closet provided access in the least obtrusive manner. (Figure 8-22 shows how well-camouflaged this addition appears.) The loss of that closet's storage area (mainly used for party equipment) was compensated for by the creation of a new closet (see Figure 8-23).

This project shows how innovative thinking and the use of products not often considered appropriate for residential design can overcome obstacles to accessibility in a cost-effective and efficient manner.

Marketing Universal Design 9

The first step in marketing universal design is insuring that the term is recognized, accepted, and understood. It is crucial that the population at large (and professionals in particular) not identify universal design with design for "special needs." As long as people view it as such, designers who seek to hasten the advent of universally designed products and environments will have little impact.

One of the most important marketing tools is the investment made in students—those future professionals who will carry new skills and attitudes into the work world. This, of course, calls for first understanding what is already known about designing universally, and then better defining and refining the discipline. To work toward this end, in 1993 the National Endowment for the Arts and the U.S. Department of Justice awarded a grant to the Boston Center for Accessible Housing to set up the Universal Design Education Project (UDEP). The schools of design at 14 universities across the United States were the first recipients of UDEP funds to set up and evaluate universal design courses. UDEP is working to disseminate the results of these first studies: Professor Roberta L. Kilty-Padgett's project at Michigan State University consisted of a course entitled "Interior Design and Human Dimensions." (Figures 9-1 through 9-4 show representative student work from the course.) Other programs that market universal design materials include Ronald Mace's Center for Universal Design at North Carolina State University, and New York's Pratt Institute's School of Art and Design, where Robert Anders and colleagues have written and published *The Universal Design Primer* and *A Universal Design Curriculum*.

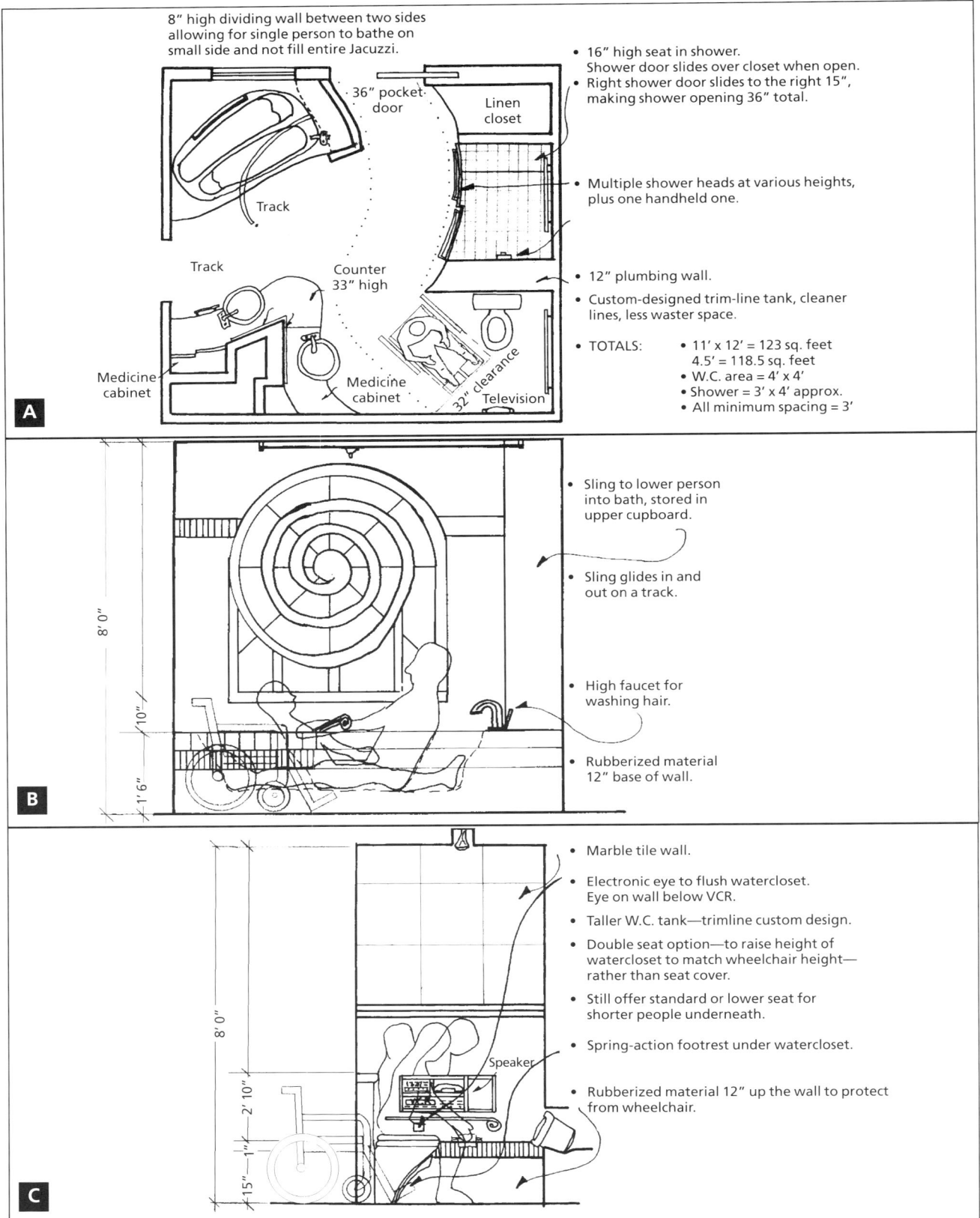

9-1. (A) Student designer Sarah Robinson's bathroom design. (B) Detail of bathtub design. (C) Taking into consideration the length of time a person might actually have to spend there, the watercloset is designed with a built-in entertainment and information center. *(Figures 9-1 through 9-4 reprinted with permission from Kenneth Klemmer and Sarah Robinson, students of Roberta Kilty-Padgett, Associate Professor Interior Design, Michigan State University.)*

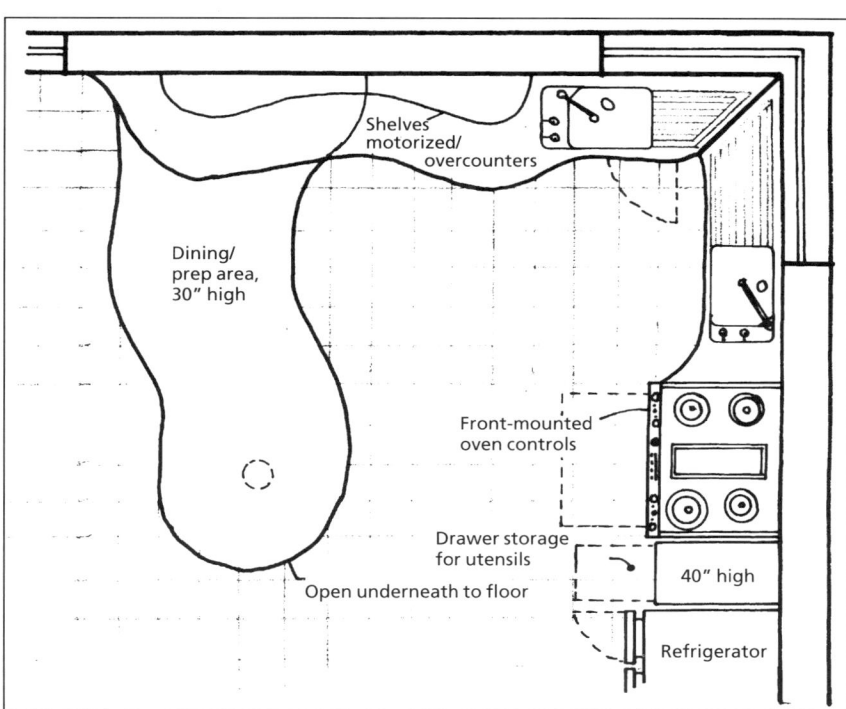

9-2. Student designer Kenneth Klemmer's kitchen design.

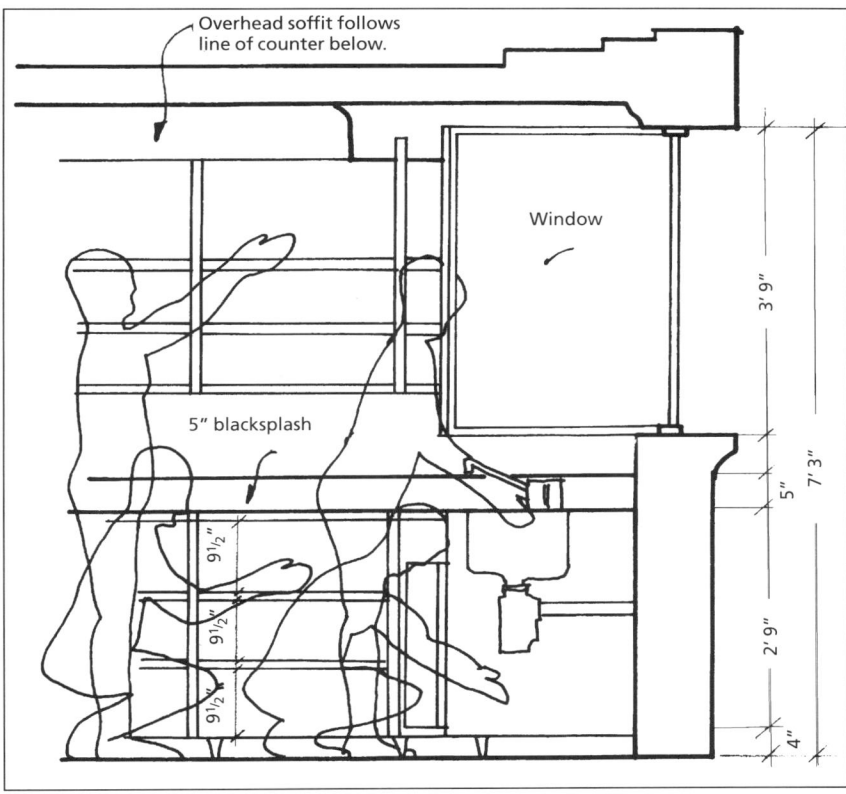

9-3. Drawing showing Klemmer's solution to the need for various shelf heights.

9-4. Klemmer's plan for using a motorized shelving unit.

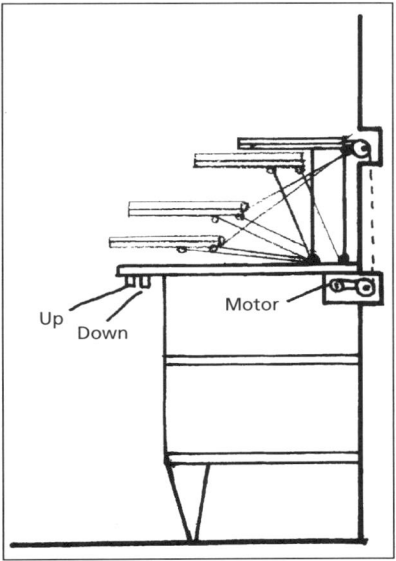

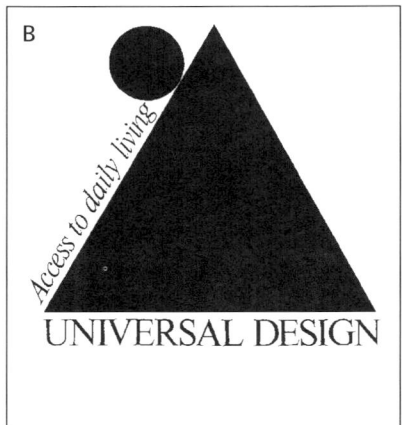

9-5. Universal design logos. (A) Whirlpool. *(Reprinted with permission from Whirlpool Corporation.)* (B) The Pratt Institute. *(Symbol design by Milton Glaser. Reprinted with permission from Pratt Institute Center for Advanced Design Research, ©1992/1993.)* (C) Three Rivers Center for Independent Living. *(Reprinted with permission from Three Rivers Center for Independent Living.)*

The term "universal design" is gaining widespread use. For the most part, it is used correctly to signify products and environments that are designed for the widest range of abilities possible (the parameters of which will change as designers learn more about individual capabilities and how to better design for them). Manufacturers use the term extensively in marketing literature (such as Whirlpool, Steelcase, Haworth). Major design journals have dedicated special issues to the concept (*Interior Design* and *Metropolis*, for example). *The Universal Design Newsletter* is published quarterly by Universal Designers & Consultants, Inc. (see Resources). Also, the Pratt Institute cosponsored the first national conference on universal design in the spring of 1992—"Universal Design: Access to Daily Living."

One interesting tool that has yet to be widely discussed is the use of a standard symbol or logo to identify a product, service, or environment as meeting universal design guidelines—similar to the International Symbol of Accessibility now familiar to all. However, one must keep in mind that such a symbol would point toward an attempt at a universal design, but would not actually signify its accomplishment. As Wm. L. Wilkoff and Laura W. Abed put it in their book, *Practicing Universal Design*, "In one sense the idea [of universal design] is utopian. Truly achieving universal design would render the International Symbol of Accessibility obsolete, since accessibility would be the norm in the built environment" (pp. 87–88; 1994).

Still, even with this limitation, there continues to be a great need for some rating system for products and designs, along with an agency or agencies (perhaps located at universities across the country) with the responsibility of establishing and providing such ratings. Several logos have appeared over the past several years, including the stylized "U" used by Cynthia Leibrock in her book *Beautiful Barrier-Free*; the varying-sized people within a house used by Whirlpool; and the abstract geometric form created for the Pratt Institute by artist Milton Glaser. (See Figure 9-5 A, B, and C for examples of these.)

Pratt's logo appears on all of its stationary and publications related to universal design as well as on the publications that have appeared as a result of the first national conference. Of that design, Glaser writes:

> The logo came out of the need to represent the issue abstractly, since I couldn't figure out how to make a more literal translation of the idea of accessibility coupled with design without being banal. The result is the convergence of several ideas: Using geometric (triangle and circle) or "universal" shapes to represent universal design; the reference to a wheel (wheelchair) moving up an inclined ramp; and the idea of a mountain as an obstacle to overcome.

Perhaps as the discipline of universal design gains more prominence and coherence, one logo will be adopted by practitioners throughout the country, allowing consumers to instantly recognize that the product or service they are being offered is created around universal standards.

This chapter presents several accounts of ventures into the business of universal design, including the design and marketing of houses, product showcases, and consulting services. Finally, existing trends and future possibilities in marketing that may reach a market ripe for universally designed products and services are examined.

Case Study
The Peaks and Valleys of Marketing Accessible Housing
by William K. Wasch

In the spring of 1986 my wife and I drove north for a brief weekend at a spa in Palm Springs. On the way we passed Carmel Mountain Ranch and stopped to see what was available for the retiree in this beautiful part of the country. Imagine our surprise to find attractive houses that were satisfactory for 50-year-olds but would be less so when residents reached their 70s and 80s. It was an up-and-down trip in and through the house, weaving around the narrow corridors and tight bathrooms on slippery tile floors into a hard-to-use kitchen, and up tricky and slippery catwalk steps to the second floor bedrooms and bathrooms. Great for that active retiree, but an increasingly difficult environment in which to function in one's later years.

Middletown House

This was the genesis of the Middletown House—a ground-level home with a lower-level accessory apartment (see Figures 9-6 and 9-7). Designed with the help of two architects and an architectural researcher (Christina Wasch), we plan to build it and live in it in our home community of Middletown, Connecticut. The idea is one that is bound to take hold as the 50-plus group in this society personally struggles with caring for their parents, often after a crisis happens, and realizes how hard it is to adapt their homes to their changed lifestyle.

9-6. Model of the Middletown House. *(Figures 9-6 through 9-10 reprinted with permission from William K. Wasch.)*

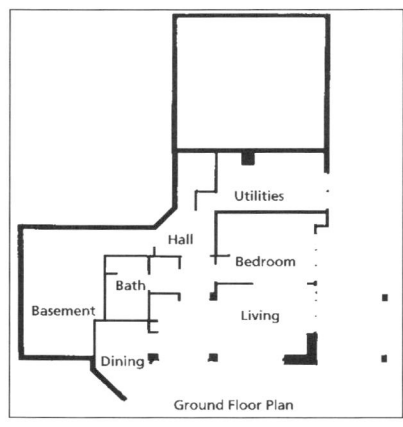

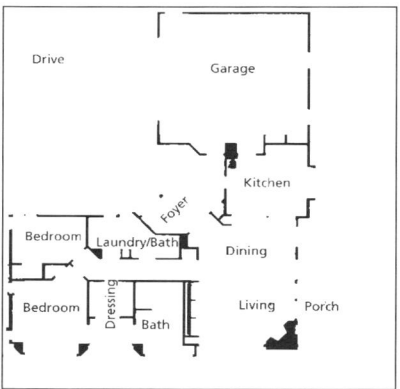

9-7. Ground and first-floor plans for the Middletown House.

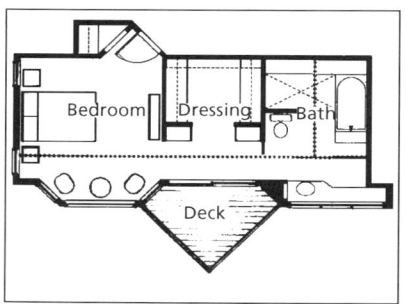

9-8. Middletown House master bedroom suite floor plan.

Universal design was the guiding principle for this adaptable house. It is built on a sloping site, featuring 2300 square feet on the ground level and a 750-square-foot accessory apartment on the lower level. It faces south for maximum solar gain. Owners of such a house could rent out the lower level apartment to a younger couple at a reduced rate in exchange for a range of services that might include driving, housecleaning, yard work, and so on, or they might use it for a live-in caregiver if necessary.

Most of the windows in the house are on the south and east side for energy efficiency; special glare-reducing glass and shades, as well as small porches on the south side for raised gardening and sitting, are built into the design. All the hallways—of which there are few—are 4 feet wide, and the house features a completely accessible kitchen and bathroom. Other features include a built-in vacuum system, an easy-to-clean and maintain storage wall in the living room, and close access from the kitchen to the garage. All of these design elements allow the residents to move and function independently with a walker or wheelchair for as long as possible while further reducing the strain and cost of caregiving.

Another important design feature is an adjoining bedroom to the master bedroom that can be used by a caregiver in case the resident is immobilized for a period of time and the caregiver needs to be nearby throughout the night (see Figure 9-8). There is also a built-in joist in the bedroom that leads right into the bathroom. While ordinarily covered by the ceiling, should the need arise, a sling can be attached for moving a person for washing, bathing, and so on. (This addition may seem extreme, but with the progression of a variety of impairments, it could be needed at certain times.)

Other important building features include plywood backing in the halls and bathrooms so that attractive grab bars can be installed easily when needed, skylights that offer glare-free light and can be opened and closed with motor controls, and a unique home control system, called Butler in a Box®, that responds to voice or touch commands and can carry out a variety of functions from several control centers throughout the house (see Figure 2-3). These functions include opening or closing windows, turning lights and appliances on and off, dialing and answering the phone, communicating with the life-line system if necessary, and controlling heating and cooling systems.

The house contains a variety of products that reduce the strain of caregiving and allow the residents to remain independent longer. These range from levers instead of knobs on doors, easy-to-use plumbing fixtures, pocket doors, easy-access closets, a side-by-side refrigerator/freezer, adjustable counters and cabinets, a side-hinged microwave oven, front cooktop controls that go from green to red with increased heat (see Figure 9-9), and a number of unique bathroom fixtures (including an adjustable sink, an accessible shower stall with seat and adjustable shower head, a Jacuzzi, and a Swiss clos-o-mat—a combination bidet/toilet—see Figure 9-10).

The Middletown House concept was presented to several conferences of gerontologists and home builders, and it was featured in many newspapers, in builder and design magazines, and in the article "An Adaptable House Spans the Generations" in *The Wall Street Journal*. It even caught the attention of Helpmate Robot builder Joseph Engelberger, of Danbury, Connecticut, who suggested that a little niche be built in the kitchen where "Roscoe" could be stored and recharged so he could wash the car and deliver to his seated owner a phone and lunch, and even lend a hand to help him/her out of his/her chair.

However, despite all the research and presentations, little is being done to build this type of house (though sometimes a letter arrives from a builder who has read about the idea). While the Lewis Home in California is a great move in the right direction (see the case study on the "Friendly Home" later in this chapter), this type of construction is still rarely done, especially in the northeast where builders continue to be conservative, especially in these tight times.

Therefore, in the fall of 1989, we went back to thinking

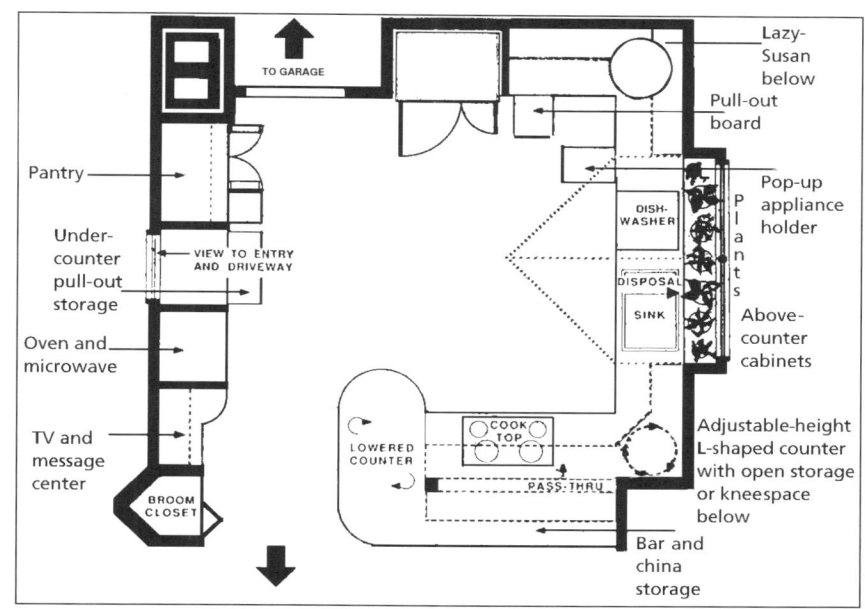

9-9. Middletown House kitchen floor plan.

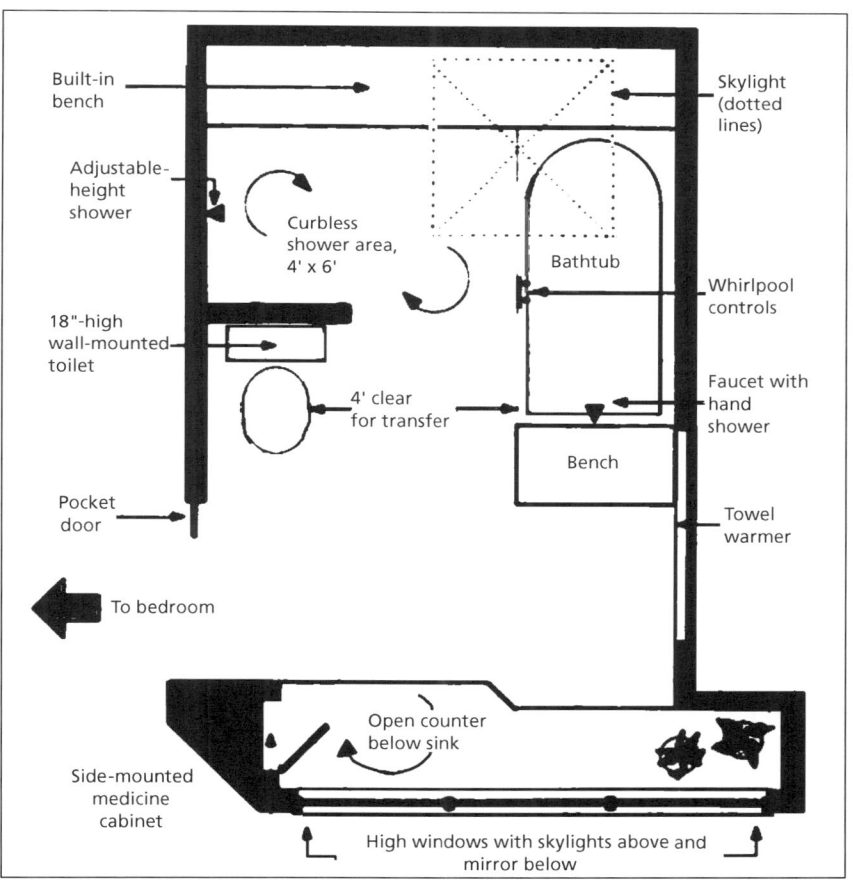

9-10. Middletown House bathroom floor plan.

about adapting existing homes. There might be changes that can be made before a crisis strikes, thus allowing people to remain in the homes in which they have lived for so many years. AARP research shows that the average home tenure for individuals over 60 is close to 20 years.

This is especially the case with the 80 percent of the elderly who choose to remain in their own homes. Our plan was to organize a way to assist individuals and multi-family senior housing owners and operators in making modifications to their homes and buildings. The goal was to enable residents who are elderly or disabled to live comfortably and independently in a noninstitutional setting. Thus in late 1989, Adapt-Your-Home was cofounded with Ron Netter in Hamden, Connecticut.

Adapt-Your-Home

Ron had started a company called Total Serve in the fall of 1988. At that time focus groups and other research techniques showed that there was a large market in the greater Hamden/New Haven area for a company that would provide a range of services to older individuals who wanted to remain in their own homes. It was obvious that many of these people had relied on a wide range of craftsmen through the years, and often these individuals were no longer in business, creating a gap in reliable service.

Ron developed a good mailing list, prepared considerable direct mail, and was quite well received in the first four or five months with a variety of gutter cleaning, minor home repair, leaf raking, and even some more extensive carpentry jobs. Total Serve filled an important niche and gradually built up a promising business. The company reached its height in the summer of 1989 when it employed over 25 individuals using 4 trucks. But supervising this many individuals, who were all doing different jobs, soon became a daunting task. Adapt-Your-Home started cutting back on general services, concentrating exclusively on home adaptation.

Several months were devoted to putting together an assessment document, and then eight Total Serve clients were visited, all of whom were older. They were then using the company for a variety of cleaning and maintenance projects. The most dramatic assessment was one done for an 85-year-old retired professor who had been living in an old farmhouse outside of New Haven for the past 40 years. He, as many of us do, enjoyed having his bedroom and bathroom on the second floor and liked to come down to his study, living room, and kitchen for his daily activities. He also enjoyed cutting wood and gardening. However, he had failing eyesight, a hearing disability, and a very severe case of arthritis which made it hard for him to go up and down the stairs and to stand up from a seated position.

The assessment was informal, but it showed there were three or four items that would make life immediately more comfortable for him. One was better illumination in his living room. The second was improving his telephones so that he could hear them better and also be able to dial out more easily using larger buttons. The third was installing an extendible handrail that would help him move between floors.

This was only one case, but it showed that the needs were immense. The company began to look at individual houses with a view to assisting the owners in making them more user-friendly for people with a variety of disabilities, including those most often associated with aging.

Many of the Middletown House ideas, particularly the products used, could be transferred to retrofits. The company was statewide, and also was fortunate to be called upon by the Department of Rehabilitation to build ramps, accessible bathrooms, and kitchens for young individuals who were disabled and wanted to remain at home and go back to work. This work gave the company a good background and simplified its business decision to concentrate on adapting both single-family and multi-family housing for people who are elderly or disabled.

Marketing Adapt-Your-Home

The next step was to organize an open house that featured some of the products selected for Middletown House. The company spent several weeks developing its showroom and offices in Hamden, displaying actual product exhibits and adaptations, including lever door handles, nonskid floor surfaces, automatic door openers, widened doorways, adjustable cabinets and counters, easy-to-use faucets, Plexiglas™ cabinet doors, and accessible appliances and sinks. There was a model bathroom with attractive grab bars, adjustable shower heads, accessible sinks, temperature controls, and barrier-free access. The company held a well-advertised open house in January 1990, inviting its congressman, the Commissioner on Aging, and all members of the aging network in Connecticut. Over 100 people attended, and there was excellent newspaper and radio publicity on the event.

The company then began to work closely with the aging and disability networks by sending mailings to all senior housing facilities (nonprofit and private), and it slowly began to see a build-up in specific contacts. The company built seven ramps for the state under their program to permit individuals who are disabled to return to the work force, and it also began working with two very old nonprofit senior housing complexes built in the 1970s, which were in need of major renovations.

The next promotional idea was to work with the Yale School of Public Health to develop a public education video that presented an assessment of an elderly housing unit to show its accessibility problems for frail elderly and to present a series of product and adaptation solutions from the company's showroom and product research.

The video was promoted statewide and representatives spoke at a variety of state and regional conferences, developing a considerable reputation for the company's assessment work, product research, and developing line of products. These products ranged from the Bathease Tub (which has a door built into it) to the Normbau and HEWI grab bar lines to a variety of accessible kitchens to electric door openers.

Other than the state work, business was slow. Employees spent a lot of time on community and social service agency education, networking with the groups representing people who are elderly or disabled, writing articles, showing the video to scores of groups, and conducting in-service training programs for various centers for independent living. But the company was getting into a major working capital problem because of the large amount of outstanding monies.

A Change in Direction

Next the company initiated a statewide program to sell its assessment and product consultation program to private elderly or disabled home owners and the operators of multi-family senior housing. It did not take long for the company to realize that most facilities built in the 1970s were almost inaccessible for frail elderly people. Simple items such as levers, handrails, and easy-use faucets and tubs were rare, even though most of the residents were frail elderly in their 70s and 80s. Even the 5 percent handicapped units in newer buildings often had grab bars installed in the wrong places or in the wrong direction. Facilities built in the 1980s showed better accessibility; there were even a few with completely accessible bathrooms. However, units continued to be tight, and simple things like levers and pressure plate-operated doors were the exception rather than the rule.

The company completed 10 major "free" senior housing facility assessments and submitted a variety of proposals for making them more accessible. In the summer of 1992, the company did an assessment for the Public Housing Authority in Enfield, Connecticut. They found 80 ground floor units built in 1962. Half were 18' x 18' efficiencies, and the rest were 20' x 23' one-bedroom units. They measured each unit, drew the basic plan with a CAD program, and then took a hard look at what was found. The company came up with a series of 20 recommendations on how to make the units more accessible and usable by a frail older population. Problems ranged from a very tight, inaccessible kitchen and bathroom to hardly any usable storage space. Recommended solutions included a pocket door in the bathroom across from a more convenient and open closet space to a Bathease Tub with door, seat, and hand-held shower. Unfortunately, the Authority chose not to proceed with the proposal. If they had done so, Adapt-Your-Home would have prepared a set of plans, recommended products, and provided an estimate on the cost for adapting from 1 to 80 of the apartments.

Legislative Developments

In the fall of 1989, representatives attended a HUD conference in Boston to learn more about compliance with Section 504 of the Rehabilitation Act of 1973 as amended, and how HUD-financed housing must become more accessible for the specific resident who is disabled or frail and elderly. They studied the Fair Housing Amendments Act of 1988, which required all new multi-family unit construction to be completely accessible, and the Omnibus Housing Act, which offered greater federal support for reverse equity mortgages and assistance in making home repairs and modifications to low-income homeowners who are elderly and disabled. The following summer the Americans with Disabilities Act was passed, raising major accessibility issues in employment, public services, transportation, private businesses, and other establishments.

Representatives realized that architects and builders are faced with a minefield of new guidelines and regulations. HUD's new accessibility guidelines are still not clear, while some states have their own more stringent set of regulations; thus the only solution is a massive research and education program.

Knowledgeable, but Still Not Selling

Despite the company's investment in community education and its efforts at promotion, it was unable to sell its private home assessment services. Seniors, their families, and caregivers did not want to spend money, even if it could be applied to future retrofit. So in December 1990, Adapt-Your-Home decided to set up an educational research and assessment center on a nonprofit basis, called the Independence Resource Center, in New Haven. This allowed the company to do assessments for senior HUD-financed housing units and to apply for both private and public grants to cover some of the overhead that it was spending on community education.

For example, the company just completed a major 504 assessment for the Middletown Housing Authority, which has a 125-unit high-rise senior housing building and a 40-unit ground-level set of senior apartments. All are over 20 years old and meet few accessibility

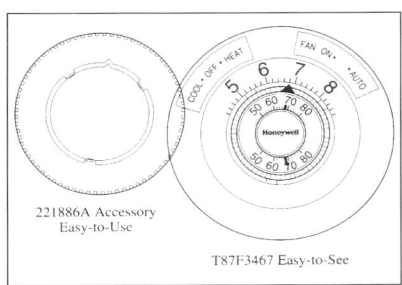

9-11. Honeywell offers thermostat controls that are both "easy-to-see" and "easy-to-use."
(Reprinted with permission from Honeywell, Inc.)

guidelines. The company ran a similar assessment for the Hartford Housing Authority (with 4000 units). They have 15 complexes, of which 4 are designated for seniors. However, Hartford also has a high proportion of people with disabilities, so it is essential for them to know the accessibility status of all of their units.

In addition to the assessments, Adapt-Your-Home has kept the product distributorships and a small group of carpenters and handymen on a contract basis so that they can do estimates, make adaptations, and provide any other services needed.

The company recognizes that multi-family housing facility managers are not yet in a major position to pay for adaptations. Their reserves are often used up, and what is available must be used for basic repair. For example, the Connecticut State Legislature recently required all multi-family housing to be equipped with sprinklers, and this has become a tremendous problem for many of the older facilities. This has to be done before they can begin to make the adaptations that were recommend in Adapt-Your-Home assessments. However, under the new guidelines, any public housing authority that applies for HUD funding under the Comprehensive Improvement Assistance Program must have a completed Section 504 report on file to be considered for these grants. So the pressure is on.

Conclusions

All of us are dealing with some major difficulties in getting this kind of business underway. Adapt-Your-Home's dream of developing a sophisticated program, marketing it, and then franchising it nationally still has a long way to go. The venture capitalists we talked to didn't think that anyone can make money in the elderly market. We know we're here at the right time, but we've got to continue to be patient; setting up the nonprofit organization will help us ride out the next year or so until we begin to see more funds made available to adapt these older facilities in compliance with Section 504 of the Housing Code.

There is a vast housing stock out there that is not even adaptable, let alone accessible. Besides the needed social programs, we must think about the environment and adapt it to meet the needs of a population that is increasingly frail and elderly or disabled. We must take advantage of the products on the market, and, in the planning stage of a project, make single-family homes more accessible. Planning and implementing a major reconstruction program for the thousands of HUD, FNMA, and State Housing Authority-financed multi-family facilities for people who are elderly or disabled is also very important.

There are four lessons we've learned that should be shared with anyone thinking about getting into this business.

1. Do a good research job up front, and research it a second time through to be sure there is a market—and that you understand how to reach that market.

2. Be very precise about what you want to offer. Don't try to do too much, and narrow your mission very carefully. We learned a hard lesson by trying to do everything.

3. Set up tight financial controls, and recognize that if you are doing state work you have to build in extra costs to cover the lag time in payment.

4. Be properly financed.

All of these are hallmarks of how you start any small business. We've learned that you can't forget any of them.

Case Study

Home ReVisions: Marketing Tools for Independent Living
by Sheila Zwelling

In November of 1992, Rick Zwelling, the president of a major building supply parts store in Columbus, Ohio, opened a relatively small side business to help solve a problem he kept running into: offering solutions to the increasingly challenging obstacles to independence that people face within their homes. He and designer Tom Price had spent the year and a half prior to the opening researching the market, studying available products, and gaining an understanding of the two main consumer groups they were targeting: the aging individual who requires home modification to remain independent, and people with varying degrees and types of disabilities who can also benefit from such modifications.

Their company, Home ReVisions, provides customized solutions for making any home more comfortable, accessible, and safe through a four-part program:

1. Home assessment (free, without obligation)
2. Products and product information
3. Design services
4. Installation

The center of the business is a products showcase set up to reflect the rooms in a typical house. This is a relatively small space (900 square feet), but it is remarkable in the diversity of products displayed.

9-12. Sheila Zwelling, co-owner of Home ReVisions in Columbus, Ohio, demonstrates the use of one of the thousands of accessible products available from her home accessibility remodeling business.

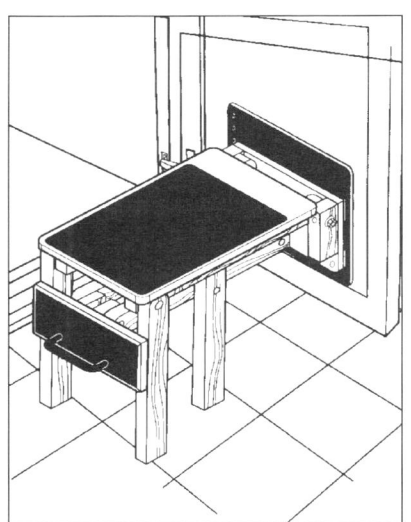

9-13. Folding stool added to inside cabinet door from Rev-A-Shelf. *(Reprinted with permission from Rev-A-Shelf, Inc.)*

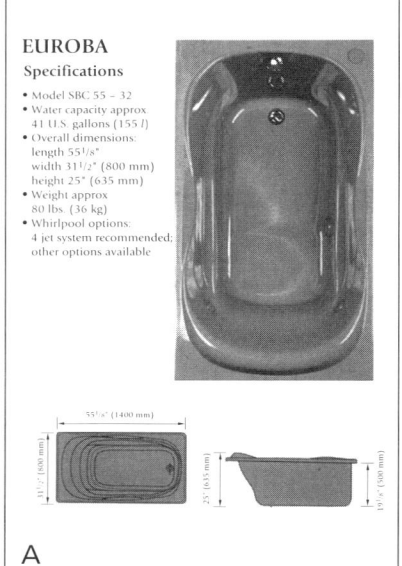

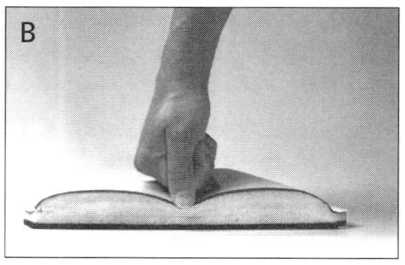

9-14. (A) and (B). The Soft Bathtub from International Cushioned Products, Inc., is on display at Home ReVisions. *(Reprinted with permission from International Cushioned Products, Inc.)*

The kitchen of Home ReVisions includes cabinet doors that are spring-loaded, opening with only a light push. Pull-out cabinet inserts are prevalent throughout, with a lazy Susan built into the corner base cabinet section, as well as a fold-out step stool (see Figure 9-13). The sink is shallower than a standard one and features an extendable, single-control faucet. Counters are given over to gadgetry, including the OXO line of kitchen tools, various door and jar opener aids, and adapted utensils. One cabinet features a motorized insert that automatically lowers items from upper shelves to the counter.

Two bathrooms are displayed, both featuring increased lighting to accommodate the changes in vision that aging people experience. One features the Soft Bathtub from International Cushioned Products, Inc. (see Figure 9-14), as well as a fully accessible shower stall that knocks down completely so it can be installed in existing bathrooms with limited door access. The second features an adaptable shower/tub unit that allows for grab bars to be installed as needed and comes with or without a seat insert and with a removable door panel for lower access. The second bathroom also presents several methods for meeting toilet needs: a higher single-unit commode as well as a relatively new insert that can be bolted underneath an existing toilet, raising it to 18 inches.

The bedroom features a pull-down bed unit that operates effortlessly and stops at any angle (see Figure 9-15). Also displayed in this room are numerous gadgets including a talking clock, a large-button telephone, and aids for putting on socks and shoes when strength for bending, reaching, and pulling is limited.

The living room consists of two Leisure Lift chairs that help the individual stand and sit without assistance, lamps with inexpensive inserts that allow them to be turned on and off at a touch, and a doorbell attached to a lamp, providing redundant cueing for people with hearing disabilities.

These are only a few of the hundreds of products on display, and they are only a small representation of the over 13,000 products that the company has ready access to and knowledge of. All of the products are attractive, blending in with the usual decor of one's home; none of them are institutional in appearance, one of the common complaints and misconceptions of products that are geared toward maintaining independence.

Home ReVisions may be unique in the United States at the moment. So far, Zwelling knows of no other business that provides all of the services and products Home ReVisions offers for independent living. Some of their success may be due to their connection to an existing, successful business and to their long-standing expertise in installation. In the future, it is likely that such companies will appear across the country as the population learns that there are ways to make better use of their homes and demands the products and services that allow them to do so.

9-15. The Sico bed opens and closes with very little effort, and it stops at whatever angle it is released—a feature that adds safety to convenience. *(Reprinted with permission from Sico Incorporated.)*

Case Study
The Friendly Home
by Gail Hartwigsen, Ph.D.

If you think back to your most memorable house, you may find yourself describing a place of fond memories, using descriptors like comfortable, cheerful, warm, familiar, and inviting—all words that convey a friendly feeling. In the dictionary, the word "friendly" also includes support, aid, not hostile or antagonistic, and serving a beneficial or helpful purpose. How appropriate, then, that the Lewis Homes' (of California) adaptable house was named the "Friendly Home." (See the floor plan in Figure 9-16.)

Recently opened as a model in Lewis' Cypress Park development in Chino, California, the Friendly Home (a joint project of Lewis Homes of California, the National Council on the Aging, and the Southern California Gas Company) was conceived as a house that would meet the needs of several constituent groups: people who are older or have disabilities, people who anticipate some degree of disability due to aging, and builders and remodelers. Why? Consider these facts:

- The 65-plus age group will more than double between the years 1990 and 2030; by 2010, it should increase by about 23 percent. This represents substantial growth, from 31 million in 1990 to almost 40 million by 2010, and to 66 million by 2030.

- Of those aged 55-plus, 85 percent say that they would like to remain in their own homes.

- The ability to perform routine daily tasks diminishes with age. Tasks that affect individual human functioning and home maintenance are most affected.

- Homes, as they have generally been built, are dangerous places, with more accidents occurring there than anywhere else. The less physically able people are, the higher their risk of injury—particularly from falls.

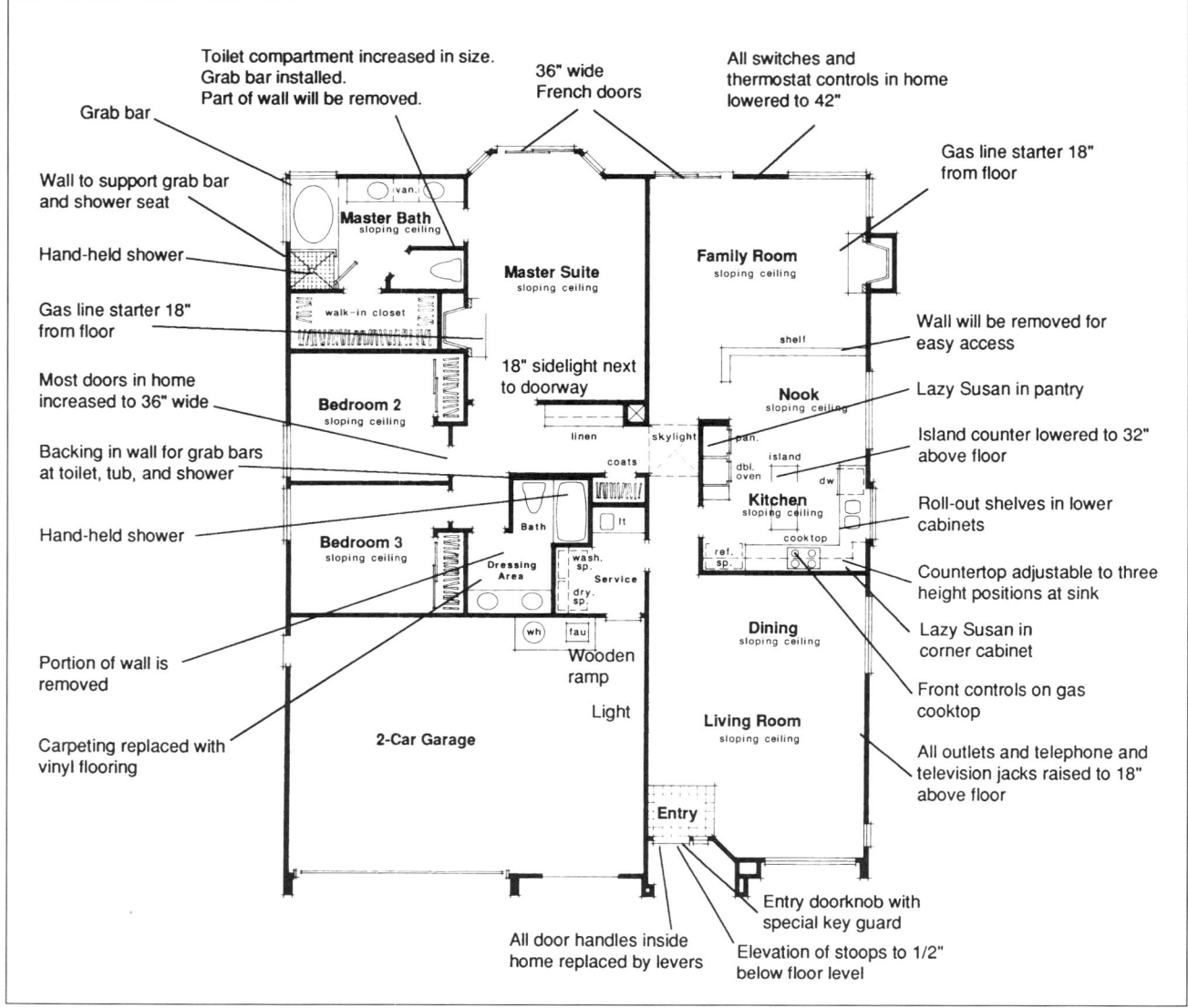

9-16. Floor plan for the Friendly Home. *(Reprinted with permission from Randall Lewis of Lewis Homes.)*

As a first attempt to meet the needs of these constituent groups, Randall Lewis incorporated design ideas into the Friendly Home that theoretically would benefit what is called the 95th percentile of disability: people with various degrees of handicap, including arthritis, diminished vision, muscle weakness, problems with bending and kneeling, temporary problems such as broken bones and joint replacements, and so on. People who use a wheelchair but still have significant upper body strength would also be accommodated for the most part, but those with severe disabilities would require additional individualized modifications.

It is important to note that Randall Lewis selected an existing floor plan to modify. One of the goals of the project was to show that a home could be modified; a custom plan was not necessary. The design selected was one already slated for construction at Cypress Park, since it met several necessary criteria of accessibility. It was a single story, having few hallways and a relatively open plan in the living/dining and kitchen/family room areas. Some structural changes were made: the removal of a half wall by the kitchen nook, the widening of most doorways, the replacement of sliding doors with French doors, the construction of a wall between the shower and tub in the master bathroom to accommodate a grab bar and shower seat, and the addition of extra support to bathroom walls to support the addition of grab bars at a later time. Other changes included lowering light switches and thermostat controls; raising electrical outlets, telephone jacks, and fireplace starters; replacing standard shower fixtures with hand-held showers; and replacing doorknobs with levers.

Most of the design attention was devoted to the kitchen, bathrooms, and master bedroom, and these are the areas found to have the best cost/benefit ratio. According to Lewis, the features of the home that have received the most praise from visitors so far have been the overall increased and accessible storage space (particularly in the kitchen through the addition of lazy Susans, corner cabinets, and customized storage), a garage ramp, and the basic changes already mentioned concerning light switch and electrical outlet placement. Positive comments concerning the rocker light switches are frequent, with people suggesting they be included in all models.

However, criticisms have also focused upon the kitchen and bathrooms; while an island in the kitchen is felt by many to be a necessity in southern California, some visitors to the Friendly Home felt that it might be a hindrance. The closed nature of the bathrooms where more open floor space is needed, was also viewed as a problem, particularly for those in wheelchairs. The compartment surrounding the toilet in the master bath and the arrangement of the shower and tub were primary areas of concern.

"Most people tend to be interested in changes that total $5000 or less," said Lewis. The Friendly Home provides more accommodation than the absolute minimum, and so the actual price charged to the consumer may exceed that figure. Lewis Homes is holding off on its judgment of reaction to the home as well as a definite pricing structure until the market improves.

Lewis says they have made some observations concerning Friendly Home shoppers: One of their realizations is that the market for this product is a vast one, with the needs of 60- and 80-year-olds being significantly different and therefore not reasonably standardized by the medium/large volume builder. Another observation is that those looking at the house are not necessarily shopping for today, but for the future. This finding taps right into the primary goal of the project: to create a home that can adapt to changing physical needs over time.

Adaptable housing is beginning to be viewed by builders of senior housing as having a marketing advantage over standard-built housing. Builders can advertise that residents can "age-in-place" in their homes and communities, a feature that is very attractive to the older buyer, the overwhelming majority of whom say they prefer remaining in their own homes to moving.

If adaptable housing is so much more supportive and satisfying for all people, regardless of age and physical capability, why hasn't it become the construction standard? Everything takes time, and construction is like any other highly developed, advanced industry: It has tried-and-true standards it has used for years, standards that have produced what is probably the most envied housing stock in the world. Millions of small builders have contributed to this effort over the years, and to say to them, "Now we have a better way to do it—we start building all adaptable housing next month"—would be silly and futile, not to mention demeaning.

All things take time; the challenge to adaptable housing and its advocates is to demonstrate its advantages to consumers and its potential market to builders: supply and demand, as usual. Once this happens and people in general become aware of the advantages of adaptable housing, the possibility of it being mainstreamed and as affordable as standard-built housing will become more of a probability.

Universal Design Strategy
Marketing Universal Design Products to an Aging Population
by Joseph A. Koncelik

Aging consumers are one of the most significant market segments. Discretionary buying power and the need for sensitively designed products make this population a key force in the marketplace. Furthermore, new technology allows manufacturers to serve a broader range of consumers than ever before.

In designing appliances for an aging population, high-technology applications to products require an increased attention to appropriate control and display design. The designer needs to understand age-related changes to sensory modalities—vision and hearing—in order to design consumer-sensitive products. Similarly, furnishing design requires an understanding of anthropometrics related to an aging population, as well as physiological changes that occur as a result of the higher incidence of arthritis and muscle/skeletal changes and disabilities.

Key Points about the Market and the Design Process

1. Aging is not uniform—the physiological processes associated with aging occur at different rates in different people.

    The majority of adults are in, and will remain in, good health for almost their entire lives. Older people are no less capable than younger people, and they tend to remain so.

    Consider that in the United States:

    - Healthy adults over the age of 55 constitute an $800 billion market.

    - Adults over the age of 45 constitute 51.3 percent of all households, 49.6 percent of all income generation, and, most importantly, 58.5 percent of all discretionary income. They are and will remain the most significant market for the design of goods.

2. The consumer products industry has no future if it neglects this market.

    Meeting the needs of this population is an economic necessity. Designers must be sure to understand the aging process in human factors.

3. The most important step in designing for this group is to identify those normal aging characteristics, which will be used as criteria for the design of all products and environments.

4. Designers must understand human factors modeling.

    Human factors is the body of knowledge about the characteristics, capabilities, and performance of the human being, meant for application to the design process.

    Aging is a process, not a state of being. Such continuous change complicates the design process. Designers must have a model that allows the maximum application of general characteristics related to the development, production, and distribution of their product.

Implications for Appliance Design

Two ubiquitous examples of poor design are the blue-light emitted figures used with many VCR displays and the black-on-black buttons of many remote controls. Both should be remedied in the near future. Gaudy, but meaningless, displays that dazzle but provide no meaningful information must also be reconsidered. They distract attention when it should be focused on other activities. For example, internal research at General Motors has proven conclusively that the time required to monitor automotive displays is negligible, but the information provided has actually increased. The shift of the eye from road to display surface is a perfect example of unreasonable accommodation.

Corrective measures can and must be taken. The most important is *redundant cueing*—the provision of stimuli to more than one sense organ to convey a signal. Most appliances and high-technology devices rely upon visual cues alone; appliances must be developed with control and display devices that signal the user through hearing, tactile sensitivity, and shape recognition as well as through alphanumeric symbols, color, and visible positioning. Current technology, which has made integrated circuitry and computer chips very inexpensive, has so far been used to primarily extend the complexity of appliances and other products instead of using it to provide redundant cueing.

Simple mistakes, such as choosing the wrong figure/ground color and contrast relationship for displays, must either be avoided or, finally, regulated. Blue-lighted figure displays should never be used: No matter what the age of the user, blue figures are harder to distinguish for an eye designed for edge sensitivity (i.e., the human eye). Also, blue-lighted figures fatigue the eye more quickly and increase the chances of error.

Controls have also become a technological issue. Membrane switches, microminiaturization, and stylistic concerns have diminished the recognition of a control and its specific position on a surface. Designers must make an extra effort to rethink control design in order to help position the hands and fingers, giving positive feedback that the control is working or has actuated the desired process. Blending the control with the surface, a stylistic cliché of the 1980s, must be changed.

Implications for Home Furnishings Design

Currently, manufacturing is highly specialized in the arena of furnishings for the elderly who are infirm. Manufacturers face high research and development costs for new products, with long-term production cycle testing and on-site product evaluations before marketing. It is difficult for many manufacturers to muster the staying power to develop and market special products for this population.

Design solutions are frequently the least difficult part in the chain of related events that must occur to provide better furnishing products to the elderly, especially those who are infirm. The Herman Miller, Inc. recently abandoned research and development of residential products for this population, not because product design and development was so difficult, but because they did not have the marketing capability, distribution network, and service expertise to be successful.

At best, manufacturers, dealerships, and distributorships find success when they are able to make sales directly to large-budget facilities just opening or deciding to refurbish their interiors. This would include senior centers, retirement communities, congregate housing facilities, apartments and housing for the elderly, and other non-medical settings that disburse funds in sufficient quantity for the manufacturer or dealership to deal direct.

Corrective Measures

- *Marketing plan*—Any manufacturer or designer contemplating the development of furnishings designated for a "special user" market should formulate a careful marketing plan that takes the following into account:

    1. How the product will be handled beyond manufacturing
    2. An effective sales strategy with carefully trained sales specialists who are in constant communications with design/marketing/engineering staff
    3. A careful plan for servicing of all products on-site or through returns
    4. A long-term extended time to allow for market development. Short-term expectations will likely prove unrealistic.

- *Design*—The design team should be fully acquainted with the human factors of aging and be willing to work with the dimensional and proportional characteristics—especially in seating design—that are atypical in the design of most furnishings. Dimensions shouldn't be altered to suit aesthetic considerations.

- *Technology*—There have been significant advances in materials and production methods that allow for small-quantity production of goods. Batch production of furnishings in high-tech materials is now possible. At least four manufacturers of fabrics are producing odor-eliminating fabrics, thus many fabrics that can be acquired are cleanable and resist bacterial growth.

- *The "special user"*—As any population ages, its physical, psychological, and sociological characteristics diversify. The population becomes heterogeneous. This makes uniformity in design unworkable—one size will most definitely not fit all. Product lines must be responsive to this diversity by emphasizing modularity or variability to meet differentiating needs.

Conclusions

Marketing professionals must take a proactive as opposed to a reactive approach to developing information about aging. In relation to product development, marketing should precede product development—not the typical relationship in the experience of designers.

Do not mix aging with infirmity. Aging is inexorable but varies in rate. Infirmity happens at any time in the life span, with higher susceptibility in infancy and in the old-old population. Most people will never be infirm, and many who are infirm have been afflicted for a very long period of their life—perhaps all of their life.

Developing an applied human factors model(s) requires consideration of the acceptability of the information on the dynamic characteristics of aging. Such a model is necessary for understanding the characteristics, capabilities, and performance of human beings. If a high degree of diversity of characteristics is misapplied to design projects that are meant for general production, distribution, and use of product, the information will go unused. Likewise, if designers compress diversity into a mold of uniformity in responsiveness of environments and products, the resulting effect is a neglectful and ultimately inhumane design.

Case Study

Marketing Universal Design as a Public Service: A Nonprofit Resource Center
by Rae Duncan-Lyle

The Housing Resource Center (HRC) is a nonprofit, tax-exempt organization in Cleveland, Ohio, that operated a demonstration house featuring displays, workshops, and information (books and its own newsletter) on all aspects of home maintenance, repair, and improvement. In conjunction with Cleveland's Services for Independent Living (SIL), this demonstration house was renovated to create an environment suitable for use by people with and without disabilities.

The following sections describe the renovations that created universal features for this demonstration home.

First Floor

- Wide doorways — 32 inches–36 inches where possible
- Carpeting — Level, dense weave
- Electrical outlets — 24 inches from floor for easy reach
- Electrical switches — 48 inches from floor for easy reach

Hallways

- Shelf and drawers — Site-built storage accessible from hall
- Drawer pulls — Wide, easy to grasp

- Baskets — Lightweight, removable storage for linens and so on
- Doorbell — Combines light and sound signal

Bathroom
- Sliding door — Replaces hinged hallway door; easy to open and provides greater access. (Note that this is not a pocket door, but rather it slides on the outside of the wall, like a barn door, an inexpensive alternative.)
- Skylight — Natural light and privacy
- Glass block tub wall — Natural light and privacy
- Mixing valve control — Reduces likelihood of accidental scalding; one-hand operation
- Hand-held shower — Usable by person in sitting or standing position
- Tub chair — Makes transferring from wheelchair possible; gives support
- Vanity and sink — Sink located so extended reach is unnecessary
- Sink control — Single-handle faucet allows easy use
- Vanity support leg — Custom-made for maximum access under vanity; integrated with overall design
- Medicine cabinet — Located low and at the side for easy access
- Mirror — Large, with 3-inch tilt at top; good visibility for standing or sitting person
- Outlet/light switch — Located on front of vanity
- Oak railing — Provides support during transfer from wheelchair to toilet; integrated with overall design
- Toilet location — Extra space on left for wheelchair access
- Vinyl flooring — Low maintenance; color doesn't show scuff marks; good traction

Kitchen
- Skylight — Provides ample natural light
- Entrance door — 36-inch width for good access

9-17. Sink with the following universal design features:
- Single-handle faucet control
- Wand attachment that can be used to fill containers without lifting them into sink
- Hot water tap with lever control, providing a safe source of hot water for tea, coffee, cocoa, and so on.

(Reprinted with permission from the San Diego Center for the Blind, CA.)

Lever handle	Can be activated with forearm, wrist, or elbow
Threshold	Only ¼-inch step up
Glass block sidelights	Provide light and view with good security
Window	Crank handle at bottom for easy operation; latch handle extended
Base cabinets	Lower than usual countertop height (34½ inches vs. 36 inches); higher, deeper toe-kick at bottom (8" x 8" vs. 4" x 4") allows closer approach in wheelchair
Range	Front-mounted controls eliminate reaching across burners
Range hood switch	Mounted on front of cabinet
Refrigerator	Side-by-side style allows for variations in reach
Pantry cabinet	Hinged shelves bring contents into reach
Sink/base cabinet	Clear space under sink when doors are open allows wheelchair to roll under
Double-bowl sink	Shallow for easy reach; rear drain location provides more space underneath for wheelchair
Sink faucet control	Single-handle for ease of use

• Water shutoffs	Located under sink at side where they can be reached from sitting position; lever-action valves for easy operation	
• Insulated hot water line	Prevents accidental burns	
• Light switches	Under sink at side; control overhead lights	
• Towel rack, shelves	Mounted on inside of cabinet doors for easy access	
• Swing-out shelves	Bring cupboard contents within easy reach	
• Cutting board	Slides out for use; large size; doubles as additional counter space	
• Knife rack	Mounted under cabinet; swings down for use	
• Eating area	Counter mounted at higher than usual table height (31 inches vs. 29 inches) for wheelchair access	
• Light switch	Under-counter light control at side of counter; rocker-type switch can be operated with hand, elbow, and so on	
• Fire extinguisher	Mounted low for easy reach from hall or kitchen	

9-18. Provence, a new line of kitchen and bar sink faucets from Kohler, has a distinctive European-influenced design. Shown here is a one-handle kitchen faucet with integral pull-out spray. *(Reprinted with permission from Kohler Co.)*

The house was open (free of charge) to the public five days a week and served as a design and research center for architects, builders, and occupational and physical therapists, as well as for people with disabilities and their families. Such demonstration facilities can go a long way toward introducing the public to the benefits of universal design and creating new opportunities for consultants, designers, architects, builders, and product manufacturers. Unfortunately, funding problems led to the recent closing of this valuable facility.

Universal Design Strategy

Marketing Universal Design as a Consultant
by Susan Behar, ASID

The concept of universal design is truly revolutionary. Universal design is not, however, a new area of expertise in the field of architecture, interior design, or product design. It is only all-encompassing good design. All structures, facilities, and buildings created with universal principles will function to the fullest extent possible for those both with and without disabilities.

It has taken a long time for this concept to become reality, but universal design has finally arrived. The Americans with Disabilities Act did not create a logical end point; rather it legitimated universal design. The purpose and intent of this powerful legislation catapulted universal design into its rightful position (Behar, 1992). Our built environment has long been designed for use by one average physical type—young, fit, and adult. The fact is that millions do not fit this mold. People with physical impairments have come to represent a large segment of the population (Universal Design: Access to Daily Living Conference, 1992). Fifty-million middle-aged baby boomers are putting a new spin on society's traditional concept of growing older, and, as society grows older, the perception of what older means is changing. By the year 2030, one out of every five Americans will be 65 or older (Brotman, 1982). Consider that 31 million Americans have arthritis, 8.5 million are sight-impaired, 21.2 million have hearing impairments (O'Conner, 1986), and approximately 2 million use wheelchairs. Finally, remember that there are millions of latchkey children; like the elderly, children have physical limitations and therefore have special safety and security needs. This leaves more than 210 million Americans who are temporarily able-bodied (TABs).

Most individuals do not consider themselves disabled. They want to choose where they live and how they live, work, and entertain. Accessible design that is also aesthetically appealing lessens the stigma of aging while minimizing disability.

Strategy/Survival: The Universal Design Approach

The universal design approach is a business enhancing strategy needed for survival and for renewed opportunities for design professionals. The four A's—*accessibility, adaptability, aesthetics,* and *affordability*—address the education and design values necessary for incorporating universal design into the environment.

- *Accessibility:* Knowledge and implementation of accessibility codes for the ADA legislation and safety, health, and welfare issues for the licensing of design professionals are essential and mandatory for practicing designers. Noncompliance with this important legislation can result in civil rights liabilities.

- *Adaptability:* Universal design incorporates flexible products and design for an environment that works best for all people and maximizes the lifespan usage of a facility.

- *Aesthetics:* The design professional's creative ability to incorporate beautiful and barrier-free design has placed the designer in an important new marketing position. Universal design focuses on function without compromising aesthetics. This approach lets those with disabilities blend more fully and equally into the American mainstream. Mainstreaming is the real challenge of the ADA.

- *Affordability:* The costs of integrating adaptable and accessible features in the early stages of a project are minimal. A universal design approach meets legislation compliance and protects the client from costly design mistakes.

Design for the disabled has always been a hard sell. Many people's views of an environment designed for people with disabilities is that of a sterile and utilitarian setting. Universal design is the tool that changes this attitude: Through education and seeing examples of aesthetically pleasing environments, more clients will come to understand its value. Until that time, design professionals must incorporate universal design into all projects. But one must also know when to market benefits and when not to. A sell can come at any phase of a project: during the design stage, after the installation, or during the post-occupancy evaluation.

Case Study 1: Morton Plant Family Care Center

The Morton Plant Family Care Center is an affiliation of a nonprofit hospital located six miles from the center. The facility has two family practice physicians who treat an entire range of patients, from infants to frail elderly. Though the building was designed before the ADA legislation, it was universally designed since the facility's goal was to be barrier free and patient friendly.

Building Description

This 3300-square-foot facility is on the ground floor of a three-story office complex. The office complex is comprised of several medical suites joined by courtyards. Spaces were designed with an open feeling to provide a friendly, spacious, accessible environment with storage space provided for wheelchairs. Low planters divide the reception, waiting room, education, and nursing areas. Other areas include doctors' offices, a staff lounge, and examination rooms.

Materials/Furnishings

The outpatient clinic has 36-inch-wide doorways for users of wheelchairs, 5-foot-wide corridors, and offices that provide a 60-inch turning radius for wheelchairs. Instead of knobs, lever handles are used on all doors and U-pulls are used on all cabinets. Level-loop carpet and floor tile are installed on the same level for safer and easier mobility. For better visibility, signage with raised letters in contrasting colors is placed at eye level. Bathrooms feature wall-hung vanities, backsplashes are eliminated so that mirrors can extend down to the countertops, walls are reinforced at the proper height so grab bars can be installed either during construction or later, sinks are installed at a 32-inch height, and nonslip ceramic tile is used for additional safety. The selection of interior materials, furnishings, and accessories creates an aesthetically friendly environment. Colored grab bars, warm peach wall coverings, aqua tiles, and non-gloss laminates both brighten and soften the medical center. Furniture selection is based on ease of use, taking into account the varied needs of the population. The waiting area's seating has armrests and firm upholstery that allow elderly persons to easily get in and out of chairs. The variety of lighting and contrasting colors define surfaces and facilitate safety and independence for persons with visual disabilities. Textured wall coverings improve acoustics to aid those with hearing difficulties. All of these features underscore the fact that this facility values patients' needs.

Even though it was constructed and furnished before the ADA, this universally designed clinic meets the necessary criteria of this important legislation. Careful planning and selection of furnishings and finishes provided accessibility and adaptability so that patients, staff, or visitors with disabilities could visit or be employed with little or no extra cost to the facility. The Morton Plant Family Care Center was farsighted in accepting these offered marketing values: barrier free and friendly.

Case Study 2: Urology Health Center

The Urology Health Center is one of the very few surgical centers in the country dedicated to the practice of urology. It is a diagnostic and surgical ambulatory center located across the street from a hospital in a two-story, stand-alone building. The facility is located in a totally renovated 10,000-square-foot area of an existing building and has a 17,000-square-foot addition with separate entrances for the diagnostic and surgery centers. The diagnostic center includes a reception area, sub-wait areas, and four physician work areas, each consisting of a consultation office, a nursing station, and three examination rooms for each of the physicians. Other areas include a library, a patient education room, and accessible rest rooms adjacent to the laboratory with a pass-through so that patients need not carry their urine cups through the public space. (Maintaining the dignity of patients was a prime consideration in the design of this center.) The surgery center offers a large reception area with a resource center and a small family consultation waiting area featuring small-scaled firm sofas, table lamps, wall sconces, mahogany bookcases, and an ash wood pedestal table and chairs to create a warm, homelike environment. Other areas include five procedure

9-19. The reception area of the Urology Health Center in New Port Richey, FL, demonstrates a commitment to universal design. The check-in counter features two counter heights to accommodate all individuals. The open reception area and French doors provide a warm and welcoming environment. *(Figures 9-19 through 9-23 reprinted with permission from Susan Behar, ASID.)*

rooms, pre-op and post-op areas, three operating rooms, and a nurse supervisor area. The shell for an elevator shaft was constructed so that the surgery center could affordably add an elevator and easily build out the second story at a future date.

This urological practice is located in a retirement area; most of the patients are over the age of 50 and the majority rely on Medicare health insurance. Because of the squeeze between revenues and operating costs, surgery centers are looking to provide cost-effective quality care for their patients (Interiors, 1993). Key goals for a patient-oriented practice included these design values for the Urology Health Center:

- A feeling of hospitality
- Comfort
- A pleasing environment
- Well organized
- Patient well-being
- Informed patients
- Compliance with the ADA
- Maintenance of independence

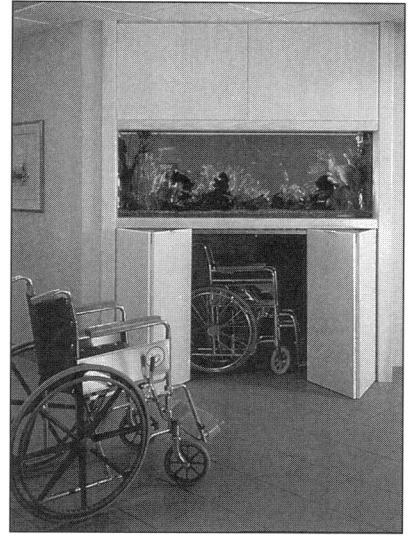

9-20. Attention to detail in the space planning process provided an area for wheelchair storage at the Urology Health Center.

The design of this center creates an agreeable mood and a sense of well-being through the use of warm ash woods, rose-toned wall coverings, soft recessed lighting, natural light, and outdoor views in the reception areas, corridors, and post-op areas. In a survey entitled "How Patients Evaluate the Quality of Ambulatory Medical Encounters: A Marketing Perspective," Kenneth Bopp points out that quality is divided into technical quality and expressive quality. A caring, efficient, supportive environment is essential to success (Bopp, 1990) and is quite evident in this health center.

Careful planning went into the design of the center in order to create a supportive environment that was in compliance with the requirements of the new legislation and with the strict code and regulations already in place. Long, maze-like corridors were eliminated, and the tactile, braille signage in contrasting colors was limited to room identification. Architectural clues help one find one's way through this large facility. A centrally-located nursing station, tile flooring to indicate directional flow, level-loop carpeting, 6-foot hallways, murals, and vaulted ceilings serve as wayfinding elements. The carpeted corridors and wall coverings also help reduce ambient noise and glare.

For this universally designed facility, accessibility considerations included custom reception counters with variable heights,

9-21. The vaulted ceiling, change in floor materials, lighting, and murals at the end of the hallway help patients and visitors maneuver through the Urology Health Center independently.

9-22. Furnishings, variety in lighting, and accessories make the waiting area at the Urology Health Center a comfortable, relaxed environment.

seating areas for users of wheelchairs to sit with friends and family, and small seating areas throughout the medical building for privacy and comfort. There are also automatic door openers, 36-inch French doors with decorative lever hardware in the reception areas, thresholds at less than ¼ inch in height, and telephones with individual volume control for patient use. Furniture systems adjust in height to accommodate the various needs of all users, and partitioned walls add flexibility and adaptability to the spaces as the facility's needs change. The large floral arrangement in the reception area provides hospitality and aesthetic appeal. An aquarium provides for passive viewing activity; a resource center and education area provide information on preventative health priorities and help create informed patients.

The cost effectiveness of this center is important to note. Efficient use of staff time stems from a good patient flow; design flexibility that can allow this facility to affordably grow into a multi-use practice in the future is an important cost-saving element. Another very important factor is achieving patient satisfaction and loyalty at an affordable price: Patients, staff, and visitors recognize, appreciate, and patronize this important medical center (Fisk et al., 1990). It serves as an exemplary model for universal design as a successful tool for implementing the ADA in a caring, patient-oriented facility.

Conclusion

The principles of universal design are powerful in their simplicity; they are held within a simple formula that uses thinking and understanding of the varying abilities of people as its base. The four A's—accessibility, adaptability, aesthetics, and affordability—are its dictums; independence, freedom of choice, normalization, value, flexibility, and improved self-esteem are its excellent results. Marketing tools for success and survival are to creatively produce structures with furnishings, interior finishes, and products that enable these results.

Universal Design Strategy

New Marketing Strategies for Universal Design
by Amy Harden, Ph.D.

Past marketing strategies that have been used to attract consumers with "special needs" (people with disabilities or those who are older) have generally not been successful. Once a product is labeled or specified as fulfilling needs of a special segment of the population, it is often doomed to failure. This phenomenon is not related directly to manufacturers' misunderstanding consumer

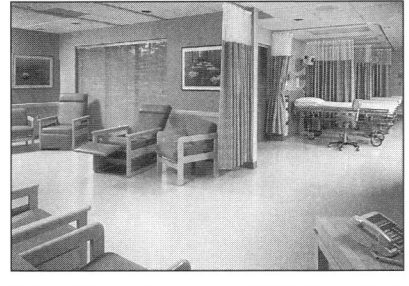

9-23. Vibrant materials and artwork were selected to encourage alertness at the Urology Health Center.

needs and not producing responsive products, or to a lack of people with those needs, but rather to the singling out of people who would buy such products as being different in some manner from the rest of "us."

Universally designed products—those that are developed to meet and adapt to consumer needs rather than having the consumer adapt to the environment—represent a first step in responding to this situation. However, much attention must be placed on the marketing of these products in order to sell to the target market. Unless the marketing strategies are changed from focusing on people who are labeled as special to a strategy that focuses on products that change or adapt the environment to meet needs of the entire population, success will probably be limited.

The primary marketing change needed is to follow the philosophy of universal design and eliminate labels identifying special segments of the population. This is especially true for those who are fighting to maintain independence and to fit into the general population (e.g., the elderly, those with disabilities). One notable example of a successful strategy change may be seen in the mail-order catalog, "Comfortably Yours: Aids for Easier Living." The products are described as convenient for everyone even though it is apparent that many of the products do meet special needs. Offered through the catalog are Swedish Rehab products such as long, jointed-handle grooming aids. Although these products are beneficial to individuals with arthritis or those with limited movement, the ad copy does not mention this aspect. Instead, the emphasis is on the convenience, rather than the necessity, of such products.

The "Comfortably Yours" catalog uses models who represent various population segments rather than just one segment in order to reinforce the philosophy that the products are useful for everyone, not just one particular group. Therefore, no label is associated with purchasers that may signify they are somehow different or lacking from others. Not only does this catalog reach its primary target of the elderly population, but it also has increased the market to include all segments with a common need that convenient products can fulfill.

In addition to changing the strategies for marketing specific products, strategies must also be adapted in order to reach older Americans and/or individuals with disabilities who could greatly benefit from new product developments without undue attention to their specific needs. One popular and accepted method of reaching target models is the use of catalogs. However, as stated above, the way in which the catalogs are developed and presented is important.

In a focus group study, consumers identified several advantages for catalog use, including the ease of locating needed products, convenience, and the variety and uniqueness of the products available. Another advantage is that it is not necessary to travel to stores to find the products desired. Catalogs come to the consumer's home (often in abundance). Once the catalogs arrive, consumers can take as much or as little time as they want looking through the product offerings.

In addition to the convenience, the products offered by catalogs generally include a variety often unavailable locally. Local retail stores carry only a select assortment of products because of limited space in which to store and display their products. Catalogs, on the other hand, are able to carry and display many more products since space is generally unlimited. Therefore, catalogs are often used to meet specific needs that are not met at local retailers. For example, catalogs for special apparel sizes are plentiful, as well as catalogs for specific products.

Although catalogs offer consumers many advantages, there are also disadvantages to catalog use. Primary disadvantages identified by focus groups were related to returns and unmet expectations. The need to repackage, ship, and pay additional postage to return an unwanted product was often mentioned. Consumers also report that products portrayed in catalogs often look different from the actual products received. The quality of product illustrations are frequently not adequate for consumers to develop realistic expectations. This is generally a problem with products that are purchased primarily for their visual appearance (most often clothing).

Another relatively new strategy that may better reach the elderly and people with disabilities is the use of TV in-home shopping (e.g., QVC, the Home Shopping Network). Consumers who participated in focus group discussions of various in-home shopping methods generally did not use this shopping method, primarily because they felt a lack of trust regarding product quality and follow-up service, as well as a fear of providing credit card numbers over the telephone.

Although consumers may presently be reluctant to use this method of shopping, it nevertheless has the potential of offering several advantages over catalog and local retail shopping. As with catalogs, shopping can be done 24 hours a day via a toll-free telephone service. Also, unique and varied selections can be made available. Most importantly, products can be demonstrated—potential customers can see clothing modeled, cooking and cleaning utensils used, and so on. Finally, a side advantage is that individuals who may have little outside contact with the world may sometimes develop a feeling of relationship with the TV hosts and customer service representatives—a connection that should not be belittled.

Disadvantages of TV in-home shopping methods are similar to those of catalog use: return of unacceptable merchandise and unmet expectations. However, seeing actual products demonstrated could eliminate some of these problems. But TV shopping may not be as convenient as catalog shopping since time has to be set aside to watch for when specific types of products are broadcast. Some networks also limit the time that a product may be purchased to just the time that the product is being displayed on the screen. Other networks seek to alleviate this difficulty by providing consumers with a schedule of types of products to be presented, giving an overview of the specific products in each segment, providing a review of products displayed, and allowing the consumer to order the product by calling any time, not just during display.

TV in-home shopping shows a great deal of potential for meeting the needs of people who may not be able to physically travel to local stores (as well as those whose schedule limits their shopping time). In order to continue and increase the success of this marketing strategy, attention needs to be given to reassuring consumers that purchasing products via TV is as safe and risk-free as any other shopping method. Once consumers try this method, they will most likely continue to use it. In addition, as technology continues to improve and interactive television becomes a reality for the mass society—allowing people to identify and search for a product they want at any time and see a demonstration of that product on demand—the disadvantages experienced at present will be eliminated.

Resources 10

Americans with Disabilities Act: Government Resources

For further information on the Americans with Disabilities Act, you should first contact the appropriate governmental agency (as listed here), each of which offers a variety of services, including primary and resource publications. One copy of each publication is available free, and all are available in alternative formats—braille, spoken, computer disk, and so on.

Title I

U.S. Equal Employment Opportunity Commission (EEOC)
Office of Communications and Legislative Affairs
1801 L Street, NW
Washington, DC 20507 (also, district offices)
202-663-4900 (voice), 800-800-3302 (TDD)

The EEOC is the primary resource for information about Title I. It can provide information, speakers, training, technical assistance, and referrals for employers and employees. It also offers several booklets, pamphlets, fact sheets, and videos, including the *ADA Technical Assistance Manual* and the *Compliance Manual* (the first copy of each is free).

Titles II and III

1. U.S. Department of Justice (DOJ)
   Civil Rights Division
   Office on the Americans with Disabilities Act
   P.O. Box 66118
   Washington, DC 20035-6118 (also, district offices)
   202-514-0301 (voice), 202-514-0381 (TDD),
   202-514-6193 (computer bulletin board)

In addition to telephone support, the DOJ publishes pamphlets, booklets, books, and fact sheets, including the *ADA Technical Assistance Manual* and *Title II and Title III Regulations*.

2. U.S. Department of Transportation (DOT)
   400 7th Street, SW
   Washington, DC 20590
   202-366-9305 (voice), 202-755-7687 (TDD)

   The DOT provides information on public and private transport services and offers a variety of materials, including *Transportation for Individuals with Disabilities, Regulations* and *ADA Paratransit Handbook*.

Title IV

The Federal Communications Commission governs the provisions of Title IV: Telecommunications. Contact it at:

1919 M Street, NW
Washington, DC 20554
202-632-7260 (voice), 202-632-6999 (TDD)

Call with specific questions, or ask for the following published materials: *Telecommunications Services for Hearing and Speech Disabled, Regulations* and *Telecommunications Relay Service—An Informational Handbook*.

ADA Technical Assistance Centers

There are ten regional centers, established by the National Institute on Disability and Rehabilitation Research, that provide information, training, and technical assistance to employers, people with disabilities, and other interested parties on issues related to the ADA. Any of these centers can provide the following:

- Information (i.e., printed and audiovisual materials)

- Referrals to local experts for questions/issues outside the scope of the center's operation

- Training for employers, people with disabilities, and others

- Technical assistance on how to comply with employment and public accommodations requirements

For a complete listing of these centers, including a breakdown by state, see either of the *Technical Assistance Manuals*.

Job Accommodation Network (JAN)

JAN is a free consultative service that offers solutions to accommodation issues. Operators can provide assistance in understanding the regulations and can help you find ways to make a workspace accessible. They also offer a computer bulletin board for fast access to products and ideas. Write to it at:

> Job Accommodation Network (JAN)
> P.O. Box 6123
> 809 Allen Hall
> Morgantown, WV 26506-6123

Also contact it for its publications. Especially useful is its publications resource list. JAN phone numbers are:

- Accommodation Information:
  (out-of-state) 800-526-7234 (voice/TDD),
  (in-state) 800-526-4698 (voice/TDD)

- ADA Information:
  (out-of-state) 800-232-9675, 800-ADA-WORK (voice/TDD),
  800-342-5526 (800-DIAL-JAN) (computer modem)

Americans with Disabilities Act: Nongovernment Resources

All of the major groups representing people with disabilities offer information and advice on ADA issues (for example, the American Foundation for the Blind, the Arthritis Foundation, Goodwill Industries of America, and so on). Their national addresses and phone numbers can be found in the *Technical Assistance Manuals.* You can also contact local branches for assistance. Other organizations that are especially helpful are as follows:

1. The Disability Rights Education and Defense Fund, Inc. (DREDF)
   2212 6th Street
   Berkeley, CA 94710
   510-644-2555 (voice/TDD)

   DREDF has been a key organization in providing training and information on disability-related issues. DREDF offers videos, books, and pamphlets and also provides legal representation to individuals with disabilities.

2. National Organization on Disability (NOD)
   910 16th Street, NW, Suite 600
   Washington, DC 20006
   202-293-5960, 202-293-5968 (TDD), (202)293-7999 (fax),
   800-248-ABLE (2253)

NOD is the only national disability organization concerned with all disabilities, all ages, and all disability issues.

Finally, of all of the privately published guides available on the ADA, the work of Patricia Morrissey is especially useful for understanding the law. She has written several books on the ADA, including *A Primer for Corporate America on Civil Rights for the Disabled* (1991), from LRP Publications (800-341-7874), and *The Educator's Guide to the Americans with Disabilities Act* (1993), from the American Vocational Association.

Organizations

1. Barrier-Free Environments, Inc.
   P.O. Box 30634
   Highway 70 West-Watergarden
   Raleigh, NC 27622
   919-782-7823 (voice/TDD)

2. The Center for Universal Design
   School of Design
   North Carolina State University
   P.O. Box 8613
   Raleigh, NC 27695-8613
   919-515-3082 (voice/TDD), 919-515-3023 (fax)

   Ronald Mace remains one of the best resources for universal design materials. He is involved with both of these organizations. They offer books, floor plans, workshops, consultations, and resource guides. Information packs on available materials related to general accessibility and universal design can be obtained from the center by calling 800-647-6777 (information only).

3. Building Owners and Managers Association, International (BOMA)
   P.O. Box 79330
   Baltimore, MD 21279-0330
   800-426-6292

   Ask for the *ADA Compliance Guidebook* and *Opening Doors*.

4. The Hartford House
   Community Affairs Department
   ITT Hartford Insurance Group
   Hartford Plaza
   Hartford, CT 06115

   The Hartford House is an exhibit built to show how accommodations can be made to create a supportive environment for people as they age in place. You can get information on the exhibit as well as a valuable product/research guide (*How to Modify a Home to Accommodate the Needs of an Older Adult*) by writing to the above address. Hartford House also has a video that can be borrowed at no cost or purchased for $25.00.

5. Pratt Institute
   Center for Advanced Design Research
   200 Willoughby Avenue
   Brooklyn, NY 11205
   718-636-3690, 718-636-3553 (fax)

   The Pratt Institute offers an accredited degree in universal design and also publishes several very useful books, including *The Universal Design Primer* and a *Universal Design Curriculum*.

Publications

1. *The Accessible Housing Design File* (1991), by Ronald Mace. New York: Van Nostrand Reinhold.
2. *Beautiful Barrier-Free: A Visual Guide to Accessibility* (1992), by Cynthia A. Leibrock (with Susan Behar). New York: Van Nostrand Reinhold.
3. *Design for Dignity: Accessible Environments for People with Disabilities* (1993), by William L. Lebovich. New York: John Wiley & Sons.
4. *Design Intervention: Toward a More Humane Architecture* (1990), by Wolfgang Preiser, Jacqueline Vischer, and Edward White. New York: Van Nostrand Reinhold.
5. *Housing Interiors for the Disabled and Elderly* (1991), by Bettyann Boetticher Raschko. New York: Van Nostrand Reinhold.
6. *Housing Publication List* (1993). Fact sheets, booklets, newsletters. PF 5033(393)-D12173. AARP Fulfillment, 601 E. Street NW, Washington, DC 20049.
7. *Metropolis—The Magazine of Architecture and Design*. P.O. Box 5052, Vandalia, OH 45377-9977: 800-344-3046.
8. *The New ADA: Compliance and Costs* (1993), by Deborah S. Kearney. Kingston, MA: R.S. Means.
9. *Nursing Home Renovation Designed for Reform* (1991), by Lorrainne G. Hyatt. Newton, MA: Butterworth-Helneman Architecture.
10. *Practicing Universal Design* (1994), by Wm. L. Wilkoff and Laura W. Abed. New York: Van Nostrand Reinhold.
11. *That All May Worship* (1992), National Organization on Disability, Religion, and Disability Program. Washington, D.C.
12. *The Workplace Workbook 2.0: An Illustrated Guide to Workplace Accommodation and Technology* (1993), by James Mueller. Amherst, MA: Human Resource Development Press.

13. *Transgenerational Design* (1994), by James J. Pirkl. New York: Van Nostrand Reinhold.

14. *Universal Design Newsletter,* Universal Designers and Consultants, Inc. 1700 Rockville Pike, Suite 110, Rockville, MD 20852: 301-770-7890, 301-770-4338 (fax).

Technology

1. ABLEDATA
   Adaptive Equipment Center
   Newington Children's Hospital
   181 East Cedar Street
   Newington, CT 06111
   203-667-5405 (voice/TDD), 800-344-5405 (voice/TDD)

   ABLEDATA offers a comprehensive database of products and assistive devices. In addition to providing fact sheets offering comparisons of similar products, it can also perform custom database searches for your specific need. The service is free for the first ten items of a search, and a small fee is charged thereafter.

2. American Foundation for Technology Assistance (AFTA)
   Route 14, Box 230
   Morgantown, NC 28655
   704-438-9697

   AFTA maintains a database of adaptive and assistive technology and can provide information on products, services, and training; discounts on purchases; and sources of financial aid for purchasing essential products.

3. *Apple Computer Resources in Special Education and Rehabilitation* (1989). Edited and published by DLM Teaching Resources, Allen, TX. Developed by the Office of Special Education Programs, Apple Computer, Inc., in association with the TRACE Research and Development Center, University of Wisconsin, Madison, WI 53706.

   This document lists computer applications by disability categories along with hardware adaptations, software, and information services.

4. Foundation for Technology Access
   1307 Solano Avenue
   Albany, CA 94706-1888

   The foundation publishes information on employment issues related to disabilities; provides referrals for services that aid equal employment opportunity; and offers information, consultation, and technical assistance on assistive technology for people with disabilities, including computer hardware and software technology and adaptive and assistive equipment.

5. Gallaudet University
   National Information Center on Deafness
   Kendall Green
   800 Florida Avenue, NE
   Washington, DC 20002
   202-651-5051 (voice), 202-651-5052 (TDD)

   Besides general information on deafness, Gallaudet offers up-to-date information on assistive devices for overcoming communication barriers including computers, alerting devices, and TDDs.

6. MAXI-AIDS
   42 Executive Boulevard
   P.O. Box 3209
   Farmingdale, NY 11735
   800-522-6294

   This mail-order catalog carries a multitude of products available for assisting people with a wide range of disabilities. Often these products are useful for everyone. The catalog features everything from kitchen gadgets to computer accessories, ranging in price from a few dollars to several hundred dollars.

7. National Rehabilitation Hospital
   102 Irvine Street, NW
   Washington, DC 20010-2949
   202-877-1932 (voice), 202-726-3996 (TDD)

   This organization plays a major role in the creation of new assistive technology—designing, testing, and evaluating tools created by others. It also offers a wide range of publications on disability-related issues.

8. RESNA
   1101 Connecticut Avenue, NW, Suite 700
   Washington, DC 20036
   202-857-1199

   RESNA provides information on rehabilitation engineering, including modifying equipment and designing new devices. It publishes a number of items on assistive technology, including a bimonthly newsletter. Ask for their:

   - *Assistive Technology Sourcebook* (1990), by A. Enders
   - *The Workplace Workbook: An Illustrated Guide to Job Accommodation and Assistive Technology* (1990), by James Mueller

9. *Sears Health Care Catalog*
   800-326-1750

   This listing is included to show the availability of products offered to the general public that are often thought of as geared to special needs publications. Sears offers a wide range of products suitable for making environments more universal.

10. *Solutions: A HyperCard Stack of Computer Resources for Individuals with Disabilities*
    Apple Computer, Inc.
    20525 Mariana Avenue, MS23D
    Cupertino, CA 95410
    408-973-6484

    This "stack" includes information on hardware products, software products, and information resources.

11. TRACE Research and Development Center (TRACE RDC)
    S-151 Waisman Center
    1500 Highland Avenue
    Madison, WI 53705

    TRACE RDC provides information on assistive and rehabilitation technology. It is an especially good source for data and products on making computers accessible for a wide range of disabilities.

Appendix A: Chemical Sensitivities

Products and Resources

1. *AFM Enterprises, Inc.* (American Formulating and Manufacturing). 1140 Stacy Court, Riverside, CA 92507. 714-781-6860 or 6861.

   Provides a product catalogue for the chemically sensitive and environmentally aware. Product catalogues include paints, stains, sealers, joint and caulking compounds, and adhesives, as well as cleaning products and strippers.

2. *Earth Tools.* 9754 Johanna Place, Shadow Hills, CA 91040. 800-825-6460.

   Provides a line of nontoxic cleaning products for the home.

3. *Eco Design.* 1365 Rufina Circle, Santa Fe, NM 87501. 800-621-2591.

   This company's catalog is "The Natural Choice." They offer a variety of natural paints, stains, and wood preservatives, including Livos products.

4. *Environmental Design Research.* 373 Wurster Hall, University of California, Berkeley, CA 94720.

5. *Environmental Health Services.* 3202 Anderson Lane, #208–249, Austin, TX 78757. 512-288-2369.

6. Good, Clinton F., 11521 Warren Lane, Fairfax, VA 22032.

   Architect and consultant for nontoxic environments.

7. *The Masters Corporation.* P.O. Box 514, New Canaan, CT 06840.

   Provides consultation on nontoxic construction.

8. *Miller Paint Co., Inc.* 317 SE Grand Avenue, Portland, OR 97214. 503-233-4491.

   Deals only in paints—low-biocide interior and exterior paint and non-fungicide paint. Contact Gary A. Wellman.

9. *Murco Wall Products, Inc.* 300 NE 21st Street, Fort Worth, TX 76106. 800-452-1451.

    Provides wall products for the chemically sensitive, joint and texturing compounds, and interior paints.

10. *Negley Paint Co., Inc.* P.O. Box 47848, San Antonio, TX 78265-8848. 210-651-6996.

    Provides fungicide- and biocide-free paints.

11. *Pace Chem Industries, Inc.* 779 S. La Grange Avenue, Newbury Park, CA 91320. 805-499-2911.

    Provides nontoxic and hypoallergenic sealers and paint for wood building products and furniture, vinyl wall coverings, and so on.

12. *Real Goods Trading Corporation.* 966 Mazzoni Street, Ukiah, CA 95482. 800-762-7325.

    Provides natural and nontoxic cleaning products.

13. Segal, Barry. RD 1, Box 22 A, 106 South Street East, Trumansburg, NY 14886.

    Consultant for nontoxic environments.

14. *Sinan Co.* P.O. Box 857, Davis, CA 95617-0857. 916-753-3104.

    Provides natural wool carpeting without chemical treatments; also the entire line of AURO products—organic paints, stains, finishes, sealers, oils, waxes, lacquers, varnishes, thinners, undercoats, primers and fillers, natural cleansers, and polishes. The firm also carries natural cosmetics, furniture, bedding, office supplies, insulation, vacuum cleaners, and so on.

15. *Terra Verde Trading Co., #1.* 72 Spring Street, New York, NY 10012. 212-925-4533; or *Terra Verde Trading Co., #2.* 420 Broadway, Santa Monica, CA 90401. 310-394-1115.

    Provides cleaning supplies with nontoxic finishes.

16. *Toxic Substances Information Line.* 800-648-6732.

17. *United States Consumer Products Safety Commission.* 1111 18th Street NW, Washington, DC 20207. 200-638-2772 (200-638-CPSC).

18. *United States Environmental Protection Agency.* 800-424-9065.

19. *W.I.S.E. Institute, Inc.* P.O. Box 317, Ephraim, UT 84627. 800-759-9473.

    Their catalog is called "Healthy Home and Body." It offers cleaning tips as well as information on nontoxic products, air purifiers, natural stains and finishes, and even cosmetics.

Books and Articles

If the previous resources cannot provide or recommend the necessary products or substitutions, the following books and articles may give you the needed information or suggest other avenues for exploration:

"Beware the Sick-Building Syndrome." *Newsweek,* 7 January, 1985. pp. 58–60.

Bierman-Lytle, Paul, AIA (1989). *Home Safe Home.* New York: Nichols Publishing.

Bower, John (1989). *The Healthy House.* New York: Carol Commission.

"Building a Healthy House" (September–October 1986). *Everything Natural.* Available from Nontoxic Lifestyles. P.O. Box 475, Inverness, CA 94937. 415-663-1685.

Dadd, Debra Lynn, and Alan S. Levin, M.D. (1982). *A Consumer Guide for the Chemically Sensitive.* San Francisco: Nontoxic Lifestyles, Inc.

——— (1990). *Non-Toxic and Natural: A Guide for Consumers.* Los Angeles: J. P. Tarcher Books.

Davidoff, Linda Lee (Winter 1989). "Multiple Chemical Sensitivities (MCS)." *The Amicus Journal,* pp. 10–30.

EPA (September 1988). "The Inside Story: A Guide to Indoor Air Quality." Washington, DC: Environmental Protection Agency and Consumer Product Safety Commission.

Healthy House Catalog (1988). Cleveland, OH: Environmental Health Watch and Housing Resource Center.

Godish, Thad, Ph.D. (Summer 1986). "Indoor Air Quality Notes: Formaldehyde—Our Houses and Health." No. 1. Department of Natural Resources, Ball State University, Muncie, IN 47306.

——— (Summer 1986). "Indoor Air Quality Notes: Residential Formaldehyde Control." No. 2. Department of Natural Resources, Ball State University, Muncie, IN 47306.

"How Healthful Is Your Home?" (July 1989). *East West,* pp. 47–71.

"Indoor Air Pollution" (October 1985). *Consumer Reports,* pp. 600–603.

Pfeiffer, Guy O., M.D., and Casimir M. Nikel (1980). *The Household Environment and Chronic Illness: Guidelines for Constructing and Maintaining a Less Polluted Residence.* Springfield, IL: Charles C. Thomas.

Rousseau, David, W. J. Rea, M.D., and Jean Enwright (1988). *Your Home, Your Health, and Well-Being.* Vancouver, BC: Hartley and Marks.

Schoonmaker, David (March–April 1989). "Are You Home Sick?" *Mother Earth News,* pp. 90–100.

References

Chapter 2

Bush-Brown, A. and D. Davis (1992). *Hospital Design for Health Care and Senior Communities.* New York: Van Nostrand Reinhold.

Gaunt, L. (1980). "Can Children Play at Home?" In P. F. Wilkinson (ed.) *Innovation in Play Environments.* London: Croom Helm.

Hildreth, G. J. and C. D. Hoyt (Winter, 1981). "Children and Privacy: Implications for Parents and Teachers." *Journal of Home Economics*, 73, pp. 31–33.

Hyatt, L. G., J. Brieff, J. Horwitz, and C. McQueen (1982). *Uses of Self-Help in Compensating for Sensory Changes in Old Age* (Grant Report). New York: American Foundation for the Blind.

Inman, M., M. Boschetti, and J. Inman (1992). "Design Criteria in the Study of the Sustainable Residential Setting for the Independent Older Adult." Paper presented at Environmental Design Research Association, Annual Meeting, Boulder, CO.

Lindberg, L. (1960). "Children in the Community." *Good Living for Young Children.* New York: New York State Council for Children.

Loo, C. (1978). "Issues of Crowding Research: Vulnerable Perceptions and Developmental Differences." *Journal of Population, 1*, pp. 336–349.

Piaget, J. (1973). *The Child and Reality.* New York: Viking Press.

Proshansky, H. (1973). "Theoretical Issues in Environmental Psychology." *Representative Research in Social Psychology, 41*, pp. 93–109.

Rohe, W. (1982). "The Response to Density in Residential Settings: The Mediating Effects of Social and Personal Variables." *Journal of Applied Social Psychology, 12*, pp. 292–303.

Rotter, J. (1971). "External Control and Internal Control." *Psychology Today, 5*, p. 37.

Sweaney, A., M. Inman, C. Wallinga, and S. Dias (1986). "The Perceptions of Preschool Children and Their Families' Social Climate in Relation to Household Crowding." *Children's Environments Quarterly, 3:4*, pp. 10–15.

Webb, N. (1984). *Preschool Children with Working Parents.* Lanham, MD: University Press of America.

Chapter 4

Mueller, J. (1993). *The Workplace Workbook 2.0: An Illustrated Guide to Workplace Accommodation and Technology.* Amherst, MA: Human Resource Development Press.

Pheasant, S. (1988). *Body Space: Anthropometry, Ergonomics and Design.* New York: Taylor & Francis.

Chapter 6

ANSI/HFS 100—1988 (1988). *American National Standard for Human Factors Engineering of Visual Terminal Workstations.* Santa Monica, CA: The Human Factors Society.

Apple Computer, Inc., in Association with the TRACE Research and Development Center, University of Wisconsin-Madison (1989). *Apple Computer Resources in Special Education and Rehabilitation,* 1989 ed. Allen, Texas: DLM Teaching Resources.

——— (April, 1993). "Buyer's Checklist: Displays & Monitors." *Modern Office Technology,* p. 51.

Becker, F. D. (1990). *The Total Workplace.* New York: Van Nostrand Reinhold.

Dainoff, M. J. and M. H. Dainoff (1986). *People and Productivity: A Manager's Guide to Ergonomics in the Electronic Office.* Toronto: Holt, Rinehart and Winston of Canada. Reprinted in 1992 by Carswell: Toronto.

——— (1992, May). "Guerrilla Ergonomics." *WordPerfect The Magazine,* pp. 42–45.

DeWitt, P. E. (October 12, 1992). "Building a Better Keyboard." *Time,* p. 72.

Hedge, A. (1992). "Australian Research Shows that Improved Posture Reduces the Incidence of Keyboard-Related CTS." *Proformix™ Research Update #004:920v1*.

Hedge, A., W. Sims, and F. D. Becker (1989). "Lighting the Computerized Office: A Comparative Study of Parabolic Lensed-Indirect Office Lighting Systems." *Proceedings of the Human Factors Society 33rd Annual Meeting, 1*, pp. 521–525.

Hembree, D. (1990, January). "Warning: Computing Can be Hazardous to Your Health." *Macworld*, pp. 150–157.

Horowitz, J. M. (October 12, 1992). "Crippled by Computers." *Time*, pp. 70–72.

Karasek, R. A. (1981). "Job Decision Latitude, Job Design, and Coronary Heart Disease." In G. Salvendy and M. J. Smith (eds.), *Machine Pacing and Occupational Stress*. London: Taylor and Francis.

Krimmer, N. (1991). "Ergonomics and Safety Issues of Computer Workstations on Campus." Unpublished presentation at the Computers on Campus National Conference, NC.

Murray, William E. (1985). "Video Display Terminals: Radiation Issues." *Library Hi Tech*, 12; 3(4), pp. 43–47. Reprinted in *NIOSH Publications of Video Display Terminals* (1991), pp. 31–35. U.S. Department of Health and Human Services.

Stellman, J., and M. Henifin (1983). *Office Work Can Be Dangerous to Your Health*. New York: Pantheon Books.

Wagner, C. G. (1992, May–June). "Enabling the 'Disabled'." *The Futurist*, pp. 29–32.

Chapter 8

Alvarez, Mark (February, 1987). "Healthy Building." *Rodale's Practical Homeowner*, pp. 30–35, 118, 120.

American National Standards Institute (Final draft, 1992). *American National Standard for Accessible and Usable Buildings (ANSI 117.1—1992)*. Falls Church, VA.

Barrier-Free Environments (1991). *The Accessible Housing Design File*. New York: Van Nostrand Reinhold.

Beall, G. T., M. M. Thompson, F. Godwin, and W. T. Donahue (1981). *Housing Older Persons in Rural America: A Handbook on Congregate Housing*. Washington, D.C.: International Center for Social Gerontology.

Connell, Bettye R., and Jon A. Sanford (1996). "Individualizing Home Modification: Recommendations to Facilitate Performance of Routine Activities." In J. Hyde and S. Landsbury (eds.), *Housing Adaptations to Accommodate Changing Needs: Research, Policy and Programs.* Newton, MA: Butterworth Press.

Department of Justice (DOJ) (1991). "Nondiscrimination on the Basis of Disability by Public Accommodations and in Commercial Facilities; Final Rule." *Federal Register,* 56(144), pp. 35544–35961.

Directory of Accessible Building Products, 2nd ed. (1992). Upper Marlboro, MD: NAHB National Research Center.

Goldsmith, S. (1984). *Designing for the Disabled* (3rd ed., fully revised). London: RIBA Publications.

Grandjean, E. (1973). *Ergonomics of the Home.* New York: John Wiley.

Kaufman, J. E., ed. (1987). *IES Lighting Handbook Application Volume.* New York: Illuminating Engineering Society of North America.

Kira, A. (1958). *Housing Requirements of the Aged: A Study of Design Criteria.* Ithaca, NY: Cornell University Housing Research Center.

——— (1960). "Housing Needs of the Aged with a Guide to Functional Planning for the Elderly and Handicapped." *Rehabilitation Literature,* 21(12), pp. 370–377, 384.

Koontz, T. A., and C. V. Dagwell (1994). *Residential Kitchen Design, a Research-Based Approach.* New York: Van Nostrand Reinhold.

Liebrock, C., with S. Behar (1993). *Beautiful Barrier-Free.* New York: Van Nostrand Reinhold.

Moore, L. J. and E. R. Ostrander (1992). "In Support of Mobility: Kitchen Design for Independent Older Adults" (Information Bulletin 225). Ithaca, NY: Cornell University, Cornell Cooperative Extension.

Null, R. L. (1987). "A Universal Kitchen Design for the Low-Vision Elderly." *Journal of Interior Design Education and Research,* 14(2), pp. 45–50.

Olson, W. W. (1989). "Selecting a Refrigerator" (HE–FO–2185). St. Paul, MN: University of Minnesota, Minnesota Extension Service.

Raschko, B. B. (1982). *Housing Interiors for the Disabled and Elderly.* New York: Van Nostrand Reinhold.

Schumacher, T. L., and G. Cranz (1975). "The Built Environment for the Elderly: A Planning and Design Study, Focusing on Independent Living for Elderly Tenants." Princeton, NJ: Princeton University, School of Architecture and Urban Planning.

Smith, E. (1993). "Entryways: Creating Attractive, Inexpensive No-Step Entrances to Houses." Atlanta: Concrete Change, 404-378-7455.

Sweet's Accessible Building Products (1992). New York: McGraw-Hill.

Uniform Federal Accessibility Standards (1984). Washington, D.C.: General Services Administration, Department of Defense, Department of Housing and Urban Development, U.S. Postal Service.

Chapter 9

Behar, S. (May, 1992). *The Human Lifespan: Growing Up/Growing Older.* Position paper presented at "Universal Design: Access to Daily Living" conference, Pratt University, pp. 36–38.

——— (July/August, 1991). "Universal Design Blends Function with Form." *Group Practice Journal*, pp. 87–88.

Bopp, K. (March, 1990). "How Patients Evaluate the Quality of Ambulatory Medical Encounters: A Marketing Perspective." *Journal of Health Care Marketing.* pp. 6–15.

Brotman, H. (1982). "Every Ninth American." House Select Committee on Aging. Washington, D.C.

Fisk, T., C. Brown, K. Cannuzzari, and B. Naftak (June, 1990). "Creating Patient Satisfaction and Loyalty." *Journal of Health Care Marketing*, pp. 5–15.

Gorman, J. (December, 1992). "Critical Condition." *Interiors*, pp. 28, 32, 36, 96.

McMillan, N. (1981). *Marketing Your Hospital, A Strategy for Survival.* American Hospital Association, p. 77.

O'Conner, G. (November, 1986). "Design: Remodeling for the Handicapped and Elderly." *Remodeling Contractor*, p. 46.

Wilkoff, Wm. L. and Laura W. Abed (1994). *Practicing Universal Design: An Interpretation of the ADA.* New York: Van Nostrand Reinhold.

Williams, F. (June, 1987). "The Future of Aging." *The Archive of Physical Medicine and Rehabilitation*, p. 335.

Contributors

Robert Anders is the Director of the Design Management Graduate Program and a Professor of Industrial Design at Pratt Institute. He has been teaching universal design since 1991 when he coauthored Pratt's "Curriculum on Universal Design" and *Universal Design*, a primer currently used in several programs nationwide. He was formerly Director, Staff Design at Bristol-Myers Co. and Director, Visual Merchandising at Revlon, Inc.

Franklin Becker, Ph.D., is a Professor and Director of the International Workplace Studies Program at Cornell University and co-leader of the Industrial Development Research Council CRE 2000 research program. Both research programs focus on the changing workplace and its effects on individuals, organizations, and communities. In particular the research has looked at new ways of working involving home-based telework, telework centers, nonterritorial offices, and team and collaborative environments. Professor Becker has conducted research, lectured, and consulted in England, Canada, Europe, Japan, Australia, and New Zealand as well as in the United States. He has served as the Academic Affairs member of the Board of Directors in the International Facility Management Association, from which he has received the Outstanding Educator award and the Distinguished Author award. In addition to his academic responsibilities, Professor Becker is a principal in @WORK Consulting Group, a management consulting firm offering a range of services related to planning, designing, and managing integrated workplace strategies.

Susan Behar, ASID, principal of Susan Behar, ASID/Universal Design in Dunedin, Florida, is a licensed interior designer committed to the practice, education, and research of universal design. Behar contributed to the nationally awarded book, *Beautiful Barrier-Free—A Visual Guide to Accessibility.* Behar lectures and teaches to professional, public, and academic audiences. She is currently involved with the Universal Design Education Project Grant.

James C. Canestaro, AIA, is a Senior Architect and Facility Planner who provides professional and instructional services to the Department of Energy. He has made numerous continuing education presentations and has authored technical articles and books on the subject of feasibility and benefit-cost analysis.

Nancy C. Canestaro, Ph.D., D.Arch., has taught at the University of Tennessee and at Michigan State University. Her areas of expertise include programming and simulation games.

Ken Cherry lives and works in Ohio as a writer and sometimes editor. He is a parent to Daniel and Jesse, and husband to Mary Cecelia.

Bettye Rose Connell, Ph.D., is the Director of Research and Design Development at the Rehabilitation Engineering Research Center for Accessibility and Universal Design in Housing, North Carolina State University, and a Research Architect and Chief of the Environmental Section at the Rehabilitation Research and Development Center on Aging at the Veterans Affairs Medical Center in Atlanta. Dr. Connell holds a M.S. degree from Cornell University (Environmental Analysis and Architecture) and a Ph.D. from Georgia Tech (Architecture). Her recent research includes studies of the impact of accessible features and home modifications on ease and independence in routine household activities for individuals with disabilities and evaluation of the appropriateness of accessible housing features for occupants' needs. She has also conducted research used to develop accessibility standards for children's environments, assembly areas, and ramps.

Owen J. Cooks is the ADA Facilities Coordinator and a Project Manager and alumnus at Purdue University, where he has been instrumental in the development and implementation of the Facilities Audit and Transition Plan for ADA compliance. He has spoken of his experiences at Association of Physical Plant Administrators conferences and workshops and the Association of ADA Coordinators. He has also made presentations at several universities and consulted with miscellaneous outside organizations.

DeVonna L. Cunningham Cervantes received her B.S. in Early Childhood Education with Teaching Certification from Oklahoma State University (OSU) in 1981. In 1991 she returned to OSU as the graduate resident of the Bartlett Independent Living Laboratory to work on the degree of Master in Environmental Design, specializing in barrier-free design, with a minor in Public Administration. She was an OSU Foundation Distinguished Graduate Student Fellow recipient for 1991/1992 and a member of Kappa Omicron Nu.

Carol V. Dagwell, Ph.D., is a Professor of Interior Design at Radford University in Virginia. She received her Ph.D. from Virginia Tech, is a member of a number of professional associations including IDEC, AAHE, and IFI, and coauthored the book *Residential Kitchen Design, A Research Based Approach*, that includes descriptions of both accessible and unviersal design kitchens.

Diane Davis taught in interior design programs for almost 14 years at Purdue University and then at Valparaiso University, where she directed the Interior Design program. She actively integrated computer-aided design into the course curricula while teaching. In the summer of 1994, Davis joined Bentley Systems, Inc., the developers of MicroStation CAD software, to design and manage their Academic Program.

Rae Duncan-Lyle is an accessibility specialist providing consultation on accessibility issues as they relate to designed environments, plan review, and on-site evaluations. The Housing Resource Center (Cleveland), the kitchen of the spinal cord injury service of the Veteran's Administration Hospital (Wade Oval), and Section 202 Apartments for Maximum Independent Living, Inc., are examples of design assignments completed by Lyle. Her areas of expertise are Titles II and III of the Americans with Disabilities Act, Section 504 of the Rehabilitation Act of 1973, and the Fair Housing Amendments Act of 1988. Lyle is a frequent presenter at ADA workshops and seminars for businesses and public entities.

Joan M. Eisenberg is an independent (consumer and industry) certified kitchen and bath design consultant in Baltimore, Maryland. She is also a certified home economist and a professional member of the American Society of Interior Designers.

Amy Harden, Ph. D., is an Assistant Professor of Retailing at Miami University who earned her B.S. and M.S. from Bowling Green State University and her Ph.D. from Ohio State University. Her research has focused on examining technology and its use in retailing. She is currently exploring consumer's attitudes toward technological advances, perceptions of dress, and in-home shopping methods used for apparel purchases.

Gail Hartwigsen, Ph. D., holds the following degrees: a B.S. in Home Economics Education from Glassboro State College, a M.A. in Housing and Interior Design from the University of Connecticut, and a Ph.D. in Family Ecology—Human Environment and Design/Gerontology from Michigan State University. She taught at Indiana State Univerity and Arizona State University. She served as Program Manager for two national Institutes of Senior Housing and Community Based Long-Term Care at the National Council on Aging. She also was Assistant Director of the National Council on Seniors Housing of the National Association of Home Builders. She was also a Staff Researcher for the National Commission on Manufactured Housing and is presently an Associate with ProSource Systems Corporation, Specialist in Resident Systems for Senior Independent Living and Care Facilities

Robert Herman is a partner in Herman Stoller Coliver Architects. Since he completed graduate studies at Harvard's School of Design in 1960 and entered private practice in 1969, the main body of his work represents a concerted effort to elevate the design quality and living standards of low-income housing to match or exceed that of the private marketplace. From a sub-specialty in the design of affordable senior housing, his writings, lectures, and teaching at UC Berkeley have described how "user-needs" surveys become a resource for creative, economical design solutions.

Karen Hirsch, Assistant Professor of Education, Northeast Missouri State University, has started two Independent Living centers. She is currently studying disability history by conducting oral history interviews with polio survivors and by examining disability experiences in the FWP ex-slave narratives, as well as interviews with southern textile mill workers.

Marjorie Inman, Ph.D., is a Professor and Chair of the Department of Apparel, Merchandising, and Interior Design at East Carolina University in Greenville, North Carolina. She received her Ph.D. from Purdue University in Lafayette, Indiana. She is a member of the ECU Gerontology Institute and the American Society on Aging as well as of the American Society of Interior Designers Allied Education, the Environmental Design Research Association, and the American Association of Housing Educators. Dr. Inman is a Certified Kitchen Designer and is a member of the AES Regional Research Committee involved with a national study of households at risk for homelessness.

Betty Jones graduated from San Diego State University in 1989 with a B.A. in Interior Design. She currently works in the hospitality industry.

Joel I. Kahn has been an engineer with Procter & Gamble in Cincinnati, Ohio, since 1974. He and his wife Susan have one son, Philip, who is ten. Kahn has been the National Multiple Sclerosis Father of Year and a National Easter Seals Community Service Award winner. He is an Adjunct Associate Professor of Engineering at the University of Cincinnati.

Roberta Kilty-Padgett, M.F.A., has been an interior design educator since 1969. Her teaching and research involvement include post-occupancy evaluations in relation to human needs, interior design programming, ergonomics, and anthropometrics.

Bradley A. Knopp is the Executive Director of the HTM Group, a research consulting firm that also provides technical writing and information management services to industry and government. With a professional background in both the humanities and the applied sciences, Knopp strives, as he puts it, "to supply prudent generalism in an overspecialized world."

Joseph A. Koncelik is a professor in the Department of Industrial Design at Georgia Tech University. Until 1995 he taught in the Interior Design program at Ohio State University. His research, design, and scholarship has covered lifespan-related products and interior design, special products for the aging and those with disabilities, and research methodology related to the design process. Koncelik has received awards of excellence from the National Endowment for the Arts, from the Institute of Business Designers, and from the Industrial Designers Society of America.

Richard G. Long, Ph.D., has been coordinator of vision research at the Rehabilitation Research and Development Center, Atlanta Veterans Affairs Medical Center, since 1988. He received his Ph.D. in special education from Vanderbilt University in 1986. Dr. Long has also worked as a clinician and administrator in rehabilitation programs serving persons with blindness and low vision. His research interests focus on outcome measurement in geriatric rehabilitation and on orientation and mobility of blind individuals.

Joseph A. Maxwell is an industrial designer of products, appliances, and accessible environments. His design firm, Joseph A. Maxwell—Industrial Design, combines the latest in human factors research with over 26 years of practical design service to the nation's aviation, health care, and housing industries.

Lee Meyer is a licensed architect and certified interior designer who holds undergraduate and professional degrees from the University of Minnesota. His work experience includes both contract and residential design, and he is a principal architect at the firm Lee Meyer Architects in St. Paul, Minnesota.

Lois J. Moore, M.S., is an architectural design research consultant specializing in independent senior housing. She is the senior author of the recent book, *In Support of Mobility: Kitchen Design for Independent Older Adults,* which illustrates 75 research-based kitchen design recommendations for ambulant older adults.

James L. Mueller is an industrial designer who has worked in the field of rehabilitation technology and design since 1974, specializing in universal product design and workplace accommodation for people with disabilities. His clients include private businesses as well as public agencies, consumer organizations, and individuals with disabilities.

Kerry A. Nelson, ASID, IDEC, is an Associate Professor of Art and the Director of the Interior Design Program at San Diego State University. A practicing certified interior designer, her projects have been published in *Contract, Interiors, Philadelphia Inquirer Magazine,* and *San Diego Home and Garden.* She has received several awards from the American Society of Interior Designers for her work.

Roberta L. Null, Ph.D., holds a bachelor's degree from South Dakota State University, a master's degree from the University of Minnesota, and a Ph.D. from Ohio State University. She has taught housing and interior design courses at Purdue University and San Diego State University, and most recently at Miami University. Dr. Null's research and teaching have focused on the design of supportive environments for special needs groups. She received the 1986 Environmental Design award from the Education Foundation of the American Society of Interior Designers (ASID) for the design of training kitchens at the San Diego Center for the Blind. She has authored over a dozen articles and has made numerous presentations of universal design at professional meetings. She is an Allied Education Member of ASID, as well as a member of the Environmental Design Research Association, the Interior Design Educators Council, and the Senior Housing Council of the National Association of Home Builders. She is also co-founder of Common Place Publishers in Columbus, Ohio, and co-editor of a proposed academic journal on universal design.

Jill Osiowy holds a BID and is currently a graduate student in the Master of City Planning program at the University of Manitoba.

Arvid E. Osterberg, D.Arch., is a Professor of Architecture at Iowa State University. He teaches courses on universal design, housing for elderly residents, and historic preservation. Dr. Osterberg was a principal investigator on comprehensive ADA surveys of ISU campus buildings, sites, and residence halls.

Edward R. Ostrander, Ph.D., is Professor Emeritus in the Department of Design and Environmental Analysis, College of Human Ecology, Cornell University. His expertise is in user responsive design research, design programming, and research-based design for the elderly.

Cindy Paulson-Schiefelbein, M.A., OTR, has a background in architecture and interior design and in cultural anthropology. She also has over 24 years experience in occupational therapy. This background, along with her own chemical sensitivities and MS condition, strengthens her long-standing commitment to barrier-free design.

Jillianne Pfeifer has a B.S. in Residential Interior Design from Ohio State University. She has worked as a designer in an interior design firm and as a self-employed interior designer. Currently, Pfeifer is employed by Surface Style as an architectural consultant for ceramic tile selection and installation.

James Postell is an Associate Professor of Interior Design at the University of Cincinnati and a registered architect. He received his Bachelor of Architecture from Rice University in 1982 and his Master of Architecture from the University of Pennsylvania in 1984. He has practiced architecture and interior design in Houston, Philadelphia, Lubbock, and Cincinnati. His research and design currently focuses on human factors, ergonomics, and furniture design.

John P. S. Salmen, AIA, is a licensed architect who has specialized in the area of barrier-free and universal design for over 18 years. He is the president of Universal Designers & Consultants, Inc., in Rockville, Maryland, and is the publisher of *Universal Design Newsletter.* He is a nationally prominent expert in the technical aspects of the ADA and its Accessibility Guidelines, and is a member of the review committees for both ADAAG and ANSI A117.1.

Elizabeth B. N. Sanders is a vice president in Research and Strategies at Fitch Inc., an international business and design consulting firm based in Columbus, Ohio. In her 12 years at Fitch, Dr. Sanders has been primarily responsible for the introduction and integration of information design, human factors, and currently, participatory design research. She holds a B.A. in psychology and anthropology from Miami University and a Ph.D. in experimental and quantitative psychology from the Ohio State University.

Jon A. Sanford, M.Arch., is the Coordinator for the Housing Evaluation Program at the Center for Universal Design, North Carolina State University, and a Research Architect at the Rehabilitation R&D Center on Aging, Atlanta VA Medical Center. Sanford is well known for his expertise in research and design for older people and people with disabilities. Recent projects include work in the areas of home modifications; accessibility guidelines for assembly areas, children's environments, and ramps; orientation and wayfinding; design of grab bars and toilets; and the design of long-term care facilities for people with cognitive, physical, and sensory impairments.

Henry Sanoff, Ph.D., AIA, is a Professor of Architecture in the School of Design at North Carolina State University. He has won numerous awards for his designs, research, and achievements as an educator, along with several Progressive Architecture design awards. He is one of the founders of the Environmental Design Research Association and the recent recipient of a Distinguished Fulbright award to Korea. Mr. Sanoff has directed projects throughout the United States and has served as a visiting lecturer at schools all over the world. He is the author of *Visual Research Methods in Design, Integrating Programming, Evaluation and Participation in Design,* and *School Design.*

Anne E. Seltz, M.A., CCC-A, is a consulting audiologist from Minnesota. With more than 30 years' professional experience, she continues to help solve patients' communication problems caused by hearing loss. Teaching them how to manage their own acoustic environment is a major part of her counseling.

Shoshana Shamberg, OTR/L, is the President of Abilities O.T. Services Inc., a consulting firm that specializes in independent living and accessibility. Shamberg consults with housing agencies, building contractors, social workers, and elderly and disabled home owners on issues related to accessibility, such as HUD 504 requirements, the ADA, functional analysis, activities of daily living, barrier-free design, and assistive technology. Shamberg was appointed to the State of Maryland Governor's Task Force on Senior Housing in 1993 and was invited to participate in the First National Conference on Home Modification Policy at the 1993 National Home Remodelers conference. She has been a visiting instructor in the graduate O.T. program of Towson State University. She is presently enrolled in a graduate degree program in Assistive Technology at the Johns Hopkins University.

Jannis Shea, Ph.D., is Director of Undergraduate Studies and Associate Professor in the Department of Child Development and Family Relations at East Carolina University in Greenville, North Carolina. She received her Ph.D. from the University of North Carolina at Greensboro and is a member of the East Carolina University Gerontology Institute and the American Society on Aging, as well as the National Council on Family Relations, the Environmental Design Research Association, and the American Association of Housing Educators.

William Sims, Ph.D., CFM, is a Professor of Facility Planning and Management and Chairman of the Department of Design and Environmental Analysis at Cornell University. He is co-director of Cornell's International Workplace Studies Program. He serves on the International Facility Management Association's (IFMA) Education Committee and the Certification and Accreditation Task Forces, and has served on the IFMA Board. Professor Sims is the author of many scholarly and professional publications, and he has consulted, conducted research, and lectured widely in North America, Europe, and Japan. Professor Sims' research interests are centered around the planning, design, and management of facilities and on their effects on individual and organizational performance. In addition to his academic responsibilities, Professor Sims is also a consultant to an international clientele of companies and government agencies related to programming and designing new facilities and major renovations; assessing the organizational and management implications of planning and management processes, facility designs, and space and furniture policies; developing and reviewing the organizational structure and nature of facility management practices and policies; and facility performance appraisal.

Eleanor Smith, after 25 years as a counselor and community college teacher, stopped teaching in 1988 and began devoting her time to the disability liberation movement. As a wheelchair user since the age of three, she is especially interested in basic access to all homes. Anyone working on this issue or interested in doing so is encouraged to write Concrete Change, 1371 Metropolitan Avenue, SE, Atlanta, GA 30316.

Timothy J. Springer, Ph.D., is the Chairperson of Human Environment and Design in the College of Human Ecology at Michigan State University. He is a recognized authority on ergonomics and the impact of the environment and technology on performance and productivity. He is a widely published researcher and author with over 40 research reports, two books, and several book chapters to his credit. He consults with a wide range of companies and organizations, including many Fortune 500 companies, on matters of facility design and planning, performance, productivity, and ergonomics.

Dr. Dana G. Stewart is the Director of the Housing Studies, Research and Development Program, and the Head of the Department of Interior Design at the University of Manitoba.

Sandra S. Thurlow, Ph.D., got her Ph.D. at Purdue and her M.S. and B.S. at Iowa State University. Currently, she is the manager of the North American Consumer Products Usability Department at

Whirlpool Corporation. Other Whirlpool assignments she has been involved in include Engineering Home Economics and Electronics Systems Development and Research.

Dr. Johan Ullman is a physician specializing in anesthesiology and intensive care and in occupational health. Dr. Ullman is also an inventor and a designer. He is a Ph.D. student at the department for occupational orthopaedics at Sahlgrenska University Hospital in Gothenbutg, Sweden. Dr. Ullman has developed his own theories about work postures, working chairs, keyboards, pens, trays, and many other aspects of working life. Initially his theories were very controversial, but they have been widely accepted by the international scientific community, and today Dr. Ullman is one of the world's leading experts in ergonomic development.

Ann Warble-Nienow received her M.S. degree in Housing and Interior Design at Purdue University. She is an independent interior designer in Hilton Head, South Carolina.

William K. Wasch is president of William K. Wasch Associates in Middletown, Connecticut. He founded the Home Outreach Ministry to the Elderly in Middletown and developed an Adapt-Your-Home program for a New Haven Company. He also served as Executive Vice President of Elderworks, which designed recruitment programs for older workers and retirees.

Margaret J. Weber, Ph.D., Professor and Associate Dean, College of Human Environmental Sciences, Oklahoma State University, received her Ph.D. from the University of Missouri. She has published extensively in housing- and interior design-related journals.

Alan P. Wier is an independent designer and former member of the Industrial Design Department at Ohio State University. He has been an educator and consultant in product and interior space design for 14 years. He is a graduate of the University of Illinois, Urbana, with a B.S. in Architecture and a M.B.A. His research interests are in human factors and focusing the use of computer visualization to enhance design communication and productivity.

Mary H. Yearns, Ph.D., is an Associate Professor and Extension Housing Specialist at Iowa State University. Her subject matter and interests focus on the housing needs of an aging population and persons with disabilities. She is co-designer of "The Home for All Ages," a three-room exhibit that has been shown throughout Iowa at home shows, fairs, and conferences. The 40-foot-long, interactive display demonstrates universal design ideas and assistive devices to make homes more convenient, comfortable, and safe for people of all ages and all abilities.

Susan Zavotka, Ph.D., is an Associate Professor in the Department of Family Resource Management at Ohio State University. She is responsible for the Residential Interior Design Program, teaching courses in residential space planning, historic furnishings, and design for people with disabilities. Her research interests focus on aesthetic preferences and the psychological impact of interior environments on behavior.

Rick Zwelling founded Home ReVisions in Columbus, Ohio, in 1991. He also owns and operates Columbus Parts Supply, a 30-year-old maintenance supply wholesaler for the multi-housing industry. The unique combination of Home ReVisions and Columbus Parts Supply's resources and expertise addresses a broad range of design needs.

Sheila Zwelling is the Director of Marketing and Market Research for Home ReVisions and has been with the company since its inception. Her contributions to Home ReVisions include the compilation, organization, and maintenance of the product resource library; education in federal requirements regarding housing and accessibility; and spreading awareness of accessible/barrier-free products and their benefits for everyone.

Index

A

Abed, Laura W., 254

AbiliCAD™, 154

Abilitech, Inc., 154

Ability-sensitive design, 74

Able Ergonomics Corporation, 160

Accessibility, 27–29, 276–277, 280
    bath design for, 240–245
    improving, 81–87
    in bath design, 30–31
    residential redesign for, 246–247

Accessible design, 28–29

Accessible sanctuary, 208

Accommodations for physical limitations and abilities, 105–106

Acoustics
    and office design, 145–146
    universal design strategies for, 205–210

Adaptability, 27–28, 276–277, 280
    in airport design, 195

Adaptable design, 28

Adaptable work centers in office design, 10

Adapt-Your-Home, 258–263

Adjustable armrests, 158

Adjustable keyboards, 28, 152–153

Adjustable monitor placement, 160

Adjustable workstation height, 155

Adjustable workstations, 28

Advertisements and universal design, 25

Aesthetics, 27, 276–277, 280
    in elderly accommodations, 39–44
    in preschool accommodations, 36

Affirmative action provisions of the Rehabilitation Act, 5

Affordability, 27, 276–277, 280
    providing for elderly, 39

AFM Enterprises, Inc., 293

Aging, characteristics of, 32

Aging population
    marketing products to, 268–272
    universal design for, 33–34

AIKCO, 15

Airport interior design
    adaptability in, 195
    convenience in, 195
    durability in, 194–195
    environmental and economic demands in, 193–194
    evaluation checklists in, 198–200
    social challenge in, 191–192
    special needs in, 192–193

Alarms, redundant, 29

Alcohol addiction, 21

Alteration, coverage of under ADA, 18

American Association of Retired Persons (AARP), 228, 258

American Ceramic Olean Tile, 30

American Ergonomics Corporation, 157–159

American National Standards Institute (ANSI) guidelines, 15

American National Standards Institute/Human Factors Society 100 Act (ANSI/HFS-100), 135–136

American Seating Company, 216

American Society for Testing and Materials, 140

American Society of Heating, Refrigeration, and Air Conditioning Engineers, 142

American Society of Interior Designers (ASID), 57, 143

Americans with Disabilities Act (ADA), 25
    and facility management, 72–80
    and high-speed railcar interiors, 210–214
    and occupational therapists, 95–96
    employment practice covered by, 6–12, 95–96
    future for, 23
    government resources on, 285–286
    individuals not protected by, 11
    individuals protected by, 11
    legislative history of, 2–3
    nongovernment resources on, 287–288
    organizations for, 288–289
    publications on, 289–290
    reasoning behind, 5
    Regional Disability and Business Accommodation Center for, 82
    restaurant efforts at complying with, 214–215
    Subtitle A: General Services, 14–16
    Subtitle B: Transportation, 16–17
    tax incentives for businesses, 19
    Technical Assistance Centers for, 286
    technology for, 290–292
    Title I: Employment, 5–12, 22, 95–96, 285
    Title II: Public Services, 13–17, 22, 192–193, 285–286
    Title III: Public Accommodations and Services, 7, 17–19, 22, 96, 285–286
    Title IV: Telecommunications, 19–20, 286
    Title V: Miscellaneous Provisions, 20–21
    universal housing design in, 225
    user considerations in a task force for, 69–70
Americans with Disabilities Act (ADA)-related legislation, 4–5, 261
Americans with Disabilities Act Accessibility Guidelines (ADAAG), 15–16, 18, 20, 46–47, 60, 72–74, 88, 94
Anderson Consulting, 137–138
Anders, Robert, 111–112, 251
Anthropometric Percentile Estimation Device, 49
Antiglare screens and filters, 149–150
Apple Adjustable Keyboard™, 153
Apple Valley Care Center, 40
Appliance design, 269–270
    customer feedback in, 113–115
Architectural and Transportation Barriers Compliance Board, 19–20
Architectural Barriers Act of 1968, 4

Armrests, adjustable, 158
Attorney fees, 21–22
Automated Closet Carousel™, 249

B

BACI®, 243
BackCare Corporation, 153, 158
Background reading in participatory design, 48
Back pain, 148
Ballpark accessibility, 216–217
Barlow-Lawson, Stephen, 110, 155
Barrier-free environments, 5, 230–231
Barrier Free Environments, Inc., 1
Barriers, eliminating, 104
Bartlett Independent Living Laboratory, 230–231
Bast, Jan, 57
Bathease Tub, 260
Bathroom
    accessibility in, 30–31, 240–245
    carpet for, 244
    comfort in, 245
    in preschool accommodations, 36
    providing for elderly, 38
    universal design for, 19, 240–245
Beasley, Kim, 216
Becker, Franklin, 133–134, 140, 164–176
Bedroom, providing for elderly, 38
Behar, Susan, 27, 275–280
Behavioral aspects of office design, 136–137
Biomorph™, 155
Biomorph™ Personal Power Podium, 110
Bisexuality, 21
Bobrick Washroom Equipment, Inc., 193, 196, 217
Bopp, Kenneth, 279
Boston Center for Accessible Housing, 251
Building Owners and Managers Association (BOMA), 144
Building systems and office design, 139–141
Built environment, design process for, 179
Business, tax incentives for, 19
Butler in a Box®, 27, 256
Butter, Reinhart, 211

C

Camden Yards Ballpark, 216–217
Canestaro, James, 72, 100–102
Canestaro, Nancy, 72, 100–102
Carpal tunnel syndrome (CTS), 98, 155
Catalog marketing, 281–282
Ceatrice Polite Apartments, 52–56
Center for Accessible Housing, 244
Center for Universal Design, 1, 251
Cervantes, DeVonna L., 230–231
Chadwick, Don, 156
Chang, En-Bair, 112
Charlotte (NC) International Airport, 202–204
Chemical sensitivities, 161–164
    books and articles on, 295–296
    products and resources for, 293–294
Child development center, redesigning, 180–190
Civil Rights Act of 1964, 2, 22
Climate control, providing for elderly, 39
Cohen, Evelyn, 229
Color and product desirability, 118–119
Colorado, University of, at Boulder, 144
Comfortably Yours: Aids for Easier Living, 281–282
Comfort in bath design, 245
Comfort™ Keyboard System, 153
Communication and office design, 137–138
Communications Act of 1934, 19–20
Communications under ADA, 197–200
Compliance attitude, 79
Compulsive gambling, 11, 21
Computer-aided design (CAD), 50, 154
Computer environment, universal design for, 147–161
Concrete Change, 221
Connell, Bettye Rose, 223
Consultant, marketing universal design as a, 275–280
Consumer market, growing a, 104–105
Convenience and airport design, 195
Cooks, Owen J., 12, 49, 88–99
Cooktop area, 236
Copy stands, 160
Cornell University International Facility Management Program, case studies, 164–176
Cost as concern in universal design, 29–30, 79
Courses, coverage of under ADA, 19
Cumulative trauma disorders, 78
Customer feedback, using, for new product design, 113–115

D

Dagwell, Carol K., 231–240
Dainoff, Marvin, 122
Danish model for sitting, 125–127
DataHand®, 153
Davis, Diane, 133, 147–161
Defense against charges of discrimination
    direct threat as, 14
    fundamental alteration to nature of goods and services as, 14
    good-faith effort as, 12, 14
    readily achievable as, 14
    undue hardship/burden as, 14
Demand-response transportation system, coverage of under ADA, 16
Dilaura, D. L., 144
Dining facilities, providing for elderly, 38
Direct threat, as defense against discrimination, 14
Disabilities
    assessment and applications for, 96–98
    definition of, 6
    enabling products for, 103–132
    problem in defining, 1
    statistics on numbers of, 1–2
Disabled Access Tax Credit, 19
discovery® seating, 120–123, 157
Discrimination
    and Equal Education for All Handicapped Children Act of 1975, 4
    and Rehabilitation Act of 1973, 4–5
    as reason behind the ADA, 5
    defenses against charges of, 14
    remedies for, 22
Display areas, providing for elderly, 39
Dispute resolution, alternate means of, 21
Door handle levers, 1, 27, 80
Dor-O-Matic Automatic Doors, 99
Dowell, William, 49
Drugs, testing for in workplace, 11
Duncan-Lyle, Rae, 272–275
Durability and airport design, 194–195
Dynamic sitting, 121

E

Earth Tools, 293

Eastern Paralyzed Veterans Association, 18

Eco Design, 293

Economics of universal design, 29–30, 79–80

Egan Visual, Inc., 110

Eisenberg, Joan M., 240–245

Elderly
designing low-income housing for, 53–56
environmental programming requirements for, 63–64
universal design for, 37–44

Electrical concerns in kitchen, 239

Electrical outlets, location of, 226

Electromagnetic radiation, protection from, 161

Elevator, residential, 247–249

Ellis, Jerry, 74–77

Empathy in universal design, 46–47

Employment
and the Rehabilitation Act of 1973, 5
coverage of under ADA, 6–12, 95–96

Enabler System, 106–110

Enabling products, 103–132
for home, 111–113
for personal hygiene, 113

Engelberger, Joseph, 257

Entertaining, providing place for elderly, 39

Environmental Design Research, 293

Environmental Health Services, 293

Environmental programming, 48, 62–66

Environmental revisions, 65

Equa™ chairs, 156

Equal Education for All Handicapped Children Act of 1975, 4

Equal Employment Opportunity Commission (EEOC), 22

Ergomax® chair, 157–159

Ergomax® System of Postural Support (SPS), 158

Ergonomics
accommodating disabled through, 105–106
definition of, 134

Ergonomic seating, 27–28, 120–123, 156–159

Essential function, 11
definition of, 7
managing employees, 8–9

Examinations, coverage of under ADA, 19

Exhibitionism, 11, 21

Eyestrain, 148–151, 161

F

Facilities management
and specific disabilities, 96–98
cultural universal design perspective in, 100–102
individual and public involvement in, 91–94
self-evaluations in, 90–91
specific examples of reasonable accommodations in, 98–99
universal design for, 72–80

Facilities managers, 71

Facilities surveys, 88–89

Facility programming, 181

Fair Housing Amendments Act of 1988, 219, 261

Family room, providing for elderly, 38

Federal Wilderness Areas, 21

Fitch, Inc., 115–120

Fixtures Furniture, 120–123

Flexibility, characteristic changes in, 32

FlexPro™ keyboard, 153

Flooring
in preschool accommodations, 36
providing for elderly, 39

Floor space
in preschool accommodations, 36
providing for elderly, 38

Focus groups and participatory design, 49–50, 119

Footrests, 159

Friendly Home, 265–268

Froescher, 120–121

Furniture
in office design, 139–141
in preschool accommodations, 36

G

Gender identity disorders, 21

General Electric, 110

General Motors, 269

General services, coverage under, 14–16

German Federal Railway Design Center, 214

German Quickborner Team, 137

Gero-Stillwell, Ann, 58

Gibralter™, 155

Girsberger Office Seating, 28
Glaser, Milton, 254
Good, Clinton F., 293
Good faith effort
    and reasonable accommodations, 12
    as defense against discrimination, 14
    documenting, 81
Governor William Donald Schaefer's Accessibility Task Force, 216
Grab bars, 31
GRAHL ergonomic chairs, 156
GRAHL Office Ergonomics, 156
Granberg Superior Systems, Inc., 227
Grandjean, Etienne, 128

H

Habitat for Humanity, 221
H'A'FELE, 148
Handrails, 54
Harassment, 20
Harden, Amy, 280–283
Hartford Housing Authority, 262
Hartwigsen, Gail, 266–268
Haworth, Inc., 29
Head-controlled input devices, 154
HeadMaster™, 154
Health Care Keyboard Company, Inc., 153
Health issues in office design, 135–136
Hearing, characteristic changes in, 32
Hearing impairment
    and acoustic environments, 205–210
    reasonable accommodations for, 13
Herman Miller, Inc., 49, 156, 270
Herman, Robert, 51, 53–56
Herman Stoller Coliver Architects, 54–55
HEWI grab bars, 260
HEWI, Inc., 177
Highline™ Lite™ PC toilet, 104, 241
High-speed railcar interiors, 210–214
Hirsch, Karen, 49, 66–68
Hodges, Anthony, 153
Home automation systems, 26
Home, enabling products for, 111–113
Home furnishings design, 270–271
Home ReVisions, 263–264

Home universal design
    and ADA, 225
    baths in, 240–245
    general suggestions for, 221
    kitchens in, 220, 222, 224, 226–228, 231–240
    philosophy in, 224–227
    residential elevator in, 247–249
    safety in, 226–227
    supportiveness conflicts in, 227
Homosexuality, 21
Honeywell, Inc., 26, 262
House of Representatives, 21
Housing Resource Center (HRC), 272
Human factors modeling, 269
Human strength, characteristic changes in, 32
Human traffic problems in shopping mall design, 63
Hyatt, Lorraine, 34, 223
HydroLoc™ door seal, 106

I

I.D./Design, 155
Impairment, definition of, 6
Independence Resource Center, 261
Indoor air quality in office design, 141–142
Information displays, changes in, to accommodate personnel, 73
Inman, Marjorie, 35–44
Input devices, head-, mouth-, and voice-controlled, 154–155
Insurance plans, and ADA coverage, 20
Interlude lavatory, 178
International Cushioned Products, Inc., 264
Interviews in participatory design, 48–49, 66–68
Invitation™ countertop lavatory, 105, 241

J

Job Accommodation Network (JAN), 12, 287
Jones, Betty, 247–249

K

Kahn, Joel I., 49, 69–70
Keyboard
    adjustable, 28, 152–153
    split and modified, 153
    tilting, 154–155

Keytronic® Corp., 153

Kilty-Padgett, Roberta L., 251–252

Kinesis Corporation, 153

Kira, Alexander, 245

Kitchen design, 220, 222, 224
    and visual impairment, 57–60
    controls and hardware in, 239–240
    lighting and electrical concerns in, 239
    low-vision users in, 240
    providing for elderly, 38
    safety in, 226–227
    storage in, 237–239
    supportiveness conflicts in, 227
    universal design for, 30, 226–228, 231–240
    work centers and counter heights in, 227, 232–237

Klemmer, Kenneth, 252–253

Kleptomania, 11, 21

Knopp, Bradley A., 177, 191–204

Kohler Co., 19, 104–106, 178, 241–242, 275

Koncelik, Joseph A., 32, 268–272

Kravtin, Benson, 112

L

Laundry facilities, providing for elderly, 39

Leibrock, Cynthia, 254

Leisure Lift chairs, 264

Lever door handles, 1, 27, 80

Levers, 111–112

Lewis Homes of California, 257, 265–268

Lewis, Randall, 266–267

LiDrizzah, Margaret, 58

Life management, 138

Lifespan, design for, 25

Lighting
    and office design, 143–145
    appropriate overhead, 150
    in bath design, 245
    in kitchen design, 239
    in preschool accommodations, 36
    providing for elderly, 39

Living room, providing for elderly, 38

Logan Graphic Products, Inc., 151

Lubidet®, 113–114

Lumbar Depth Adjustment, 159

Lumbar Height Adjustment, 159

Lumex, 31, 243

Lumex Tub-Guard® Tall bathtub rail, 243

M

Mace, Ronald, 1, 25, 33, 251

Macro environment, 178–180

Mainstreaming, 4

Maintenance
    in preschool accommodations, 36
    providing for elderly, 39

Major life activities, definition of, 6

Mandal, A. C., 125

Marketing strategies for universal design, 31
    case studies in, 255–265
    catalogs in, 281–283
    consultant in, 275–280

Marketing to an aging population, 268–272

Maryland Stadium Authority, 216

Masters Corporation, 293

MasterShower™ tower, 242

Material, chemical, and finish toxicity, 142–143

Maxwell, Joseph A., 177, 191–204

Mayline Company, Inc., 97

McKiel, Frank, 154

Mendelsohn House, 52–56

Meridian, Inc., 152

Meyer, Lee, 246–247

MicroComputer Accessories, Inc., 97

Micro environment, 178, 180

Microwave oven, 237
    location of, 226–227

Middle environment, 178, 180

Middletown House, 255–259

Middletown Housing Authority, 261–262

Miller Paint Co., Inc., 293

Mini-focus groups in universal design, 119

Minneapolis Rehabilitation Center, 154

Mirrors in bath design, 243

Mistrick, R. G., 144

Mobility, characteristic changes in, 32

Modeling, 50

Modular house, universally designed, 33

Monitor placement, adjustable, 28, 160

Monk Restaurant, 214–215

Montag, Diane, 60
Moore, Lois J., 224–229
Morton Plant Family Care Center, 277–278
Mouse pad supports, 154–155
Mouth-controlled input devices, 154
Mueller, James L., 10, 71–73, 103–113
MultiResource Centers, Inc., 154
Murco Wall Products, Inc., 294
Murray, William, 161

N

NASA Neutral Body Posture (NBP), 158
National Council on the Aging, 265
National Electric Code and bath design, 244
National Kitchen and Bath Association, rules of bathroom design, 241
National Lighting Bureau, 143
Negley Paint Co., Inc., 294
Nelson, Kerry A., 58, 177–180
Netter, Ron, 258–259
New construction, coverage of under ADA, 18
New product design, customer feedback for, 113–115
Noise reduction, aids for, 161
Nonstructural barriers, 95
Non-territorial office, 166–171
Normbau grab bars, 260
Norwegian model for sitting, 127–128

O

Observation in participatory design, 49
Occupational therapists and the ADA, 95–96
Office design
    acoustics in, 145
    building and furniture systems in, 139–141
    case studies in, 164–176
    chemical sensitivities in, 161–164
    communication and productivity in, 137–138
    computers in, 147–161
    eyestrain as problem in, 148–151, 161
    health, safety, and welfare issues in, 135–136
    indoor air quality in, 141–142
    lighting in, 143–145, 150
    material, chemical, and finish toxicity, 142–143
    post-occupancy evaluations in, 140–141
    psychological and behavioral aspect of, 136–137
    universal design in, 133–176
Omnibus Housing Act, 261
Open risers, 228
Opportunity elements, 37
Opsvik, Peter, 127
Oral history interview as a universal design technique, 66–68
Oral hygiene devices, 112
Osterberg, Arvid E., 81–87
Ostrander, Edward R., 224–229
Outdoor space
    in preschool accommodations, 36
    providing for elderly, 39
Ovens, 236, 238
OXO International, 34

P

Pace Chem Industries, Inc., 294
Palm rests, 155
Panasonic, 113–114
Paralyzed Veterans of America, 216
Paratransit system, coverage of under ADA, 16
Participatory design
    background reading in, 48
    conducting research in, 47
    determining needs in, 48
    establishing goals in, 47
    focus groups in, 49–50, 119
    interviews in, 48–49, 66–68
    observation in, 49
    post-occupancy evaluation in, 60–61, 140–141
    questionnaires in, 49, 91–96
    research in, 47
    stating problems in, 48
    surveys in, 49, 88–89
    uncovering concepts in, 48
Paulson-Schiefelbein, Cindy, 133, 161–164
Pedophilia, 11, 21
Peerless Electric Company, 144
"People first" approach, 26, 46
People in Architecture award, 53
People with disabilities, language choices in referring to, 26
Perfect sitting position, 124–125
Personal control in office design, 138–139

Personal Harbor™ Workspace, 51, 98

Personal hygiene, enabling products for, 113

Personalization
    in preschool accommodations, 36
    providing for elderly, 38

Pfeifer, Jillianne, 214–215

Pheasant, Stephen, 78

Physical limitations and abilities, accommodating, 105–106

Physiological disorders, definition of, 6

Piaget, Jean, 35–37

Playroom, modeling, 182–183

Podiums, 110

Polsky, Norman, 120

Postell, James, 120, 134–147

Post-occupancy evaluation (POE), 51–54, 56, 60–61, 179
    and office design, 140–141

Post-occupancy survey, 55

Precedence™ bath whirlpool, 106, 241

Prentke Romich Company, 154

Preschool child, universal design for, 35

Price, Tom, 263

Prime location
    in preschool accommodations, 36
    providing for elderly, 38

Privacy
    in preschool accommodations, 36
    providing for elderly, 38

Private clubs, coverage of under ADA, 17–18

Product design criteria, 116

Productivity and office design, 137–138

Proformix™, 151

Programming in participatory design, 47–48

Proxemics, definition of, 134

Psychoactive substance use disorders, 11, 21

Psychological aspects of office design, 136–137

Public accommodations under ADA, 7, 96

Public and commercial environments
    built environment in, 179
    case studies in, 180–204, 210–217
    defining and designing, 178–180
    team approach in, 179–180

Public Housing Authority, 260–261

Public service
    and marketing universal design, 272–275
    coverage of under ADA, 13–17

Public transportation, coverage of under ADA, 16–17

Purdue University's ADA Compliance Plan, 12, 88–95

Pynoos, Jon, 228–229

Pyromania, 11, 21

Q

Qualified individual, identifying, 7

Questionnaires
    individual and public involvement in, 91–94
    in participatory design, 49

Quiet spaces, providing for elderly, 39

QWERTY keyboard layout, 152–153

R

Ramps, 79

Readily achievable, as defense against discrimination, 14

Real Goods Trading Corporation, 294

Reasonable accommodation, 11–13
    categories of, 13
    examples of, 13, 98–99
    in managing employees under ADA, 8–9

Redundant alarms, 29

Redundant cueing, 270

Reflectance in the office environment, 145

Regional Disability and Business Accommodation Center, 82

Rehabilitation Act of 1973, 4–5, 7, 13, 20–22, 261

Religious organizations, coverage of under ADA, 7, 17–18

Remcraft, 243

Repetitive strain injury (RSI), 155

Residential elevator, 247–249

Residential redesign for accessibility, 246–247

Restaurants and ADA compliance, 214–215

Retaliation, 20

Rev-A-Shelf, Inc., 264

Rheumatoid arthritis, 98–99

Risers, open, 228

Robinson, Sarah, 252

Role playing, 50

Russell, Susan, 115–120

S

Safety, 29
    in bath design, 240–245
    in office design, 135–136
Safety-oriented design, 29
Salmen, John P. S., 216–217, 228
San Diego Center for the Blind, 50, 56–62, 223
Sanders, Elizabeth B. N., 115–120
Sanford, Jon A., 223
Sanoff, Henry, 177, 180–190
Sanoff, Joan, 190
Sauvant, Lutz, 111
School lunch kit, re-creating, 115–120
Scott, John M., 208
Seating
    ergonomic, 27–28, 120–123, 156–159
    posture theories on, 124–132
Seating design, new directions in, 201–204
Security
    in preschool accommodations, 36
    providing for elderly, 38
Segal, Barry, 294
Self-evaluations, 90–91
Seltz, Anne E., 205–210
Senate, 21
Senior housing design, 207
Serber, Hector, 157, 159
Services for Independent Living, 272
Shamberg, Shoshana, 72, 95–99
Shared office studies, 165
Shea, Jannis, 35–44
Shimuzu Institute of Technology, 137–138
Shopping center, universal design process for, 63–66, 179–180
Sick building syndrome, 142, 161–164
Sico bed, 265
Side-by-side refreigerators, 29, 227, 234
Signage, as aid to wayfinding, 79
Sims, William, 164–176
Simulation game in facility management, 100–102
Sinan Co., 294
Site and building access, 180
Sitting positions
    conversational, 130
    Danish model for, 125–127
    feet on the table, 131
    free, unfettered, 131–132
    Norwegian model for, 127–128
    perfect, 124–125
    sack of potatoes slouch, 129–130
    standing model for, 129
    Swiss model for, 128–129
    tilting backward, 130
    tilting forward, 130
    writing desk, 130–131
Skilled Nursing Facility, 40–41
Small business
    guidelines for making accessible, 81–87
    tax incentives for, 19
Smith, Eleanor, 221
Socialization, design for, 37
Social space, in preschool accommodations, 36
Soft Bathtub, 264
Southern California Gas Company, 265
Spacial arrangements, 80
Spacial planning, 184–186
Special needs, problems with phrase, 26
Springer, Timothy J., 72–80, 120
stackABLE™ Monitor Risers, 160
Stairways, providing for elderly, 39
Standing model for sitting, 129
Static charge buildup, 143
Steelcase, Inc., 51, 98
Steps, hazards of, 79
Storage spaces
    in preschool accommodations, 36
    providing for elderly, 39
Stove controls, location of, 226
Structural barriers, 95
Stumpf, Bill, 156
Substantially limits, definition of, 6
Supportive design, 28
Supportiveness as criteria for universal design, 227
Surveys, and participatory design for, 49, 88–89
Swedish Rehab Products, 281
Swiss model for sitting, 128–129
Symbols, for universal design, 254–255
Systems furniture, 80

T

Tacit office environment, 135–139
Takach, Richard M., 208
Tampa International Airport, 191, 195, 202–204
Tax deduction to remove barriers, 19
Tax incentives, 81
Team approach to universal design, 179–180
Technical assistance manuals and programs, 21
Telecommunication devices for the deaf (TDDs), 19–20
Telecommunications, coverage of under ADA, 19–20
Telephone aids, 160
Terraces of Los Gatos, 40–41
Terra Verde Trading Co., 294
Territoriality
    in preschool accommodations, 36
    providing for elderly, 38
Thermos Company, 115–120
Thief River Falls Technical College, 154
Thurlow, Sandra, 113–115
Tillman, Robert and Elizabeth, 248
Tilting keyboard, 154–155
TONY™ keyboard, 153
Total Serve, 258
TOTO, 113–114
Toxic Substances Information Line, 294
Trakker™, 29
Transportation, coverage of under ADA, 7–9, 16–18
Transsexualism, 11, 21
Transvestitism, 11, 21
Travel hair dryer, 112
TV in-home shopping, 282–283

U

Ullman chair, 131–132
Ullman, Johan, 124–132
Ultratec, Inc., 20
Undue hardship/burden as defense against discrimination, 9, 14
United Methodist Church, 74
United States Consumer Products Safety Commission, 294
United States Environmental Protection Agency, 294
Universal design, 25–27
    accommodating through, 105–106
    aesthetics of, 31
    and the ADA, 74, 78
    controls and hardware in, 239–240
    cornerstones of, 27–29
    criteria by which to plan and judge, 80
    cultural differences in, 100–102
    definition of, 25
    economics of, 29–30, 79–80
    empathy in, 46–47
    environmental programming in, 62–66
    for aging population, 33–34, 37–44
    for baths, 240–245
    for kitchen, 30, 226–228, 231–240
    for low-vision users, 240
    for preschool child, 35
    for shopping center, 63–66
    for the computer environment, 147–161
    implications for facility management, 72–80
    in advertisements, 25
    in the office, 133–176
    lighting and electrical concerns in, 239
    logos for, 254–255
    marketing strategies for, 31, 280–283
    oral history interview in, 66–68
    organizations for, 288–289
    participatory design in, 47–50
    process of, 45–70
    publications for, 289–290
    storage in, 237–239
    team approach in, 179–180
    technology for, 290–292
    work centers and counter heights in, 232–237
Universal Design Education Project (UDEP), 251
Universal footprint studies, 165, 171–175
Urology Health Center, 278–280
User considerations in an ADA task force, 69–70
Utley, James, 190

V

Value contrast, 240
Vari-Task™ Workcenter, 97
Video display terminals (VDTs), 136
    antiglare screens for, 149
    back pain and, 148
    filters for, 149
    placement of, 143–145, 148–151
    universal design in, 147–148
Vision, characteristic changes in, 32
Visual impairment, 107
    reasonable accommodations for, 13
    universal design for, 56–62

Voice-controlled input devices, 154

Volunteers for Medical Engineering, 216

Voyeurism, 11, 21

W

Wake Community College Child Development Program, 181

Warble-Nienow, Ann, 62–66

Wasch, Christina, 255

Wasch, William K., 255–263

Washer-dryer combinations, 113

Wayfinding, 58–59, 66
    signage as aid to, 79

Weber, Margaret J., 230–231

Welfare issues in office design, 135–136

Wheelchair accessibility, 105
    and reasonable accommodations, 13
    residential redesign for, 246–247

Whirlpool, 254

Whirlpool Corporation, 29, 59, 110
    customer usability laboratory operated by, 103, 113–115

White Home Products, Inc., 249

Wier, Alan, 17, 50, 177–178, 210–214

Wilke, Harold H., 3

Wilkoff, Wm. L., 254

Wilsonart, 155

Window glare, 148–149

Windows, providing for elderly, 39

W.I.S.E. Institute, Inc., 294

Woolf House, 52–56

Work centers and counter heights in kitchen design, 227, 232–237

WorkManager™ System, 97

Workstation heights, adjustable, 155

World Health Organization, 142

Wrist fatigue, 152

Wrist rests, 155

Y

Yale School of Public Health, 260

Yearns, Mary H., 81–87

Z

Zaininger, Mark, 112

Zavotka, Susan, 178, 214–215

Zwelling, Rick, 263–264

Zwelling, Sheila, 115–120, 263–264